LONDON

Michael Jackson

Second
edition
of the
American
Express
Pocket
Guide

Mitchell Beazley

The Author
Michael Jackson's previous works include *The English Pub*, *Michael Jackson's Pocket Cocktail and Bar Book* and *The World Guide to Beer*, and his latest projects include a book on whisky. He writes regularly for *Travel & Leisure*, *Food & Wine* and *Playboy*. He has also acted as a consultant on food and drink projects for the English Tourist Board.

This book is dedicated to the memory of Maggie O'Connor Jackson (1943–81), who loved London.

Contributors
John Roberts (Sights and places of interest, for both editions)
Fiona Duncan (other additional text for second edition)

Acknowledgments
The author and publishers would like to thank the following for their invaluable help and advice: Stephen Clark, Valerie Cumming of the Museum of London, Pamela Fiori, Kidsline Projects, London Tourist Board, Ila Stanger.

Quotations
The author and publishers are grateful to Faber and Faber (UK) and Harcourt Brace Jovanovich (USA) for their kind permission to reprint the quotation from *The Waste Land* by T. S. Eliot on p58.

Few travel books are without errors, and no guide book can ever be completely up to date, for telephone numbers and opening hours change without warning, and hotels and restaurants come under new management, which can affect standards. While every effort has been made to ensure that all information is accurate at the time of going to press, the publishers will be glad to receive any corrections and suggestions for improvements, which can be incorporated in the next edition.

Series Editor David Townsend Jones
Editor (first edition 1983) David Arnold
Editor (second edition 1986) Leonie Hamilton
Researcher Catherine Palmer
Art Editor Eric Drewery
Designer Sarah Jackson
Illustrators Jeremy Ford (David Lewis Artists), Illustra Design Ltd, Rodney Paull
Production Androulla Pavlou

Edited and designed by
Mitchell Beazley International Limited,
14–15 Manette Street, London W1V 5LB,
for the American Express Pocket Travel
Guide Series

© American Express Publishing
Corporation Inc. 1983
New revised edition © American Express
Publishing Corporation Inc. 1986
Reprinted 1987
Text, except for Sights and
places of interest © Michael Jackson
All rights reserved
No part of this work may be reproduced
or utilized in any form by any means,
electronic or mechanical, including
photocopying, recording or by any
information storage and retrieval system,
without the prior written permission of
the publisher.
ISBN   0 85533 599 8

Maps in 4-colour by Clyde Surveys Ltd,
Maidenhead, England, based on
copyrighted material of John
Bartholomew & Son Limited. London
Transport Underground Map,
Registered User Number 83/008.
Typeset by Vantage Photosetting Co.
Ltd, Eastleigh, England.
Printed and bound in Hong Kong by
Mandarin Offset

Contents

How to use this book

The American Express Pocket Guide to London is an encyclo-
paedia of travel information, organized in the sections listed on
the previous page. There is also a comprehensive **index** (pages
212–219), which is accompanied by a **gazetteer** (pages
220–224) of the most important streets that are shown in the
full-colour **maps** at the end of the book.

For easy reference, all major sections (**Sights and places of
interest, Hotels, Restaurants**) and other sections as far as
possible are arranged alphabetically. For the organization of the
book as a whole, see *Contents*. For individual places that do not
have separate entries in *Sights and places of interest*, see the
Index.

Abbreviations

As far as possible only standard abbreviations have been used.
These include days of the week and months, points of the
compass (N, S, E and W), street names (Ave., Pl., Rd., Sq., St.),
Saint (St), C for century, and measurements.

Bold type

Bold type is used in running text primarily for emphasis, to
draw attention to something of special interest or importance. It
is also used in this way to pick out places – shops or minor
museums, for instance – that do not have full entries of their
own. In such cases it is usually followed in brackets by the
address, telephone number, and details of opening times.
Similarly, in *Hotels* and *Restaurants*, it is used to identify
places mentioned in one entry which have an entry of their own
elsewhere in these sections.

Cross-references

A special type has been used for cross-references. Whenever a
place or section title is printed in sans serif italics (for example
Tower of London or *Basic information*) in the text, this
indicates that you can turn to the appropriate heading in the
book for further information. For added convenience, the

How entries are organized

Belgravia
*Map **16**&**17**H–K. Tube Hyde Park Corner, Knightsbridge,
Sloane Square, Victoria.*
London's most magnificent terraces, once the town houses of
dukes, make up the great squares of Belgravia, the area around
Belgrave Sq. developed by Thomas Cubitt in a frenzy of activity
following the establishment of nearby *Buckingham Palace* as
the royal residence in the 1820s.

Belgrave Square itself forms the centrepiece of the fairly
regular plan, with its massive Classically decorated blocks by
George Batesi and grand corner houses by other architects
surrounding the private sunken gardens. Eaton Sq., to the S, is
a long rectangle with the King's Rd. running through the
middle of its massive stuccoed terraces. To the S again is Chester
Sq., to some eyes the most appealing of the three.

In Motcomb St. Seth-Smith's Doric-fronted pantechnicon of
1830 looks back on Wilton Crescent, built by the same architect
3yr earlier. For refreshment, go to **The Grenadier** (see *Pubs*).

running heads, printed at the top corner of the page, always correspond with these cross-references.

Cross-references always refer either to sections of the book – *Basic information*, *Planning*, *Hotels*, *Shopping* – or to individual entries in **Sights and places of interest**, such as *Tower of London* or *Chelsea*. Ordinary italics are used to identify sub-sections. For instance: see *Time Chart* in *Culture, history and background*.

Map references

Each page of the colour maps at the end of the book has a page number (2–24) and each map is divided into a grid of squares, which are identified vertically by letters (A, B, C, D, etc.) and horizontally by numbers (1, 2, 3, 4, etc.). A map reference identifies the page and square in which the street or place can be found – thus the **Tower of London** is located in the square identified as Map **13**G17.

Price bands

Price bands are denoted by the symbols ☐ ☐☐ ☐☐☐ ☐☐☐☐ and ☐☐☐☐☐ which signify cheap, inexpensive, moderately priced, expensive and very expensive, respectively. In the cases of hotels and restaurants these correspond approximately with the following actual prices, which give a guideline at the time of printing. Although actual prices will inevitably increase, in most cases the relative price category – for example expensive or cheap – will be likely to remain more or less the same.

Price bands	Corresponding to approximate prices	
	for **hotels** *double room with bath and breakfast; singles are somewhat cheaper*	for **restaurants** *meal for one with service, VAT and house wine*
☐ cheap	under £30	under £7
☐☐ inexpensive	£30–50	£7–15
☐☐☐ moderate	£50–70	£15–20
☐☐☐☐ expensive	£70–90	£20–30
☐☐☐☐☐ very expensive	over £90	over £30

— Bold blue type for entry headings.
— Blue italics for address, practical information and symbols, encapsulating standard information and special recommendations. For list of symbols see p6.

— Black text for description. Bold type used for emphasis.
— Sans serif italics used for cross-references to other entries.

Entries for hotels, restaurants, shops, etc. follow the same organization, and are usually printed across a narrow measure.
In hotels, symbols indicating special facilities appear at the end of the entry. ——

Merryfield House ☐
42 York St., W1 ☎ *935 – 8326. Map* **8***E6* ☐ ☐ *7* ☐ *7. Tube Baker Street.*
Location: Marylebone, near Oxford St. According to the proprietress, "This isn't a luxury hotel – no complimentary handkerchiefs – but I'll boil yours for you and hang them out. I have to go now; I'm having lunch with one of the guests, a widow who is here on her own." A friendly guest-house, immaculately kept.
☐

5

Key to symbols

- ☎ Telephone
- ⑫ Telex
- ★ Not to be missed
- ☆ Worth a visit
- ♣ Good value (in its class)
- *i* Tourist information
- 🚗 Car parking
- Ⓗ Hotel
- 🏠 Simple (hotel)
- 🏤 Luxury (hotel)
- ▭ Cheap
- ⫽▭ Inexpensive
- ⫽▭⫽ Moderately priced
- ⫽⫽⫽⫽ Expensive
- ⫽⫽⫽⫽ Very expensive
- ⟳ Number of rooms
- ▭ Rooms with private bathroom
- ▤ Air conditioning
- 🛏 Residential terms available
- AE American Express
- CB Carte Blanche
- ⓓ Diners Club
- ⓜ MasterCard/Access
- VISA Visa/Barclaycard
- ▤ Secure garage
- ⇌ Own restaurant
- 🍽 Meal obligatory
- ☁ Quiet hotel
- ↕ Lift
- ⅊ Facilities for the disabled
- ▭ TV in each room
- ▱ Telephone in each room

- 🦮 Dogs not allowed
- 🌿 Garden
- ⋘ Outstanding views
- ⇌ Swimming pool
- ⤴ Tennis court(s)
- ✓ Golf course
- 👥 Conference facilities
- Ⓡ Restaurant
- 🍴 Simple (restaurant)
- △ Luxury (restaurant)
- ▱ A la carte available
- ▦ Set (fixed price) menu available
- ⬛ Good for wines
- 🍽 Open-air dining available
- 🏛 Building of architectural interest
- † Church or cathedral
- 🔲 Entrance free
- 🔳 Entrance fee payable
- 🔳 Entrance expensive
- 🚫📷 Photography not permitted
- 𝒦 Guided tour available
- 🎫 Guided tour compulsory
- 🍴 Cafeteria
- ✳ Special interest for children
- 🍸 Bar
- ⦿ Disco dancing
- 🎵 Nightclub
- ✾ Casino/gambling
- ♫ Live music
- ✌ Dancing
- 📓 Revue

6

Before you go

Documents required

Visitors from EEC countries need only an identity card to visit Britain. Otherwise, a valid passport is all that is needed. Citizens of the USA, the Commonwealth and most West European and South American countries do not need visas; an International Certificate of Vaccination is seldom required.

International driving licences are not required to drive personal or hired cars, only your full valid national licence. Your own car should be properly insured; bring also the vehicle registration certificate (logbook), an insurance certificate or green card, and a national identity sticker.

Travel and medical insurance

Make sure that you take out an insurance policy covering loss of deposits paid to airlines, hotels, tour operators, etc., and emergency costs, such as special tickets home and extra nights in a hotel.

Visitors from countries with no reciprocal health agreement are not covered for any medical help other than accidents or emergencies, and even then will be expected to pay if they have to stay the night in hospital. They should be properly insured. No charge is made for visitors from countries with a reciprocal arrangement, such as EEC member countries.

Money

There is no exchange control in Britain, so you can carry any amount of any currency through customs in or out of the country.

The unit of currency is the pound sterling (£), divided into 100 pence (p). There are coins for 1p, 2p, 5p, 10p, 20p, 50p and £1, and notes for £1, £5, £10, £20 and £50.

Travellers cheques issued by American Express, Thomas Cook, Barclays and Citibank are widely recognized; make sure you read the instructions included with your travellers cheques. It is important to note separately the serial numbers of your cheques and the telephone number to call in case of loss. Specialist travellers cheque companies such as American Express provide extensive local refund facilities through their own offices or agents.

Major international credit cards, such as American Express, MasterCard (linked in Britain with the Access card), Visa (linked with Barclaycard) and Diners Club are widely accepted for most goods and services. Carte Blanche is less common.

Customs

If you are visiting the United Kingdom for less than six months, you are entitled to bring in, free of duty and tax, all personal effects which you intend to take with you when you leave, except tobacco goods, alcoholic drinks and perfume. Make sure that you carry dated receipts for valuable items, such as cameras and watches, or you may be charged duty.

Duty-free allowances at the time of writing for import into Britain are given below. The figures shown in brackets are the increased allowances for goods obtained duty and tax paid in EEC countries. In all cases travellers under 17 are not entitled to the allowances on tobacco goods and alcoholic drinks.

Tobacco goods 200 (300) cigarettes *or* 100 (150) cigarillos *or* 50 (75) cigars *or* 250 (400)g tobacco. Or if you live outside

7

Basic information

Europe, 400 cigarettes *or* 200 cigarillos *or* 100 cigars *or* 500g tobacco.

Alcoholic drinks   1 (1.5) litres spirits or strong liquor (over 22% alcohol by volume) *or* 2 (3) litres of alcoholic drink under 22% alcohol, fortified wine or sparkling wine *plus* 2(5) litres of still table wine.

Perfume   50g/60cc/2 fl oz (75g/90cc/3fl oz)

Toilet water   250cc/9fl oz (375cc/13fl oz)

Other goods   Goods to the value of £28 (£163)

Prohibited and restricted goods include narcotics, weapons, obscene publications and videos.

If you have anything in excess of the duty free allowances you must pass through the channel with red 'Goods to declare' notices, otherwise pass through the green 'Nothing to declare' channel.

For exemption from Value Added Tax (VAT) on goods bought in Britain for export see *Shopping.*

Getting there

London's Heathrow Airport is one of the busiest in the world, and there are regular flights from most countries on a wide range of international airlines. Gatwick, the city's second airport, is also heavily used, and both are within an hour of the city centre (see *From the airport to the city* opposite). Air fares vary enormously, so consult your travel agent.

Only Cunard now operates frequent transatlantic sailings, but it is possible to sail to English ports (usually Liverpool or Southampton) on other less regular routes. An efficient network of short-distance passenger, car and train ferries links Britain with France, Belgium, The Netherlands, West Germany, Ireland and Scandinavia. The main ports of entry are Dover, Folkestone, Harwich, Felixstowe, Portsmouth, Plymouth and Fishguard.

Climate

English weather is rarely given to extremes, but it is unpredictable, and can change character several times a day. Average daytime temperatures range from 6°C (43°F) in winter (Dec–Feb) to 21°C (70°F) in summer (June–Aug), only occasionally going below 0°C (32°F) or above 27°C (80°F). There is an annual rainfall of 24in (60cm), most of it in winter but liable to arrive at any time.

Clothes

In summertime light clothes are adequate, but remember to include some protection against showers and a sweater or jacket for cool evenings. During the rest of the year, bring warm clothes and hope you won't need them all, although in winter overcoats, gloves, etc. will usually be necessary.

London has given the world some bizarre fashions, and is consequently relaxed about dress, but restraint is expected in some institutional buildings, the older hotels and restaurants, casinos and some clubs. If you are attending any formal or particularly grand occasion, full evening dress, which the British refer to simply as 'black tie', may be expected, so do check first.

Poste restante

Poste restante (general delivery) can be addressed to any post office. (See *Post offices p15* for the two main post offices.)

Getting around

From the airport to the city

Heathrow is the terminal station of the underground's Piccadilly Line, and frequent trains link the airport with all parts of the city between 5.00 (6.45 Sun) and 23.30. The journey to the city centre takes about 40min.

The M4 motorway is the other main link, the trip to the centre taking 30min–1hr depending upon traffic. London Regional Transport operates a 24hr bus service to Liverpool St. via South Kensington, Piccadilly and Fleet St., various coach companies run services to Victoria Bus Station, and some airlines run buses to meet arriving flights and connect with their various passenger terminals in central London. A more expensive alternative is to take a taxi, always readily available at the airport, but make sure you take a black metered cab and not one of the 'pirate' operators who may overcharge.

Gatwick is farther out of the city and the easiest way into London is to take the Gatwick Express, the British Rail service from the airport station. This reaches Victoria Station in London in 30min and all parts of the city are easily reached from there. The airport is by the side of the M23 motorway, an hour or more from central London, and there are bus services around the clock. Because of the distance from London a cab is not a practicable proposition, and could be expensive; ask the driver first how much the fare will be.

Arriving by other means

By rail: London's several major stations encircle the centre, and all have underground interchanges, taxi ranks and bus stops. (See *Railway services p12*.)

By road: The roads into London plough through the sprawling suburbs, after which signposting for 'West End' indicates the centre. Try to avoid driving anywhere in the rush hours (8.00–9.30 and 17.00–19.00). The biggest bus terminus in London is at Victoria, and most cross-country coaches make for there.

Public transport

London Regional Transport's network of buses and underground ('tube') trains is extensive and efficient, although the usual warnings must be made about travelling in the rush hour. Free bus and tube maps and details of services are available at the Travel Information Centres located at the following tube stations: Heathrow Central, Euston, King's Cross, Piccadilly Circus, Oxford Circus, St James's Park and Victoria. There is also a telephone information service ☎222–1234: you may have to wait a while for an answer as the calls are stacked and dealt with in rotation.

Various special tickets are available, and it is wise to visit a Travel Information Centre and get details of them early in your visit. The tickets include flat-rate passes for bus or tube or both for various periods from three days to one month. See *London for children* for further information on children's fares.

When using public transport remember to join the queue.

The underground

The underground (see *Map 24*) is the easiest and fastest way to get around the city, if not the most interesting. The stations are easily recognized by the London Regional Transport symbol, a horizontal line through a circle. On maps, each line

Basic information

always has its own colour (Circle line yellow, Central line red, etc.), so it is easy to plan your journey, noting where you have to change lines. The fare depends on how many zones you enter; see *Buses*. Buy your ticket before travelling, either from a ticket office or a machine in the station, where the fares will be on display. Show your ticket to a collector or, if it is a yellow one, put it in the automatic entry gate and walk through, picking it up as you go – you will need to present it at the end of your journey. Follow the signs to the platform for the line you want. Check with the indicators above the platform and on the front of the train that it is going to your station; some trains do not go to the end of the line, and some lines divide into two or more branches. Trains stop at every station, with only a few exceptions at weekends. The first tube trains run at about 5.00, and they begin to close down after 23.30, when you might have trouble with connections. Smoking is forbidden in underground trains and in all stations that are underground.

Buses

(See table of central bus routes, *Map 22–23*.) London's red buses are usually slower than the tube, but are cheaper and more interesting, offering a good view from the upper deck. Do use them and don't be discouraged by the complex network of routes: people waiting in the queue will usually help you, and the conductor will answer your questions and tell you when you have reached your destination if necessary. Each bus runs along part or all of a numbered route – find out which route you want from the map at the bus stop, and look at the indicator on the front of the bus to check that it is going far enough along the route for you. There are two types of bus stop; a normal stop, with the LRT symbol on a white background, where all buses stop; and a request stop, with a red sign bearing the word 'Request', where the bus will stop only if you raise your hand or, if on the bus, ring the bell. Fares are tied to zones; a small flat fare is payable for every zone you enter. Children under 16 pay less, and those under five travel free. Usually the conductor will come round and collect your fare during the journey, but sometimes you will have to pay as you enter. Smoking is allowed only upstairs on double-decker buses. The buses run between about 5.00 and 23.30, although there are a few night buses on special routes, running once an hour or so.

Green Line Coaches run from central London into the country outside London Regional Transport's area. They stop only rarely in London, and are more expensive than red buses. Ask at a Travel Information Centre for details of routes.

Taxis

London's distinctive black taxis are driven by some of the best drivers in the world, who have to pass an exam to prove their detailed knowledge of the city before they get a licence. They can be hailed as they cruise the streets (a cab which is free illuminates its yellow light), and you will also find them on ranks at stations and outside hotels and large stores, etc. Once they have stopped for you, taxis are obliged to take you anywhere you want to go within six miles of the pick-up point, provided it is within the metropolitan area. The fare, always shown on the meter, consists of a basic hiring charge and subsequent additions according to the length of your journey; there are additional charges for extra passengers, night or weekend hire and for baggage. In all cases notices will be displayed inside the taxi with details of all charges. Give the driver a 10–15% tip.

10

Some black taxis and many private taxis (known as 'minicabs') cannot be hailed but must be ordered by phone. You will find the numbers by some public telephones and in directories, hotels and clubs, etc.

It is best to stick to the black taxis if possible; the strict regulations governing fares for black taxis do not apply to minicabs, so if you have to use a minicab try to agree the fare with the driver at the start of the journey to avoid problems when you reach your destination.

Getting around by car

Driving in London is as aggressive as in most large cities, with an additional difficulty for foreign visitors in that everyone appears to be on the wrong side of the road. London has a totally unplanned road system and an abundance of one-way systems. If you can face all of that, make sure that you are carrying your licence, that your tyres have at least 1mm of tread, and that all your lights are working.

You must drive on the left and only ever overtake on the right. The speed limit in London and all built-up areas (i.e. streets with lamp posts) is 30mph (48kph) unless otherwise indicated. Standard international road signs are generally used. A solid white line across the road means that you must stop, a broken white line that you must give way; a solid white line down the centre of the road must not be crossed at all, but a broken line can be crossed if it is safe to do so. Pedestrian crossings are marked by black and white zones across the road and are sometimes controlled by traffic lights. In either case pedestrians have the right of way and traffic must stop to let them cross, unless there is a green traffic light showing, in which case drivers have priority. Observe lane division rules, i.e. slower traffic on the inside (left), faster traffic on the outside, and be sure to get into the correct lane coming up to junctions, as different lanes may be controlled by different traffic signals. Car horns must not be used from 23.30−7.00 except in emergencies, and the wearing of seat belts in both front seats is compulsory.

Parking is extremely difficult on streets in central London, usually possible only at meters for a maximum of 2hr. Two yellow lines by the roadside means no parking at all, one yellow line no parking in the working day (8.00−18.30, Mon−Sat). Always look for an explanatory sign when it is a restricted zone: there will be one giving details of the maximum stay allowed, or indicating that the space is for residents only. Parking is always prohibited near pedestrian crossings and junctions. If you are violating parking regulations, you may be fined (but not on the spot). Or you may have your car immobilized by a wheel clamp; instructions on how to get it released will be displayed on the windscreen, but you will have to pay a fine, on the spot, and wait until it is unlocked. In rare cases the police may tow away your car to a pound and exact a greater fine.

Off the streets, there are various car parks and garages, often indicated by a blue sign with a large P. Charges for these should be set out clearly somewhere near the entrance.

If you belong to an FIA-affiliated motoring organization and are bringing your own car, the services of the two main British motoring organizations will be at your disposal:

Automobile Association   5 New Coventry St. WC2
☎954−7373

Royal Automobile Club   49 Pall Mall, SW1 ☎839−7050

11

Basic information

Renting a car

Renting a car is probably not worthwhile if you do not intend to go outside London. To rent one, you must be over 21 and hold a full valid national licence. You can opt for either a daily rate plus a mileage charge, or a weekly rate with unlimited mileage, often more economical. Insurance is usually included, but check before you leave. You may be asked to leave a cash deposit larger than your likely eventual overall charge, from which the difference will be refunded when you return the car.

The head offices of the major car firms are: *Avis*, Trident House, Station Rd., Hayes, Middlesex ☎848–8733; *Europcar*, Bushey House, High St., Bushey, Watford ☎950–5050; *Hertz*, 1272 London Rd., SW16 ☎542–6688.

All these companies can arrange for cars to be waiting if you arrive by aircraft or train.

Getting around on foot

Although many Londoners ignore them, it is best to use zebra crossings, where pedestrians have priority, or subways.

A few outer areas are unsafe for pedestrians after nightfall: if you are walking outside the city centre after dark, stick to the main streets.

Railway services

British Rail offers a fast Inter-City service between major towns throughout the UK, as well as Motorail and sleeper trains. Reduced-rate tickets are available for off-peak day or weekend trips, and the Britrail Pass, on sale only outside the UK through travel agents, offers unlimited travel on the whole network for weekly periods up to one month.

British Rail Travel Centres (visitors only)
4–12 Regent St., SW1. (*Map 10G10*)
407 Oxford St., W1. (*Map 9F8*)
Major British Rail stations in London
S and SE England (Information ☎928–5100)
Charing Cross, Strand, WC2. (*Map 10G11*)
Waterloo, Waterloo Rd., SE1. (*Map 11H13*)
Victoria, Buckingham Palace Rd., SW1. (*Map 17J9*)
East Anglia (Information ☎283–7171)
Liverpool Street, Liverpool St., EC3. (*Map 13E16*)
SW and W England, S Wales (Information ☎262–6767)
Paddington, Praed St., W2. (*Map 7F5*)
Midlands, NW England, N Wales, W Scotland (Information ☎387–7070)
Euston, Euston Rd., NW1. (*Map 4C10*)
St Pancras, Euston Rd., NW1. (*Map 4C11*)
NE England, E Scotland (Information ☎278–2477)
King's Cross, Euston Rd., NW1. (*Map 4B11*)

Domestic airlines

The principal airline operating from the capital to other major cities is British Airways. Other airlines include British Caledonian, British Midland Airways and Dan-Air. Unless you wish to go to one of the country's extremities, like Aberdeen in Scotland, it is often easier to go by car or train and arrive directly in the city centre.

Ferry services

The only ferry services in London are pleasure cruises on the Thames (see *River and canal trips p16*).

On-the-spot information

Public holidays
New Year's Day, Jan 1; Good Friday; Easter Monday; May
Day (first Mon in May); Spring Bank Holiday (last Mon in
May); August Bank Holiday (last Mon in Aug); Christmas
Day, Dec 25; Boxing Day, Dec 26. Most places are closed.

Time zones
London time is GMT in winter and changes to European
Summer Time (EST), 1hr ahead of GMT, from the end of
Mar to late Oct.

Banks and currency exchange
All banks are open Mon–Fri 9.30–15.30. Money can also be
exchanged outside these hours at *bureaux de change* found as
small separate shops and in hotels, railways stations, travel
agencies and airports, although the exchange rate might not be
as good as that offered by the banks. Travellers cheques are
widely accepted, the exchange rate being roughly the same as
for cash.

Shopping hours
Most shops are open Mon–Sat 9.00–18.00, and some open Sat
9.30–12.00. Many large city-centre shops stay open late on
Wed or Thurs (see *Shopping*). Office hours are Mon–Fri
9.30–17.30. A few small shops and some large stores may open
on Sun, particularly in the weeks before Christmas.
   Outside the city centre shops may close at lunchtime,
usually 13.00–14.00, and for one afternoon during the week.

Rush hours
The rush hours are approximately 8.00–9.30 and 17.00–19.00
on Mon–Fri only. Unlike some cities, London does not
become totally choked, but getting around will take longer.

Post and telephone services
Post offices are usually open Mon–Fri 9.00–17.30, Sat
9.00–12.30, with the notable exception of the 24hr post office
in William IV St., off Trafalgar Sq. (*Map 10 G11*).
   Stamps are available at post offices and occasionally from
machines. There are two classes of inland mail, but as the
second class is only a little cheaper and sometimes a lot slower
and more unreliable, it is best avoided. You will also have to
specify which rate you want for international mail, as it will not
automatically go air mail. When sending a parcel out of the
country you will have to fill in a customs form declaring the
contents. Besides the boxes in post offices, mail can be posted
in the red boxes placed at regular intervals on main streets.
There are various special services available, such as express or
recorded or guaranteed delivery. Ask for details.
   Public telephones are found in kiosks and in booths on main
streets and in post offices, hotels, pubs, stations, etc. They
should all have London telephone directories; if you want a
number outside London, dial 192 and Directory Enquiries will
supply it. There is always an area code, which may have up to
six numbers. It is not necessary for local calls but must be used
when telephoning from outside the area – London's is 01.
Most international calls can be dialled direct from public
telephones; if the codes are not displayed in the booth then call
the operator (100) and ask for International Directory
Enquiries for the country you require.

13

Basic information

Public telephones take 2p, 10p and 50p coins, so have a supply ready. Follow the instructions displayed by the telephone. In the older telephone boxes you must insert the money after you hear the call answered and when a series of rapid pips is heard. In the newer booths you must insert the money before dialling and when the light flashes; you will be refunded any unused coins. The ringing tone is a repeated double trill, and an intermittent shrill tone means that the line is engaged. See also *Telephone services*, opposite.

Public lavatories

The public conveniences found in main streets (often in French-style, automated 'superloos'), parks and underground stations can often be dirty and vandalized, although there are some exceptions. Well maintained conveniences that can be used by anybody will be found in all larger public buildings, such as museums and art galleries, large department stores and railway stations. It is not acceptable to use the lavatories in hotels, restaurants and pubs if you are not a customer. Public conveniences are usually free of charge but you may need a small coin to unlock a lavatory or to use a proper washroom.

Electric current

The electric current is 240V AC, and plugs have three square pins and take 3, 5 or 13 amp fuses. Foreign visitors will need adaptors to use their own appliances which should be bought before departure.

Customs and etiquette

The English are a tolerant people, and London is a cosmopolitan city, so foreign visitors are unlikely to offend by tripping up on some part of etiquette. The most important custom is that of queuing – the British queue for everything and if you do not wait your turn they will not take it kindly.

Tipping

Tipping is customary in a few cases. A tip of 10–15% is usual in hotels and restaurants, unless a service charge is already incorporated into the bill. Taxi drivers also expect about 10–15% of the fare. You need only give small tips to porters, hairdressers, cloakroom attendants and commissionaires.

Disabled visitors

Prior information is important. A useful publication is *Access in London*, published by Nicholson, and there is a Disabled Information Service run by *The Royal Association for Disability and Rehabilitation (RADAR)*, 25 Mortimer St., W1 ☎637–5400.

Local and foreign publications

The weekly entertainments magazines, such as *Time Out*, *City Limits* and *What's On & Where to Go*, are the most comprehensive guides to events and entertainments of all sorts. London's daily evening newspaper, the *London Standard*, also features a wide range of entertainments. Programmes of special events (free concerts, ceremonies, etc.) are usually available from Tourist Information Centres (see opposite) and are listed in *The Times*.

Morning newspapers are produced for national circulation, and do not necessarily cover local London events.

Foreign newspapers are widely available from newsagents, the *International Herald Tribune* and many others on the day of publication, and most of the others a day or two later.

14

Emergency information

Emergency services (call free from any telephone)
Police   ☎999 (no coins needed).
Ambulance   You will be asked which service
Fire   you require

Hospitals with casualty departments
Middlesex Hospital   Mortimer St., W1 ☎636–8333
St Mary's Hospital   Praed St., W2 ☎262–1280
St Thomas's Hospital   Lambeth Palace Rd., SE1
☎928–9292

Other emergencies
If your complaint does not warrant an ambulance or
hospitalization you will have to ring up a doctor or dentist.
Consult the 'Yellow Pages' of the telephone directory under
'Physicians and Surgeons' and 'Dental Surgeons'.

Late-night chemists
Boots   Piccadilly Circus, W1 ☎734–6126
Bliss   50 Willesden Lane, NW6 ☎624–8000

Help lines
Capital Help Line   ☎388–7575. Referral service.
Release   ☎354–3127. Drug problems, legal and practical.
The Samaritans   St Stephen's Church Crypt, 39 Walbrook,
EC4 ☎283–3400 (24hr). Talk out problems.

Motoring accidents
— Do not admit liability or incriminate yourself.
— Ask any witnesses to stay and give a statement.
— Contact the police.
— Exchange names, addresses, car details and insurance
   companies' names and addresses with other driver(s).
— Give a statement to the police who will compile a report
   which insurance companies will accept as authoritative.

Car breakdowns
Call one of the following from the nearest telephone.
— The nearest garage/breakdown service.
— The police who will put you in touch with the above.
— The number you have been given if you hired the car.

Lost passport
Contact the police immediately and your consulate (see
p15) for emergency travel documents.

Lost travellers cheques
Notify the local police at once, then follow the instructions
provided with your travellers cheques, or contact the
nearest office of the issuing company. Contact your
consulate or American Express if you are stranded with no
money.

Lost property
Report your loss to the police immediately (many insurance
companies will not recognize claims without a police
report). There are some special lost property offices:
British Rail   At main stations. (See *Railway services p12*.)
Heathrow Airport Lost Property Office   ☎759–4321
London Regional Transport   200 Baker St., NW1.
Taxi Lost Property Office   15 Penton St., NW1.
(Visitors only)

17

Introduction

To see the pageantry of London, or the architecture, to visit the theatre or the places of government and jurisdiction, is to be immersed for a moment in a city which was capital of half the world, and which enjoyed that position rather more recently than Athens, Rome or Constantinople. Nor has London cast aside the robes of her recent eminence. She may be wrinkled in some places, face-lifted in others, and over-painted here and there, but she has retained dignity in her middle age.

The attitude of Londoners to their own city can puzzle the newcomer. There is a defiant defensiveness in the proclamation "I love New York"; Londoners are cooler and ostensibly more detached, but inclined nevertheless to be deeply and irremovably in love with their city. They will rightly evince anger at the handiwork perpetrated by planners and developers in the post-war period, but the irony is that such licensed vandalism prospered so long without restraint simply because the profusion of fine and historic architecture seemed inexhaustible.

To the newcomer, London is an overwhelming jumble of antiquity, a labyrinthine junkshop with 'finds' hidden all over the place, often apparently unnoticed and gathering dust. Sometimes it seems that every house was the birthplace of someone famous, or the scene of an invention, each corner the site of an important speech, a battle or an especially vile crime, each name one which has passed into the language.

The irrepressible curiosities of London manifest themselves from Greenwich in the E to Richmond in the W, two of the most interesting and pleasant little towns in England. Both maintain their identities while remaining parts of London, although they stand about 20 miles apart (London is at some points 35 miles from end to end), and each can be reached by pleasure boat from the heart of the capital.

London grew from the river; the Thames was its first thoroughfare, its lifeline and its mean of social irrigation. Because the first route to London was up the river, successive waves of immigrants, Italians, Jews, Huguenots and many others, settled in what became known as the 'East End', a series of waterside, working-class communities which has nurtured its own culture, patois and social mores. They settled in the E because, as foreigners, they were barred in times past from entering the city. Yet there were older immigrants in London from the beginning; Romans founded the settlement nearly 2,000yr ago, and many a Cockney today has a discernibly Roman nose.

This is how the city was born. Yet when Londoners talk about 'The City', they mean specifically and exclusively that part which was originally walled and still vestigially is, and which covers no more than one square mile, between Tower Bridge and Blackfriars Bridge. The City is the financial district, the 'Wall Street' of Britain. The Lord Mayor of London represents only this square mile, and its streets are patrolled by the separate City Police. The City does not include the famous shopping streets, or theatreland, and does not care. It is an entity within itself, parochial yet worldly, with its own rituals and customs, and its preoccupation with bulls and bears and commodity prices.

London is governed not from The City but from County Hall, in Lambeth, and from the town halls of its more than 30 boroughs. Britain is governed not from The City but from

Westminster, a mile up-river. Westminster, too, was once a small city, but it spread far from the river, and today takes in Covent Garden, Soho, theatreland and the main shopping streets of central London. Yet, because of its geographical relationship with the original walled city, today's centre is known as the 'West End'.

While The City remained fiercely independent and intro-spective, Westminster was the royal seat, and London has good reason to be grateful. The royal residences of Westminster (St James's, Buckingham Palace and Clarence House) are joined to those of Kensington (Kensington Palace) by a long swathe of royal parks. Through St James's Park, Green Park, Hyde Park and Kensington Gardens, you can walk miles across the great metropolis amid the greenery. With Holland Park, Regent's Park, and the squares of Bloomsbury, Chelsea and Kensington, developed during the Georgian and Victorian periods, London has a remarkably green inner city.

Born from two separate cities on the river, modern London is, not surprisingly, a complex patchwork of villages. To any-one from outside, Chelsea is probably the most familiar district name in the capital. It is also a neighbourhood which perfectly demonstrates London's enigmatic charm, contriving simul-taneously to be grand and yet to be a pristine, dolls-house village. At one moment, it spreads itself elegantly on the riverside; in another it hugs itself in narrow streets, cosy as a cat. It has been smart, then bohemian, and is now both, and yet richer than ever. It has the most discreet streets in London, yet its main thoroughfare, King's Road, is bereft of caution. It is always unmistakeably Chelsea, yet it has many moods. London is like that; a face which is unforgettably familiar, but which has an expression for every emotion.

London, that great sea, whose ebb and flow
At once is deaf and loud, and on the shore
Vomits its wrecks, and still howls on for more
Shelley, *Letter to Maria Gisborne*, 1819

The changes of mood can be sudden. South Kensington has some of the wealthiest streets in Britain, North Kensington some of the poorest. Yet deprivation has not bred dullness, nor isolation; s of the river, Brixton, too, is less than a ghetto, despite its occasional tensions. In the delightful Brixton mar-ket, you can buy jellied eels, an old cockney delicacy, as well as yams and breadfruit.

The river may no longer influence population trends, but the underground lines do. Parts of s London became places of cheap housing when they were ignored by the underground systems, but when the new Victoria line went s in 1969, these neighbourhoods suddenly became attractive to a new genera-tion of young, professional people who no longer wished to live out in the suburbs. The same 'gentrification' has taken place in several districts which were built for the artisan; the social classes are as identifiable in London as they are anywhere else in Britain, but nowhere else do they quite so readily live together.

Strangers get lost in London. So do Londoners, unless they are cab drivers. It is a city in which to lose oneself, an engrossing experience. People who are afraid of getting lost, who believe that every city should be built as a piece, at a single stroke, to a well-ordered plan, should not come. London was not built for efficiency. It is a city for explorers.

19

Time chart

AD 43	The invading Romans under Claudius defeated the Celtic tribes of SE Britain and bridged the Thames close to the site of the later London Bridge. By AD 60, London was a thriving port and settlement at the centre of the Roman road network.
60	Revolt by Iceni tribe from East Anglia, under Queen Boadicea, culminated in destruction of London before Romans regained control.
200	England's capital, and a prosperous city of traders, London was fortified by the Romans. Walls from modern sites of Tower to Aldgate, along London Wall to Barbican and down to the river at Blackfriars.
200– 400	Romans used Germanic mercenaries to help defend this outpost of their weakening empire.
410	Romans withdrew, and London reverted to a farming town under the Angles and Saxons, warrior kings.
700– 820	England gradually reunited under kings of Wessex, from Winchester. London an important provincial market town. Christianity slowly reintroduced, and stimulated learning.
836	London sacked by Vikings. For almost two centuries it was a border-land pawn in their struggle with the western Saxon kingdoms, with divided loyalties usually determined by self-interest.
1014	London taken by storm for the last time; Olaf, an Anglo-Saxon, tied his boats to London bridge and sailed downstream to destroy it. (Hence the song *London Bridge is Falling Down*.)
1052	Disgusted by London's switching of support to his enemies, King Edward the Confessor started to build a new abbey and palace named Westminster on Isle of Thorney. Tension between City and Crown was born.
1066	Norman invasion. William did not attack the well-fortified London, but forced it into submission by destroying surrounding farmlands.
1066– 1100	London accepted and thrived under the civilized Norman rule. William I built Tower of London.
1140 –90	As political stability was undermined by factionalism among the king and powerful barons, London exacted a price for its support. It won the power to raise taxes and elect its own governors. The powerful guilds, confederations of merchants, controlled trade.
1215	London accepted Charter of Incorporation from King John, confirming authority of the Lord Mayor, elected annually by 24 aldermen. Displeased by heavy taxes, it supported barons in drafting Magna Carta.
1217	First stone bridge over Thames, London Bridge.
1263	Trade guilds took control of city from aldermen during turbulence of baronial wars, and reinstituted government by citizens' assembly (Anglo-Saxon idea).
1269	Henry II began construction of new Westminster Abbey after boundary dispute with City.
1280	Old St Paul's Cathedral completed, half as tall again as current St Paul's. Precincts housed sports arena, markets and a brewery. 126 parish churches plus monasteries inside city displaced population.
1326	The new urban pressures of the city erupted in riots against the king. Foreigners and Jews attacked.

1338	Edward III made Westminster the regular meeting place of Parliament, previously irregular.
1348	Black Death. Half city's 60,000 population died.
1381	Peasants' Revolt. Seeking an end to feudalism, a working class 'army', led by Wat Tyler from Kent, took over London for two days. Tyler killed by mayor.
1399	London supported Parliament in forcing deposition of the absolutist and heavily-taxing Richard II.
1411	Work began on Guildhall, the city's 'royal palace'. Professional soldiers and tradesmen formed new wealthy class threatening the old feudal aristocracy.
1461	London's support essential to Edward IV, victor of Wars of the Roses, in struggle to restore stability to country and its trade. King knighted many London citizens in return for support.
1500– 1600	Population exploded from 50,000 to 200,000 during economic boom of relatively stable Tudor period. New slum areas arose outside London, all ungoverned suburbs, including red-light district of Southwark.
1533	Henry VIII's Reformation. New gentry class snapped up land vacated by dissolution of the monasteries. Henry founded downriver naval bases.
1553 –58	Queen Mary reinstated Catholicism. Citizens martyred at Smithfield. London then supported the parsimonious Protestant Elizabeth I for 45yr.
1600 –70	The new gentry, now aristocracy, began to develop their new land, moving westwards, building on the edge of the countryside in Piccadilly and Leicester Sq.
1603 –42	Puritanism flourished in the city as a reaction against the autocratic Stuart kings, James I and Charles I.
1642 –49	London financed Parliament in Civil War. London and Westminster both embraced by new fortifications, and the citizens manned defence. London was the setting for Charles I's execution in 1649.
1649 –60	The Commonwealth (republic). London traders gradually reacted against the religious radicals' egalitarianism, and supported the restoration of Charles II in 1660.
1665 –66	The Great Plague. The last and worst outbreak. At least 100,000 died in just over a year.
1666	The Great Fire. Medieval London destroyed after fire, started in king's baker's in Pudding Lane.
1666– 1700	Reconstruction with stone buildings and wider streets. Wren's plan of grid of streets with piazzas infringed too many property rights; private ownership shaped new landscape. Instead Wren built 51 churches, culminating in St Paul's. By 1700, the 300,000 population was widely dispersed after the fire.
1700 –50	Both the new urban poor and the fashionable elite pushed up the population to 675,000 by 1750. The villages of Knightsbridge and Marylebone were incorporated, and St James's and Mayfair were developed. To the E and S were slums, where gin consumption averaged two pints per person per week and only one child in four lived beyond five.
1774	The City, still self-governing, returned the radical John Wilkes as Mayor after his being expelled from Parliament three times. It still distrusted the cultured West End and the almost omnipotent Parliament.
1780	The Gordon Riots. Anarchy in London for a week, but

	still no police force with day-to-day authority.
1780– 1820	Middle and upper classes moved ever more to the suburbs in the w, as slums and urban pressures increased. Still no comprehensive local government.
1829	The Metropolitan Police or 'Peelers', the first police force, founded. City founded its own force in 1835.
1820 –38	Prince Regent, later George IV, and architect Nash developed Regent's Park and Regent St., Buckingham Palace and The Mall.
1835	Britain given local councils. London was exempted from this, and continued to be 'governed' by over 150 parishes, encompassing 300 administrative bodies. Slum clearance still partially executed by the Commissioner for Woods and Forests.
1839	New Palace of Westminster, the present one, was started after old one was burnt down.
1844	Controlling monopoly in printing money granted to the Bank of England.
1832 –66	Cholera killed thousands: various Public Health Acts had no effect on London, until Metropolitan Board of Works founded in 1855. Destitution worsened by clearance of land for railways.
1851	The Great Exhibition in the Crystal Palace in Hyde Park celebrated British supremacy in trade, science and industry. Consolidated by Prince Albert's development of the museums and learned institutions of South Kensington.
1863	Railways available to working class for first time, and opening of first underground line. Increased mobility and belated public health and education measures.
1889	London County Council formed, giving London comprehensive local government for first time.
1897	Victoria's Diamond Jubilee. London described as "centre of an empire on which the sun never sets".
1900 –05	Opening of four new electric underground lines began rapid expansion into sprawling suburbs.
1914 –18	Women took over many services in London during the War, and the suffragettes won the vote in 1918.
1920 –30	'Homes for Heroes' programme was part of growth of vast new estates quadrupling size of London.
1940	The Blitz. London bombed, mainly in The City and East End; St Paul's stood alone amid rubble.
1945 –55	Private and local government re-development of the city resulted in fast modernization.
1951	Festival of Britain, one of the first world fairs. Royal Festival Hall built.
1955 –65	Boom years for property developers, who erected prestigious skyscrapers while London County Council concentrated on housing in suburbs. Population of central London lowest for centuries.
1956	Clean Air Act created smokeless zones and marked the end of central London as an industrial area.
1960 –70	'Swinging London'. Economic boom, immigration and changing values and wealth patterns made London more cosmopolitan. In 1965, Greater London Council succeeded LCC.
1970 –80	Local government gained strength, tempering modernization through such projects as Covent Garden.
1984 –85	Labour GLC threatened with abolition by Conservative government.

22

Architecture

London was not the vision of an emperor or king. To their surprise, visitors who know by repute its showcase architectural masterpieces find not a city of grand avenues and broad boulevards, but a family of villages, offering delightfully distracting details more often than panoramic views. Its uniquely pervasive grandeur derives from this blending of a rich heritage of fine buildings into the everyday life, past and present, of a bustling city.

A chronology of English architectural styles

Norman (1060–1200)   Sturdy buildings around massive piers; round arches; carved geometrical ornament; square towers and keeps.
Gothic (1180–1540)   Lighter, more dynamic buildings: flying buttresses, pointed arches and windows, spires. Main periods are: **Early English** (1180–1260), marked by simplicity and airiness; **Decorated** (1250–1370), extensive surface ornament and window tracery; and **Perpendicular** (1300–1540), with slender columns stressing vertical line, fan vaulting and panelled windows.
Tudor (1540–1603)   The Renaissance influenced only decoration, with strapwork and carved gables. Brick buildings with symmetrical plan, often E or H; large mullioned windows.
Jacobean (1603–25)   Extravagant wood and plaster decoration.
Classical (1615–66)   Inigo Jones introduced Palladian style. After Great Fire, Wren worked in styles from Classical simplicity to dignified but sophisticated Baroque.

But withal understand that in London many stately palaces, built by noblemen upon the river Thames, do make a very great show to them that pass by water; and that there be many more like palaces, also built towards land, but scattered and great part of them in back lanes and streets, which if they were joined to the first in good order, as other cities are built uniformly, they would make not only fair streets, but even a beautiful city, to which few might justly be preferred for the magnificence of the building.

Fynes Moryson, 1617

English Baroque (1690–1720)   Fluidity of Continental Baroque was tempered by Classical and Medieval elements.
Palladianism (or Georgian) (1720–1820)   Italianate buildings with columns and porticoes, often relatively plain, combined with new art of landscape gardening.
Neo-Gothic (1740–80)   Brief vogue for Classical decoration gave way to Rococo-like frivolity and novelty.
Regency (1780–1830)   Simplistic Classicism with delicate interior ornament, often in stucco relief.
Victorian (1830–1900)   Extravagantly treated historicist themes, especially Neo-Gothic, contrast with functional public and industrial structures in iron and glass.
Domestic Revival (1870–1920)   Direct simplicity in domestic architecture, using brick, stone and wood.
International Modern (1930–60)   Functional airy buildings often worked into English gardens.
Modernist (1945–present)   Imaginative use of space and new materials; concern for social basis of architecture.

23

Culture, history and background

London is still blessed with the stones and mortar of its Roman founders in the remnants of the 2ndC city wall, especially near the Barbican. Defence was still the vital consideration when the Norman conquest of 1066 was followed by the construction in 1078 of the huge, square White Tower, one of the best existing examples of a Norman keep.

Westminster Abbey, begun in 1245, is London's finest remaining medieval building, the E arm epitomizing the elegant Early English style, with the later nave in the Perpendicular style. Timber roofing, one of the glories of the English Gothic, survives in the hammer-beam roof of Westminster Hall, and the Great Hall of Hampton Court (1536), along with St James's Palace, a superb red-brick example of the ornate Tudor adaptations of Gothic.

Inigo Jones, born in 1573 in Smithfield, brought the vigour and sophistication of Italian Renaissance styles to London, most notably the elegant symmetry of Andrea Palladio. Jones' particular contribution to the building of London was the development of Covent Garden, especially the Piazza (1631–39), and the first two Palladian buildings in London, the

The White Tower (1078) in the Tower of London, the first of the square Norman keeps, is built of Caen stone.

The hammer-beam roof in Westminster Hall (1399), the only surviving part of the old Palace of Westminster.

The Anne Boleyn gatehouse of Hampton Court Palace (1540), built for Henry VIII in Tudor red brick.

The Banqueting House, Whitehall (1622), Inigo Jones' strictly Palladian masterpiece, incorporates Ionic columns.

24

Banqueting House in Whitehall (1619–22), and the delightful Queen's House in Greenwich.

Sir Christopher Wren (1632–1723), an Oxford-educated scientist, and later Surveyor of the King's Works, was entrusted with the rebuilding of The City after the Great Fire. On the churches of The City he designed towers and steeples to lead the eye to the dome of St Paul's Cathedral. In his buildings, Wren used elements of the classical Renaissance style, but was obliged to adapt its geometrical grandeur and piazzas to the framework of the medieval city's alleys and courtyards.

Wren's secular buildings include the Royal Naval Hospital, Greenwich (1696–1702), and the Royal Hospital, Chelsea (1681–91). His assistant Nicholas Hawksmoor designed several churches that are increasingly appreciated; a fine example is St Mary Woolnoth (1716–24). Wren also influenced Sir James Gibbs, a leader of the English Baroque, and the combination of styles is exemplified by St Martin-in-the-Fields (1722–26).

In the Georgian period, fashion swung away from Baroque back to the rules and conventions of Classical architecture, a move typified by Palladian Chiswick House (1725–29), which

St Paul's (1675–1710) has vast circular crossing, over which arches on piers support inner and outer domes.

St Mary-le-Strand (1714–17), by Gibbs, has Italianate steeple on Classical base.

Chiswick House (1725–29), by Burlington and Kent, has Palladian columned portico.

25

also has a garden landscaped by William Kent. The same notions of refinement and good taste were evident in the Georgian terraces built at this time. The dominant designer was Robert Adam (1728–92), one of a family of influential architects, whose terraced town houses were unified by an elegant facade.

In the later part of the Georgian period, the Regency architect John Nash (1752–1835) used these themes to give a sense of shape and elegance to the heart of modern London. Seen from Piccadilly Circus, the bold, sweeping curve of Regent St. echoes Nash's plan for a triumphal 'Royal Mile' from the Prince Regent's residence at Carlton House to Regent's Park. At either end of this mile are two pristine examples of Nash's work: Carlton House Terrace (1827–32) and Park Crescent (1812–22). These elegant terraces and crescents were mirrored in the development of Belgravia and Chelsea, largely by Thomas Cubitt, in the 1820s and 1830s.

The sterner values of the Victorian period were reflected in church-like buildings such as the Houses of Parliament (1840–50, Sir Charles Barry and Augustus Pugin). This Gothic

20 St James's Sq., a Georgian terraced town house, with strictly Classical facade.

Cumberland Terrace (1825), Regent's Park, by Nash, has massive Classical pediments with stucco decoration.

The Palace of Westminster (1840–50) has a classically balanced plan decorated in Perpendicular Gothic style.

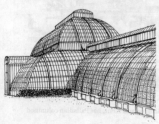

The enormous **conservatory** or **palm house** (1844–48) at Kew Gardens, a functional but elegant Victorian structure.

Revival architecture had moments of fantasy, as the spires of St Pancras Station (1868–74, Sir Gilbert Scott) happily show. The railway era also brought some breathtaking examples of civil engineering, and the interior of Paddington Station (1850–4, Brunel) remains a proud memorial to the best of these. Similarly inspired use of cast-iron and sheet glass is seen in the magnificent conservatory at Kew Gardens (1844–48, Decimus Burton).

The 20thC has so far produced little exciting architecture in London, although the passing of time is leading to a greater appreciation of 1920s and 1930s industrial buildings like the Hoover factory on Western Avenue, and Battersea Power Station. Bauhaus refugees founded the design group Tecton, which designed Highgate's Highpoint Flats (1936), described by Le Corbusier as "a vertical garden city". Notable post-war buildings, both of which have provoked controversy, include Oxford Street's dominant Centrepoint (1965, Richard Seifert), which became a symbol of profligate speculation, and the National Theatre (1967–77, Denys Lasdun), in the cold, horizontal style of the South Bank complex.

The Hoover factory (1932) shows influence of Art Deco.

Barbican (begun 1955) is a housing and social development with walkways between many levels and gardens.

The National Theatre (1967–77) has superbly organized interior, with complex vertical and horizontal creation of functional spaces.

Centrepoint (1962–66), whose honeycomb tower rises above a piazza.

London and literature

The resonances of a city through its life are caught and kept in its literature, and few pavements echo these sounds as pervasively as those of London. The streets themselves are dotted with blue plaques to mark the homes and working places of writers, and the British Museum is heavy with the manuscripts of classics.

It was from London that English literature began its journey; from the Tabard Inn in Southwark, whence Geoffrey Chaucer (1340–1400), a court official and customs officer in London, despatched his garrulous pilgrims with their *Canterbury Tales*. In so doing, he created a specifically English literature, graphically realistic and vernacular. The Tabard became the Talbot Inn, which survived until the 1870s, and Talbot Yard is still there, with six centuries of exits and entrances to remember. It is easy to perceive Chaucer's London in his descriptions of the walled city of Troy in *Troilus and Criseyde* – there is something familiar about a city surrounded by countryside but inside bursting with wonders like those detailed in the contemporary but anonymous *Piers Plowman*.

A tradition was established. Even for the great Renaissance writers, steeped in classical learning, London, noisy, fast and aggressive, dictated its own style, often drama. Shakespeare (1564–1616) worked in the circular galleried theatres of Southwark, thought too rowdy for The City proper, where art was brought for almost the first time to the working class, the 'groundlings' who stood in the 'pit' (see *Bear Gardens Museum*). He would also perform for more exclusive audiences – both *Twelfth Night* and *A Midsummer Night's Dream* are thought to have been first performed privately in the Inns of Court. The plays of his contemporary Ben Jonson give perhaps the best idea of London, where the cunning and clever prosper, especially *The Alchemist*, *Bartholomew Fair* and *Every Good Man in his Humour*, which includes a scene in Paul's Walk, the central aisle of St Paul's. Jonson and others would often retire to The Mermaid Tavern, which stood where Bread St. meets Cheapside, but they sometimes wound up in Southwark's prisons, The Clink or Marshalsea, for writing plays which displeased the Crown. Others met a worse fate: much of Sir Walter Raleigh's finest writing was done during his 13yr in the Tower before his execution in 1618, and Christopher Marlowe was stabbed to death in a tavern in Deptford in 1593.

John Donne (1573–1631), whose early lyrics have such sense of place, is claimed by some to symbolize London's temporary 'decline' into intellectualism by turning to religious poetry and in 1621 becoming Dean of St Paul's. Admittedly, London only housed and did not inspire Milton and the great metaphysical poets. Yet, from the ashes of the medieval city (burnt in 1666) and Puritanism rose arguably the greatest works about London, certainly two of the best diaries ever written, both social history and literature: those of Samuel Pepys and John Evelyn.

> The stones of St Paul's flew like grenades, and the lead melted down the streets in a stream. The very pavements glowed with fiery redness, and neither horse nor man was able to tread on them.

Evelyn's description is one of the highlights, but everyday life is also vividly pictured – that of Pepys so honestly that he always wrote in a secret shorthand not deciphered until 1820.

With the 18thC post-fire development of the West End came
a new Augustan 'Age of Reason', when London, a new Rome or
Athens, inspired learned, urbane works. But its vigorous,
down-to-earth character shone through. Satire became the new
mode, irreverent modern classics about people not gods, such
as *The Dunciad* by Pope (1688–1744), often to be found at
Chiswick House with his patron Lord Burlington; or *London*
by Dr Johnson (1709–84), an archetypal English blend of
common sense and classicism (see *Johnson's House*). Cliques
need meeting places, and the most famous surviving one is the
Cheshire Cheese on Fleet St.; Russell St., Covent Garden,
housed the most renowned coffee houses.

But the age of reason was not all it thought itself. In 1679
Dryden was beaten up outside the Lamb and Flag pub in Rose
St., WC2 (since nicknamed 'The Bucket of Blood'), having
offended the Earl of Rochester, a fellow-writer, in a satire. At
Swift's suggestion, John Gay wrote *The Beggar's Opera* in 1728
as a 'Newgate pastoral', depicting with a new moral stringency
the slums of Covent Garden and the notorious Newgate prison.
Henry Fielding, a pioneer of the new novel form with *Tom
Jones*, was an innovative magistrate in Bow Street, trying to
protect the same slum dwellers. Even writing had its seamy side
– buried under the Barbican is the site of Grub Street, still the
imagined habitat of ill-paid hack writers.

London is enchanting. I step out upon a tawny coloured magic
carpet . . . . it takes up the private life and carries it on, without
any effort . . . .

Virginia Woolf in her diary, 1926

Although Wordsworth was moved to write "Earth has not
anything to show more fair" (*On Westminster Bridge*, 1802), and
Keats (1795–1821) found peace enough in Hampstead to write
Ode to a Nightingale (see *Keats' House*), it was urban squalor
which moved Charles Dickens (1812–70), the most obsessive
writer about London. Like that of his own Sam Weller,
Dickens' "knowledge of London was extensive and peculiar".
In his novels London is most often a brooding, malevolent
presence, too powerful for the people in it, a city of slum
tenements, an evil ruling class, prisons and 'London
particulars' or 'pea-soupers', poisonous mixes of fog and smog.
To balance this, there is the comedy and vitality of his
unforgettable Cockneys, like Sam Weller, Mr Micawber and
Bill Sykes, with their own unique language. Yet underneath
speaks the morally appalled social reformer. The references are
endless (see *Dickens' House*), but some idea of his feelings can
be gained from his treatment of the Thames, along which Abel
Magwitch tries in vain to escape in *Great Expectations* and which
is so often the recipient of corpses – as in the superb opening
scene of *Our Mutual Friend*. On a boat trip downstream to
Greenwich, one can still feel the spirit of Dickensian London
among the deserted warehouses of dockland, and an eerie
feeling it is.

By the inter-war years, things had changed. Virginia Woolf
(1882–1941) wrote: "I ask nothing better than that all the
reviewers . . . . should call me a highbrow. If they like to add
Bloomsbury, WC1., that is the correct postal address". In
Bloomsbury's leafy Georgian squares, Lawrence, Yeats, Eliot
and Forster found a calming peace, which is still there and can
be felt in the modernist literature forged in the area.

29

Royal London

Like the pussy cat in the nursery rhyme, people go "up to London to look at the Queen". For the visitor from other parts of the realm, the rituals, pageantry, and palaces of royal London are the tangible demonstration not only of a heritage but also of a unique record of stability. The monarchy has survived not because the kingdom is quiescent but because the Crown itself is a stabilizing influence. It has had its nadirs, of course: it was replaced by the Commonwealth from 1649–60; and more recently the abdication of Edward VIII in 1936, before his coronation, provoked something of a crisis of confidence in the institution. Today, most Britons regard it as the keystone of the state. That phenomenon is not unique, but it is rare.

. . . . for within the hollow crown
That rounds the mortal temples of a king
Keeps Death his court, and there the antick sits,
Scoffing his state and grinning at his pomp . . . .
I live with bread like you, feel want,
Taste grief, need friends: subjected thus,
How can you say to me I am a king?
William Shakespeare, *Richard II*, c.1593

The kingdom is not, of course, England, otherwise the Queen's husband and son and heir would not be the Duke of Edinburgh and the Prince of Wales. The Queen is head of state of many countries in the Commonwealth, too, but arguably the most important job of the monarchy is to represent the family of nations which together, and by consent, comprise the United Kingdom. Because they have smaller populations, Scotland and Wales are numerically less represented in Parliament than England, but they are equal in the sight of the Crown. In countries of less age, national unity can be an objective in itself, but Britain is neither young nor one nation, and needs some means by which it can articulate its wholeness.

There will soon be only five kings left – the Kings of England, Diamonds, Hearts, Spades and Clubs.
King Farouk of Egypt, 1951

At the time of the wedding of the Prince of Wales in 1981, Charles Douglas-Home, writing in *The Times*, conceded that the Queen has "almost no executive function to perform", but concluded that she has "a 'presence' in the highest reaches of the political process". Until now, the Queen has always been able to appoint as Prime Minister the leader of which ever of the two parties, Conservative and Labour, won the election. If the party system fragments further, however, the Queen might find herself required either to find a Prime Minister out of a confusion of minority parties, or decide whether to dissolve a hung Parliament. The monarchy, Douglas-Home pointed out, "is not yet constitutionally allowed to slip back into a world of sumptuous ceremonial".

Where to see the Royal Family

The daily Court Circular, which gives details of all the Royal Family's public engagements, is printed in *The Times* and the *Daily Telegraph*. Apart from this, the Queen presides at certain

annual events, often accompanied by other members of her
family.

The State Opening of Parliament, at the beginning of each
new session of Parliament, usually late Oct, is the most
apparently political of the Queen's regular duties, in that she
announces in her speech a programme of proposed legislation.
In fact, the measures outlined are put forward not at the
discretion of the Queen but on behalf of her government.

Remembrance Sunday, on the Sun nearest Nov 11, sees the
Queen placing wreaths on the Cenotaph in Whitehall to
commemorate the dead of the two World Wars.

Trooping the Colour takes place on a Sat in mid-June to
honour the Queen's official birthday on June 13. Each year a
different Guards regiment presents itself for inspection; the
'colour' is its regimental flag. The Queen rides on horseback to
Horse Guards' Parade off Whitehall, receives the salute amid
marching bands, and often makes an appearance on the balcony
of Buckingham Palace on her return.

Royal residences

Buckingham Palace did not become the principal royal
residence until the time of Queen Victoria (1836–1902), but it
had been used by monarchs since George III bought it in 1762.
Before Victoria, St James's Palace, built for Henry VIII
(1509–47), was the sovereign's official residence. Its status is
still honoured in the accreditation of foreign diplomats to "the
court of St James", and it is the headquarters of the Gentlemen
at Arms, who form a personal bodyguard for the Queen, and the
home of the Yeomen of the Guard. These, rather than the
Tower Yeomen, are the true 'Beefeaters', a word probably
derived from 'buffetier', meaning an attendant at royal buffets.
St James's Palace also includes Clarence House, home of Queen
Elizabeth the Queen Mother, one of the most dearly loved
members of the Royal Family in recent decades.

Kensington Palace was acquired as a home by William III,
who wanted a place in the country around London. It was the
home of the sovereign from 1689–1760, and is now the home of
Princess Margaret, the Queen's sister, and of other royals.

Windsor Castle (see *Excursions*) is still used extensively by
the Royal Family. Originally the home of Edward the Confessor
(1042–66), it is a country home much closer to London than
Balmoral in Scotland, or Sandringham in Norfolk.

Who's who in the Royal Family

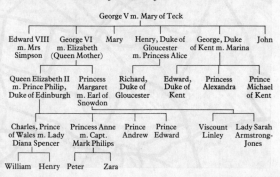

31

Orientation map

Hertford
Stansted Airport

A10

Highbury

Islington

Upper St.

Camden
Town

Pancras

King's
Cross

Angel

City Rd.

Bethnal
Green

Euston Rd.

Old St.

A11

Bloomsbury

Cambridge

British
Museum

High Holborn

Liverpool St.

tham Ct.

Fleet St.

St Paul's

The City

Whitechapel

A13

ho

Covent
Garden

Victoria Embankment

algar
q.

Charing
Cross

Waterloo
Br.

London Br.

Tower of
London

St Katharine
Docks

St James's
Park

Waterloo

Southwark

stminster
Abbey

Pal. of
Westminster

Elephant
& Castle

stminster

Tate
llery

Old Kent Rd.

Oval

A2

dsworth Rd.

A202

A23

Canterbury
Dover

Lambeth

Camberwell

Brixton

0   2 miles

3

0   1   2   3 km

Dulwich

33

Calendar of events

See also *Sports and activities* and *Public holidays* in *Basic information.*

January

1st week. Jan sales. Most stores offer good reductions; the most voracious shoppers camp out overnight in queues. Some now start late Dec

International Boat Show. Earls Court, SW5. Leisure boats

Jan 29. Charles I Commemoration. Whitehall, SW1. On the anniversary of his execution, the unofficial King's Army parades from the statue at Charing Cross to the Banqueting House

Jan/Feb. Chinese New Year. Chinatown, around Gerrard St., W1. Dragons, lanterns, flags, torches and the Lion Dance

Jan/Mar. Rugby Union Internationals. Twickenham. On two Sat afternoons England play

February

Cruft's Dog Show. Earls Court, SW5. The world's biggest, most prestigious show

Annual Clowns Service. Holy Trinity Church, Dalston, E8. The Clowns International Club attends its church in full costume to honour its founder, Joseph Grimaldi. All welcome to free clown show afterwards

Shrove Tuesday, 11.00. Pancake races. Lincoln's Inn Fields, WC2. Pancakes, made of fats forbidden in Lent, are tossed in races by teams of beauty queens, chefs and housewives

Folk Music Festival. Royal Albert Hall, SW7. Weekend of concerts

March

Mar 1. St David's Day. Windsor Castle. A member of the Royal Family presents the Welsh Guards with the national emblem, a leek

Ideal Home Exhibition. Olympia, W14. A huge exhibition of everything, but everything, found in and around the home

Camden Festival. The borough, from Bloomsbury to Hampstead, sponsors concerts, plays, etc.; always attracts big jazz names

2nd Tues. Bridewell Service. St Bride's, Fleet St., EC4. The Lord Mayor and Sheriffs attend this thanksgiving service for the Bridewell children's home, now moved out of London

Oranges and Lemons Service. St Clement Danes, Strand, WC2. As a reminder of the nursery rhyme, children are presented with the fruits during a service

Royal Film Performance. Royals and celebrities attend a gala premiere for charity

Mar 17. St Patrick's Day. Pirbright, Surrey. The Irish Guards are presented with shamrock by the Queen Mother

Country Music Festival. Wembley Arena. Festivities last for a week

Mar/Apr. Boat Race. Putney to Mortlake. Oxford and Cambridge University eights battle upstream with awesome power

Mar/Apr. Head of the River Race. Mortlake to Putney. A full day's racing between teams from all over Europe

April

Maundy Thursday (Thurs before Easter). Maundy Money. At a different church every year, the Queen presents specially-minted coins to the elderly and to groups of children

Good Friday. Butterworth Charity. St Bartholomew the Great, Smithfield, EC1. After 11.00 service, hot cross buns and coins are laid out on tombstones for local children

Easter Day. Easter Parade. Battersea Park. Climax of the day-long fair is the huge colourful parade at 15.00. Also fairs on Hampstead Heath and Blackheath. Tower Church Parade. Tower of London, EC3. After 11.00 service, the Yeoman Warders have an official inspection

Easter Monday. Procession and Easter carols. Westminster Abbey, SW1

Harness Horse Parade. Regents Park, NW1. A morning parade of heavy working horses in superb, gleaming brass harnesses and plumes

2nd Wed after Easter. Spital Sermon. St Lawrence Jewry, EC2. A service attended by all The City's pomp, Lord Mayor included, in full regalia

Apr 21. Queen's Birthday. 21-gun salutes in Hyde Park and on Tower Hill at 12.00. Troops in parade dress

May

FA Cup Final. Wembley Stadium. Showpiece soccer match

Rugby League Cup Final. Wembley Stadium. Showpiece rugby league match

Beating Retreat. Horse Guards Parade, SW1. Military massed bands and marching

Summer Exhibition. Royal Academy, Piccadilly, W1. An extensive *pot pourri* of much that is happening in British art. To Sept

Ascension Day. Beating the Bounds. The boundary stones of parishes were traditionally 'whacked' with a stick in defiance. Today it happens around the Tower, and All-Hallows-by-the-Tower, EC3, one of the marks of which is in mid-river but is whacked notwithstanding

Private Fire Brigades Competition. Guildhall Yard, EC4. They spray targets with hoses. Again in Sept

Glyndebourne Opera Season. Sussex. Exclusive performances in a country house, with champagne picnics during intervals. To Aug

Chelsea Flower Show. Royal Hospital, SW3. A massive and superb 4-day horticultural display May 29 or soon after. Founder's (Oak Apple) Day. Royal Hospital, Chelsea, SW3. The Chelsea Pensioners' annual parade

June

1st Wed. The Derby. Epsom Downs. This great horse race is on common land, and so is attended by fairs, gypsies, and huge crowds

June 4. Samuel Pepys Memorial Service. St Olave, EC3. Lord Mayor and Co., 17thC band, all flock to Pepys' own church

Test match. Lords, NW8. 5-day international cricket match

June 11 or nearest Sat. Trooping the Colour. Horse Guards Parade, SW1. The Queen, in uniform, rides from Buckingham Palace in procession to receive the Colour from her Foot Guards amid full pageantry

3rd Week. Royal Ascot. The Berkshire racecourse sees some fine racing but more important for royalty on parade and 'society' out to impress each other and enjoy themselves

3rd Mon. Garter Ceremony. St George's Chapel, Windsor Castle. The 24 members of The Very Noble Order of the Garter attend a service, invest new members, and pay homage to the Queen

June 22 or near. Election of the Sheriffs of The City of London. Guildhall, EC2. Full pageantry and procession

June/July. Wimbledon Tennis Championships. The world's top players

Outdoor concerts. In all major parks, Kenwood Lakeside, Hampstead Heath, and Crystal Palace Bowl. Until Sept

July

1st week. Henley Royal Regatta. Henley, Oxfordshire. Another sporting event (rowing) which is also part of the 'season'

Royal Tournament. Earls Court, SW5. All the Armed Forces join in displays of gymnastics, motor cycling and military skills. On the Sun before it begins, they all parade along The Mall, SW1

Promenade Concerts. Royal Albert Hall, SW7. Until Sept. See *Concerts* in *Nightlife*

Royal International Horse Show. Wembley Arena. Show jumping

3rd week. Swan Upping. London Bridge to Henley. The Dyers Company and Vintners Company, who share ownership of all swans with the Queen, take six boats upriver counting and marking the birds

Vintners Roadsweeping. St James Garlickhythe, EC4. Wine porters sweep the road in front of the procession marking the inauguration of their new Master

August

Bank Holiday Weekend (last in Aug). Horse Fair. Clapham Common. Bank Holiday Fair. Hampstead Heath. A traditional fairground. The Notting Hill Carnival. Ladbroke Grove, W11. West Indian street carnival

September

Test match. Kennington Oval, SE11. 5-day international cricket

Last Night of the Proms. Royal Albert Hall, SW7. See *Concerts* in *Nightlife*

Autumn Antiques Fair. Chelsea Old Town Hall, Kings Rd., SW3

Sept 21. Christ's Hospital Boys March. Church of the Holy Sepulchre, Holborn Viaduct, EC1. The pupils and band of this ancient school march to Mansion House in 16thC 'bluecoats'

Private Fire Brigades Competition. EC4. See May

Sept 28. Admission of Sheriffs. See June; in another ceremony they are admitted to the Guildhall

Sept 29. Election of the Lord Mayor. Guildhall, EC2. Beforehand, the whole corporation proceeds in state from Mansion House

October

Oct 1 or 1st Mon. Judges Service. Westminster Abbey, SW1. At the start of the legal year, the judiciary process from Westminster Abbey to breakfast in the Palace of Westminster, and then parades in the afternoon at the Royal Courts of Justice in the Strand, WC2

1st Sun. Pearly Harvest Festival. St Martin-in-the-Fields, WC2. The brightly caparisoned Pearly Kings and Queens, Cockney folk leaders, in full uniform

Horse of the Year Show. Wembley Arena. Show jumping, featuring top international competitors

2nd Sun. Harvest of the Sea Thanksgiving. St Mary-at-Hill, EC3. Billingsgate dealers fill the church with fish, and The City attends in state

Quit Rents Ceremony. Royal Courts of Justice, WC2. An official receives token rents on behalf of the Queen; the ceremony includes splitting of sticks and counting of horseshoes

Oct 21. Trafalgar Day. National Service for Seafarers at St Paul's Cathedral, attended by Admiralty top brass; and a naval ceremony in Trafalgar Sq., WC2

National Brass Band Festival. Royal Albert Hall, SW7. A type of music at which the British excel

Oct/Nov. State Opening of Parliament. The processional route is Buckingham Palace, The Mall, Horse Guards Parade, Palace of Westminster. Usually the entire Royal Family attend; full regalia, ancient gilded coaches

November

1st Sun. London to Brighton Veteran Car Run. Hyde Park Corner, SW1. An early start (8.00) for the 50yr-old-plus cars

Nov 5. Guy Fawkes Night. To celebrate the 1605 Gunpowder Plot to blow up Parliament, fireworks and bonfires all over town, with effigies of the conspiracy's leader burnt on top

Sun nearest Nov 11. Remembrance Sun. The Queen and State attend an 11.00 ceremony at the Cenotaph, Whitehall, SW1. The previous evening there is a moving Festival of Remembrance at the Royal

Albert Hall, SW7

Fri nearest Nov 12. Admission of Lord Mayor Elect. Guildhall, EC2. The outgoing mayor hands over the insignia

Sat nearest Nov 12. Lord Mayor's Show. Guildhall to Law Courts, Strand, WC2. The state coaches follow the many colourful floats in this huge carnival

London Film Festival. National Film Theatre, South Bank. To Dec

Late Nov. Switching on of Christmas lights in Regent St. and Oxford St. Until Jan 6

Nov/Dec. Benson & Hedges Tennis Championships. Wembley Arena

December

Royal Smithfield Show. Earls Court, SW5. Agricultural show

Norwegian Christmas Tree. Trafalgar Sq. Carol-singing on most evenings beneath the tree

Dickens Drive. Dickens House, Doughty St., WC1 to St Peter's, Eaton Sq., SW1. A costumed afternoon drive in stage and horses followed by mime and music

Dec 31. Watch Night. St Paul's Cathedral. Scots gather on steps for Hogmanay. Trafalgar Sq. is the other traditional spot for high-spirited revellers

Weekly events

Mon. Bric-a-brac and antiques at Covent Garden market

Wed. Camden Passage antique market. Late-night shopping in Knightsbridge (see Shopping). Some theatre matinees

Thurs. Late-night shopping in Oxford St. and Regent St. Some theatre matinees

Fri. Bermondsey (New Caledonian) antique market (see Shopping)

Sat. Portobello Rd. antique market and Covent Garden crafts market (see Shopping). Theatre matinees. Evening open-air concerts in June-July at Kenwood House, Hampstead Heath

Sun. Petticoat Lane, Camden Lock markets (see Shopping)

Daily events

11.00 (10.00 Sun). Changing the Guard. Horse Guards Parade

11.30 (only alternate days in winter). Changing the Guard, Buckingham Palace

21.50 Ceremony of the Keys. Tower of London. Another ceremonial changing of guards. Write to Resident Governor for free ticket

When and where to go

Unlike the folk of some cities, Londoners do not all choose to take their holidays at the same time, so the capital never 'closes down'. It does, on the other hand, become very crowded at the height of summer. Consider side-stepping this stampede: the British climate may be unpredictable but it is rarely extreme and London, being in the mildest part of the country, can be very pleasant in the spring and autumn. Moreover, a whole series of outdoor sporting (and social) events takes place from March (see *Calendar of events*).

Outdoor institutions, like the open-air theatre in *Regent's Park*, begin to brave the elements in May, and in the same month Glyndebourne's opera season starts. The crowded months are July and Aug, but theatre-lovers will want to avoid the summer in favour of autumn and winter, often better times for new shows and certainly for accommodation. Even in winter, London remains alive with activity, and several of the main exhibitions take place at this time of year. One famous winter institution which London has cast aside is the pea-souper fog, vanquished by clean-air legislation, and little else remains to stop Londoners going about their daily rounds.

The main airport being on the western side of the city, and the longer rail and road routes running into the W and N, those compass points have a powerful influence on activity in London. The greatest number of hotels are in the W, whether in suburbs like *Chiswick*, inner districts like *Kensington*, *Chelsea* and Victoria, or in the West End, the area which most Londoners regard as the centre by virtue of its shops, restaurants and theatres. Further E, *The City*, though it is jewelled with historical sights, is seen by the Londoner as being primarily a business district which empties in the evenings and at weekends. In much the way that The City is a buffer to the E, so is the river to the S. The implantation of the *Barbican* Centre in The City and the *South Bank Arts Centre* across the river were both conscious attempts to extend the geographical spread of nocturnal life. Beyond these staging posts, however, central London fades in The City and only half-heartedly crosses the Thames. Central London does not formally define itself, but most inhabitants would probably accept the Circle line on the tube system as a fair boundary.

Few Londoners live within that circle, however, and their districts of residence outside it are the source of much local rivalry. Not only does the topography of fashionable northern suburbs like *Hampstead* and *Highgate* provide their inhabitants with elevated notions, but it is also true that many Londoners feign disinclination to cross the river. Certainly many of the 'south-of-the-river' districts closer to London have little to recommend them to visitors, although among these are some residential enclaves that are gradually becoming fashionable. Nevertheless there are no recommended tourist hotels at present S of the river; nor indeed are there many to the E of *Tower Bridge*. So for accommodation the visitor has to stick to the centre, the N or the W.

Each of the compass points appears in the beginning of the postal codes and is also printed on street signs. Much of the West End is W1 (West One), addresses in The City usually carry EC (East Central), and so on. Nevertheless the system is not as logical as it might be and spoken directions will tend to be given in terms of the area's or the district's name.

Area planners

The City

Home not only of Mammon (in the Bank of England and the *Stock Exchange*) but also of God (in *St Paul's Cathedral* and the numerous churches) and the Godless (in *Fleet Street*). The *Royal Courts of Justice* and the *Old Bailey* are to be found in The City, and the whole square mile is guarded by the *Tower of London*.

The West End

Unlike The City, the West End has no precise borders, though it is divided by its main thoroughfares into clearly-defined neighbourhoods. Simply by crossing the street it is possible to leave behind a neighbourhood of one character and enter what seems to be another world. See *Orientation map* for area limits.

Mayfair is the neighbourhood of exclusive hotels, expense-account restaurants, embassies, *haute couture* houses and casinos, and its denizens usually ride in chauffeur-driven cars. Its 'village' shopping street is Bond St., with South Molton St. for the younger folk, and North and South Audley Sts. for the extra-extravagant. In hilly, elegant Brook, Mount and Curzon Sts. are smaller, old-established exclusive shops. The alleys of Shepherd Market offer pavement cafes for rest and refreshment on sunny days.

Soho is seductive not for its sex shops, which are no more inviting nor less sleazy than those in any other city, but for its delicatessens, patisseries, moderately–priced restaurants, and a gossipy confluence of Italian waiters, Cockney film editors, lengthy lunchers and other miscreants. Its trendiness has long attracted media folk. Over Shaftesbury Ave., its cosmopolitanism hardens into Chinatown.

Covent Garden has, despite the misgivings of purists, proved to be one of the most successful examples anywhere of a discarded facility (in this instance a wholesale fruit and vegetable market) being turned into an area for strolling, eating and shopping. The most fiercely community-conscious of all the inner city areas, it has come to stand for everything opposed to big business and development.

Bloomsbury has a bookish dignity which once hid all manner of intensity. It also has the *British Museum* and the nucleus of London University, whose visitors and students find perfect peace in its many green squares.

Belgravia is the most elegant part of the West End, with its early 19thC houses; Belgrave Sq., from which it takes its name, has beautiful gardens. Even the very rich who have always lived here are feeling the pinch and today the area is dominated by embassies. Belgravia's 'neighbourhood shop' is Harrods, round the corner in Knightsbridge.

St James's is gentlemen's clubland, with Jermyn St. as its shopping thoroughfare. The name is broadly applied to the neighbourhood around St James's St., and St James's Sq., on the hill running down from Piccadilly to *St James's Palace*, constituting an area which has perhaps changed less than any other over the last 50yr.

Westminster is media shorthand for Parliament, in much the way that its *Whitehall* is used to denote the Civil Service and *Downing Street* to suggest the Prime Minister. Apart from *Westminster Abbey*, all the dominant buildings in this area are concerned with government. No shops, few residents – just a rich seam of pomp and circumstance.

Inner London
Beyond central London, several inner districts make their own unique contributions to metropolitan life. The most obvious are the two which give their name to the Royal Borough of Kensington and Chelsea. *Kensington*, with its famous museums, also extends to Notting Hill and Portobello Rd., eventually giving way to Hammersmith, which has a couple of respected theatres. *Chelsea*, elegant and fashionable, with its clothes shops and restaurants, spills over into Fulham. All these districts are in the w; in the N, Islington has emerged as the outstanding example of the arty rejuvenation of London's old working-class inner boroughs.

Outer London
Intellectual *Hampstead* and *Highgate* in the N, maritime *Greenwich* in the E, villagey *Dulwich* in the S, riverside *Richmond* in the w. . . . all are to varying degrees outer districts, though London stretches yet further in an exhausting sprawl of mainly 1930s suburbs.

Walks in London

Although London is vast in area, it is also a marvellous city for walking in. Perhaps the chief reason for this lies in the close proximity of the many separate and characterful neighbourhoods that it comprises, and a number of these – *Chelsea, Holland Park*, Little Venice, *Greenwich, Hampstead,* among others – make walks in themselves (see A–Z of *Sights and places of interest*).

In a city that reached its prime before the days of motor transport, walking is also, quite naturally, the most effective way to see and learn about London. For information about walks for this purpose – routes, subjects of theme walks, starting times – ☎730–3488: London Visitor and Convention Bureau. Similar information is also published on the back page of *The Times* in The Times Information Service.

The walks described in detail on the following pages have a different and special purpose: to give a taste of a Londoner's London – its river, parks and pubs, and its cultural, especially literary, heart.

As an introduction to this historic city, however, or to refresh the memory after a long absence, the following stroll through its City of Westminster, centre of government and tradition and cornerstone of the West End, links many of London's most famous landmarks and serves as a convenient orientation tour as well.

Walk 1/Introduction to London
Allow 2–3hr. Tube Westminster. See Maps **9–10**.
Begin by walking along Bridge St., past the statue of *Queen Boadicea*, symbol of patriotism, on to Westminster Bridge itself, from where the best view of the *Palace of Westminster* and **Big Ben** can be gained. Look also to your right along the Victoria Embankment to see the fine government buildings. Let your gaze move round in full circle to cross the river with the Charing Cross railway bridge; beyond it is the *South Bank Arts Centre* and, on this side, **County Hall**, headquarters of the Greater London Council. The panorama continues past the

huge stone lion at the E end of Westminster Bridge to the new St Thomas' Hospital, and crosses the river again by Lambeth Bridge.

From the foot of Big Ben, walk back round the w side of the Palace of Westminster past Westminster Hall and then cross over the road to St Margaret's Church to arrive at *Westminster Abbey*.

Continue around Parliament Sq. almost to Bridge St. again, before turning left into Parliament St., which leads to *Whitehall*. The second street on the left, past the Cenotaph, is *Downing Street*, where the policeman at the door identifies 'Number 10'. Going N along Whitehall, the *Banqueting House* (1622) is on the right, nearly opposite the Whitehall entrance to *Horse Guards Parade*. At the N of Whitehall is *Trafalgar Square*, dominated by **Nelson's Column**, and a crowded area of constant activity.

As you cross the square towards the *National Gallery*, notice also James Gibbs' beautiful church of *St Martin-in-the-Fields* (1726). St Martin's Pl., in front and to the right of the church, has the central Post Office on its right; to the N, up St Martin's Lane, is the globe-topped spire of the **Coliseum**, home of the English National Opera (see *Nightlife*). Leading round to the left, however, past the entrance to the *National Portrait Gallery*, is Charing Cross Rd. Follow this road as far as Leicester Square tube station, then turn left along Cranbourn St. into **Leicester Sq.** itself.

The route continues along the N side of Leicester Sq. as far as the Swiss Centre, where a right turn up Wardour St. leads past Lisle St. and Gerrard St., the two main arteries of **Chinatown**, to Shaftesbury Ave., the heart of theatreland and the southern boundary of *Soho*. Turn left on Shaftesbury Ave. and walk down to **Piccadilly Circus**.

Arriving at Piccadilly Circus, pause a moment to orientate yourself between Shaftesbury Ave., Regent St., curving majestically to the w and N, and *Piccadilly* itself, leading w towards *Mayfair*, *Belgravia* and Knightsbridge. It is the fourth major street that you must follow, however: Lower Regent St. to the S, which borders *St James's* on the right, and crosses Pall Mall to the Duke of York Monument, at the top of the steps that run down past the elegant and imposing **Carlton House Terrace** to *The Mall*.

At the foot of the steps look left towards Admiralty Arch, and Trafalgar Square beyond it. Notice also the ivy-clad wartime extension to the Admiralty, the Citadel, beyond which can be seen the expanse of Horse Guards Parade. Then walk w along The Mall, with *St James's Park* on your left, towards the gilded **Victoria Memorial** and beyond it *Buckingham Palace*, passing *Marlborough House*, *St James's Palace*, Clarence House and *Lancaster House* on the way. Walk round the S side of Buckingham Palace to Buckingham Gate and Buckingham Palace Rd., to the entrances to the **Queen's Picture Gallery** and the **Royal Mews**.

To complete the walk, either continue along Buckingham Palace Rd. to Victoria Station, or retrace your steps to follow Birdcage Walk along the S side of St James's Park in front of the newly restored Wellington Barracks. The first street on the right, **Queen Anne's Gate**, leads to St James's Park tube station. To continue along Birdcage Walk into Great George St. takes you to **Parliament Square** and Westminster tube station, where the walk began.

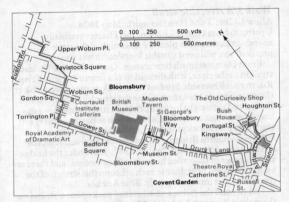

Walk 2/London's cultural heart

Allow 1–2hr. Tube Temple. Map 10–11.

The central areas of *Covent Garden* and *Bloomsbury* have always been nurseries of artistic endeavour and achievement.

Begin at the Aldwych, where **Bush House**, facing up Kingsway, is an appropriate symbol of British cultural prestige; from this building the BBC runs its foreign radio services. On the right, Houghton St. leads to Portugal St., and **The Old Curiosity Shop**. It is not certain that Dickens based his novel on this antique shop, but he knew it well.

Back on the Aldwych, turn up **Drury Lane**. The **Theatre Royal**, down Russell St. to the left and on the corner of Catherine St., was founded in 1663. Also in **Russell St.** were the famous coffee houses of the 18thC; Dr Johnson and Boswell first met in a bookshop at no. 8 in 1763. Drury Lane continues until it turns into Museum St. and pushes on into more elegant *Bloomsbury*, passing on the right in Bloomsbury Way the church of **St George**, used by Dickens as the setting for his Bloomsbury christening in *Sketches by Boz*.

Return to Museum St. and turn right, passing an occult and magic bookshop, the Rudolf Steiner Library, and a couple of famous publishing houses. At the far end is the **Museum Tavern**, at different times favoured by Karl Marx and Dylan Thomas. Turn left here, past the *British Museum*, and then right into Bloomsbury St., passing the peaceful and unspoilt **Bedford Sq.**, the home at times of many distinguished people and therefore of a crop of blue plaques. Continue down Gower St., pausing to see the statues of tragedy and comedy outside the **Royal Academy of Dramatic Art**.

A right turn into Torrington Pl. passes Dillon's University Bookshop and Woburn Sq. on the right, home of the *Courtauld Institute Galleries*. Gordon Sq., on the left, was a stamping-ground of the Bloomsbury Group. Torrington Pl. leads on to Tavistock Sq.; the garden has as its focal point a statue of *Mahatma Gandhi*, and a tree planted by Pandit Nehru. Turn left along the far side of the square to Upper Woburn Pl. On the right, a blue plaque marks the site where Dickens lived from 1851–60, now the headquarters of the British Medical Association. Farther on the right, turn into **Woburn Walk**, with its bowfronted shops and brass plaque in memory of the poet W. B. Yeats, who lived here at the turn of the century.

A left turn leads back to Euston Rd., for a bus or tube.

Walk 3/A riverside stroll

Allow 1–2hr. Tube Hammersmith. Map **20**C4.

Upstream from central London, the Thames gradually abandons business for pleasure. As much of the route is unpaved you will need suitable footwear in wet weather.

From Hammersmith tube station, Queen Caroline St. leads straight to the river, with the option of a detour left into Crisp Rd. to visit **Riverside Studios** for a drink or snack, or a look at the art gallery or bookshop. Cross the river by Hammersmith Bridge and turn right for a surprisingly rustic walk along the overgrown bank to the **Bull's Head** pub at Barnes, or stay on the N side for historical and architectural interest.

Hammersmith Bridge is one of the most attractive on the river; a suspension bridge built in 1887. Just under the bridge are a number of balconied houses and boathouses, and there are a couple of pubs next door to each other on this stretch of the river; the most interesting is the **Blue Anchor**.

Just beyond the pubs, a small area of park opens out, and on the right is **Wescott Lodge** (1700), a former vicarage. Farther away to the right, across the main road, is the handsome 1930s facade of **Hammersmith Town Hall**.

On the river, an ugly iron jetty marks the spot, indicated by a plaque, where a creek and a small natural harbour gave birth to the village of Hammersmith. The path winds to the right, then an inlet to the left leads suddenly into a tiny Georgian street which once lay at the heart of Hammersmith, **Upper Mall**. On the left is the **Dove** pub, and on the right is **Kelmscott House**, once the home of William Morris. Over the coach-house door is a sign commemorating the Hammersmith Socialists, and the building is still the headquarters of the William Morris Society. The same house can also boast of having witnessed the first demonstration of the electric telegraph.

The riverside walk continues past the crow's-nest lookout post of the Corinthian Sailing Club, through a modern cloisterlike construction under a block of apartments, past the balconied **Ship** pub, a pumping station and another pub called

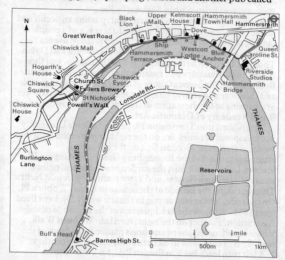

the **Black Lion**; this pub has associations with the humorist and essayist A. P. Herbert. Leaving behind a panoramic view of the river, the path then deserts the Thames for a moment to follow the fine Georgian terrace, **Hammersmith Terrace**. As the river comes back into view, from Chiswick Mall a ramp can be seen from which it is possible to walk at low tide to a small island, **Chiswick Eyot**. On the right is Fuller's brewery, then **St Nicholas** church, where Whistler and Hogarth are buried. Enter the churchyard from the river and the tomb of *Hogarth* is on the left, surrounded by a railing. Walk round the church into the new graveyard, and the green, bronze tomb of *Whistler* is near the ivy-covered wall. The path leading out of the church, Powells Walk, leads to a main road, Burlington Lane, across which is *Chiswick House*. Back on the opposite side of the church, Church St. leads to **Chiswick Sq.**, on the left, said to be the scene of an episode in Thackeray's *Vanity Fair*. Round the corner is *Hogarth's House*.

Walk 4/The parks

Allow 1–3hr. Use Maps **6–10** to enjoy the parks and wander off the skeleton route described. Tube Piccadilly Circus.
A few minutes' walk from Piccadilly Circus tube station, London's royal parks begin, and they spread themselves airily to *Kensington*.

Stroll down Lower Regent St. to the very end, passing the Crimean War memorial and crossing *Pall Mall* into **Waterloo Pl.** Descend the steps to *The Mall*, with the **Institute of Contemporary Arts** on the left and the Admiralty building diagonally across the road. Cross the road, and enter *St James's Park*.

This small but pretty park is dominated by its lake, alive with waterfowl. Follow the lake to the opposite end of the park to leave by the gateway to the right, in front of *Buckingham Palace*. Renegotiate The Mall to enter **Green Park**, opposite. Walk diagonally across this hilly little park, bearing left to enter the pedestrian subway at Hyde Park Corner.

This subway emerges by the triumphal **Wellington Arch**, on an island of history surrounded by a tangled urban road system. It is best to leave this island, after a look at its imposing monuments, by another hole in the ground, this one signposted for Hyde Park Corner tube station. By-passing the station itself, emerge by *Hyde Park*, backtracking to enter by the triple archway, then take one final subway to arrive in grassy safety. On this corner is *Apsley House*.

Inside the park, the thoroughfare to the left is **Rotten Row**, for horse riders. Straight ahead is the path that leads to the **Serpentine**, the descriptively-named lake popular for boating, which also boasts two adequate restaurants. Follow the lake as far as the bridge carrying the main road, and cross to the other bank. A few steps beyond the bridge is the **Serpentine Gallery**, noted for its exhibitions of contemporary artists. Behind the gallery are paths to the bandstand and Round Pond, with a striking view en route of the *Albert Memorial and Royal Albert Hall*. Return to the water's edge, on the Kensington side, to see the Art Nouveau statue of *Peter Pan*, whose whimsy pervades the gardens. At the head of the waters is a paved garden, and beyond them the Elfin Oak, a tree-stump carved with elves. Don't leave the gardens without visiting *Kensington Palace*. From this end of the park, it is not far to Bayswater or Kensington High St. tube stations, to the N and S respectively.

Sights and places of interest

London's major sights are every bit as enjoyable as their worldwide reputation suggests, but remember that this is also a city of wonderful diversity, so try to take in some of the less well-known attractions too.

Opening hours are fairly regularly adhered to, although entry may not be allowed near closing time. Churches' hours may vary more than those of other buildings, especially in *The City*, and are always subject to closure for services. Rules on photography vary, but often only flash is prohibited.

Major sights classified by type

Ancient buildings
Apsley House
Banqueting House
Buckingham Palace
Chiswick House
Eltham Palace
Fenton House
Gray's Inn
Guildhall
Ham House
Hampton Court
Kensington Palace
Kenwood House
Lambeth Palace
Lancaster House
Leighton House
Lincoln's Inn
Mansion House
Marble Hill House
Marlborough House
Orleans House
Osterley Park
Royal Hospital, Chelsea
Royal Naval College, Greenwich
St James's Palace
Somerset House
Staple Inn
Strawberry Hill
Syon House
Temple
Tower of London
Westminster, Palace of

Churches
Brompton Oratory
St Bartholomew-the-Great
St George's, Bloomsbury
St James's Piccadilly
St Martin-in-the-Fields
St Mary Abchurch
St Mary-le-Bow
St Mary-le-Strand
St Paul's, Covent Garden
St Paul's Cathedral
St Stephen Walbrook
Southwark Cathedral
Westminster Abbey
Westminster Cathedral

Districts
Belgravia
Bloomsbury
Chelsea
Chiswick
The City
Covent Garden

Greenwich
Hampstead
Highgate
Kensington
Mayfair
Richmond
St James's
Soho
Westminster

Museums and galleries
Apsley House/Wellington
    Museum
The Bear Gardens Museum
HMS Belfast
Bethnal Green Museum
The British Museum
Commonwealth Institute
Courtauld Institute Galleries
Dickens' House
Dulwich College and Picture
    Gallery
Geffrye Museum
Geological Museum
Hogarth's House
Imperial War Museum
Dr. Johnson's House
Keats' House
Kenwood House/Iveagh Bequest
London, Museum of
London Transport Museum
Madame Tussaud's
Mankind, Museum of
National Gallery
National Maritime Museum,
    Greenwich
National Portrait Gallery
Natural History Museum
Public Records Office Museum
Royal Academy of Arts
Royal Air Force Museum, Hendon
Science Museum
Sir John Soane's Museum
Tate Gallery
Victoria & Albert Museum
Wallace Collection
Whitechapel Art Gallery

Parks/gardens
Holland Park
Hyde Park
Kew Gardens
Regent's Park
Richmond Park
St James's Park
Zoo

Albert Memorial and Royal Albert Hall Ⅲ

Kensington Gore, SW7 ☎ *589–8212. Map 15|4. Tube Knightsbridge, South Kensington.*

These fine examples of Victoriana are dedicated to Victoria's consort, who encouraged the institutionalization of arts and sciences which gives this corner of *Kensington* its character. The Albert Hall was erected in 1867–71, and today its huge amphitheatre is used for everything from boxing to concerts, most notably the summer 'Prom' season (see *Nightlife*); visitors are allowed in when the hall is not in use.

Its bold, simple red outline is offset by a solemn ceramic frieze showing the triumph of the arts and sciences. Although the ornate spire of the *Albert Memorial* over the road sits uneasily on the huge Gothic canopy, and although the statue of Albert himself is utterly uninspired, there are endless details to admire in the inventive melange of granite, marble, bronze and semi-precious stones, especially since the recent restoration.

Apsley House, The Wellington Museum Ⅲ ☆

149 Piccadilly, W1 ☎ *499–5676. Map 9|H8* 🚾 *Open Tues–Thurs, Sat 10.00–17.50, Sun 14.30–17.50. Tube Hyde Park Corner.*

Once the first of a row of aristocratic houses a traveller from the w would encounter when approaching the city, and hence known as 'no. 1, London', Apsley House still puts on a brave show, despite being surrounded on three sides by London's busiest roads. Inside, the visitor is still ensured of calm in the majestic rooms once occupied by the Duke of Wellington, Britain's greatest soldier.

Built by Robert Adam in 1771–78 for Baron Apsley, the brick-fronted mansion was bought in 1807 by Lord Wellesley, Wellington's elder brother who sold it to the duke in 1817. Wellington transformed the elegant house into a palace with the help of his architect Benjamin Wyatt, who clad the exterior with Bath stone and added the large portico in 1828; the house was clearly intended to impress at a time when the duke's political career was at its height (he was Prime Minister from 1828–30), and impress it did – during the Reform crisis of 1832, a mob stoned the house, and iron shutters replaced the windows.

Because of the transformation, two complementary styles are to be found in the interior. Adam's work has a fine elegance, whereas Wyatt's changes and additions are on a grander scale. This contrast is not too obvious on the ground floor, where the duke's personal mementoes and his fine collection of porcelain and dinner services are displayed in rooms which retain some air of domesticity, but it strikes one forcibly on reaching the stair-well, where the graceful curve of Adam's design is offset by Wyatt's heavy and ornate bannister. The stair now houses Antonio Canova's massive Neo-Classical statue of the nude *Napoleon as a Roman Emperor.*

The best example of Adam's interior work is the **Piccadilly Drawing Room** at the top of the stairs, with its vaulted ceiling, decorated with characteristically delicate Classical mouldings, and curved apsidal e end. Wyatt's work is best seen in the splendid **Waterloo Gallery**, with an elaborate ceiling in his grand 'Versailles' manner. The eight large windows have shutters which slide out to reveal mirrors, turning the room into a glittering hall of light in the evenings. The **Dining Room**, also on the first floor, was adapted by Wyatt from 1816–29 to house the fantastic table service given to Wellington to commemorate his Portuguese victories by the Prince Regent of Portugal in 1816. The complete service consisted of about 1,000 pieces, of which the most important is the centrepiece to be seen on the large oak table.

The fine paintings at Apsley House are largely those of the first duke, with a few additions and loans. Velazquez dominates the Spanish collection with *A Spanish Gentleman* and the profoundly serene *Water Carrier of Seville* (Waterloo Gallery). Murillo and Ribera are also represented, as are many Dutch and Flemish artists: look out for Jan Vermeer of Haarlem's *Landscape with Bleaching Grounds* (Yellow Drawing Room) and Elsheimer's haunting *Judith and Holofernes* (Piccadilly Drawing Room). There are a great many portraits of Wellington's illustrious contemporaries, including several of Napoleon and a fine equestrian study of the duke himself by Goya (Waterloo Gallery).

Banqueting House 🏛 ★

Whitehall, SW1 ☎*930–4179. Map **10**H11* �(*Open Tues–Sat 10.00–17.00, Sun 14.00–17.00. Tube Westminster, Charing Cross.*

The old prints in the entrance hall show this superb Palladian building as the focal point of the great royal palace of Whitehall; the single hall to survive a fire of 1688, it is today in a very different setting, across busy *Whitehall* from *Horse Guards Parade* and dominated by large government offices. Built by Inigo Jones in 1619–22, the Banqueting House has a Classical solemnity and clarity of design that was entirely novel in its day, marking the final triumph of Italian Renaissance ideas in England.

On the ceiling are the giant canvasses commissioned from Rubens by Charles I of the apotheosis of his predecessor and father, James I. Installed in 1635, their incredible scale and vigorous movement are entirely Baroque in feeling, contrasting strongly with Jones' Classicism. Rubens received a knighthood and a pension; Charles I, ironically, was led to his execution in 1649 from the window of this hall.

Barbican

☎*628–8795. Map **12**E15. Tube Barbican, Moorgate.*

The Barbican now rises as London's boldest piece of Utopian planning. It was a barren bomb site when, in 1956, it was chosen to reintroduce housing to the almost totally commercial City centre. On a bad day, it can seem grim and forbidding, a monument to the failed dreams of modern architecture, but it does have a certain excitement, with angular towers soaring upwards and walkways sweeping across. And sometimes the concrete comes to life: the Barbican Centre contains the London Symphony Orchestra's concert hall, the Royal Shakespeare Company's theatre (see *Nightlife*), cinemas, a gallery, conference halls, a roof garden and cafeterias and restaurants. Opened in 1982, its complex design and sumptuous interior constitute the largest social and arts centre of its type in Europe. Also within the complex is the superbly designed new Museum of London (see *London, Museum of*).

Incongruous amid the concrete stand remains of bastions of the old City wall, and the church of **St Giles Cripplegate**, the gutted shell of which survived the fire-bombing. The 15thC tower is surmounted with a brick top storey of 1683 and an attractive central turret and weather vane.

Battersea
*Map **21**D4. Train to Battersea from Waterloo, or bus no. 19, 39, 45, 49.*
Very little remains of the old Thameside village of Battersea, now an industrial sprawl. Down by the river, **Battersea Park** is well laid out, with sculptures by Henry Moore and Barbara Hepworth, and is the site of the Easter Parade (see *Calendar of events* in *Planning*). Overlooking the river is an attractive **Japanese Peace Pagoda** completed in 1985. A dominant and increasingly admired landmark is the vast **power station**, brick-built in the modern, monumental style of the 1930s.

The Bear Gardens Museum and Arts Centre
*1 Bear Gdns., Bankside, SE1 ☎ 928–6342. Map **12**G15 ▨ ▨ ✗ ⚹ Open Fri–Sun, 10.30–17.30, Wed–Thurs by appointment. Closed Mon–Tues. Tube London Bridge.*
Until the 18thC, Southwark acted as London's pleasure centre, an area of taverns, brothels and theatres. The museum, named after a bear-baiting arena on the same site, houses an exhibition on the circular theatres of the area where Shakespeare worked, including a replica of a 1616 stage where performances are held.

HMS Belfast
*Symons Wharf, Vine Lane, SE1 ☎ 407–6434. Map **13**G17 ▨ Open daily Apr–Sept 11.00–17.20, Oct–Mar 11.00–16.40. Tube London Bridge.*
This World War II warship, a Southampton class cruiser, saw action in the Battle of North Cape in 1943, when the *Scharnhorst* was sunk, in the Normandy landings and even in the Korean War. Now she is a floating tribute to all that, and to wartime naval life in general. Conditions on board were cramped, and the visitor has to weave and duck through hatches and up ladders, but the imagination can run riot on the navigation bridge or next to the massive main guns.

Belgravia
*Map **16**&**17**H–K. Tube Hyde Park Corner, Knightsbridge, Sloane Square, Victoria.*
London's most magnificent terraces, once the town houses of dukes, make up the great squares of Belgravia, the area around Belgrave Sq. developed by Thomas Cubitt in a frenzy of activity following the establishment of nearby *Buckingham Palace* as the royal residence in the 1820s.
Belgrave Square itself forms the centrepiece of the fairly regular plan, with its massive Classically decorated blocks by George Batesi and grand corner houses by other architects surrounding the private sunken gardens. Eaton Sq., to the s, is a long rectangle with the King's Rd. running through the middle of its massive stuccoed terraces. To the s again is Chester Sq., to some eyes the most appealing of the three.
In Motcomb St. Seth-Smith's Doric-fronted pantechnicon of 1830 looks back on Wilton Crescent, built by the same architect 3yr earlier. For refreshment, go to **The Grenadier** (see *Pubs*).

Bethnal Green Museum of Childhood ☆
*Cambridge Heath Rd., E2 ☎ 980–2415. Map **21**C5 ▨ ⚹ Open Mon–Thurs, Sat 10.00–18.00, Sun 14.30–18.00. Tube Bethnal Green.*
In the heart of the authentic East End, off the usual tourist track, this museum was opened in 1875 as an extension of the

Victoria & Albert Museum. There are numerous old toys to study, including board games, toy ships, trains and dolls from many periods. Among the dolls' houses, the **Tate Baby House** stands out, a fully furnished Georgian mansion in miniature dating from about 1760.

The museum is not exclusively devoted to children. Upstairs there is a good **costume collection**, with children's and adult clothes on show; the superb wedding dresses span two centuries. Decorative arts exhibits include 19thC continental furniture and Art Nouveau objects.

Blackheath
Map 21D5. Train to Blackheath from Charing Cross.
This common near the royal residences of *Greenwich* and *Eltham Palace* used to be as grim a place as its name suggests. However, in the 18thC it became a fashionable country address, and now the refreshingly open high clearing is surrounded by the fine, plain and elegantly unadorned Classical houses of that period. On the SE side, a semi-circular arrangement, known as the **Paragon**, is quite stunning. Probably dating from the 1780s, it consists of a series of blocks linked by single-storey colonnaded arcades.

To the NE of Blackheath is the superb red-brick **Charlton House** ☆ (☎ 856–3951 ▢ ◪ open by appointment Mon–Fri), the best Jacobean house in London. Built in 1607–12, it is entirely regular, with a central arched doorway, exuberant Mannerist carvings, and flanking towers.

Bloomsbury
Map 4C–E. Tube Euston, Russell Square, Holborn.
Bloomsbury, like so many other areas of London, is a 'village' with a reputation. The Bloomsbury Group were as well known for their mores as for their writings, but their patch of London remains the literary capital, housing a host of publishing companies and centred on the London University and the *British Museum*. It is also enjoyed for its Georgian squares.

One of the most fashionable addresses in the 18thC, Bloomsbury was an inconspicuous residential area when Virginia and Leonard Woolf, Roger Fry, Lytton Strachey and Maynard Keynes made it their fortress in the inter-war years. Before long, other voices were heard there: T.S. Eliot, Bertrand Russell and D.H. Lawrence were inevitably drawn to the centre of the action, even if they did not agree with 'The Group'.

Bloomsbury Sq. is where it all began, when the Earl of Southampton built a palace for himself there in 1660. No original buildings survive, although the gardens are pleasant. **Bedford Square**, to the w past *St George's, Bloomsbury*, was built in 1775; it survives virtually intact as London's finest square. Its plain, almost severe terraces are built of dark brick with stucco pedimented centres. The lush garden is exquisite, although private. The much larger Russell Sq., at the top of Bedford Pl. with its huge plane trees, has fared less well. South of the square, the enchanting streets around Museum St. are full of secondhand bookshops. To the N, Woburn, Gordon and Tavistock Squares all boast good gardens and some terraces surviving from the early 19thC. A short walk to the E brings you to the **Jewish Museum** (☎ 388–4525 ▢ open Tues-Fri 10.00–16.00, Sun 10.00–12.45) and Cartwright Gdns., with a fine crescent-shaped terrace. A little further on is Brunswick Sq., a major modern public housing development with brutal but interesting architecture, and the *Coram Foundation* (the Foundling Hospital Art Museum).

The University has buildings throughout Bloomsbury, of which the best is the oldest, the original **University College** in Gower St. It is a splendid Classical building with dome and portico, dating from 1827–29. The Senate House in Malet St., by contrast, is an essay in 1930s Classicism. Also within this 'open campus' is the University Church of Christ the King in Gordon Sq., 1853 Gothic with an impressive cathedral-like interior. Nearby are two University art collections, the *Percival David Foundation of Chinese Art* and the *Courtauld Institute Galleries*, on either side of Torrington Pl.

The British Museum 🏛 ★   *Russell Sq. better*
Great Russell St., WC1 ☎ *636–1555. Map* **10**E11 📷 💻
Open Mon–Sat 10.00–17.00, Sun 14.30–18.00. Tube
Russell Square, Tottenham Court Road.

Despite its age and venerable traditions, the British Museum is constantly changing, for this is one of the most adventurous of the world's great museums. It was founded in 1753 around the 80,000 items collected by Sir Hans Sloane, a successful physician. Sloane's will allowed the nation to purchase his collection for £20,000, well below its value, thus beginning a sequence of generous bequests. The nucleus consisted of Sloane's broad-ranging cabinet of curiosities: zoological and mineral specimens, antiquities, manuscripts, books and drawings. Natural history was best represented, but in time the museum became orientated more towards archaeology.

In 1823 George III's huge library was given to the nation by his heir and the decision was taken to build a new and grand edifice to display the nation's collected treasures. With the young Robert Smirke as architect, the intention was to create a Neo-Classical structure around a quadrangle, which was completed by 1838. The quadrangle was later filled in with the famous Reading Room (see **British Library**).

The move of the natural history exhibits to the *Natural History Museum* in the 1880s and the ethnographic exhibits to the Museum of Mankind (see *Mankind, Museum of*) in 1970 has coped with much of the museum's space problem; both are still administered by the British Museum.

A comprehensive catalogue would fill a bookcase. A selective visit should include the following.
Greece and Rome ★
The best place to start a visit; turn left in the entrance hall and for the moment pass through the Assyrian section. This leads to one of the best laid-out sections, offering an excellent chronological survey and including some of the finest examples of Greek art in the world. It starts with simple idols of the 3rd and 2nd millennia BC (**Rm. 1**) found in the Cyclades. Bronze Age Greek art (**Rm. 2**) is followed by early ceramics (**Rm. 3**) that show a developing sophistication – as in the fine wine jar by Exekias (c. 540 BC), decorated with mythological scenes in black on a red-earth background. The exit to this room is through the Room of the Kouroi (**Rm. 4**), named after two superb **statues of naked young men** (6thC BC). In **Rm. 5**, ceramics of about 500 BC, now with red figures on black, demonstrate that Greek artists had achieved a full understanding of the forms and movements of the human body.

The next room chronologically is the **Duveen Gallery** (**Rm. 8**), which contains some of the finest examples of Greek

49

The British Museum

art: a sizeable group of the sculptures that once adorned the Parthenon in Athens, dating from c.440 BC when Pericles was beautifying Greece's greatest city. They have become world famous as the **Elgin Marbles★** now the subject of controversy, with the Greek government making strenuous appeals for them to be returned to Athens. The Parthenon was ruined by an explosion in 1687; in 1803 Lord Elgin rescued the shattered fragments of the pediment sculptures, frieze and metopes and brought them to London. The **frieze**, displayed at eye level around the outside of the gallery, consists of marvellously natural figures and horses in a rhythmic procession to Mt. Olympus. The superb **pediment sculptures** recount the birth of Athena and the foundation of Athens.

Among the innumerable treasures of this collection is a **caryatid from the Erectheion** in Athens (c.410 BC) in **Rm. 9**. In **Rm. 7** are fragments of the great **Nereid Monument** (5thC BC) from a Greek colony at Lycia in Asia Minor, reconstructed into a facade. The Nereids themselves, wind spirits, are portrayed as dancing maidens with flowing garments clinging to their energetically moving bodies. In **Rm. 12** is a **frieze of the Battle of the Greeks and Amazons** from the Mausoleum of Halicarnassus, an extraordinary tomb of the late 4thC BC, built for Mausolus, which was one of the Seven Wonders of the Ancient World.

The smaller collection of Roman art (**Rms. 14 and 15**) begins with the famous **Portland Vase** (c.1stC BC), a cameo glass production, with the top white layer carved to reveal the blue underneath. There are also wall paintings from Pompeii, pleasant little architectural landscapes, and sculptures. Rooms above house smaller Greek and Roman antiquities, including fine figurines, busts, vases and household items. Particularly good are the Roman portraits in **Rm. 70**; the representations of Greek and Roman life in **Rm. 69**, with a small fountain actually in operation and a Roman waterwheel from Spain; and the Greek vases in **Rms. 72 and 73**.

Ancient Mesopotamia ★

The collections from the ancient cities of Assyria rival those of Greece in importance – Britain's close relations with Turkey in the mid-19thC made extensive excavations possible. Contrasted with the Greeks, the Assyrians seem to have been interested in a static, formal approach to representation, and the changes in style through the period are much less striking. The Nimrud Gallery (**Rm. 19**) has huge **reliefs from the palace of Ashurnasirpal II** (9thC BC), which show highly-ritualized hunting and military scenes. From a century later are two huge winged bulls with human heads (**Rm. 16**), once forming an entrance to the palace at Khorsabad. The best observed and most enjoyable details to be found in the Assyrian sculptures are not shown in the king and his countless soldiers but in the animals, particularly the lions in the **relief series from Ninevah** (7thC BC), taken from Sennacherib's palace (**Rm. 17**).

Upstairs in **Rm. 54** can be found the smaller archaeological finds from Sumeria and Babylon. From the Sumerian city of Ur in modern Iraq comes the extraordinary figure of a goat resting its legs in a tree (c.2500 BC), and a charming box inlaid with figures known as the **Standard of Ur**.

Ancient Egypt ☆

The nucleus of this collection of 70,000 objects fell into British hands after Napoleon's defeat at the Battle of the Nile in 1798. The large **Egyptian Sculpture Gallery** (**Rm. 25**) gives an

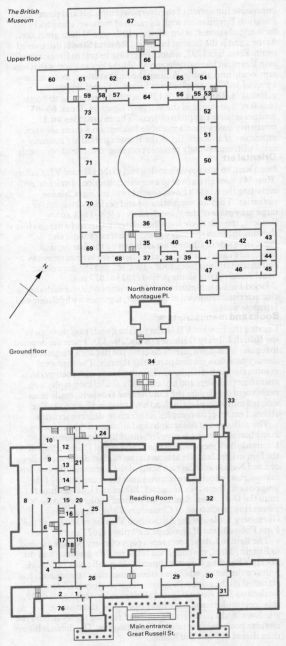

impressive indication of the overpowering scale and stern quality of Egyptian art with its ranks of massive, shiny and hard-edged statues, often showing little sign of their great age. At the s end is the famous inscribed **Rosetta Stone**, discovered by the French in 1797, which, by giving its text in Greek as well as in Egyptian hieroglyphs, provided the key to a script that was previously unreadable. Among the huge **statues**, look out for a pair of 3rdC BC granite lions found at Gebel Barkal, a colossus of **Rameses II** (c.1250 BC) and a giant scarab beetle (c.200 BC), an image of the sun god. Upstairs, **Rms. 60–65** contain smaller Egyptian objects. The **mummies and mummy cases** have a macabre fascination – there are even mummies of animals. From the Roman period are mummy cases with unnervingly realistic portraits of the dead occupants.

Oriental art

From **Rm. 66** it is possible to descend to the Edward VII Gallery (**Rm. 34**), now given over to a superb collection of oriental art, including the world's finest assembly of ancient **Chinese ceramics**. They are sophisticated and perfect – look out for a **large grey plate** of the Ming dynasty (1368–1644 AD), a flawless, smooth circle with the faintest pattern of a dragon just showing through the milky glaze. A more dramatic and expressive side of Chinese art is shown by the fine ceramic horses and camels, and even more fierce are bronze weapons and chariot fittings from 1500–1000 BC, and the impressive ritual vessels of the Shang period (1523–1027 BC).

Good Indian sculptures are also on display, some with the characteristic eroticism of Hindu art, together with Islamic and Japanese works.

Books and manuscripts ★

Leaving the Edward VII Gallery at the E end, pass through to the **British Library Galleries** (**Rms. 29–33**). These are devoted to regularly changed selections from the library's vast store of literary treasures around particular themes. The medieval manuscripts in particular are breathtaking, with their perfect miniature paintings and unbelievably skilful caligraphy – on permanent display are the **Lindisfarne Gospels**, made in an isolated monastery on England's NE coast in about 698. The abstract mazes of its complex illustrations deserve scrutiny.

The collection of holographs and annotated typescripts of many literary classics is supplemented by other treasures: Leonardo da Vinci's sketch book, and one of Dürer's; two of the four originals of the Magna Carta; the last dying scribblings of Lord Nelson and Captain Scott of the Antarctic; the two 5thC manuscripts which were important in the compilation of the gospels; and there are chronicles, Bibles and legal documents from the Dark Ages. Among the printed books are Caxton's pioneering production of *Canterbury Tales*, the famous Gütenberg Bible and the Authorized Version of 1603, and the First Folio edition of Shakespeare's plays (1623).

The **British Library** receives a copy of every book published in Britain. Thus, the collection is the world's greatest, and the library's **Reading Room ★** (open to the public only by guided tours on the hour), which is entered from the entrance hall, has attracted all the greatest scholars, most notably Karl Marx, who worked on *Das Kapital* in its hallowed calm. Opened in 1857, this spectacular room has a huge iron dome and massive windows, and a radial arrangement of reading tables around the circular bookcases containing the catalogue. The dome is bigger than that of St Peter's in Rome.

Prehistory and early Britain

From the British Library Galleries one returns to the main entrance hall; upstairs to the E are the rooms devoted to prehistoric and Romano-British objects (**Rms. 36–40**). Stone Age products include carvings on mammoth and walrus tusks from France, and there is a rich collection of early metalwork. Look out for the superbly twisted electrum **torque** of the 1stC BC, found in Norfolk, and the exquisite Roman silver of the **Mildenhall Treasure** (**Rm. 40**), including several superbly embossed platters.

Medieval and later

Rms. 41–7 are devoted to medieval (post-Roman) and later material. Some of these rooms are darkened, with the exhibits spotlit, an effect which helps the visitor recognize the great quality of the items that may be easily overlooked. The technique works very well with the **Waddesdon Bequest**, for example, in **Rm. 45**, which consists of elaborately wrought metal, glass and ceramic work from the Renaissance and Mannerist periods.

In **Rm. 41** is the famous **Sutton Hoo Treasure★** – a 7thC Angle burial ship unearthed in Suffolk in 1939. On display are finely wrought items of jewellery and weaponry, and a forbidding **helmet**, now reconstructed. Their craftsmanship speaks of a sophistication which belies the common image of the 'Dark Ages', as they are usually called.

Famous objects in the medieval section include the late Roman **Lycurgus Cup** (**Rm. 41**) and the **Franks Casket**, an Anglo-Saxon whalebone carving (**Rm. 42**). Also in **Rm. 42** is the Flemish parade shield of the 15thC showing a knight kneeling before a fairy-tale damsel; a skeleton looks over the knight's shoulder, and the inscription, representing the knight's words, can be translated as 'You or death'. Also in this room is the fabulous **14thC Royal Cup** of the kings of England and France, decorated with scenes from the life of St Agnes in enamel.

The museum also possesses numerous important prints and drawings, including works by Michelangelo, Botticelli and other important masters. A periodically changed display can be found in **Rm. 67**, above the Edward VII Gallery. Sadly, only a fraction of the collection is shown at any one time.

British Telecom Tower See *Post Office Tower.*

The Brompton Oratory 血 †
Brompton Rd., SW3 ☎589–4811. *Open 7.00–20.00. Map* *16J6. Tube South Kensington.*
Converts are supposedly the most zealous adherents of any faith: certainly the Oxford Movement, a group of Victorian intellectuals turned Catholic, allowed no half-measures when they created this huge church in 1884. All the drama of the Italian Baroque is here, in an interior dark with rich marbles, heavy with gilded detail. Some of the atmosphere is genuine – the huge marble *Apostles* (1680) by Mazzuoli come from Siena Cathedral.

Buckingham Palace 血 ☆
☎930–4832. *Map 17I9. Not open to the public. Tube* *Victoria, Hyde Park Corner.*
The royal standard flying signifies that the monarch is in residence, and many a hopeful eye scans the windows of the palace to catch a glimpse of a member of the Royal Family. On

the whole, however, visitors are satisfied by the splendours of the palace, with the *Queen Victoria Memorial* and *The Mall* at their backs, and the solemn facade, guarded by soldiers in scarlet tunics and bearskins, behind railings to the front. (For the **Changing of the Guard**, see *Calendar of events* in *Planning*.)

Its familiarity and setting give it a certain grandeur, but in reality Buckingham Palace is an undistinguished example of early 20thC official architecture – it might be a rather large town hall. Behind, however, there is John Nash's older palace. In 1762, George III bought Buckingham House from the Duke of Buckingham, and Queen Charlotte moved in. In 1825 his son, the Regent, commissioned Nash to rebuild on a larger scale. The *Marble Arch* was built as the entrance (later moved), but by 1850 the project was still incomplete, and Nash was sacked under some suspicion for having squandered huge amounts of money and having bought building materials from his own companies. The best parts of the palace are still his, however. To the right of the palace, there is a large arch leading to the gardens – the clearest part of Nash's work that can be seen from outside.

When Queen Victoria came to the throne in 1837, the palace became the official residence, and it has been so ever since. It was her need for additional accommodation that led to the large side wings and front being built, although it was more humble until the facade was added in 1913.

To the left of the palace is Buckingham Gate and the **Queen's Gallery** (◼ open during exhibitions only Tues–Sat 11.00–17.00, Sun 14.00–17.00), where exhibitions of treasures from the fabulous royal art collections are mounted.

Farther along, the road becomes Buckingham Palace Rd., and here can be found the **Royal Mews** (◼ open Wed–Thurs 14.00–16.00), which can be visited when state processions are not taking place; on display are the Queen's beautiful carriages and harness. The state coaches are a great attraction; the star is the gilded and painted **Gold State Coach**, dating from 1762.

Cabinet War Rooms   See *Whitehall*.

Carlyle's House
24 Cheyne Row, SW3 ☎ *352–7087. Map* **16**L6 ◼ *Open Apr–Oct Wed–Sun 11.00–17.00, last admission 16.30. Tube Sloane Square.*

The houses in Cheyne Row were built in 1708, making them some of the oldest surviving residences in *Chelsea*, and when the Scottish writer Thomas Carlyle (1795–1881) was looking for a London home he was evidently impressed. He lived here from 1834 until his death, and the house can be seen today much as it was then, crammed with memorabilia and manuscripts of the famous, although now little-read, essayist and historian. It can also be enjoyed as a perfect example of a comfortable Victorian home. The **attic study**, with its double walls, was added in 1853 to provide a quiet working place.

Central Criminal Court   The imposing building is
universally known as the *Old Bailey* after the street in which it stands.

Charing Cross
Map **10**G11. *Tube Charing Cross.*
At the s end of *Trafalgar Square*, a statue of *Charles I* looks down *Whitehall* to the place of his execution and occupies the

site of the original Charing Cross, from where all distances to London are measured. This was the last of the Eleanor Crosses put up by Edward I in 1291 to mark the resting places of his queen's funeral cortege on its way to Westminster Abbey; Charing is a corruption of *chère reine* (dear queen). The original cross was destroyed in the Civil War in 1647, but when E.M. Barry designed Charing Cross Station Hotel nearby in 1863–64, he added a Victorian Gothic Eleanor Cross to the forecourt, where it still stands.

Chelsea ★
Map 15&16K–L. Tube South Kensington, Sloane Square.
Chelsea is London's most fashionable address. On the one hand, the pretty, well-maintained houses in its quiet streets retain the feel of an elegant backwater, almost a country village; by contrast, the King's Road is *outré*, noisy and Bohemian in a way nowhere else can imitate.

Only in the later 18thC did the quiet village nestling on the river's edge become a part of London. Charles II built the *Royal Hospital* from 1682 as a restful place of retirement for old soldiers. The military connection remains, with two large barracks and the *National Army Museum*.

Apart from the Hospital, only little remains of old Chelsea. The area around *Cheyne Walk* includes the few old houses there are, such as **Lindsey House** of about 1674, and Cheyne Row of 1708, where *Carlyle's House* can be visited. Most of Chelsea's housing dates from the 19thC, some very grand (Cadogan Sq.), and some mere artisans' cottages, now so sought after.

In the late 1800s, Chelsea became known as an artists' colony. Pre-Raphaelites such as Rossetti, Burne-Jones and Morris lived here. Whistler painted his *Nocturnes* of the evening river here, and Oscar Wilde lived in Tite St. Americans, such as Henry James and Jack London, were attracted. The blue plaques marking the former abodes of the famous are everywhere.

After World War II the avant-garde again made this their home. The 'angry young men' grabbed attention at the **Royal Court Theatre** in 1956 (see *Theatres* in *Nightlife*), artists crowded into Finch's pub in the Fulham Rd., and, most significantly, Mary Quant began selling clothes in the King's Rd., which subsequently became and remained a major centre for high fashion clothes (see *Shopping*).

Cheyne Walk ☆
SW3. Map 15M5–6. Tube Sloane Square.
There were grand houses here before the famous and beautiful terrace was built in the late 17thC. **Lindsey House** (nos. 95–100), built about 1674, gives some idea of the detached stateliness of the even bigger Tudor mansions of *Chelsea*, built when this land sloped uninterrupted down to the waterline.

Once the red-brick Georgian terrace was built, Cheyne (pronounce the last 'e') Walk's rural charm went largely unnoticed until the 19thC, when it suddenly became a haven for artists. Turner lived at no. 119 from 1846 until his death in 1851, under the name of Puggy Booth, and D.G. Rossetti moved into no. 16 in 1862. In 1880 the novelist George Eliot died in no. 4, a house dating from 1717. James McNeill Whistler lived at no. 104 from 1863, and at no. 96 from 1866–79, painting many of his most famous pictures here, including the series of the river itself, known as *Nocturnes*.

One of the most remarkable buildings, however, is earlier.
Crosby Hall (☎352–9663 ☒ open daily 10.00–12.00,
14.00–17.00) was built between 1466–75 by Sir John Crosby, a
wool merchant, as the great hall of his residence in Bishopsgate
in The City. It was moved to its present site in 1910 to save it
from demolition. It has a superb **gilded wood ceiling** and a
three-storey **oriel window**, and displays a copy of Holbein's
lost portrait of *Sir Thomas More and his Family*. Next to it,
Chelsea Old Church contains a charming monument to *Thomas
Hungerford* (1581) and Sir Thomas More's chapel (1528).

Between Crosby Hall and the church is Roper's Garden, next
to an unusually ugly modern statue of *Sir Thomas More*, whose
own gardens once occupied the site. There is a relief by Jacob
Epstein in the garden. At the E end is Cheyne Row and *Carlyle's
House*, and the gardens at the w end lead to **Albert Bridge**
(1873), a decorative piece of Victorian suspension engineering.

Chiswick

Map 21C4. Tube Stamford Brook, Turnham Green.
Although on the main routes into the capital from the w, parts
of the old riverside village of Chiswick survive, in a still and
dreamy quarter to be found by turning sharp left into Church
St. at the monster roundabout where the Great West Rd. traffic
is forced to pause. **St. Nicholas** church has a 15thC tower,
although the rest is a Victorian reconstruction; buried in the
churchyard are the painters James McNeill Whistler and
William Hogarth. Back on the Great West Rd. is *Hogarth's
House*, and just beyond it *Chiswick House* (see *Walk 3*).

Chiswick House 🏛 ★

*Burlington Lane, W4 ☎995–0508. Map 21C4 ☒ summer
only. Open mid-Mar to mid-Oct daily 9.30–13.00,
14.00–18.30; mid-Oct to mid-Mar Wed–Sun 9.30–13.00,
14.00–16.00. Tube Turnham Green, Chiswick Park.*
The Palladian architecture so favoured by 18thC English
gentlemen, with its forms reduced to simple geometrical shapes
and all detail ruthlessly contained, reached near perfection in
this ravishingly beautiful mansion in *Chiswick*. Set in its own
park, it retains the feel of a country house. The first Earl of
Burlington bought the Jacobean mansion here in 1682, and
little was changed until the third Earl of Burlington, an
enthusiastic student of Classical art, decided to add a villa to one
end of the house. It was built to his own designs in 1725–29,
with an interior by William Kent.

The villa consists of an octagonal dome rising from a simple
square block, with a portico and stairs forming the entrance.
The link building and summer parlour survive at the E side,
showing where the villa was joined to the main body of the old
house. Through a low-ceilinged and severely Classical
octagonal room one enters the three rooms that served as the
earl's **library**. An interesting exhibition of engravings, plans
and documents relating to the villa occupies the rooms on this
floor. The upper rooms are reached by a spiral stair, and
immediately the style changes: these reception rooms, designed
by Kent, are brighter in colour, with richly patterned velvet
wallpapers and heavily decorated cornices, architraves and
fireplaces. At the rear is the three-chambered gallery and, to the
sides, the dramatic **Red and Green Velvet Rooms**. In the
centre is the impressive **dome**, with elaborate coffering.
The **garden** has grown to the modern, wilder taste.

The City ★

Map 12&13E&F. Livery company halls, and some other institutions, do not have regular opening hours, and will admit visitors only if they make an appointment through this tourist office **i** *St Paul's Churchyard, EC4* ☎ *606–3030 ext. 2456/7.*

For centuries it was just what its name suggests, and although London has now vastly outgrown it, The City retains its identity, its influence, and, to a degree which invariably surprises newcomers, its self-government.

Today, 'The City' is shorthand for money; this is where the great banking, insurance and commodity trading concerns are based. During the day, over four million people work here, but at night and weekends it can be a concrete and glass desert, with a resident population of less than 5,000. As a result, it may be best to visit The City at a weekend, when it is easier to find and enjoy the hidden, almost secret places that give the area its appeal. Be warned, however, for while the streets may be free of traffic, it may be hard to find a pub or restaurant that is open. Even the famous Wren churches are often closed on Sun – the best time to visit them is weekday lunchtimes.

The City does not easily yield up its past. First the Great Fire of 1666, then the bombs of 1940 and, most recently, the zeal of developers have swept away much that was old. In its place, there is an ostensibly haphazard collection of office blocks, for the most part demonstrating the poverty of modern architecture. As Sir Nikolaus Pevsner has pointed out, the skyline has none of the excitement of New York or Chicago, but has more in common with that of an unimportant Mid-West town. On the other hand, *St Paul's Cathedral* is too great a building to be dominated by its taller neighbours, Wren's churches too interesting not to be visited, and history proclaims itself too loudly even from the street names. And, of course, The City does have its own unique geography, described by a uniquely English phrase – nooks and crannies.

The key to exploring The City is not to content yourself with its obvious beauties. To an astonishing extent it retains elements of its medieval character. Within the area bounded by the old walls (the gates were at Ludgate, Newgate, Aldersgate, Cripplegate, Bishopsgate and Aldgate) one can easily work out what was where. Cheapside, for example, with the surrounding Milk St., Poultry and Bread St., marks the site of the main medieval market. The government of The City has not even changed on the surface. The Guildhall is still its parliament, Mansion House the palace of its head, the Lord Mayor. He is selected annually by a complex system based on ancient privileges rather than mere residence. City livery companies, descended from medieval trade guilds, have an important part to play in choosing and providing the aldermen and sheriffs from whom the Lord Mayor must come. The liveries still have their own halls, their own constitutions, and their own regalia, even though they are hardly ever connected with their original trades. The City still has its own police force (look at the badges on their helmets, different from those elsewhere in London), and on royal ceremonial occasions the monarch will not enter The City unless greeted on its borders by the Lord Mayor.

The square mile is a large area to visit on foot, with its many sites of interest widely scattered. To make it more manageable, it has here been divided into four parts, each of which can be seen separately.

57

The City: east

The City to the E of a line taken from London Bridge to
Liverpool Street Station in the N includes many fine churches,
but the predominant tone is set by the great maritime trading
interests. Until the 19thC almost all the trade goods landed at
London were brought ashore between London Bridge and the
Tower of London. **Lloyd's**, the headquarters of a business
largely founded on insuring ships and their cargo, is in a new
building in Leadenhall St. Lloyd's grew, amazingly, from a
coffee house; now its huge hall (open to parties by appointment)
is a beehive of activity, centred around the 18thC Lutine Bell,
traditionally struck once for news of disaster of a missing ship,
and twice for a safe arrival. Lloyd's Shipping Register, where
the capacity and whereabouts of all the world's shipping is
monitored, is in nearby **Fenchurch St**. In Mincing Lane is the
Commodity Exchange of Plantation House.

In the SE corner of The City is the *Tower of London*. Just to
the N is **Trinity Square** with at its E side a well-preserved
portion of Roman wall. Opposite is **Trinity House**,
headquarters of the charity operating Britain's lighthouses and
lifeboats. To the W of Trinity Sq., in Byward St., is the church
of **All-Hallows-by-the-Tower**; the attractive tower dates from
1658–59. The church is actually much older, dating back to the
7thC, and there is a Saxon arch at the tower base, revealed by
bomb damage. Inside is a quite beautiful **font cover** of 1682 by
Wren's great carver Grinling Gibbons.

Further W along the river front towards *London Bridge* is the
large **Customs House** of 1812–25, its Classical facade best seen
from London Bridge. Opposite, up St Dunstan's Hill, is the
ruined church of **St Dunstan-in-the-East**, converted into a
delightful garden; Wren's extraordinary spire of 1698,
supported on flying buttresses, still stands. Back on Lower
Thames St. the next building along from the Custom House is
Billingsgate Market, a typical 19thC covered market, closed in
1982, when the fish market which existed there since medieval
times moved further E into dockland. A little farther along is the
church of **St Magnus Martyr**, designed by Wren in 1671–76
although altered since. The tower is massive, with a spire of
1705.

O City city, I can sometimes hear
Beside a public bar in Lower Thames Street,
The pleasant whining of a mandoline
And a clatter and a chatter from within
Where fishermen lounge at noon: where the walls
Of Magnus Martyr hold
Inexplicable splendour of Ionian white and gold.

                                    T.S. Eliot, *The Waste Land*, 1922

Over Lower Thames St. is Fish St. Hill and Wren's *The
Monument*. At the top of Fish St. Hill is the major
thoroughfare of Eastcheap, site of a medieval market. Some
fanciful Victorian commercial buildings deserve study – nos.
33–35, for example, all brick Gothic and gables. To the S is the
splendid Wren church of **St Mary-at-Hill**, hidden in a maze of
charming lanes, which forms a moving contrast with the great
space and harmony of Wren's beautiful interior, built in
1670–76. The church is unique in that it still has box pews and
is noteworthy for some wrought-iron sword-rests and a carved
organ screen.

Back on Eastcheap, another Wren church will be discovered a little further along on the left, **St Margaret Pattens**, named after a special type of shoe made here. This time the exterior, with a fine spire of 1687, has more to offer than the interior. A pretty early 19thC shop and house (now an American bank) next to the church completes an attractive corner. To the N is the Commodity Exchange, with its facade in Fenchurch St., and behind the new Clothworkers' Hall up Mincing Lane on the left is the small 15thC tower of **All Hallows Staining**, incongruously surrounded by large buildings. Nearby in Hart St. is **St Olave**, an attractive 15thC church, damaged in the Blitz but well restored. It contains several good monuments, especially those to *Sir James Deane* (1608) and *Peter Cappone* (1582). Samuel Pepys the diarist used the church and there is a monument to his wife (1669). Hart St. leads into Crutched Friars, which passes under Fenchurch Street Station ('crutched' means 'crossed' – there was a priory here). No. 42 is a fine early 18thC house.

North of Fenchurch St., **Leadenhall Market**, off Lime St., provides City workers with a welcome shopping area. Leadenhall St., a little further N, contains Lloyd's and the churches of **St Andrew Undershaft**, mostly early 16thC, and **St Katharine Cree**, a survivor from the early 17thC, but with a medieval tower.

This section of The City, straddling the course of the Roman and medieval wall along Camomile St. and Bevis Marks, contains three churches. **St Helen Bishopsgate** is an outstanding convent church dating back to the 13thC. Its many interesting features include an attractive W front topped by a little 17thC bell-tower, a poor box of about 1620 in the form of a one-armed beggar, and remarkable monuments. The other churches in Bishopsgate are **St Ethelburga**, with medieval fragments and a tower of 1775, and **St Botolph-without-Bishopsgate**, a pleasant 18thC building where Keats was baptized. The **Spanish and Portuguese Synagogue** in Bevis Marks deserves a visit; it dates back to 1700–1, and contains some lavishly decorated appointments of that period.

The City: south

This segment covers the central area between *St Paul's Cathedral* and London Bridge, s of Cheapside, Poultry and Cornhill.

The waterfront W of London Bridge, Upper Thames St., is now one of London's least attractive roads, bearing great quantities of traffic through a windy and noisy desert. The narrow alley of **Broken Wharf**, however, leads down to a good view of the river and the **Samuel Pepys pub** in an old warehouse. There is also a riverside walk to the W of this. But to the N, only the slender pinnacled tower of **St Mary Somerset** and the much-restored church of **St Nicholas Cole Abbey**, both by Wren, relieve the monotony.

Just beyond Queen St., the approach to Southwark Bridge, there are some smaller and older streets s of Mansion House Station. Wren's **St James Garlickhythe** (1676–83) in Garlick Hill (where that herb was sold) has a fine tower, looking rather like a lighthouse with a stone lantern on top; it contains some fine ironwork. **Beaver Hall** in Great Trinity Lane is the centre of the fur trade, the premises of which cluster in these narrow streets. Facing Upper Thames St. is the **Vintners' Hall**, one of the best of a number of livery company halls in this area. It was built in 1671, and although much restored has a fine panelled hall and a superb carved staircase. Queen St. itself contains two magnificent Georgian houses (nos. 27 and 28).

Between Queen St. and Cannon Street Station there is another maze of little lanes, around the church of **St Michael Paternoster Royal**, built by Wren but much restored after war damage. Some good interior fittings have survived, including a carved pulpit and reredos. Three livery companies have their halls in Dowgate Hill, just w of St Michael: the Skinners (with a late 18thC facade), the Dyers, and the Tallow Chandlers (the last two are Victorian).

Between Cannon Street Station and King William St. (which leads on to London Bridge) is yet another fascinating maze of small streets, with several historic pubs and wine bars. **Laurence Pountney Hill** to the E has two of the most beautiful early 18thC houses in London, dated 1703, with elaborately decorated doorways and cornices. Other attractive buildings are to be found around the pleasant little churchyard left by the vanished church of St Laurence; the **Olde Wine Shades** bar in nearby Arthur St. offers good refreshments. Next to London Bridge is the **Fishmongers' Hall** of 1831–34, the best sited and grandest livery company hall, with an imposing Classical facade overlooking the river.

Just N of Cannon St. are **St Clement Eastcheap**, containing some superb wood carving, and the extraordinary *St Mary Abchurch*, both by Wren. Farther N is Lombard St., an important banking street named after the Italian money-lenders who set up business here in the 14thC. It contains two fine churches: **St Mary Woolnoth** and **St Edmund the King**. The latter is again by Wren, with a harmonious exterior and well-preserved woodwork inside. St Mary Woolnoth was built by Nicholas Hawksmoor in 1716–27 and occupies its prominent corner site with a dramatic monumental facade. The interior, with massive Corinthian columns, is Baroque in feeling. North of Lombard St. are several attractive lanes: St Michael's Alley, Castle Court and Ball Court. Old hostelries tucked away in this enclave include **Simpson's**, the **George and Vulture**, and the **Jamaica Wine House**. There are two churches on the s side of Cornhill: **St Michael Cornhill** has a pretty churchyard, but is itself an unhappy mixture of styles by Wren and later architects; **St Peter-upon-Cornhill** by Wren is best seen from its little churchyard.

Moving w, large offices again dominate the area s of Cheapside and Poultry. The remains of the **Roman Temple of Mithras** (see the marvellous sculptures in the Museum of London, under *London, Museum of*) can be seen in Queen Victoria St. Nearby is the church of **St Mary Aldermary**, completed by Wren in 1692 in an extraordinary version of Gothic, with a tall tower, nave and aisles. The fan-vaulted roof uses a very free interpretation of the medieval style, with shallow domes between the fans, all richly covered with delicate tracery. On Cheapside is the major church of *St Mary-le-Bow*, with the grandest of Wren's steeples. Where Cheapside joins Poultry is the *Mansion House*, the Lord Mayor's official residence, with the important *St Stephen Walbrook* behind.

The City: north

The northern part of The City contains a number of important institutions and a great many lesser offices. As a result, it is less an area to stroll through than other parts of The City. In the N are Liverpool Street Station and the post-war developments of London Wall and the *Barbican*. To the s, really the centre of

The City, are the financial and administrative institutions, the *Guildhall*, the Bank of England, the Royal Exchange and the *Stock Exchange*.

In Foster Lane, N of Cheapside, is **St Vedast**, a Wren church of 1670–97 but reconstructed after war damage. Its finest feature is the elaborate and effectively sinuous spire. To the N is **Goldsmiths' Hall** built with a massive Classical exterior by Philip Hardwick in 1829–35. Frequent exhibitions of the livery company's unmatched collection of historic and modern plate make it possible to see the palatial interior, with its tremendous dome-covered staircase of coloured marble.

On nearby Gresham St. is the interesting Wren church of **St Anne and St Agnes**, built of brick in 1680 on a square with a central dome supported on columns. In Wood St., to the E, there is a lonely Wren tower in the Gothic style, all that remains of the church of **St Alban**. Next to the *Guildhall* in Gresham St. is **St Lawrence Jewry**, again by Wren (1671–87).

Lothbury, next to the **Bank of England**, the nation's controlling bank, contains Wren's **St Margaret Lothbury**. Good features include the 17thC screen brought from another Wren church, with its beautiful twisted columns. Look out for no. 7 Lothbury – Victorian architecture at its imaginative best. Lothbury leads into Throgmorton St., with the *Stock Exchange* on the right, which then becomes Old Broad St. This contains the tallest and most exciting and dramatic of The City's new office buildings, the recently completed **National Westminster Bank tower**. Its soaring height, emphasized by vertical ribbing, balances unnervingly on a narrowed base with a clear glass facade.

The northern section of The City is dominated by the undistinguished Victorian pile of Liverpool Street Station with its large hotel. Nearby in Bishopsgate is **St Botolph-without-Bishopsgate**, rebuilt in 1727–29 and with a 19thC interior. **All Hallows London Wall** (1765–67) to the W has a fine simple and light interior, with an ornate plaster ceiling.

The City: west

Most of the western part of the modern City falls outside the old Roman walled town, including the whole section W of Ludgate Circus to the beginning of the *Strand* and Smithfield Market, the capital's wholesale meat market, housed in a fine Victorian building, to the N. Of prime interest are *Fleet Street*, the Inner and Middle *Temple* extending S to the river, and *St Paul's Cathedral*.

The stretch of riverside to the S of St Paul's is disfigured by the traffic of Upper Thames St., although **St Benet's** (1677–83) remains as one of the most delightful and best preserved of Wren's churches, small and simple in the Dutch style. Nearby in Queen Victoria St. is the 17thC *College of Arms*, together with the **British and Foreign Bible Society Library**. The church of **St Andrew-by-the-Wardrobe** stands on St Andrew's Hill to the W. Built by Wren in 1685–93, it is abutted by the offices of the men who maintained the state apparel.

To the S is the new **Mermaid Theatre** (see *Nightlife*), surrounded by the raging traffic of Puddle Dock. There is a fine Victorian pub in Queen Victoria St., called the **Black Friar** (see *Pubs*). In Blackfriars Lane next to the station is the **Apothecaries' Hall**, a fine livery company building with a facade of 1684 (altered in 1779). North again is Ludgate Hill, site of the medieval 'Lud Gate' until 1760–61; it offers the best view of the portico of St Paul's. **St Martin Ludgate**, a Wren church of 1677–87, has a most attractive lead-covered spire and some good carved woodwork inside. Just behind is the **Stationers' Hall**, a building of about 1667 with a stone facade of 1800.

Another of the old roads out of The City passed through Newgate, site of the notorious gaol and now the *Old Bailey*. Newgate St. leads into Holborn Viaduct, built to span a little valley in 1863–69. Its heavy, ornate ironwork can be seen best from Farringdon St. The church of **St Sepulchre** on the N side of Holborn Viaduct is unusually large, with a great (although restored) 15thC tower. **St Andrew Holborn** on the S side is a Wren church with a 15thC tower restored in 1703.

North of Holborn Viaduct is Smithfield, long the site of the famous medieval St Bartholomew's Fair, about which Ben Jonson wrote his play in 1614, and the place where Wat Tyler and his rebel peasants confronted Richard II in 1381; Lord Mayor Walworth showed The City's customary independence by simply drawing his sword and killing Tyler. Nearby are **Smithfield Market** and *St-Bartholomew-the-Great*. St Bartholomew's Hospital opposite dates back to the Middle Ages. Its church, **St Bartholomew-the-Less**, has another 15thC tower. Behind Bart's, as it is known, at the end of Little Britain, is **St Botolph Aldersgate**, rebuilt in 1788–91 and with a well-preserved interior. The **National Postal Museum** is in King Edward St.

Cleopatra's Needle
Victoria Embankment, WC2. Map **11**G12. *Tube Embankment.*

Now appropriately sited by another symbol of timelessness, the Thames, this pink granite obelisk was made in Heliopolis in Egypt in 1500 BC, pre-dating Cleopatra by centuries. Presented to Britain by Egypt in 1819, it was eventually towed by ship to its present site and erected in 1878. There is a similar obelisk in Central Park, New York.

The College of Arms 🏛
Queen Victoria St., EC4 ☎ *248–2762. Map* **12**F15 ⊡ *Hall only open Mon–Fri 10.00–16.00. Tube Mansion House.*
The official body controlling the heraldry of the United Kingdom is housed in an interesting building constructed in 1671–88 following the Great Fire, which destroyed the older house given to the college by Mary I in 1555. The wrought-iron gates and railings, of uncertain date, are particularly splendid; the brick pilasters with carved stone capitals preserve some of its grandeur. As a professional body, the College of Arms will investigate queries relating to genealogy and heraldry – nobody knows more about argent chevrons, batons sinister or griffins rampant. Only the entrance hall is open to the public.

Commonwealth Institute 🏛
230 Kensington High St., W8 ☎ *602–3257. Map* **14**I2 ⊡ 🅿 ✳ *Open Mon–Sat 10.00–17.30, Sun 14.00–17.00. Tube Kensington High Street.*
With its extraordinary green copper roof, all peaks and eliptical curves, the Commonwealth Institute is an appropriately unusual tribute to a unique association, the Commonwealth. It was opened in 1962 as a study and display centre, and houses a permanent exhibition representing its peoples, customs and economics. There is a fine library, together with a cinema and

restaurant. The exhibition area is open-plan, consisting of a large circle of galleries on different levels around a central concourse. Each country has a display, with stuffed animals, models of oil refineries and craft objects, variously expressing the cultural traditions or economies of the nations.

The Coram Foundation *(Foundling Hospital Art Museum)* ☆
40 Brunswick Sq., WC1 ☎ *278–2424. Map* **5D12** 📰 *Open Mon–Fri 10.00–16.00 (check first). Tube Russell Square.*

In the 18thC London was full of destitute children, and their plight moved nobody more than Thomas Coram, a retired sea captain who set up a foundling hospital in 1739. The original buildings were shamefully demolished in 1926, but the magnificent **Court Room** can be seen in the Foundation's modern offices, along with a model of the original complex. After its foundation, artists led by Hogarth tried to raise funds. Consequently, it has a fine collection of pictures, of which the highlight is Hogarth's **portrait** of the sanguine philanthropist *Coram*☆ There are also works by Gainsborough and Reynolds, a study by Raphael, and a manuscript of Handel's *Messiah*.

Coram's Fields, a children's playground, is entered from Guildford St. through the hospital's original gateway.

Courtauld Institute Galleries ★
Woburn Sq., WC1 ☎ *580–1015. Map* **4D10** 📰 📷 *with flash. Open Mon–Sat 10.00–17.00, Sun 14.00–17.00. Tube Euston, Russell Square.*

When the textile industrialist Samuel Courtauld helped found London University's main art history department, the Courtauld Institute, in 1931, he provided the nucleus of an important art collection. Swelled by several subsequent bequests, this has grown into an exceptional, broad-ranging group of pictures.

The first rooms contain the Princes Gate paintings. The outstanding feature is a group of no less than 32 paintings by Rubens (1577–1640), including a fine portrait of the *Family of Jan Brueghel the Elder*, a moving *Entombment* and the incomparable *Landscape by Moonlight*, famous for its eerie beauty. Rubens' pupil Van Dyck is also well represented, and earlier Flemish art is superbly exemplified by the brilliant, jewel-like *Madonna* by Quentin Massys and two rare paintings by the Elder Brueghel – a perfect imaginary landscape and a deeply human grisaille rendering of *Christ and the Woman Taken in Adultery*. Italian paintings include a well-preserved triptych by Bernardo Daddi, a poetic and sensuous *Venus* by Palma Vecchio and 12 paintings by Tiepolo. The drawings are also excellent; there are six by Michelangelo.

Samuel Courtauld's collection amounts to one of the best publicly accessible groups of both Impressionist and Post-Impressionist paintings. Impressionist works include examples by Monet (*Autumn at Argenteuil*), Sisley, and Renoir, including the superbly-coloured *La Loge*. Manet is represented by a large oil sketch for the celebrated *Déjeuner sur l'Herbe* and the sumptuous *A Bar at the Folies-Bergère*. Two large sketches by Degas show to perfection the artist's ability to fix an ordinary moment in time. The Post-Impressionists are represented by no fewer than nine Cézannes on one wall, a Van Gogh self-portrait (with bandaged ear) and two haunting studies of Tahitian women by Gauguin, including the dreamy *Te Rerioa*.

Covent Garden ★

Map 10&11F–G. Tube Covent Garden.

Until 1974, London's fresh fruit and vegetable market was Covent Garden's chief fame, and the pubs stayed open all night for the thirsty workers, and others. When the market and its heavy traffic left to go to a new building s of the river at Nine Elms, a bitter struggle for the future of Covent Garden began. Conservationists and local residents were ranked against the developers, for whom this was a prime site for office buildings (dressed up, of course, with token community schemes). To the enormous relief of everyone but those who stood to profit, the attempt to turn the delightful and historic chaos of decaying buildings into a 'planned' desert was defeated. But it may have been a Pyrrhic victory – skirmishing continues, new buildings continue to eat away at the old, and the population of the area is falling. Even so, the best buildings remain, and although some pricey shops and bars have brought their smart set to invade the area, it retains an earthy feel of real old London, and there is some discerning and tasteful modern patronage. For visitors and Londoners alike, this is where the action is.

Until the 16thC, Covent Garden was an enclosed kitchen garden belonging to Westminster Abbey. The land was granted to Sir John Russell, later Earl of Bedford, in 1630, and a descendant of his obtained the right to develop it under the aegis of the great Classical architect Inigo Jones in 1670. The plan was ambitious – a huge piazza on the Italian model surrounded with arcaded houses. All that survives today is the church of *St Paul's, Covent Garden*. The present **market buildings** appeared in 1828–32, with the fine iron and glass canopies added later. In its restored state, the marriage of its severe Classicism to the more ornate roof creates a stunning effect. Other later market buildings surround the piazza. The best, the **Floral Hall** (1858) is to the NE, a superb example of the iron and glass architecture that sprang up in emulation of the Crystal Palace that housed the 1851 Great Exhibition.

The **market** itself is now given over to twee little shops and restaurants, with market stalls in the middle; it is at its liveliest at lunchtime. Leave it by Russell St. to the E, lined with fashionable wine bars thick with young advertising executives and publishers not so different from the *monde* who congregated in its famous coffee houses in the 18thC. Russell St. crosses Bow St., so notorious for its street crime in the 18thC that it saw the foundation of the first police force, the Bow Street Runners. Its inspiration was the novelist Henry Fielding, a magistrate at the busy courts which are still there in a newer building. To the left is the splendid facade of the Floral Hall and next to it the **Royal Opera House** (see *Nightlife*); amazingly, both are by the same architect, the Victorian E.M. Barry. The present is the third theatre on the site – built in 1857–58, its grand Corinthian portico has a frieze by J. Flaxman and statues from the previous building of 1809.

Fittingly for a quarter of such vitality, Covent Garden is traditionally London's theatre area, and its church, *St Paul's*, is the actor's church. (For *Theatres*, see *Nightlife*.)

Continuing along Russell St. will take you to the other old royal theatre, the **Theatre Royal, Drury Lane**, founded in 1663 by Charles II, whose Nell Gwynne was, of course, an orange-seller in Covent Garden. The present building dates from 1810–12, and is by general agreement London's most beautiful theatre. Covent Garden is also bordered by two of

London's main theatrical streets; to the s is the *Strand* and to
the w, St Martin's Lane, where the largest theatre is the
imposing **Coliseum** of 1904, now home of the English National
Opera. A good example of an ornate late Victorian pub,
complete with cut glass and mirrors, is the **Salisbury**, a little
further up to the left (see *Pubs*). At the top of St Martin's Lane,
Garrick St. to the right includes the solemn and grimy building
of the famous Garrick Club, a gentlemen's club with theatrical
associations. Up tiny Rose St. on the left is the **Lamb & Flag**,
the area's oldest and best pub (see *Pubs*).

The northern continuation of St Martin's Lane is drab
Monmouth St., which leads to Seven Dials, the scene of
Hogarth's 'Gin Lane' of drink and vice in the 18thC and the
cholera outbreaks of the 19thC. A little to the NW is **St Giles-in-
the-Fields**, a fine Classical church of 1731–33, with a
supremely calm interior. Near Seven Dials is **Neal's Yard** and
Neal Street, with craft shops, vegetarian restaurants and health
food stores.

Dickens' House ☆
48 Doughty St., WC1 ☎ *405–2127. Map 5D12* 🎨 *Open
Mon–Sat 10.00–17.00. Closed for two weeks Dec–Jan.
Tube Russell Square, Chancery Lane.*
When Charles Dickens lived at Doughty St. between 1837–39,
he was experiencing his first taste of success. The *Pickwick
Papers*, which brought him sudden prosperity, was still being
published, and he also worked on his first novels while in the
house: *Oliver Twist, Barnaby Rudge* and *Nicholas Nickleby*.

In Dickens' time, Doughty St. had gates at either end tended
by liveried porters. It is still a handsome house but,
unfortunately, the interior preserves almost nothing of its
original appearance; instead, however, there is an extensive
museum of Dickens memorabilia. There are pieces of furniture
from later houses, such as the table on which he was writing his
unfinished *The Mystery of Edwin Drood* the day before he died.
There are numerous letters and manuscripts, portraits of the
writer and his family, and contemporary illustrations of his
famous characters.

Downing Street
SW1. Map 10H11. Tube Westminster, Charing Cross.
There must be something significant about the way Downing
Street, the Prime Minister's residence, is so overwhelmingly
dominated by the massive government buildings of *Whitehall*.
In fact, the interior of 'no. 10' is more elegant and spacious than
the unassuming facade might suggest, and from its Cabinet
Room the country has been run since Sir Robert Walpole
accepted the house *ex officio* from George II in 1735. No. 11,
home of the Chancellor of the Exchequer, is the only other
survivor of Sir George Downing's original terrace of 1683–86.
Steps at the end of the street lead to *St James's Park*.

Dulwich
Map 21D5. Train to West Dulwich from Victoria.
The charming village of Dulwich, with wooden signposts,
broad open spaces and historic buildings, is a jewel preserved in
the rock face in a way typical of London. The presence of
Dulwich College is strong here: in **College Road** there are
several 18thC houses of considerable style, nos. 103–107 dating
from around 1700, and nos. 57 and 97, also substantial

Georgian homes. College Rd. heads s across the refreshing Dulwich Common through a toll gate. In Lordship Lane is the **Horniman Museum** (☎699–2339 ○ ⬛open Mon–Sat 10.30–18.00, Sun 14.00–18.00), in an Art Nouveau building of 1902. It houses a bizarre variety of objects: dolls, tribal art, stuffed animals, and a fine collection of musical instruments.

Dulwich College and Picture Gallery 🏛 ☆
*College Rd., SE21 ☎ 693–5254. Map **21**D5 🔲 ⚑ Open Tues–Sat 10.00–13.00, 14.00–17.00, Sun 14.00–17.00.*
In 1619, Edward Alleyn, a successful actor and colleague of Shakespeare, founded the 'College of God's Gift' at Dulwich, and the large almshouses that were part of the original bequest have been added to, making Dulwich College today one of London's greatest schools.

Of particular interest is the remarkable **Picture Gallery**, in a severe Neo-Classical building designed by Sir John Soane in 1811–14 which incorporates a mausoleum for the college's benefactors. The Dutch school of the 17thC is especially well represented: there are six Cuyps, for example, including some fine landscapes. Look out for the majestic *Landscape with Sportsmen* by Pynacker and important works by Poussin; also represented are Watteau, Claude and Canaletto. There are Rubens sketches, and English portraiture, including works by Gainsborough, and Reynold's amusing portrait of his era's great actress, *Mrs Siddons as the Tragic Muse*. But pride of place goes to the awe-inspiring **Rembrandts**, including *Titus*, a moving portrait of his sick son.

Eltham Palace 🏛 ☆
*Eltham ☎859–2112. Map **21**D5. Open Nov–Mar Thurs, Sun 11.00–16.30; Apr–Oct 11.00–18.30. Train to Eltham from Charing Cross.*
History has played some teasing games with this medieval palace near *Blackheath* and *Greenwich*. A favourite royal hunting retreat until the time of Henry VIII, it must have witnessed some huge banquets, such as when Henry IV received the Byzantine Emperor here in 1409. By the 1600s, it fell into ruins; only the Great Hall survived the Civil War, and that because it made a good barn. In the 1930s it was rescued by the Royal Army Educational Corps, who now occupy the site. You pass a lovely group of half-timbered houses in the outer court, known as the **Lord Chancellor's Lodgings** after Cardinal Wolsey, and cross a 15thC bridge over a moat with swans and geese. At the heart stands the **Great Hall** on the mound of the palace, with its superb **hammerbeam roof** and the two great **oriel windows** at either side of the dais.

Fenton House 🏛 ☆
*Hampstead Grove, NW3 ☎435–3471. Map **21**C4. ⬛ Open Mar Sat, Sun 14.00–17.00; Apr–Oct Mon–Wed, Sat 11.00–17.00, Sun 14.00–17.00. Closed Thurs, Fri, Nov–Feb. Tube Hampstead.*
Although *Hampstead* is rich in fine houses, this is its jewel. Dating from 1693, Fenton House is a brick mansion of disarmingly simple design, hardly changed except for the benign addition of the Classical portico to the E front soon after 1800. The luxurious Regency decor of the interior reflects the alterations carried out by James Fenton in about 1810. Among older items of furniture, look out for the charming little

'grandmother' clock of about 1695 on the stair landing. Meissen and Nymphenburg ware as well as English pieces are among a fine **porcelain collection**. Also kept in the house, and perhaps its crowning glory, is the **Benton-Fletcher Collection of Musical Instruments**, mainly early keyboard instruments.

Fleet Street
*EC4. Map **11**F13–14. Tube Aldwych, Temple, Blackfriars, St Paul's.*

Leading from the *Strand* into *The City*, Fleet Street, named after the small river which now flows unseen beneath its pavements, is famous as the home of British journalism, although only two major newspapers and some press agencies now have offices in the 'street of shame' itself. Fleet Street begins at Temple Bar, the western limit of The City. Walking eastwards, the gateways to the *Temple* on the right date from the 17thC. On the left, **St Dunstan's in the West** is a fine example of an early Victorian church in the Gothic style; it incorporates an extraordinary clock with giants striking bells (1671) and a statue of *Elizabeth I* (1586). **El Vino's** wine bar on the right (see *Nightlife*) is famous for providing newspapermen with liquid inspiration. Further along on the left (in Wine Office Court) is the **Cheshire Cheese**, an ancient pub frequented by Dr. Johnson and Boswell. Soon after comes the unusually ugly Daily Telegraph building of 1928, followed by the Daily Express of 1931, aggressively modern with its entirely plain, shiny black facade. Towards the end of Fleet Street, the wonderful wedding-cake spire of **St Brides** is visible over newer buildings on the right. Built to Wren's design in 1701–03, it is the tallest and one of the most elaborate of his spires.

Geffrye Museum
*Kingsland Rd., E2 ☎ 739–8368. Map **21**C5 ⬚ 🚇 Open Tues–Sat 10.00–17.00, Sun 14.00–17.00. Tube Old Street.*

Shoreditch, in the East End, was traditionally the home of the furniture industry, and this museum was opened in 1914 not only to pay tribute to that past, but also to provide models for local craftsmen of the 20thC. The buildings are interesting enough, with a fine set of almshouses built in 1715 at the bequest of Sir Robert Geffrye, a former Lord Mayor whose statue stands over the door of the central block containing the coverted chapel. The collection is imaginatively arranged as a series of rooms representing different periods, and household items and pictures give a lived-in feeling. Look out for the fine chimneypiece in the Elizabethan room and the splendidly fussy Victorian parlour.

Geological Museum
*Exhibition Rd., SW7 ☎ 589–3444. Map **15**J5 ⬚ Open Mon–Sat 10.00–18.00, Sun 14.00–18.00. Tube South Kensington.*

Founded in 1837, the Geological Museum opened in its present building in 1935, appropriately sited between the *Natural History Museum* and *Science Museum*. The traditional displays upstairs on the regional geology of Britain and world economic mineralogy are of limited interest compared with the stunning exhibitions on the ground floor. Here, the collection of **gemstones** includes some beautiful specimens, both crude and cut. There is also an adventurous exhibition entitled 'The Story of the Earth'.

Grand Union Canal ☆
Maps 2–7.
At the end of the 18thC, London was triumphantly linked to the industrial Midlands by canal, then the most efficient form of travel. The canal is still there, ignoring and largely hidden by the roads that have superseded it.

Its walks offer particularly interesting views of a London not normally seen by visitors: the backs of houses, gardens rich and poor, crumbling industrial buildings of the 19thC, and the many details of the working canals themselves, such as brightly painted narrowboats, locks, bridges and tunnels. Camden Lock is a good place to start – you can take a boat trip (see *Useful addresses* in *Basic information*) or walk either to the w (*Regent's Park* and Little Venice) or to the E (*St Pancras Station* and Islington).

Gray's Inn
High Holborn, WC1 ☎*405–8164. Map 11E12. Hall and chapel open when not in use, check first. Tube Chancery Lane.*
This ancient society of lawyers, one of the four *Inns of Court*, has occupied this site since the 14thC. South Sq., the first quadrangle encountered, has one old set of chambers (no. 1), dating from 1685. Opposite is the hall, badly burned but accurately restored. The fine carved late 16thC screen perhaps formed a backdrop to the first performance of Shakespeare's *Comedy of Errors* here in 1594. In the centre of South Sq. is a modern statue of *Francis Bacon* (1561–1626), the great Elizabethan statesman and scholar, one of the Inn's most distinguished former members. Beyond the hall is Gray's Inn Sq., full of the calm grandeur of legal London; at the s end is the frequently restored and curiously characterless chapel. More appealing is Field Court, with no. 2, a most attractive house of about 1780, and the dignified wrought-iron gates of 1723 that lead to the gardens. Designed in formal style by Francis Bacon himself, the gardens are the best of the Inns of Court, with a grand central walkway flanked by huge plane trees.

Greenwich ★
Map 21C5. Best approached by river boat – see Useful addresses in Basic information; alternatively train to Greenwich from Charing Cross.
It is no longer regarded as the centre of the world, despite the continuing primacy of the Greenwich Meridian (0° longitude) and Greenwich Mean Time (GMT), and yet the sheer self-confidence of this most easterly of the Thames-side royal residences suggests otherwise. Bold and grand in every way, the metropolis' most spectacular architectural ensemble sweeps down to the riverside through fine parkland, unifying its blend of splendid buildings in an elegant Classicism.

It owes its prominence to its position as the capital port of a great seafaring nation, and its maritime character strikes the disembarking visitor in the tall form of masts of a great British ship. The *Cutty Sark* (☒ open Mon–Sat 11.00–17.00, Sun 14.30–17.00), built in 1869, was one of the greatest of the graceful tea clippers which raced to bring back tea from the Orient. Inside the hold is a display on the ship's history and a collection of old ships' figureheads. Nearby is the diminutive *Gypsy Moth IV* (☒ hours as *Cutty Sark*) in which Sir Francis Chichester sailed around the world in 1966.

Dominating the river is the magnificent Baroque creation of the **Royal Naval College**. It was begun in 1664 as a replacement for the old royal palace, was designated a royal hospital for navy seamen in 1694, and not completed until well into the 18thC. The original plans were by Wren, but other leading architects, including Vanbrugh and Hawksmoor, made substantial contributions. Of the interior, the amazing **Painted Hall** and the **chapel** can be visited (✆ open Mon – Wed, Fri – Sun 14.30 – 16.30, closed Thurs). Sir James Thornhill's **hall** of 1708 – 27 is a Baroque tour de force. The enormous painting on the ceiling represents the glory of the Protestant monarchy, the effect increased by the rich grey columns and pilasters, with illusionistic painted flutings. The **chapel** opposite is in a much lighter Neo-Classical style; it was redecorated in 1779 – 89 after a fire.

Farther back from the river are the main buildings of the **National Maritime Museum** centred on the **Queen's House** (✆ open Tues – Sat 10.00 – 18.00, Sun 14.00 – 17.30). Henry VIII was born here, as were his two daughter queens, Mary and Elizabeth. James I gave the palace to his queen, Anne of Denmark, in 1613, and it was completely rebuilt to the designs of Inigo Jones between 1616 – 35. The Queen's House is a building of extreme Classical simplicity, in the Palladian style, quite revolutionary in its day. The most interesting rooms are the entrance hall, a perfect cube, and the graceful circular stairwell. To the sides are two wings added from 1807 – 16.

The National Maritime Museum housed here is the greatest seafaring museum in the world. Its extensive collections range from the finds of marine archaeology to an entire paddle tug. The main entrance is in the East Wing, which is devoted to the era of Britain's greatest maritime power, the 19th – early 20thC. Outstanding among the many fine model ships is one of the early iron steamship, *Great Britain*, of 1843. The galleries upstairs include a selection of the museum's excellent 19thC marine paintings. The Queen's House, reached through the open arcade, has pictures and models of the 16th – 17thC, in keeping with the architecture, and also paintings by Turner, Romney and Reynolds. The West Wing is dominated by the New Neptune Hall, with the 1907 paddle tug, *Reliant*. Exciting displays here include the decorated royal river boats: Queen Mary's shallop of 1689 and Prince Frederick's barge of 1732.

After the Queen's House, you pass into **Greenwich Park**, crowned with several hills and sloping down steeply towards the river. One hill is topped by a Henry Moore statue, others by the buildings of the Royal Observatory.

The **Royal Observatory** (✆ hours as Maritime Museum) was established in 1675 – 76, when Wren was commissioned by Charles II to build a house for the first Astronomer Royal, John Flamsteed. A well-proportioned red-brick building with a fine octagonal room on the top floor, it commands extensive views down over Greenwich and the river. On top of one of Flamsteed House's towers can be seen a large red ball mechanism erected in 1833. Each day the ball falls at exactly 13.00 to enable ships in the river to set their clocks accurately. At the rear of the house is a 19thC extension topped by a huge bulbous dome of 1894 which houses a 28in (71cm) refracting telescope, one of the largest in the world. The astronomers have moved to Sussex and more modern equipment, and Flamsteed House is now a museum, with exhibits that include clocks and telescopes used by Halley, Herschel and other royal astronomers.

Next to Flamsteed is the mid-18thC **Meridian Building**, where there is also a display on the theme of time, for this is the site of the meridian on which all the world's clock time is based through Greenwich Mean Time; visitors can have a foot in each hemisphere.

At the top end of the park is **Ranger's House** (📷 open daily 10.00–16.00), its front fringing *Blackheath* on Chesterfield Walk. Built of red brick, the stone centre framing the main doorway dates from the early 18thC, while the bow-fronted wings to the side were added by the Earl of Chesterfield in about 1754. The best room is in the s wing, and contains pictures of the Suffolk Collection, including a number attributed to William Larkin of members of the Jacobean aristocracy.

Chesterfield Walk leads into Croom's Hill, which proceeds back down to Greenwich town. This old road has several detached houses and terraces of the 17th–18thC along its steep slope. Near Ranger's house are **Macartney House** and the **Manor House**, both of the early 1700s. Greenwich has an attractive town centre a little inland from the *Cutty Sark*, with wine bars and antique shops. Its massive and monumental parish church of **St Alfege** was built in 1711–30.

Downstream is **Woolwich**, with a large naval dockyard. It is also the traditional home of the Royal Artillery. The **Royal Arsenal**, **Military Academy** and **Artillery Barracks** of the 18th–early 19thC are extraordinarily large and imposing buildings. Nearby is the **Rotunda** (📷 open Mon–Sat 10.00–12.45, 14.00–16.00, Sun 14.00–16.00), a strange tent-shaped building of 1814 moved here from St James's Park in 1820, which now houses a collection of artillery pieces from the 17thC to the present day. The river is straddled by the **Thames Barrier**, an extraordinary engineering achievement opened in 1984, which will protect London from flooding. A free exhibition demonstrates how it works.

Guildhall 🏛 ☆

Aldermanbury, EC2 ☎ *606–3030. Map* **12***E15* 📷 *Open Mon–Fri 10.00–17.00, Sat 10.00–16.00 (check first). Tube Bank, St Paul's, Moorgate.*

Despite being hidden away in its own yard in *The City*, the Guildhall has been parliament and palace for the Corporation of The City of London for almost 1,000yr. The present facade is not the one which would have greeted the powerful medieval Lord Mayors such as Dick Whittington; it was constructed in 1788–89 to the design of George Dance, an attractive but bizarre melange of 18thC Gothic ideas. The entrance porch, however, dates from the 15thC building, as do parts of the **Great Hall**. The most entertaining of the statues inside are the giants Gog and Magog, new versions of old mythical figures. Below is the large 15thC crypt, notable for its Purbeck marble columns supporting a vaulted roof.

The **Guildhall Library**, in an unremarkable new building on the w side, houses a sumptuous collection of books, leaflets and manuscripts giving an absorbing and unparalleled view of London. This building also houses the **Clock Museum** of the Worshipful Company of Clockmakers. For reasons of space, most of the display is of watches, often more like delicate works of art than time-pieces. There are two 15thC German clocks, a clock with a rolling ball for a pendulum, and a watch in the shape of a skull, the jaws of which open to reveal the time: dating from 1600, it allegedly belonged to Mary Queen of Scots.

To enter the **State Apartments** is to move on to a different age – the walls and ceilings of the King's Staircase are decorated with exuberant frescoes, with gods and heroes of the ancient world swirling illusionistically through Corinthian columns. They were painted after 1700 by an Italian artist, Antonio Verrio. Next comes a huge **Guard Chamber**, its walls decorated with 3,000 pistols, muskets and swords. A door from here leads into some of the rooms of Wolsey's palace, with the 16thC linen-fold panelling, but this brief diversion ends with the formal sequence of rooms designed by Wren. **William III's bedroom** has a ceiling by Verrio, a soaring Baroque bed and gilded furniture originally designed for the room. Rich and heavy tapestries still hang on some of the walls: in the Cartoon Gallery are tapestries made to Raphael's famous designs (for which the room was planned; the designs now hang in the *Victoria & Albert Museum*). In the **Communication Gallery** are a number of paintings by Lely, the so-called *Windsor Beauties* court portraits.

The Cumberland Suite shows a different taste, that of the 18thC, with regal pomp giving way to elegant comfort. An important collection of paintings hangs throughout these rooms, largely from the Italian High Renaissance. Titian, Tintoretto, Correggio, Raphael and Duccio are all represented; perhaps the most striking are Mantegna's series *The Triumph of Julius Caesar*, but look out also for the chilly gloss of Parmigianino's *Minerva*. Other schools of painting are also to be seen: Brueghel's *Massacre of the Innocents* and Cranach's lovely *Judgement of Paris* stand out. There are also works by Holbein, an artist associated closely with the Tudors. There are splendid views over the park and on to **Fountain Court**, a first glimpse of Wren's superb architecture in pink brick and white stone.

Before emerging, three rooms of special interest are encountered, all dating from the Tudor period. The small **Wolsey's Closet**, probably the cardinal's study, has panelled walls, a finely wrought ceiling of timber and plaster and recently discovered paintings from the 16thC. The **chapel**, also built by Wolsey, is then seen from the Royal Pew; it has an elaborate ceiling added by Henry VIII, with pendants carved in the form of angels. The reredos was designed by Wren and its marvellously carved plant forms are the work of Grinling Gibbons. Finally, as a suitable climax, there is Henry VIII's **Great Hall** of 1531–36, hung with contemporary Flemish tapestries and with a **hammerbeam roof**. Small rooms which help make the place come alive are the authentically-equipped **kitchen** and Henry VIII's **wine cellar**.

Emerging into Clock Court, an arch at the opposite end leads through to Fountain Court past the **Queen's Staircase**. Here Wren's bold but harmonious use of the contrast between stone and brick can be seen to dramatic effect from the cloister along the little courtyard. Another arch leads through to the centre of the **East Front** and the lake, **Long Water**.

All around the buildings are spectacular gardens in the various styles of different periods, some sunken and enclosed, others broad and open, some in the Tudor 'knot' pattern, others with great avenues of trees. Note the 200yr-old vine in its special greenhouse (its stem is 78in (2m) thick) which produces 600 bunches of grapes yearly, and the maze, dating in its present form from 1714. The Chestnut Avenue stretches for over 1 mile (1.5km), and flowers spectacularly in May.

Highgate ☆
Map 21B4. Tube Highgate, Archway.

This twin village of *Hampstead*, looking down on London from the N, takes its name from a tollgate that used to be near its centre and its dizzying height, best appreciated by approaching steep Highgate Hill or Highgate West Hill. Highgate Hill has a few fine mansions, most notably **Cromwell House**, a red-brick house in Dutch style of about 1637–40. Here also is **Whittington Stone** where, according to legend, Dick Whittington rested on his way home in c.1390, gazed down at The City and heard the bells chiming, 'Turn again Whittington, thrice Mayor of London'.

The High Street also has good 18thC terraces, and South Grove on the left leads past the attractive Waterlow Park and Pond Sq. to the junction with West Hill and **The Grove**, with a good terrace built around 1700. A plaque commemorates Coleridge who lived in one of the houses; his tomb is in the aisle of the nearby church of St Michael, an imposing 19thC Gothic (1832) edifice with Highgate Cemetery (see below) behind it. In complete contrast with these charms are two large and influential blocks of flats to the N on North Hill, the Highpoint flats, built in 1936 and 1939 by the Tecton group.

Highgate Cemetery is one of the most extraordinary relics of Victorian London gone to seed, a romantic wilderness that pays tribute to nature's power to reclaim its own. The newer E side is open every day but the W side, where the buildings are in a dangerous condition, is kept closed except for four days a year, when literally thousands of people take the opportunity to visit its weird Gothic chapel and Egyptian catacombs. The most famous grave on the E side is the **grave of Karl Marx**, now surmounted by a nasty monument erected in the 1950s. Many other well known people are buried here, including George Eliot, whose grave is near that of Marx.

Hogarth's House
Hogarth Lane, W4 ☎ 994–6757. Map 21C4 ▣ Open Apr–Aug Mon, Wed–Sat 11.00–18.00, Sun 14.00–18.00; mid-Sept to early Dec, Jan–Mar Mon, Wed–Sat 11.00–16.00, Sun 14.00–16.00. Tube Chiswick Park, Turnham Green.

The painter William Hogarth (1697–1764) was an urban artist, and only lived in the delightful riverside village of *Chiswick* in the summer. The house which he occupied from 1749–64 is now stranded between industrial buildings on the noisy Great West Rd. Inside the pretty old building, however, a quieter atmosphere prevails as an ironic background to the good selection of Hogarth's bustling, sarcastic and sometimes scurrilous engravings. The house also contains some contemporary furniture, and the artist himself is buried in the nearby village churchyard.

Holland House and Park
Map 6H1. Tube Holland Park.

Although Holland House has hardly survived, its park retains the elegance of its prime. Narrow paths wind among mature woods, peacocks and other ornamental birds appear to roam freely, a formal flower garden, with a traditional pattern of box hedges, is decorated with statues, and music drifts from the Orangery in summer.

The bombs of 1941 destroyed most of the house and now only

the E wing stands complete, with its attractive Dutch gabled roof line. There is also a marvellous arched loggia, with strangely chequered carvings and fleur-de-lys crenellations. The Classical gateway (1629) was designed by Inigo Jones.

Horse Guards Parade 血
Map 10H11. Tube Westminster.

The Horse Guards of Whitehall is a curiously jumbled Classical building of the mid-18thC, all arches, pediments and separate wings. Troopers of the Household Cavalry will be seen mounting guard in resplendent uniforms astride their equally well-groomed horses. The large parade ground beyond the central arch sees the great **Trooping of the Colour** ceremony in June (see *Calendar of events* in *Planning*); past the Guards' Memorial, it leads into *St James's Park*. State buildings surround the other three sides. Looking back from the park, the Old Admiralty is on the left, an ugly brick and stone extravaganza of 1894–95; to the right of the Horse Guards is the more dignified Scottish Office, actually a fine mid-18thC house; and further right are the Treasury and the rear of no. 10 *Downing Street*.

Hyde Park
Map 7G–H. Tube Marble Arch, Hyde Park Corner, Lancaster Gate.

You can stand in the middle of the largest open space in London, formed by Hyde Park and Kensington Gardens, and see nothing but wooded, rolling grassland, punctuated only by the lake known as the **Serpentine**, made in 1730.

Rotten Row, along the southern edge, was *the* place to parade in the 18th–19thC, and is still used by horse riders, although it sadly has lost its trees to Dutch Elm disease. In the SE, at Hyde Park Corner, is *Apsley House* and a graceful Ionic screen that once formed an entrance to the park's carriageway. A little to the N there is an absurd statue of *Achilles*, made in 1822 from captured French cannons. A much better statue is *Rima* by Jacob Epstein (1922) near the Hudson Bird Sanctuary in the centre of the park. On the NE is *Speakers' Corner*.

Imperial War Museum 血
Lambeth Rd., SE11 ☎ 735–8922. Map 19J13 ▣ ▣ ✳
Open Mon–Sat 10.00–17.50, Sun 14.00–17.50. Tube Lambeth North.

'Lest we forget', the Imperial War Museum was established soon after the end of World War I to preserve the relics and memory of that terrible conflict. Since then, its terms of reference have been expanded to include all wars involving Britain or the Commonwealth since 1914. We should not forget, either, that war means more than fighting; there are exhibits about life on the home front, an unparalleled display of newspapers, photographs and films, and even an important collection of modern art – pictures by artists such as Henry Moore, Paul Nash, Stanley Spencer and Augustus John, who were commissioned to record their impressions of wars in progress.

The museum's Lambeth building used to be the central range of the Bethlem Royal Hospital, built in 1812–15, appropriately perhaps as an asylum for the insane, successor to the notorious 'Bedlam' in The City. The present building's portico and large dome were added in 1835–40.

The most appealing exhibits are on the ground floor, from
models of warships and battles to full scale displays built up
with manikins in authentic uniforms around genuine tanks and
guns. Great attention is paid to realism, with foliage,
camouflage and props carefully inserted. Of particular interest
are three mobile command centres used by Montgomery in
World War II. The museum displays a number of famous
aircraft: a Sopwith Camel from the 1914–18 war, a Spitfire
from the Battle of Britain, a Focke-Wulf 190 and a
Messerschmitt Me 163 jet fighter. The upper floors are devoted
to temporary exhibitions, a room of documents, including the
German surrender signed in 1945, and the art galleries.

Inns of Court
All barristers must belong to one of these
four institutions, and many work from their dignified ancient
buildings. They are: *Gray's Inn*, *Lincoln's Inn*, and the Middle
and Inner *Temple*.

Dr. Johnson's House
17 Gough Sq., EC4 ☎ *353–3745. Map* **11F13** 🔳 *Open
Mon–Sat May–Sept 11.00–17.30, Oct–April 11.00–17.00.
Tube Blackfriars, St Paul's.*

In this substantial terraced house, dating from about 1700,
lived Dr. Samuel Johnson, from 1748–59, the man of letters
par excellence and the centre of a whole literary world which
flocked to see him here and in the nearby **Cheshire Cheese** (see
Pubs) in *Fleet Street*. In the large gabled attic, he and his six
assistants worked on the celebrated *Dictionary*.

Unfortunately, little can be seen of the house's original
contents – a few chairs and tables, however, do give some idea of
its historic atmosphere. Pictures and memorabilia give a picture
of literary life in 18thC London. Look out for a first edition
copy of the *Dictionary* and Johnson's will.

Keats' House
Keats Grove, NW3 ☎ *435–2062. Map* **21C4** 🔲 ✗ *Open
Mon–Sat 10.00–13.00, 14.00–18.00, Sun 14.00–17.00.
Tube Hampstead, Belsize Park.*

The Romantic poet John Keats (1795–1821) was already in the
grip of tuberculosis when, in 1820, he left the house in
Hampstead where he had spent his two most productive years
to journey to Italy, where he died ten months later.
Nevertheless, the house is a monument to his happiness and the
rural seclusion that inspired *Ode to a Nightingale* and other
poems. At the time it was split into two cottage homes sharing a
garden; in the other half lived Fanny Brawne, with whom Keats
fell famously and poetically in love. The engagement ring she
wore until her own death is part of the memorial collection, as
are Keats' manuscripts and annotated books, and letters to and
from friends such as Shelley.

Kensington ☆
Map **14&15**. *Tube South Kensington, High Street
Kensington.*

Modern Kensington is pleasant and prosperous, with a few
enclaves of ostentatious wealth, but the predominant pattern is
of good 19thC terraces and villas, large late-Victorian and
Edwardian apartment blocks, shopping centres that include the
better department stores, and little streets of classy boutiques
and antique shops – good taste abounds.

In the 17thC, two great houses emerged from the manors scattered among the fields: *Holland House and Park*, and Nottingham House, which became *Kensington Palace* in 1690 when William and Mary moved there and gave the impetus to a new crop of aristocratic houses. **Kensington Square** was one such development, of about 1700, and a few attractive houses are preserved, such as no. 29. The part just s of Kensington Palace is a lovely enclave, **Canning Place** in particular. **Kensington Palace Road**, running N just to the W of the palace, is known as 'Millionaires' Row'; it was begun in 1843 and consists of grand detached mansions, now largely occupied by embassies or their staff, and is a private road. The public road running N from **Kensington High Street**, a busy shopping area, to Notting Hill Gate is **Kensington Church Street**, with its many good antique shops and clothes boutiques (see *Shopping*). Nearby are *Leighton House* and the *Commonwealth Institute*.

The central part of Kensington, thought of as **South Kensington** as that is the name of the tube station which serves it, is dominated by a complex of museums and colleges set up on land bought with the proceeds from the Great Exhibition held in Hyde Park in 1851. Albert, Prince Consort to Queen Victoria, was the leading sponsor of the scheme and much of the character of this monument to Victorian optimism comes from his vision. His memory is honoured by the *Albert Memorial and Royal Albert Hall*.

Next to the Albert Hall is the **Royal College of Art**, a supposedly 'brutal' but in fact dull building of 1960–61. A little to the E of the Albert Hall is the **Royal Geographical Society**, an attractively informal house in Dutch style designed by Norman Shaw in 1874. Statues show *David Livingstone* and *Scott of the Antarctic*, both fellows of the RGS.

To the s is Prince Consort Rd. Here, at the centre of the large 20thC buildings of **Imperial College** (London University's leading science department), is the **Royal College of Music**, a red-brick pseudo-medieval building of 1883–84. The 280ft (85m) **Queen's Tower** is a spectacular survivor of the 1887–93 Imperial Institute buildings.

South of Imperial College are the great museums that, together with the colleges, represent the fulfilment of Albert's dream: the *Science Museum*, the *Geological Museum*, the *Natural History Museum*, one of London's finest buildings, and the *Victoria & Albert Museum*.

The eastern part of Kensington is predominantly residential. Beyond the Victoria & Albert Museum is the *Brompton Oratory*, with the shopping centre of the Brompton Rd. beyond, and the incomparable **Harrods** department store. Behind the main road, attractive housing of the 19thC stretches up to Knightsbridge and s into Brompton. An interesting building, well worth a detour, is **Michelin House**, an Art Nouveau gem of 1910, on Fulham Rd. Its ceramic decorations include panels with charming scenes of early motor races.

Kensington Palace 🏛

Kensington Gdns., W8 ☎937–9561. *Map 6H3* ■■ ✍☎ *Open Mon–Sat 9.00–16.15, Sun 13.00–16.15. Tube High Street Kensington, Queensway.*

Kensington Palace was first made a royal residence when it was bought by William and Mary in 1689. The house had large grounds, now **Kensington Gardens** (see *Walk 4*), and was next to the expanse of *Hyde Park*. Sir Christopher Wren was instructed to enlarge the palace and, apart from further work in the 1720s, most of what is seen was built under his supervision. It is a simple building, around three courts, and surprisingly unpretentious for a royal palace. Perhaps the most striking building is the **Orangery** of 1704, a little to the NE, probably designed by Nicholas Hawksmoor.

The interior is mostly private but the State Apartments can be visited. Some of the rooms are largely as Wren left them, others were made grander by William Kent in the 1720s. Kent's own Baroque paintings adorn several walls and ceilings, most notably in the **King's Staircase**, the **King's Gallery** and **King's Drawing Room**. One of the most attractive rooms is the **Queen's Bedroom**, sumptuously but intimately decorated, with fine 17thC furniture including the bed made for James II's queen. Look out for the fine carving by Grinling Gibbons, Wren's carver, over the fireplace in the Presence Chamber, enhanced by Kent's 'Etruscan' ceiling, and also the wind-vane above the fire in the King's Gallery. There is an interesting display of paintings of and exhibits from the Great Exhibition of 1851 in the **Council Chamber**. Several good paintings are on show in addition to the fine furniture: most notable is Van Dyck's seductive *Cupid and Psyche* ✿ but look out for Artemisia Gentileschi's powerful *Self-portrait*, an important work by a woman artist.

The royal tradition is kept up by the Prince and Princess of Wales, who have their London home here.

Kenwood House *(The Iveagh Bequest)* 𝕀𝕀𝕀 ★
Hampstead Lane, NW3 ☎ ☎348–1286. *Map* **21C4** ☑ ✗ ▣
Open daily Apr–Sept 10.00–19.00; Oct, Feb–Mar 10.00–17.00; Nov–Jan 10.00–16.00. Tube Highgate.
After a short walk through old and well-established woods, on *Hampstead* Heath, the exquisite 18thC mansion comes into view, with Robert Adam's superb Classical facade flanked harmoniously by wings containing the Orangery and library. Adam was commissioned to adapt an old Stuart house in 1766 by the first Earl of Mansfield. The result was some of the Scottish architect's finest work, including the South Front, with its decorated pilasters and the stucco portico that forms the main entrance. Several Adam details survive; the **library** is outstanding. The room was intended for 'receiving company' as well as housing books, and this explains its splendour.

Kenwood was saved from the interest of speculative builders in 1925 when the first Earl of Iveagh (Edward Cecil Guinness, of brewing fame) bought the house. He died only 2yr later, leaving the house, a sizeable bequest and a collection of pictures to the people of London. Apart from the library, the house is now laid out as an art gallery.

English 18thC painting is best represented, with excellent examples of Gainsborough and Reynolds in particular; Gainsborough's sumptuous *Mary, Countess Howe* is a masterpiece of the artist's elegant later style. Kenwood's real stars, however, are Dutch paintings, with fine examples by Cuyp and Van de Velde. Linger over Vermeer's **Guitar Player** and, supreme, Rembrandt's **Self-portrait** of c.1663. Other notable artists represented include Van Dyck, Guardi, Boucher and Turner.

In summer, concerts are given by the lake (see *Nightlife*). Dr. Johnson's summerhouse was moved here in 1968.

Kew

Map 20D3. Tube Kew Gardens, or train to Kew Bridge from Waterloo.

Close to the ideal of an English country village, Kew Green is not as rustic as it first seems. It is actually flanked by 18th–19thC detached and terraced houses which lend an air of substantial prosperity, and its unusual parish church, **St Anne's**, was built under royal patronage in 1710–14 (and extended in 1770). An interesting feature is the Royal Gallery above the w door, donated by George III in 1805.

At the narrow end of the green is the **Herbarium** (open only to professional botanists), the library and collection of some five million dried plant specimens which presages the area's great attraction, **Kew Gardens**, by whose gate it sits.

Providing a contrast to the natural splendours of the Gardens, **Kew Bridge Engines and Water Supply Museum** (Kew Bridge Rd., Brentford ☎ 568–4757 ▨ open Sat, Sun 11.00–17.00) boasts some fine 19thC steam engines used to supply London's water.

Royal Botanic Gardens ★

☎ 940–1171 ▨ ✿ *Open daily, gardens 10.00 to sunset, glasshouses, galleries, museums 11.00–17.30 or sunset if earlier.*

The full name of Kew Gardens comes as a salutary reminder to those who know it well, for they are apt to be seduced by its supreme beauty and forget that it is a scientific institution. As such, it is unmatched, studying, classifying and cultivating a vast number of plants from all around the world. Its walks are superb and its views dreamlike; in spring it is sublime.

Kew Gardens was formed from the grounds of two royal residences: Richmond Lodge and Kew Palace. George III united the two estates and from 1772–1819 Sir Joseph Banks, who had accompanied Captain Cook to the South Seas, established a true botanic garden in the large park, sending young botanists all over the world in search of specimens. It was with the help of Kew Gardens that breadfruit was introduced to the West Indies and rubber to the Malay Peninsula. In 1841, the gardens were handed over to the State and the first director was formally appointed. Further grants of land by the Crown in 1897 and 1904 took the total to over 300 acres (121.5ha). Expansion continues, for a fine new building project now underway will greatly extend the facilities for visitors. The design effectively mirrors the Gardens' famous glasshouses.

Begin at the main gates by Kew Green. For a short visit, proceed up the Broad Walk, which turns left at the Orangery, leading to the pond and Palm House, returning by smaller paths through flower-filled woodland, rock, iris and other gardens.

A more extensive tour will take in the many extra attractions. On the right of the Broad Walk is the **Aroid House**, a Nash-designed glasshouse in Classical style brought here from Buckingham Palace in 1836; inside is recreated a dense and lush tropical rain forest. Farther along on the right is the **Dutch House**, all that remains of the buildings of **Kew Palace**, the rest of which was demolished in 1802. The Dutch House actually predated the main palace buildings, being built in red brick with steep Dutch gables by a wealthy merchant in 1631. To the rear is the **Queen's Garden**, an accurate reconstruction of the type of garden the house might have had in the 17thC, with tightly-clipped hedges and aromatic herbs. Back at the Broad Walk, the **Orangery** (1761) contains temporary exhibitions.

Instead of continuing along the Broad Walk, bear to the right. The long Riverside Ave. here passes through cedar, plane and oak planted woods. A detour to the left will take in the **rhododendron dell** (if you are visiting in spring, it is almost a crime to miss this), the bamboo garden and azalea garden, with the beautiful lake to the S. Walk around the riverside to obtain a fine view across the Thames to *Syon House*. Farther along to the SW are the grounds of **Queen Charlotte's Cottage**, thatched in rustic style and built in the 1770s as a focal point for elaborate garden parties. It is now surrounded by an area left wild as natural habitat for native British plants and wildlife. Walking to the E leads to the **Japanese Gateway**, a fine replica erected in 1910 on a little hill, and surrounded by pines and flowering azaleas. Further E again is the **Pagoda**, built in a more fanciful oriental style in 1761–62, at 163ft (50m), pushing up through the surrounding woods.

From here, Pagoda Vista returns towards the entrance. On the way, take in the **Temperate House**, a large 19thC complex of glasshouses containing fine camellias, with the **Marianne North Gallery** to the E, home of an extraordinary collection of botanical paintings. A little further N, mock temples and ruins survive from the 18thC garden layout. The **Palm House** then comes into view – a magnificent and graceful iron and glass construction of 1844–48 by Decimus Burton. It contains a fabulous collection of tropical plants, many of which have grown to great size. Between the Palm House and the main entrance to the N are numerous little gardens and complexes of glasshouses devoted to particular types of plants; particularly impressive are the fine **water lilies**.

Lambeth Palace 🏛

*Map **19**J12. Open only to organized groups booking in advance ☎928–8282, usually Wed or Thurs 14.15–15.30. Tube Lambeth North.*

In the possession of the Archbishops of Canterbury since 1197, Lambeth Palace grew into prominence as the Primate's residence in the later Middle Ages. In 1547, Thomas Cranmer wrote the English Prayer Book here, but caused great controversy by eating meat during Lent in the Great Hall. The superb red-brick **gatehouse** dates from 1495, and next to it stands the 15thC tower of the now closed church of St Mary Lambeth. Beyond the walls can be seen the Classical stonework decorating the **hall**, rebuilt after the Civil War.

Lancaster House 🏛

*Stable Yard, The Mall, SW1 ☎839–3488. Map **9**H9 🗺 Open occasionally Easter to Nov Sat, Sun, public hols 14.00–18.00; subject to irregular closure. Tube Green Park.*

Previously known as York House and Stafford House, according to the aristocrat in residence, Lancaster House (begun in 1820) is the most westerly of the palaces of *The Mall*, with its facades overlooking Green Park to the w and *St James's Park* to the S. Benjamin Wyatt designed the exterior in cool Bath stone with massive and severe Classical porticos similar to his *Apsley House*, together with the imposing stairwell. Charles Barry, who took over in 1838, completed the interior in a much more grandiose and highly-decorated Baroque style. Paintings by Veronese and Guercino, brought to the house to decorate ceilings of the antechamber and gallery, conform to this taste for richness.

Law Courts The popular name for the fine Victorian
Gothic *Royal Courts of Justice* on the *Strand*.

Leighton House ▥
*12 Holland Park Rd., W14 Map 21C4 ☎ 602–3316 ▣
Open Mon–Sat 11.00–17.00. Tube High Street Kensington.*
Looking like one of several plain red-brick houses in a street
once favoured by successful artists, Leighton House contains a
remarkable surprise. Lord Leighton was the most famous of
Victorian artists and, in building his house from 1865, he gave
vent to his taste for the exotic, creating a rich interior in
Moorish style. It is fantasy, a harem in London. The highlight
is the **Arab Hall**, with its two storeys culminating in a dome,
and its walls covered with rich 13th–17thC Islamic tiles.
Interesting Victorian paintings on show include works by
Leighton himself and Edward Burne-Jones.

Lincoln's Inn ▥ ★
☎ 405–1393. Map 11E12 ▣ ▦ Open Mon–Fri
*9.00–18.00; apply at porter's lodge; Old Hall open Mon–Fri
9.00–12.00, 14.30–18.00. Tube Holborn, Chancery Lane.*
Reminiscent of one of the grander Oxford or Cambridge
colleges, this most unspoilt of the *Inns of Court* was founded in
the 14thC. The best entrance is from Chancery Lane, through a
gatehouse (with the original gates) of 1518 and the Tudor
red-brick **Old Buildings** (before 1520). Opposite the gate is the
Old Hall (1490–92) which contains an uncharacteristically
serious painting by Hogarth and a fine wooden roof. On the N
side of the court is the **chapel**, dating from about 1619–23,
standing on an open undercroft of Gothic vaulting with rich
ribbing. Its high-backed boxed pews, and its stained-glass
windows of numerous coats of arms of treasurers dating back to
the 17thC, contribute to a deep serenity. To the sw is **New
Square**, not originally built as part of the Inn but a large and
remarkably well-preserved square of about 1685–97; its
dignified brick houses, with decoration restricted to the open
pediments above the doors, enclose a splendid lawn. To the s is
a gateway of 1697 leading into Carey St. The northern part of
the Inn includes the great bulk of Stone Buildings of 1774–80,
with a severe Classical facade on the w side; the large sun-dial on
this wall is dated 1794. Opposite are the Inn's attractive private
gardens, together with the impressive Victorian brick-Gothic
library and New Hall. Beyond these lie the open spaces of
Lincoln's Inn Fields, one of London's largest public squares.

London Bridge
Map 13G16. Tube Monument, London Bridge.
London's *raison d'être*, one might call it – the Romans
discovered that this was the farthest downstream they could
easily cross the river, and built their town accordingly. In fact,
their wooden bridge was almost certainly a little to the E of the
present structure, but survived with periodic reconstructions
until the medieval stone bridge appeared in 1176–1209. This
stood for over 500yr, encrusted with houses, shops, even
chapels, and the famous iron spikes where traitors' heads were
displayed. Eventually, all its buildings were removed and the
bridge modernized in about 1749, at the same time as London's
second bridge was built at Westminster. A new bridge, now
moved to an amusement park in Arizona, was built in 1825–31.
The present structure of three arches dates from 1967–73.

London Dungeon

London Dungeon
34 Tooley St., SE1 ☎ *403–0606. Map 13G16* 🚻 🍴 *Open daily Apr–Sept 10.00–17.30; Oct–Mar 10.00–16.30. Tube London Bridge.*

Enjoying the London Dungeon requires a special sense of humour – and a strong stomach. Its location in a series of dark, damp vaults under railway arches has been carefully chosen to foster discomfort, and is ideally suited to its exhibits on the 'darker side of British history'. The vaults echo to the recorded sounds of screams and moans, and even the rumble of the occasional passing train! The ancient British heroine Boadicea, for example, is shown thrusting a blood-smeared spear into the throat of a gurgling victim. Not for the faint-hearted.

London, Museum of ★
150 London Wall, EC2 ☎ *600–3699. Map 12E15* 📷 🍴 ♿ *Open Tues–Sat 10.00–18.00, Sun 14.00–18.00. Tube Barbican, Moorgate, St Paul's.*

Recently reorganized, and moved to a new building on the corner of the *Barbican*, this museum traces the social history of London from prehistory to the present day in a 'social' manner.

The museum possesses a substantial part of the stock of important archaeological finds made in London, and is chronologically arranged so visitors follow a single winding course, with the two floors joined by a glass walkway.

Archaeological finds from the **Stone, Bronze and Iron Ages**, most originating from sites in the Thames Valley to the w of London, are grouped in settings that show the purposes to which they were put by ancient people. Axe-heads, for example, have been fitted with handles to demonstrate how they would have been used. Models and drawings reconstruct the appearance of prehistoric settlements and explain early hunting methods and agriculture.

Roman London is well represented in the museum and, as an added surprise, a carefully-placed window looks down on one of the best-preserved parts of the Roman wall outside, with its medieval bastions. Inside, the display ranges from leather sandals to board games to the superb sculptures found buried in the floor of the Temple of Mithras discovered in 1954 during the construction of an office block in Queen Victoria St. The **head of Serapis** is particularly exquisite. A famous **mosaic floor** found in 1869 can be seen in a reconstructed room setting, with reproduction furniture showing the luxurious Roman life-style.

The displays of **Anglo-Saxon and medieval London** begin with the strange gravestone in the Viking Ringerike style, inscribed with runes dating from the 11thC. An excellent model of the original Tower of London shows it as a single stone tower surrounded by a wooden palisade. A model of old *St Paul's Cathedral* is even more impressive, and shows how the great Gothic cathedral must have been before its destruction in the Great Fire of 1666.

A Ming porcelain cup mounted on a silver-gilt stand and an exquisitely embroidered glove show the sophisticated tastes and superb workmanship of the **Tudor and Stuart** periods. Also noteworthy are a copper plate of c.1558, engraved with a contemporary map of London, and the Cheapside Hoard, a collection of 16thC jewellery. Politics now feature more prominently: the Civil War, Great Plague and Fire of London all receive ample attention. A darkened room with a large model

82

graphically shows the progress of the fire; old London actually appears to disintegrate as you watch, with a commentary from Pepys' diary. The exhibits from the **18th–20thC** are even more varied, if more familiar. **Shop fronts and interiors** are reconstructed, including a superb 18thC barber's, a 19thC pub, and an early broadcasting studio. There are some extraordinary barred doors from the notorious Newgate Gaol, an 1862 fire engine, and even an Art Deco elevator from Selfridge's department store. On a smaller scale, look out for some charming Victorian Christmas and Valentine cards and toys. However, grandeur steals the show: the **Lord Mayor's Ceremonial Coach★** (1757), removed once a year for the Lord Mayor's Show, stands resplendent with its elaborate painted and gilt decoration.

London Toy and Model Museum
23 Craven Hill, W2 ☎*262–7905. Map* **7F4** ◫ ▣ ✱ *Open Tues–Sat 10.00–17.30, Sun 11.00–17.00. Tube Queensway, Lancaster Gate.*
This remarkable new museum appeals as much to adults as to the children for whom the exhibits were originally intended. Many of the toys on display can be activated at the touch of a button. There are dolls, nursery toys, mechanical toys – and a stunning ensemble of model railway locomotives.

London Transport Museum
The Piazza, Covent Garden, WC2 ☎*379–6344. Map* **10F11** ▦ ✗ ▣ *Open daily 10.00–18.00. Tube Covent Garden.*
As part of the renovation of *Covent Garden*, the Flower Market, built in 1871–72, now houses a large number of historic public transport vehicles in its spacious galleries. The museum chronicles the history of the capital's transport, with illustrations, photographs, relics such as tickets and posters, and fine models of everything from the 'wherries' that plied the river to electric trams. The real stars, however, are the vehicles themselves. There is a replica of the first omnibus of 1829, a development London copied from Paris. Then there are two genuine horse-drawn buses of the late 19thC, with open-top decks. Early motor buses and trams follow, also with open-top decks and with the driver still exposed to the elements. By then, they were painted in the familiar fire-engine red of today. From the tube there are engines and carriages going back to the 19thC.

Madame Tussaud's ☆
Marylebone Rd., NW1 ☎*935–6861. Map* **2D7** ▦ ▣ ✱ *Open daily 10.00–17.30. Tube Baker Street.*
The redoubtable Madam Tussaud lived to be 89. Having begun her wax modelling in France with the aristocracy and royalty of the *ancien régime*, and having continued to work through the Revolution (the severed heads of king and queen as modelled by Madame can be seen in the museum's Chamber of Horrors), she came to England in 1802 and settled her waxwork museum in London in 1835.

It is now linked to the *Planetarium*. The modern display combines the old and the new: a famous tableau called 'the Sleeping Beauty' has a central figure cast from one of Madame Tussaud's oldest moulds, thought to have been made of Madame du Barry, Louis XV's mistress, with a mechanism which simulates breathing. More recent celebrities include

Michael Jackson, Joan Collins, Martina Navratilova and
Gorbachov, the Russian leader. Nowhere are the visitors
quieter than in the greatest draw, the **Chamber of
Horrors**, with among other terrors a reconstruction of the
dark streets of Whitechapel where Jack the Ripper stalked.

The Mall ☆
Map 10H10. Tube Charing Cross, Green Park.
Whenever pomp and circumstance are on hand, the Mall is
where the crowds gather. Originally laid out by Charles II in
1660–62 as a formal avenue through *St James's Park*, it is now
a triumphal processional way leading from *Trafalgar Square* to
Buckingham Palace. As such, it is largely the work of one man,
Sir Aston Webb, between 1900–11.

Majestically lined with London planes, it slopes gently but
impressively down along the side of the park to the Victoria
Memorial and Buckingham Palace facade, both also designed
by Webb. Looking from Admiralty Arch, the first building on
the right is **Carlton House Terrace**, built by John Nash in
1827–29 on the site of his earlier Carlton House, the great
palace built for the Regent. Its pair of massive stucco facades are
separated by the Duke of York Steps. The view is best from St
James's Park – the balancing ranges, with their Corinthian
colonnades, broad terraces at raised ground floor level, and
supporting dumpy Doric columns, are one of London's most
exciting architectural views. On the s side of The Mall is the
Admiralty of 1722–26 with the aggressively concrete Citadel
next to it, a bold bomb-proof structure from World War II.

The rest of The Mall is surrounded by the park, but with the
palaces that are scattered along its N side visible on the right.
Marlborough House, of stone-dressed red brick, is followed by
the complex making up *St James's Palace* and then the white
stucco of **Clarence House**, built by Nash in 1825–27 for the
Duke of Clarence, later William IV, and now the home of the
Queen Mother. *Lancaster House* follows, in more solemn
yellow Bath stone. The **Victoria Memorial** occupies a circus at
the end of the avenue, a huge structure covered with elaborate
sculpture of high quality in the florid Edwardian style. Queen
Victoria's likeness faces up The Mall towards Admiralty Arch,
topped by a gilded statue of *Victory*. The circus was laid out in
1900–01 and the memorial built in 1911.

Mankind, Museum of
*6 Burlington Gdns., W1 ☎437–2224. Map 9G9 ⊡ Open
Mon–Sat 10.00–17.00, Sun 14.30–18.00. Tube Piccadilly
Circus, Green Park.*
The museum is the result of the recent upsurge of interest in
non-European cultures. Since 1972 the British Museum's
ethnographic collections have been based in this elaborate
Victorian building, decorated with statues of British
philosophers, built in 1866–67 as a part of London University.
Its sandstone and Portland stone facade looks good since
cleaning. At present, the museum is organized as a series of
temporary exhibitions on particular cultures or themes, but
they achieve considerable depth of coverage.

The British Museum's ethnographic collection is
outstanding in African textiles, pottery, and sculpture,
American art from Plains Indians and those of the northwest
coast, and Pre-Columbian Central and South America. From
the Pacific Ocean, the collection is strengthened by objects

brought back in the 18thC by Captain Cook. From Indonesia
there is the important collection of puppets, masks and other
items built up by Sir Stamford Raffles in Java in the 19thC. A
permanent exhibition of the museum's greatest treasures is kept
in **Rm. 8**, including from Nigeria an incomparable Benin ivory
mask and bronze head, Aztec turquoise mosaics in the forms of
a skull-mask and double-headed serpent, and an extraordinary
carved thunderbird from the Kwakiutl tribe of the northwest
coast of America. A hauntingly beautiful object is the life-sized
skull carved from a solid piece of crystal from Mexico.

Mansion House
*Walbrook, EC4 ☎626–2500. Map 13F16 🔟 Visitors
usually admitted Tues–Thurs on written application to
Assistant Private Secretary. Tube Bank.*

As if in reference to the ancient city states, the residence of the
Lord Mayor of London, symbol of the independence of *The
City*, is Classical in character. It owes its Palladian simplicity to
George Dance the Younger who designed it in 1739–53. Its six
giant columns support the only decoration, a pediment with
sculptures representing the dignity and opulence of The City.
The interior, by contrast, is extremely ornate, with a series of
state rooms leading back from the portico to the grand climax of
the **Egyptian Hall** – Roman in style, despite its name. The
annual **Lord Mayor's Show** which arrives here in Nov (see
Calendar of events in *Planning*) is the climax of a still largely
medieval system of government, and during the year you can
see here the liverymen, aldermen and sheriffs who choose the
Lord Mayor, parading at various antiquated ceremonies. But
their power is real – this is the only private residence in the
kingdom with its own court and prison cells.

Marble Arch
Map 8F7. Tube Marble Arch.

Now in the centre of a major traffic island, the Marble Arch
retains only part of the grandeur intended when John Nash
built it in 1828 as the entrance to Buckingham Palace. Modelled
on the Arch of Constantine in Rome, it was moved to its present
site in 1851 when the palace was enlarged by Queen Victoria. Its
traffic island was also the site of Tyburn Tree, London's
traditional place of execution from the Middle Ages until 1783.
A plaque marks the site of the permanent large triangular
gallows where regular hangings, drawings and quarterings
attracted large crowds. *Speakers' Corner* is close by on the
corner of *Hyde Park*.

Marble Hill House 🏛
*Richmond Rd., Twickenham ☎892–5115. Map 20D3 🔟
Open Mon–Thurs, Sat, Sun 10.00–17.00; Nov–Jan 10.00–
16.00. Tube Richmond, train to St Margarets from Waterloo.*

A house of elegant Palladian regularity, this fine riverside
mansion w of London began life with some 'irregular'
occupants: it was built for George II's mistress, the Countess of
Suffolk, in 1723–29, and then Mrs Fitzherbert, George IV's
secret wife, lived here in the 1790s. Its stuccoed, pristinely
white exterior has little decorative detail – the rear, garden side
is particularly impressive – and it stands in a fine open park.

The interior of the house is quite beautiful, with a series of
lovely rooms culminating in the splendid **Countess of Suffolk's
Bedroom**, with Corinthian columns framing the alcove

intended for the bed. A small amount of attractive furniture has
been put back into the house, together with some interesting
paintings, including good copies of Van Dyck portraits.
Flanking one side of the park is the exquisite **Montpelier Row**,
a perfect terrace of 1720.

Marlborough House 🏛

Pall Mall, SW1 ☎*930–2100. Map* **10**H10 🖼 ⛩ 𝒦 *Tours by
appointment only; house subject to irregular closure. Tube
Green Park, St James's.*

This red-brick house with bold stone dressings, the finest of the
palaces bordering *St James's Park*, was built by Sir
Christopher Wren for the Duke and Duchess of Marlborough
in 1709–11, following the duke's series of victories over the
French in the War of Spanish Succession which also won him
Blenheim Palace near Oxford (see *Excursions*). Various
additions were made in the 18thC–19thC, notably the attic
storeys, but Wren's powerful conception can still be
appreciated when viewed from the park. The entrance on the
Pall Mall side, however, is curiously unimpressive. Most of the
present decoration dates from the 19thC, but a series of original
murals depicts Marlborough's battles, and the ceiling of the
Blenheim Saloon is decorated with Gentilleschi's series painted
for the Queen's House at *Greenwich* in 1636. The house now
serves as the Commonwealth Centre.

Marylebone

Maps **8**&**9**D–F. *Tube Baker Street, Great Portland Street.*

During the 18thC, the fashionable West End expanded N to
surround the village of St Marylebone (St Mary-le-bourne
meaning St Mary-by-the-brook). The streets form a near
perfect grid, with the major ones running N–S from *Regent's
Park* towards Oxford St. It now consists largely of smart houses
and apartment blocks, with some busy shopping streets.
Although it has several squares and some good buildings, it is a
curiously anonymous area. The first part to be laid out was
Cavendish Sq. in 1714. St Peter's Chapel nearby in Vere St.
was designed in 1721–24 by James Gibbs, and prefigures *St Martin-
in-the-Fields*. The finest houses are **no. 20 Portman Square**,
designed by Robert Adam in 1775–76, and **Hertford House** in
Manchester Sq. (the *Wallace Collection*). Other famous
addresses are **Harley Street** where top doctors and clinics are
based, **Baker Street**, of Sherlock Holmes fame, and **Wimpole
Street**, where Robert Browning wooed Elizabeth Barrett. On
Marylebone Rd. are *Madame Tussaud's* and the *Planetarium*.

Mayfair ☆

Map **8**&**9**F–H. *Tube Bond Street, Green Park.*

The very name is synonymous with wealth and elegance –
nowhere in London will you see more Rolls Royces or more fur
coats. It was not always so. The annual fair which lent its name
to the area was suppressed by George III in 1800, so riotous had
it become. Mayfair today is a roughly square-shaped section of
the West End, bordered by the shopping streets of Oxford St,
Regent St. and Piccadilly, and Park Lane, lined by large 20thC
hotels and the backs of grand 19thC mansions. Inside this area
are expensive shops, luxurious hotels, casinos, and homes of the
rich.

The development of this area began in about 1700, and by
1800 it was largely filled with squares and terraces. **Grosvenor**

Square is the largest, without its original houses and with the large United States Embassy of 1961 at its western end. Of the squares, **Hanover Square** is the oldest, of about 1715; original houses survive in **St George's Street** to the s. **Berkeley Square** is best known, thanks to its mythical nightingale; it has huge plane trees (almost 200yr old) in its fine gardens and attractive 18thC houses surviving in the sw corner. Only one really grand mansion survives among the houses: **Crewe House** in Curzon St., begun in 1730. Two churches date back to the early development of the area: **St George's, Hanover Square**, in St George's St., of 1721–24 (notice the grand portico and bronze hunting dogs standing guard); and **Grosvenor Chapel** in South Audley St., a more modest edifice of about 1730. The Jesuit **Church of the Immaculate Conception** of 1844–49, in the same street, is worth a visit, with a high altar designed by Pugin.

The shopping streets scattered through Mayfair best preserve its reputation for high living. Around Bond St. (New and Old) are found the best art and antique dealers. Savile Row has the world's finest gentleman's tailors (see *Shopping*). **Shepherd Market** is a 19thC enclave of alleyways lined with smart shops and cafés.

The Monument 🏛 ☆
Monument St, EC3. Map 13G16 🚇 Open Apr–Oct Mon–Sat 9.00–18.00, Sun 14.00–18.00; Nov–Mar Mon–Sat 9.00–16.00. Tube Monument.

Deprived of its commanding appearance by the many modern buildings that surround it, The Monument, on its little hill close to the river, nevertheless retains the Baroque drama of its conception. Designed by Wren and built in 1671, it commemorates the Great Fire of London which began on Sept 2, 1666 in the bakery in nearby Pudding Lane. A relief on the base plinth shows Charles II in Roman dress protecting the citizens of London; the original inscription unjustly blamed the disaster on a Catholic plot. A giant Doric column, 202ft (62m) high, contains 311 steps up to a balcony and a gilded urn. It is a stiff climb but still worth it for the view.

National Army Museum
Royal Hospital Rd., SW3 ☎ 730–0717. Map 16L7 🚇 ✗ 🚇 Open Mon–Sat 10.00–17.30, Sun 14.00–17.30. Tube Sloane Square.

Opened in 1971 in a new building close to the *Royal Hospital, Chelsea*, the National Army Museum brings together objects from several older collections. A self-contained exhibition called **'Arms and the Army'** displays a comprehensive collection of small arms used by the British Army from the 17thC to the present day; the use of both edged weapons and hand guns, from muskets to self-loading rifles, is expertly explained. **'The Story of the Army'** takes the visitor through army history, with maps and models of campaigns, uniforms, weapons and other mementoes. There is also an impressive **uniform gallery**, a picture gallery and a reading room.

National Gallery ★
Trafalgar Sq., WC2 ☎ 839–3321. Map 10G11 🚇 ✗ 🚇 Open Mon–Sat 10.00–18.00, Sun 14.00–18.00. Tube Charing Cross.

Recently enlarged with its northern extension and now possessing over 2,000 pictures, the National Gallery is one of the world's greatest collections of art. Few rivals can boast such a comprehensive account of western art, and the way the paintings are shown provides a model for other great national collections: they are clean, clearly labelled, well-lit and given adequate space.

This freshness of approach accords with the National Gallery's relative youth. When most great European capital cities already had public collections, in 1823, the threat of the sale of John Julius Angerstein's great collection to William of Orange forced a tight-fisted parliament to produce the money to found a national collection. Angerstein's pictures were bought for £57,000 and housed with other bequests in Angerstein's house in Pall Mall. By 1832, with the collection growing, a larger building was needed. It was designed by William Wilkins and completed in 1838, stretching the full length of the N side of *Trafalgar Square*, but was never the imposing building intended, and has frequently been expanded since. Most recently, the northern extension – completed in 1975 – is superbly functional, with excellent hanging space making it possible to put on temporary exhibitions.

The collection of pictures has expanded steadily, with its character changing in accordance with the taste of the different periods of acquisition. After some exploratory Italian forays in the 1840s, the pioneering director, Sir Charles Eastlake, purchased many early Italian works from 1855–65, a time when these pictures were little known. As a result the gallery has a collection of Italian art unequalled outside Italy. In 1861, Queen Victoria gave 20 German and Flemish pictures in memory of her husband Albert; this inspired a new round of acquisitions, resulting in a magnificent group of Dutch and Flemish works. In the 20thC attempts have been made to strengthen the French collection.

British art is the speciality of the *Tate Gallery*, as is modern art, but the National Gallery does have some fine 18thC British masterpieces. There are also outstanding Spanish works.

Since 1946, the National Gallery has had a conservation department and this has been in the forefront in applying science to the care and restoration of paintings. As a result, a high proportion of National Gallery paintings can be seen in the most beautiful condition, cleaned of dirt or past overpainting. Temporary exhibitions bring in pictures on loan to develop particular themes. One especially interesting feature is the occasional series of exhibitions called 'Painting in Focus', in which a single masterpiece is isolated in a separate gallery with other works relating to it, and photographic displays explain its history and significance.

The turning to the left from the main entrance leads into the early Italian section. In **Rm. 1** is the *Wilton Diptych* ✪ which is actually not Italian but was put here because of its early date (c.1395). Probably French, it shows the English monarch Richard II being presented to the Virgin and Child, with saints and angels in attendance. The other glowing medieval icons are further testimony to faith as well as artistic genius; Duccio's **Maestà altar-piece panels** ★ from Siena Cathedral are outstanding. **Rms.** 2 – 6 show the transition to a more realistic style. In **Rm. 2**, Lorenzo Monaco's *Coronation of the Virgin* is in the graceful International Gothic style, while Masaccio's innovative *Virgin and Child* ★ has the spiritual gravity and solid forms of the Renaissance, thrown into relief by Paolo Uccello's *Battle of San Romano* (**Rm. 3**), with its unsuccessful attempt at

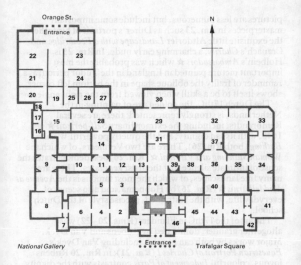

Orange St.

N

National Gallery

Entrance

Trafalgar Square

realistic perspective. The Renaissance can also be seen emerging in Botticelli's early *Adoration of the Magi* (**Rm. 4**) and Piero della Francesca's *Baptism of Christ* (**Rm. 6**). In **Rm. 7**, Leonardo's famous and beautiful black-chalk *Cartoon* ★ is shown in protective lowered lighting.

In **Rms. 8–14**, the superb collection of Italian Renaissance art unfolds. Among too many highlights to list are: Michelangelo's unfinished *Entombment*, a rare easel picture; Raphael's *Pope Julius II* ★ which was only recently discovered to be the original among several versions around the world; Correggio's charming *Mercury instructing Cupid before Venus*★; Leonardo's mysterious *Virgin of the Rocks* ★ and Bronzino's *Allegory*, with its chilly eroticism and obscure subject. One of the original pictures bought from the Angerstein collection is Sebastiano del Piombo's huge *Raising of Lazarus*, for which the artist received guidance from Michelangelo. Of the Venetian works in **Rm. 9**, Titian's breathtaking *Bacchus and Ariadne* ★ is ablaze with colour and movement. Other important Venetian works include Tintoretto's dramatic *Origin of the Milky Way* and Veronese's *Family of Darius before Alexander*. From the 15thC, Botticelli's *Mars and Venus*★ is admired for the purity of its line, and Mantegna's *Agony in the Garden*★ for its dramatic interpretation of the subject. All the greatest masters of the period are represented.

The Renaissance was not such an Italian monopoly as is sometimes supposed. The carefully observed naturalism of northern painters greatly influenced their Italian counterparts; the Dutch and Flemish collection in **Rms. 15–28** illustrates this better than anywhere else in the world. The most famous work here is Jan Van Eyck's *Arnolfini Marriage* ★ (**Rm. 24**), full of realistic but symbolic detail. In the same room is a beautiful jewel-like altarpiece by Memling showing the *Virgin and Child with Saints and Donors*. As a reminder of the range of the northern painters, look out for a wonderfully grotesque *Adoration of the Kings* by Brueghel (**Rm. 25**), and a weird rocky *Landscape with St Jerome* by Patinir (**Rm. 28**). The German pictures are less numerous, but include some important masterpieces in **Rm. 23** such as Dürer's **portrait of his father**, the exquisite little Altdorfer *Landscape with a Footbridge* and Cranach's *Charity*, a charming early nude. In **Rm. 25** is Holbein's *Ambassadors* ✫ which was probably the most important picture painted in England in the Tudor period; as a reminder of frailty the oblique shape in the bottom left corner shows itself to be a skull when viewed from the right angle.

The Dutch 17thC, the golden age of painting in the Netherlands, is strongly represented: there are several Rembrandts, including the extraordinary *Self-portrait* ★ of 1640, with its sad dignity, and the quietly powerful *Woman Bathing* (both **Rm. 26**). There are two Vermeers, of which the *Woman Standing at a Virginal* ✫ (**Rm. 26**) best demonstrates the sense of intimate silence that the artist generates. There are many fine landscapes, of which the most famous is the *Avenue at Middelharnis* ✫ (**Rm. 26**) by Hobbema, and also scenes of everyday life, with the restrained, precise style of the Dutch school.

The art of the 17thC in Flanders (**Rms. 20–22**) was altogether grander, dominated by Rubens and Van Dyck. Major works by both can be seen, including Van Dyck's *Equestrian Portrait of Charles I* (**Rm. 21**); in **Rm. 20** Rubens' joyous, colourful *Judgement of Paris* contrasts with the dignity of his landscape *Château de Steen* ✫ and his ribald *Drunken Silenus supported by Satyrs* widens the range further.

Rms. 29, 30 and 37 are occupied by 17th–18thC Italian works. Caravaggio's *Supper at Emmaus* ★ (**Rm. 29**) shows the artist's revolutionary use of naturalism in religious art: the disciples are seen as real working people with coarse clothes; look at the drama in even the hands. A popular recent acquisition, found on the ceiling of a London house, is Tiepolo's *Allegory with Venus and Time* (**Rm. 37**), full of light and air.

French painting of the 17th–18thC (**Rms. 32–33**) is shown with emphasis on Poussin and Claude, both of whom have been assiduously collected in Britain. Poussin's *Bacchanalian Revel* demonstrates his influential cool Classicism. Claude's mysterious and peaceful landscapes are altogether more approachable; the recently acquired *Enchanted Castle* ✫ has an astonishing, dreamlike quality, achieved largely by superb mastery of light. The French 18thC is poorly represented by National Gallery standards; even so it boasts Watteau's *La Gamme d'Amour*, Chardin's acute *Young Schoolmistress* ✫ and Boucher's *Landscape with a Watermill*.

The gallery's strongest English period is the 18th–19thC (**Rms. 35–36, 38–39**). Outstanding works include Hogarth's satirical *Marriage à la Mode* paintings, the basis for the more famous series of engravings, and magnificent examples of that period's two best genres, Gainsborough's portrait of *Mr and Mrs Andrews* ★ and Constable's landscape *The Hay Wain* ★ Turner opens new vistas with this magical *Rain, Steam and Speed* ★ and *The Fighting Temeraire*.

In **Rms. 41–42** are a small number of Spanish pictures of extraordinary quality. El Greco's *Christ driving the Traders from the Temple* of about 1600 is the finest of several paintings by this remarkable artist. From the later 17thC there is Velazquez's sensual tour-de-force, *The Rokeby Venus* ★ and a portrait of *Philip IV*, together with Zurbarán's *St Francis*, showing the dark religious passion so characteristic of Spanish art. There are also several good Goyas, including the famous portrait of the *Duke of Wellington*.

Rms. 43–46 now house the gallery's acquisitions charting the emergence of modern art. An impressive collection of Impressionist works include Renoir's *Les Parapluies* ★ (periodically moved to Dublin) and Monet's stunning *Lilies* ☆ as well as Degas' *Combing the Hair*. Van Gogh's intense, dynamic *Sunflowers* introduces a Post-Impressionist collection which also includes Seurat's *Bathers, Asnières* ★ with works by Gauguin, and a recent acquisition, Klimt's *Hermina Gallia*.

National Portrait Gallery ☆
2 St Martin's Pl., WC2 ☎ *930–1552. Map* **10**G11 ▣ 🚩 *with flash. Open Mon–Fri 10.00–17.00, Sat 10.00–18.00, Sun 14.00–18.00. Tube Charing Cross.*

Opened in 1859 as a kind of "national pantheon", the emphasis was placed from the start on the subjects of the pictures rather than the artists or art for art's sake. Nevertheless, the intention to obtain the best portraits has meant that the collection has acquired many fine paintings and drawings. Since 1968, photographs have been systematically included and caricatures are now also accepted. In fact, the emphasis on history gives great coherence to the exhibition, which is arranged chronologically with relevant background material, such as a pictorial essay on the Industrial Revolution. The excellent **temporary exhibitions** (🖼) also expand on themes or figures from the starting point of the portraits.

The present buildings were constructed next to the *National Gallery* in 1896 and extended in the 1930s. The collection begins at the top (several flights of stairs have to be climbed), with a room devoted to medieval portraits. Portraits in a modern sense were not produced in the Middle Ages, so the images are few in number; a copy of the fine representation of *Richard II* in Westminster Abbey dominates. Portraits became common from the Tudor period and perhaps the most interesting examples in the whole collection come from this early section. There is an excellent version of *Henry VII* by Michel Sittow of 1505, painted for the Holy Roman Emperor when Henry was seeking his daughter's hand in marriage. Perhaps the finest work of all is Holbein's magnificent cartoon for a lost fresco at Whitehall Palace showing *Henry VIII with his father Henry VII* ☆ There is an exquisite full-length image of *Lady Jane Grey*, who was executed in 1554 after being declared queen at the age of 17. Several portraits of Elizabeth I are in the incredibly detailed style of the period, with the queen decked out in rich clothes and encrusted with jewellery. A portrait of *William Shakespeare*, dated about 1610, is the only one with any real claim to authenticity.

The gallery continues through the Jacobean and Stuart periods, with the increasing formality of the court painters, giving way to the more lively images of the 18thC. Figures from the arts and sciences increase gradually in proportion to the political and military leaders. This was another golden age of English portraiture; look out for Hogarth's *Self-portrait*, several works by Gainsborough and Reynolds, and pictures of *Dr. Johnson* and *Charles James Fox*. A fine unfinished portrait of *Nelson* by Sir William Beechey and a romantic one of *Byron* in Greek costume show the greater concentration on the individual that becomes apparent in much of the 19thC work. Royalty, however, is still shown in highly idealized fashion:

Victoria and Albert sculpted in the costume of ancient Saxons is the most amusing example.

The portraits from the last years of the 19thC and later are varied in style. There are superb studies of *Edith Sitwell* by Wyndham Lewis, and some fine bronze busts by Epstein. Royalty, however, is still treated with idealized deference.

National Theatre ▥

Upper Ground, South Bank, SE1 ☎ *633–0880. Map 11G12* ▣ *✗* ▨ *Tours: up to five times a day. Tube Waterloo.*
It is a blessing that the institutionalization of the theatre in London has not led to a stultifying subservience to the establishment. The drama remains as true to its nature of subversiveness as when it was banished to the South Bank in the Middle Ages, and this latest addition to the *South Bank Arts Centre* created its own furore. The building itself, designed by Sir Denys Lasdun in 1970–75, is a prime example of the Brutal style, a lumpy abstract sculpture in concrete. The interior, however, is much more universally admired, with a superb intersection of horizontal and vertical planes creating a honeycomb of useful and interesting space.

See *Theatres* in *Nightlife*.

Natural History Museum ▥ ★

Cromwell Rd., SW7 ☎ *589–6323. Map 15J5* ▣ ▨ ♣ *Open Mon–Sat 10.00–18.00, Sun 14.30–18.00. Tube South Kensington.*
When the *British Museum* was formed from Sir Hans Sloane's collections in 1753, a high proportion of material consisted of plant, animal and geological specimens. Appropriately, these categories grew at enormous speed (they still do, at the rate of 300,000 items each year), and in 1860 it was decided to split off the natural history collections. Between 1873–80 the present building was erected in South Kensington with Alfred Waterhouse as architect. His creation is a cathedral to nature, a vast Romanesque construction with a central porch opening on to a great iron-roofed nave. Unlike a cathedral, however, there are two immensely long side wings creating an impressive facade along the Cromwell Rd. Once criticized as austere and heavy, cleaning has revealed the bright colours of the cream and blue terra cotta tiling, and the countless relief details that cover the exterior – a fitting showcase for the treasures housed within.

In the 1970s, a new policy was adopted by which the museum shows a series of self-contained exhibitions, rather than attempting to show all of its millions of specimens in old-fashioned cabinets. On entering the museum, however, parts of an older, dramatic display have survived: the giant central hall, with huge dinosaur skeletons towering over the visitor. There they stand, absurd and terrifying, the centre of an exhibition about their evolution and disappearance. The left side of the hall is given over to an exhibition explaining the theory of evolution. Also on the ground floor is an exhibition of British birds arranged by habitat, and an exceptionally lively presentation on every aspect of human biology. Look out for the display on British insects, and the **Whale Hall**. This is one of the museum's most effective sections, although unmodernized, containing the vast skeletons and jaw bones of the great mammals and a life-sized model of a blue whale.

A monumental staircase leads from the Central Hall to the upper floor, where an exhibition traces a controversial subject: the evolution of man. Another, on the origin of the species, covers Darwin's work with admirable thoroughness. The traditional hall, devoted to minerals, rocks and gems, serves as an effective contrast to the newer exhibition techniques, and is notable for the incredible diversity and beauty of its specimens.

Old Bailey *(Central Criminal Court)*
Old Bailey, EC4 ☎ *248–3277. Map* **12***F14* 👓 🐾 ▣ *Open Mon–Fri 10.30–13.00, 14.00–16.00. Tube St Paul's.*

The Old Bailey's famous gilt figure of *Justice*, complete with scales and sword, looks down on a site with a grim history. The Central Criminal Court replaced Newgate Gaol, dating from the Middle Ages, for many years a place of execution and eventually the 19thC reformers' ultimate symbol of penal squalor. The current Portland stone building dates from 1900–07. Inside its heavy Baroque frame justice can be seen to be done from the public galleries, but you will have to queue early when a major criminal case is being heard – the crowds of Newgate gallows have their modern counterparts.

Orleans House Gallery ▥
Orleans Rd., Twickenham ☎ *892–0221. Map* **20***D3* 🚉 🐾 *Open Apr–Sept Tues–Sat 13.00–17.30, Sun 14.00–17.30; Oct–Mar Tues–Sat 13.00–16.30, Sun 14.00–16.30. Tube Richmond, train to St Margaret's from Waterloo.*

Although it takes its name from the Duc d'Orleans, later King Louis Philippe of France, who lived here in the early 19thC, this house in Twickenham, near *Strawberry Hill*, dates from 1710. Regrettably, most was demolished in the 1920s, but the superb **Octagon** survives amid attractive woodland. It was designed by James Gibbs in 1720. The interior is richly decorated with Baroque stucco work: heads of George II and Queen Caroline can be seen on medallions. The Octagon is now a gallery, and a few fine early English landscape paintings are on show, although the building is generally used for temporary exhibitions. Nearby is *Marble Hill House*, and the grander *Ham House*, which can be reached by ferry.

Osterley Park ▥ ☆
Isleworth, Middlesex ☎ *560–3918. Map* **20***C3* ■■ ▣ *in summer. Open Apr–Sept Tues–Sun 14.00–18.00; Oct–Mar 12.00–16.00. Subject to alteration. Tube Osterley.*

Already one of the finest country houses in the London area, Osterley gained more prestige after being completely refurbished between 1761–82 by the great Scottish architect Robert Adam for the banker Francis Child, who was trying to emulate the other country houses nearby, such as *Syon House*. It still contains much of the furniture he designed for it, and is set in a large area of parkland, with lakes and woods, and an attractive brick stable block to one side, which probably contains the buildings of the medieval manor house which originally stood on the site. Adam's building is a large hollow square, with corner turrets and a great portico that opens to the central courtyard. This unusual scheme for the 18thC was dictated by the existing house, built with great magnificence by Sir Thomas Gresham (the wealthy merchant who founded the Royal Exchange) in the 1570s. By Adam's time it had fallen into decay, and he completed the covering of the exterior with an entirely new skin of brick, and built the portico.

At the end of the courtyard the main door leads into the **hall**, the centrepiece to the whole design, beautifully decorated in Adam's Classical style, with white stucco reliefs on a grey background. At either end, copies of ancient Roman statues inhabit niches within apses. Note how the ceiling decoration is echoed in the marble floor pattern. Beyond the hall is the great **gallery**, a plainer room probably designed a few years earlier by Sir William Chambers. The remaining rooms open to the public are by Adam, who even designed the door handles and friezes. The **Drawing Room** has a ceiling of extraordinary richness and contains fine original commodes. The **Tapestry Room** is hung with works from the French royal Gobelins workshop, in extravagant pink with Rococo designs from paintings by Boucher. The **State Bedchamber** has an absurdly elaborate four-poster bed. Plainer, but just as effective, is the **Etruscan Dressing Room**, with delicately painted walls.

Pall Mall
Map 10H10. Tube Charing Cross, Green Park.
When *St James's Palace* became the main royal residence in the 17thC, this avenue quickly became established as its main route into London and the site for the favourite Stuart game of palle-maille, resembling modern croquet. The street is now the most important in *St James's*, famous for the traditional gentlemen's clubs that line its s side, a sequence of stern Classical buildings reflecting the importance of tradition in this most conservative of areas.

From the *Trafalgar Square* end, Pall Mall becomes interesting beyond the soaring glass slab of **New Zealand House** (1957–63). This is at the bottom end of John Nash's great city planning scheme of the early 19thC that stretched up Regent St. and incorporated *Regent's Park*. Just past New Zealand House will be found the delightful little **Opera House Arcade**, built by Nash in 1816–18 and the first in London; note the splendid wrought-iron lamps. At Waterloo Pl. the **Duke of York's Column**, built by Benjamin Wyatt in 1831–34, can be seen in front of the steps of **Carlton House Terrace**.

Back on Pall Mall, the gentlemen's clubs begin. These uniquely English and very exclusive institutions, designed to provide the gentleman with a 'country house' haven to which he can retire in the city, thrive unchanged, still offering, in various mixes, snoozing, business talk and witty conversation, and hallowed peace. The corners with Waterloo Pl. are occupied by the impressive **United Services Club**, designed in 1827 by Nash (now the Institute of Directors), and the **Athenaeum** of 1828–30, traditionally the clergy and academics' club. Farther along in a dignified terrace come the **Travellers' Club** (1829–32), a Victorian version of Italian Renaissance for those who have been more than 1,000 miles from London; the **Reform Club** (1837–41), a Liberal political grouping formed after the 1832 Reform Act; and then more modern buildings, including the **Royal Automobile Club** of 1908–11. Beyond comes **Schomberg House**, built in 1698, a tall brick structure with projecting wings. Other clubs are the **Army and Navy** on the N side, jokingly known as 'The Rag' after the toughness of its meat; and the **Oxford and Cambridge** on the s; along with the **Junior Carlton**, a waiting post for the famous senior Tory (Conservative) club. Pall Mall ends with the lower, brick buildings of *St James's Palace*, past the entrance to *Marlborough House*.

Parliament, Houses of See *Westminster, Palace of.*

The Percival David Foundation of Chinese Art
53 Gordon Sq., WC1 ☎ *387–3909. Map **4**D10* 📷 🎫 *with flash. Open Mon 14.00–17.00, Tues–Fri 10.30–17.00, Sat 10.30–13.00. Tube Euston.*

Gathered with scholarly precision by Sir Percival David and given by him to the University in 1951, this remarkably rich collection of Chinese ceramics of the 10th–19thC is aptly sited in *Bloomsbury*, surrounded by intellectual and artistic endeavour. Unfortunately, the presentation of the collection is rather too scholarly, and the great numbers of bowls, jars, vases and figurines grouped in display cabinets by classification tend to cancel each other out by their profusion. But the individual items are of great beauty, glazed in rich and subtle colours.

Piccadilly
*Map **9**G–H. Tube Piccadilly Circus, Green Park.*

As the famous 'hub of Empire', **Piccadilly Circus** puts on a pretty poor show, with a motley collection of buildings covered in illuminated signs. But the **Trocadero** centre, with its variety of shops and restaurants offering specialities from different countries, has brought a new sense of life. The focus of the Circus is the *Shaftesbury Monument*, a statue and fountain of *Eros* (1893) around which international youth likes to gather while temporarily dropping out. Piccadilly itself, stretching w to Hyde Park Corner, is lined with imposing commercial buildings. Some of the stores are justifiably famous: **Hatchard's** for books, **Simpson's** for clothes and **Fortnum and Mason** for anything expensive (see *Shopping*). In addition, there are arcades of smart little shops, with the Piccadilly Arcade of 1909–10 to the s and the most attractive Burlington Arcade of 1815–19 to the N. Wren's *St James's*, the **Ritz** (see *Hotels*) and Green Park are of greatest interest on the s side; Burlington House (the *Royal Academy*) on the N. By Hyde Park Corner is *Apsley House.*

Planetarium
Marylebone Rd., NW1 ☎ *486–1121. Map **2**D7* 🎫 📷 🎟️ *'Starshows' every 45min 11.00–16.30. Tube Baker Street.*

Attached to *Madame Tussaud's*, the Planetarium's great green copper dome is a striking landmark, providing convincing displays and 'starshows' on astronomy. The auditorium inside the great dome is at the top of a long ramp through the Astronomers' Gallery, past imaginative displays on the great astronomers. But the highlight for all visitors is the moment they tip back their seats and gaze at the heavens projected on the dome above them.

Post Office Tower ▥
*Cleveland St., W1. Map **9**E9. Not open to the public. Tube Great Portland Street.*

Renamed British Telecom Tower, but still faithfully known as the Post Office Tower, this 619ft (189m) landmark has a purpose beyond display, having been erected in 1964 to achieve effective TV and radio telephone broadcasting above surrounding buildings. Sadly its revolving restaurant and observation platform are now closed. The architecture is pleasantly familiar to Londoners, neither inspired nor pretentious, with a jumble of transmitters and radio masts above an elongated cylinder.

Public Records Office Museum ⅲ
Chancery Lane, WC2 ☎*405–0741. Map 11F13. Tube Chancery Lane.*

Most of the public records are now kept at Kew, but in this successful example of Victorian Gothic official architecture one room and a corridor are given over to a museum, unimaginative in its presentation but boasting some remarkable treasures. Outstanding are the two volumes of the **Domesday Book**, the great survey of England carried out for William the Conqueror in 1086, from Apr 1986 the centre of an extensive exhibition commemorating its ninth centenary. Among later documents are a copy of the Magna Carta, Guy Fawkes' confession to participation in the Gunpowder Plot, and William Shakespeare's will. There is an extensive display of royal seals, with their elaborate designs showing the image of the king, a knight in armour or suchlike. Several monuments from the Rolls Chapel, which used to stand on the site, include an example of early Renaissance sculpture by Pietro Torrigiano, showing the recumbent figure of *John Young*, a Master of the Rolls (d.1519), in a Classical architectural surround. There are also fine medieval and later strong-boxes.

Regent's Park ☆
Maps 2&3A–D. Tube Regent's Park, Baker Street.

Regency London was certainly sophisticated; and the legacy is one of the most impressive examples of town planning in the country. Marylebone Fields, a hunting chase of Henry VIII's, reverted to the crown in 1809, and the Prince Regent's friend, John Nash, was put in charge of an ambitious scheme that would link it with Carlton House to the s via the new Regent St. Carlton House has gone but the park retains much of the original plan. It is approached from Portland Pl., leading into the elegant terraces of **Park Crescent** and **Park Square**, built from 1812–23. To E and w around the flanks of the park stretch magnificent Classical terraces, mostly built in the 1820s. To the w is the amazing length of **York Terrace** and, best of all, the imaginative, almost oriental-looking **Sussex Place** with its octagonal domes. The dome motif is repeated in copper on the brand new **Mosque** nearby. On the E side of the park, **Chester Terrace** and **Cumberland Terrace** are ostentatiously grand, with vast porticos decorated with stucco reliefs and sculptures.

The park itself is attractively landscaped, with a massive straight **Broad Walk** continuing the line of Portland Pl. through the centre. Two circular roads (the Inner and Outer Circles) carry road traffic; on the Inner Circle, **St John's Lodge** incorporates parts of a villa of about 1818. Here too is the marvellous **open air theatre** where superb productions of Shakespeare's plays can be enjoyed in the summer months (see *Nightlife*). There is a small lake in **Queen Mary's Gardens** within the Inner Circle, and a larger one with islands to the w. Across the N side of the park is a branch of the *Grand Union Canal*, picturesquely incorporated as part of Nash's plan, and the *Zoo*.

Registry of Births, Deaths and Marriages
St Catherine's House, 10 Kingsway, WC2 ☎*242–0262. Map 11F12* 📷 ✈ *Open Mon–Fri 8.30–16.30. Tube Aldwych, Temple.*

With perseverance and a little money, it is possible to trace ancestry in England or Wales back to 1837, the date centralized registration of births, deaths and marriages began. To go further back, local records have to be consulted. The system is not difficult but it is time-consuming, a factor which seems to discourage few people, for the offices are always busy. Simply look up the reference for yourself or an ancestor born in England or Wales (listed alphabetically by year) and order the birth certificates, which takes about two days. This will usually give the names, addresses and occupations of the parents. By searching for their marriage certificate or birth certificates it is possible to repeat the process back into history.

Richmond ☆
Map 20D3. Tube Richmond.
The Palace of Sheen was first occupied by Henry I in 1125, beginning an important royal connection which gave impetus to the growth of this still beautiful Thames-side town. The name came later; after a fire in 1499, Sheen was rebuilt as Richmond Palace by Henry VII, the title coming from his former title as Earl of Richmond (in Yorkshire). Henry died in the palace, as did Elizabeth I in 1603. Charles I was the last king to live there, moving his court during a 1634 plague; it then fell into decay.

Of the great Tudor palace, the most magnificent before the building of Wolsey's nearby *Hampton Court*, very little remains. What there is can be seen on the western side of **Richmond Green**. A Tudor gatehouse marks the position, but within are private houses of later date which, in some cases, incorporate portions of the old brickwork – the fine early 18thC pedimented facade of **Trumpeters' House** predominates. Richmond Green itself boasts exceptional 18th–19thC houses on all four sides – most notable is **Maids of Honour Row** of about 1724, built for the companions of Caroline, wife of the future George II, who then lived at Richmond Lodge in Old Deer Park in *Kew* to the N. Richmond Theatre, built in 1899, lies across the green to the W. Old Palace Lane leads down to the river, where the attractive ochre **Asgill House**, a mansion of the 1760s, can be seen on the left.

Richmond's busy and crowded shopping centre, with its infuriating traffic system, contains some 17thC almshouses in The Vineyard near au interesting church with a 16thC tower, St Matthias, and, up Hill Rise, the fine Queen Anne terrace of Ormond Rd. To the S of the noble 18thC bridge rises **Richmond Hill**, offering one of London's most remarkable views. The preservation of this unspoiled vista over *Marble Hill House* and *Ham House* across the wooded expanse of the Thames Valley is a rare and triumphant planning success. It has been painted by several of Britain's greatest artists, such as Reynolds, Turner and Constable. Some good 18thC houses can be seen at the top of the hill, including **Wick House**, built for Reynolds by Sir William Chambers in 1772.

A gate into **Richmond Park** of 1700 is thought to have been erected by Capability Brown. The park is the most telling reminder of Richmond's royal connection; with over 2,000 acres (814ha) first enclosed by Charles I and still a royal park, it is the most natural stretch of green land in London. Its rough heath and woodland contain a great variety of native plants, birds and animals, even protected herds of red and fallow deer. The highest points offer excellent views NE across London. The several private houses in the park include **White Lodge**, built for George II in 1727–29, now the Royal Ballet School, and **Pembroke Lodge** of about 1800, now a restaurant.

Royal Academy of Arts 血

Burlington House, Piccadilly, W1 ☎ *734–3471. Map 9G9*
✖ ★ ● *Open daily 10.00–18.00. Tube Piccadilly Circus,
Green Park.*

First built as a mansion for the first Earl of Burlington in the
newly-developed Piccadilly area in about 1665, Burlington
House was remodelled in 1717–20 in the elegant Palladian
style. The third earl made this as celebrated a forum for the
artists whose patron he became as his *Chiswick House*; Pope,
Arbuthnot, Gay, all often attended. Unfortunately, between
1868–74 the exterior of the Georgian house was obliterated by
the rebuilding that marked its adoption by the Royal Academy
of Arts. This new building is in the Victorian Renaissance style,
with a screen along *Piccadilly* opening on to a forecourt with a
statue of *Sir Joshua Reynolds* in the centre. Other learned
societies occupy the buildings to right and left.

The Royal Academy was founded in 1768 with Reynolds as
its first and greatest president to foster the arts of Britain.
Except for a few decades after its foundation, however, the most
interesting developments in British art have consistently taken
place outside of, and even in opposition to, the dictates of the
Royal Academy. This is still true: the Academy's free-for-all
Summer Exhibition (see *Calendar of events* in *Planning*) may
be popular and enjoyable, but no one would claim that it does
much to influence developments in art. The modern academy
consists of 40 academicians and 30 associates, the country's
most successful establishment artists. Today a most important
function is as a home for major temporary exhibitions.

The academy has an important collection of works of art,
including much by past academicians: Reynolds,
Gainsborough, Constable and others (not on public display
except during exhibitions in the private rooms, otherwise by
appointment). Works that form part of the decorative schemes
of its grand interior include some by artists such as Benjamin
West and Angelica Kauffmann in the entrance hall, and Marco
Ricci. The academy's outstanding treasure is Michelangelo's
beautiful relief tondo depicting the *Madonna and Child*★

Royal Air Force Museum, Hendon

Grahame Park Way, NW9 ☎ *205–2266. Map 21B4* ⊡ ●
*Open Mon–Sat 10.00–18.00, Sun 14.00–18.00. Tube
Hendon Central.*

The northern suburb of Hendon itself lays claim to the interest
of aircraft enthusiasts: there was a pioneering flying school here
before World War I, and it became one of the first aerodromes,
staging regular air displays and becoming famous as the starting
point for the first non-stop London to Paris flight in 1911. The
museum was opened in 1972 in an excellent modern building
which incorporates two historic World War I wooden hangars.
Interesting displays trace the history of flight and show the
development of the R.A.F., with its vital role in two world
wars.

However, it is the aircraft themselves that take pride of place.
They range from a manned observation kite from before World
War I to what is, incredibly, its descendant, the prototype of the
successful Harrier 'Jump-jet'. There is a Blériot XI, similar to
that in which Louis Blériot made the first cross-Channel flight
in 1909, and a replica of the Vickers Vimy in which Alcock and
Brown first crossed the Atlantic non-stop.

Famous World War I aircraft include a Sopwith Camel from

Britain, a Fokker D VII from Germany and a Hanriot HD1
from France. From World War II there is the oldest surviving
Spitfire Mk 1, which fought in the Battle of Britain, the only
known Wellington bomber, a Mosquito fighter bomber and the
towering bulk of an Avro Lancaster, mainstay of the British
bombing of Germany. Next to it are two of its heaviest bombs,
one of 12,000lb (5443 kilos) and the 24,000lb (10886 kilos)
'Grand Slam'. More modern jet aircraft include the early
Gloster Meteor and a Canberra bomber.

Nearby are the separate **Battle of Britain Museum** and
Bomber Command Museum (☎) with further rare aircraft
and explanatory displays.

Royal Courts of Justice ▥
Strand, WC2 ☎405–7641. *Map* **11**F13 ⬚ ✵ ▣ *Open
Mon–Fri 10.00–16.30; entry depends upon use of courts.
Tube Temple, Chancery Lane.*

Better known as the Law Courts, this extravagant complex in
the *Strand*, built by G.E. Street in 1874–82, houses the courts
where important civil, as opposed to criminal, law cases are
heard. They are now looked on by many with admiration, after
long being despised as an example of Victorian plagiarism – for
they are in Early English Gothic style. Cleaning has helped, as
the rich colours and intricate patterns in the stone can be
appreciated. More than that, they do have a dignity suited to
their purpose, and their complex irregularity and inventive
detail feast the eye. Inside, the sheer scale of the **great hall** is
every bit as impressive as the exterior.

Royal Hospital, Chelsea ▥ ☆
Royal Hospital Rd., SW3 ☎730–0161. *Map* **16**L7 ⬚ *indoors.
Grounds open 10.00 to sunset, Sun 14.00 to sunset, chapel
and dining hall Mon–Sat 10.00–12.00, 14.00–16.00, Sun
14.00–16.00. Tube Sloane Square.*

Amply surrounded by parkland and retaining all the dignity of
its riverside setting, Wren's stately Royal Hospital buildings of
1682–92 are still a majestic sanctuary of calm, although now
surrounded by *Chelsea*. It was founded by Charles II in 1682 as
a refuge for aged and disabled soldiers on the model of Louis
XIV's Les Invalides in Paris. It now houses some 400
pensioners, including a dwindling number of World War I
veterans, who can be seen round and about Chelsea in their
old-fashioned uniforms, red in summer and blue in winter; and
in May it stages the **Chelsea Flower Show** (see *Calendar of
events* in *Planning*).

The best view is from the s, where an open courtyard looks
down the extensive gardens towards the river. At the centre of
the courtyard is a statue of *Charles II* as a Roman emperor by
Grinling Gibbons, Wren's master carver. The hospital is
entirely symmetrical and quite plain, its red-brick facades
embellished with minimal stonework. At the centre of each
block is a tall white portico of four columns or pilasters, and
the central block is capped by a graceful, spire-like lantern.

The **vestibule**, a severely domed room, lit by the lantern
above, is entered through the portico in the courtyard. To the
right is the **chapel**, little altered since Wren's time. It has a fine
carved reredos in dark wood, matching the organ gallery at the
entrance end and, in the apse, a painting of about 1710–15 by
Sebastiano Ricci, *Christ in Majesty*, a colourful burst of Baroque
splendour. The **Great Hall** occupies the corresponding space to

the chapel on the other side of the vestibule. It is more solemn, with panelled walls and military standards hanging from the ceiling. At the far end, there is a dark and ponderous painting by Verrio showing *Charles II* with mythological companions in front of the hospital buildings. A small museum in one of the eastern wings covers the hospital's history.

St Bartholomew-the-Great 🏛 ✝ ★
Little Britain, EC1. Map 12E14. Tube Barbican.
The churchyard through the 15thC gateway with the charming Tudor house on top used to be the nave of this, one of the oldest churches in London. Now only the chancel and transepts remain with their 19thC refacing of flint and Portland stone. The church belonged to a wealthy medieval priory, founded in 1123 by a courtier of Henry I, Thomas Rahere, who had a vision of St Bartholomew during a bout of malaria in Rome. The priory was sacked in 1529, one of the first to suffer in the Dissolution. Inside, many original features have survived. Rahere's church must have been impressive, for the high, massive **nave** of the present building was only the choir of the original. Huge columns support a Romanesque triforium, surmounted by a clerestory built in 1405 in Perpendicular Gothic style to replace the original; the cool grey stone in three regular tiers has a peaceful solidity typical of Norman architecture. A lighter touch is given by the late Gothic **oriel window** built into the triforium on the s side of the choir. It dates from 1517 and was built by Prior Bolton, whose rebus is carved upon it – a crossbow bolt piercing a wine tun.

Beyond the altar is the **Lady Chapel**, dating to 1335. This has been much rebuilt after the depredations of the intervening centuries, during which it was not part of the church at all but used as a workshop; in 1725 Benjamin Franklin worked here.

At the w entrance, the massive crossing which once supported a huge stone tower can be seen. The present tower in brick is above the s aisle and dates from 1628, by which time surviving parts of the old priory were being used as a parish church. Five medieval bells are housed in the tower, making this one of the oldest peals in the country. On either side of the crossing are the much restored transepts. The best preserved is to the s, and from this stretches one side of an elegant cloister, almost entirely 19thC restoration work, imitating the style of the few original stones that survived long use as a stable and forge. A plain but beautiful font stands in the s transept, dating from the early 15thC.

There are a number of fine monuments, including the medieval tomb of the founder, *Rahere*, which has a delicate canopy of 15thC Gothic tracery. Outstanding examples of later tombs include a Renaissance monument of 1589 in Italian marble to *Sir Walter Mildmay*, founder of Emmanuel College, Cambridge, and that of 1615 to *Sir Robert Chamberlayne*, whose marble effigy kneels in ceremonial armour beneath a carved canopy. The monument to *Edward Cooke*, who died in 1652, actually weeps in damp weather as a result of condensation – a phenomenon referred to in the inscription.

St George's, Bloomsbury 🏛 ✝
Bloomsbury Way, WC1. Map 10E11. Tube Holborn.
This splendid church compares well with the near contemporary but much more famous *St Martin-in-the-Fields*. Built by Nicholas Hawksmoor in 1720–31, it is in some ways an

even more dramatic design than Gibbs', with a huge portico of Corinthian columns and a layer-cake spire, topped by a statue of *George I as St George*, a typical piece of Baroque overstatement. The interior repeats the boldness of the exterior – simple shapes, plenty of light and more giant columns. Notice the fine patterned inlay of the wooden reredos.

St James's
Map 10G – H. Tube Piccadilly Circus, Green Park.

Despite being unprotected by conservationists, there are still in the world examples of that strange breed, the English gentleman. Come to St James's, and you would never know that they are rare, for this is *their* district, still existing to provide the quiet, comfortable life long enjoyed by the upper-class.

Occupying the area between *St James's Park* and *Piccadilly*, the land was granted to the Earl of St Albans in 1665 in recognition of his loyalty while the king was in exile. The earl began building straight away, and the proximity of the palace ensured that his square and streets soon became fashionable. The centrepiece was **St James's Square**, with a large central garden. No 17thC houses survive, but there are several fine examples from the 18thC: **Lichfield House**, no. 15, with its Classical facade, is the best. At the centre of the gardens is an equestrian statue of *William III* of 1807. To the N up Duke of York St. is the area's church, *St James's, Piccadilly*.

To the S, running parallel to the park, is *Pall Mall*, a splendid road lined with gentlemen's clubs. *St James's Palace* is at the western end, with **St James's Street** stretching N to Piccadilly. Here are many more of the gentlemen's clubs built in the 19thC: **White's**, for hard-drinking Conservatives; **Boodles**, a famous gambling club in the days of Beau Brummell, the Regency dandy; **Brooks'**, the Whig club founded in 1788; and the **Carlton**, the Conservatives' club.

> Those mausoleums of inactive masculinity are places for men who prefer armchairs to women.
> V.S. Pritchett on London clubs

St James's Place leads off to the W towards Green Park, a quiet street lined with 18thC houses and with the magnificent **Spencer House** (1756–66) overlooking the park at the end. Opposite is one of the two most interesting modern office developments in St James's – aggressively modern, in fact, and built in 1959–60. The other is the **Economist** complex, built around a central plaza just to the W of St James's St.

Another feature of St James's is the shops, with the most traditional approach to service and quality in London (see *Shopping*). For refreshment, try the Victorian **Red Lion** pub in Duke of York St. (see *Pubs*).

St James's Palace ▥ ★
Pall Mall, SW1. Map 9H9. Not open to the public. Tube Green Park.

Despite its much greater antiquity, London has an architectural threshold formed by the plague and fire of 1665–66. This royal palace is unique in surviving intact, unadorned, and preserving a glimpse of Tudor London. There it sits, sandwiched by its larger offspring of *St James's* and *The Mall*, and yet dwarfing them, for all their grandeur and boldness, by its very antiquity and history. The official residence from 1698, when Whitehall

101

Palace burned down, until *Buckingham Palace* took over in
1837, its seniority is still recognized; the Queen's court is 'the
Court of St James's' and new monarchs are still proclaimed
from this palace. Today it consists of 'Grace and Favour'
quarters for yeomen-at-arms, lords and ladies-in-waiting, and
the Lord Chamberlain.

Henry VIII took over the site from a leper hospital in 1532,
and had his palace built entirely in brick, with battlements and
diapering (diagonal patterning in the brickwork). Even the
State Rooms added by Wren in the 17thC, also with
battlements, maintain the low, informal approach, echoing the
domesticity of Tudor architecture. The best original feature,
visible to the public from *Pall Mall*, is the tall **gatehouse**, with
its octagonal corner towers. The interior is closed to the public
but includes some fine features: the Throne Room has an
overmantle by Grinling Gibbons; both the Armoury and
Tapestry Room were decorated by William Morris in 1866–67;
and the Chapel Royal, home of the Queen's liveried choir and
scene of many royal weddings – George IV and V and Victoria –
has a ceiling by Holbein. The **Queen's Chapel**, across
Marlborough Rd. but originally within the palace, is in an
entirely different style to the rest of the buildings. Designed by
Inigo Jones, it was built from 1623–27 in the Classical manner,
with rendered white walls and Portland stone dressings. The
beautiful interior boasts some more ornate Baroque work from
the 1660s, including fine carving by Gibbons. To the w,
attached to the palace, is **Clarence House**, built in 1825–27 by
Nash and now the Queen Mother's home; when she is in
residence, a piper (bagpipes) plays in the garden at 9.00. The
palace is flanked by two grand mansions from later periods:
Marlborough House to the E and *Lancaster House* to the w,
with *St James's Park* to the s.

St James's Park ☆
Map 10H–I. Tube St James's Park.
London's first royal park was always nearer to art than nature.
In 1536 Henry VIII drained a marsh to make a park between *St
James's* and Whitehall Palaces, filled with deer (for ornament
rather than hunting). In 1662, Charles II made it a public
garden, laid out in the formal style of the period with avenues of
trees, *The Mall* as a carriage way, and a long straight canal. In
1828, it was remodelled on the present pattern by John Nash,
who created the lovely complex of trees, flower beds and views
across the natural-looking lake that we see today. The
waterfowl, some of which breed on Duck Island at the E end,
have always continued the contrivance – there are even
pelicans. The view from the bridge over the lake back towards
Whitehall is one of the most beautiful in London.

St James's Piccadilly 🏛 †
*Piccadilly, W1 ☎ 734–5244. Map 10G10. Tube Piccadilly
Circus, Green Park.*
When *St James's* was developed as a residential area after
1662, Sir Christopher Wren was commissioned to build the new
church, completing it in 1684. It is basically one great room
with plain galleries, with a vaulted ceiling decorated with
plaster mouldings. Although damaged by bombs in 1940, the
church has been well restored and preserves some fine fittings.
The organ is 17thC, moved here from the old Whitehall Palace,
and topped by gilded figures carved by Grinling Gibbons, who

also produced the marvellous marble **font**, with its virtuoso relief of Adam and Eve, and the rich floral arrangements carved on the wooden **reredos**. In the crypt is the **London Brass Rubbing Centre**(☎ open Mon – Sat 10.00 – 18.00, Sun 12.00 – 18.00), where rubbings can be made from replicas of medieval monumental brasses.

St Katharine's Dock ☆
Map 13G18. Tube Tower Hill.
While confusion hangs over the future of the vast area of dockland downstream, St Katharine's Dock, next to the *Tower of London*, already has an entirely new role. Originally built in 1827 – 28 by the great engineer Thomas Telford, this was for many years one of the leading docks in the Pool of London, with the advantage of being closest to The City. Today, St Katharine's again profits from its proximity to The City – as a residential and tourist centre and a yacht marina. The large modern World Trade Centre looks down on the brick-brown sails of the Thames sailing barges and gleaming hulls of luxury yachts moored in the docks. Telford's **Ivory House** (later modified) shows off 19thC industrial architecture at its best, and has been tactfully connected to house flats, shops and an exhibition area. A timber-built warehouse is now the Dickens Tavern, and several blocks of fashionable flats sit between the docks and the river.

There is now a fine collection of old ships to lend a flavour of the ocean to the modern docks. On show are a steam tug and a lightship, a sailing barge, a steamer of 1890 and a sailing schooner of 1900. Pride of place goes to *RRS Discovery*, the ship Scott captained on his research expedition to Antarctica in 1903 – 4. Further E are the marvellous warehouses, wharves and pubs of Wapping (see *Pubs*) – well worth the walk for a taste of the Victorian industrial landscape.

St Martin-in-the-Fields 🏛 †
Trafalgar Sq., WC2. Map 10G11. Tube Charing Cross.
The first buildings in a new architectural style often seem oddities, and this church has maintained its non-conformity. Today, it is the centre of a folk music society, and a shelter for vagrants and drug addicts, as well as a church. The broad views allowed by *Trafalgar Square's* open spaces make enjoyment of this magnificent church's proportions possible, and it is now recognized for the seminal building it was. Designed in 1722 – 26 by James Gibbs (the foundation goes back to 1222) in a solemnly Classical style, it is very close to a Roman temple, except for the novel placing of a tower and spire above the Corinthian portico. The interior is similar to Wren's churches of a few decades earlier – spacious and light, with galleries to the sides and a splendidly moulded ceiling. The crypt contains several interesting relics, including a whipping post dating back to the 18thC.

St Mary Abchurch †
Abchurch Lane, EC4. Map 13F16. Tube Cannon Street.
With a small cobbled churchyard, simple brick exterior and lead spire, the glories of St Mary Abchurch's interior are unexpected. Built by Sir Christopher Wren in 1681 – 86, it consists of little more than one huge dome on top of a square room, creating a sense of space with architectural detail kept to a minimum. The dome was painted in Baroque style by William

Snow between 1708–14, and shows the name of God in Hebrew surrounded by figures representing the virtues. Although damaged in World War II, the church has been expertly restored; the **reredos** carved by Grinling Gibbons, for example, was rebuilt from fragments. Note the richly carved pulpit, the panelling and some original pews.

St Mary-le-Bow 🏛 †

*Bow Lane, Cheapside, EC2. Map **12**F15. Tube Bank, St Paul's.*

When Wren rebuilt London's churches after the Great Fire of 1666 he put particular emphasis on their steeples, and this is the most magnificent. A great tower capped by an intricately designed stone spire, it is still prominent among the larger modern buildings around. The church was built in 1670–80, with the tower separated from the body of the church by a vestibule. The design and execution of the two doors to the tower which serve as the porch are particularly fine. The interior is large and simple, much restored after gutting during the war, and the crypt retains elements from the original Norman church. St Mary's bells are of sentimental importance to Londoners – being born within range of their sound is the qualification for being a Cockney. The bells were destroyed in the Great Fire of 1666 and again in the Blitz, although the current ones include recasts from remnants salvaged in 1941.

St Mary-le-Strand 🏛 † ☆

*Strand, WC2. Map **11**F12. Tube Aldwych, Temple.*

It is hard to imagine a more ironic fate for a jewel of the Baroque: the island in the middle of the *Strand* is so small that the continuous traffic passes within inches of its walls, which now, as a result, need drastic renovation. James Gibbs built this in 1714–18 fresh from the joys of Rome. The facade especially is a delight: from the portico, with its ornate capitals, the eye sweeps up to the triangular pediment and the bold layered spire. The interior has a richly coffered ceiling with two tiers of columns and a pediment dramatically framing the apse. Notice the fine carving of the pulpit, which was originally on a taller base with a scallop-shell sounding board behind, all part of the grand theatrical effect.

St Pancras Station 🏛 ☆

*Euston Rd., NW1. Map **4**C11. Tube King's Cross St Pancras.*

That a railway station could be made into a Gothic fortress speaks much of the Victorians' confidence. St Pancras Station, with its accompanying hotel building (now used as offices), was the glory of Victorian London. It was designed by Sir George Gilbert Scott in 1868–74, freely using the northern Italian and French Gothic styles. Notice the harmony of its red bricks with the pink and grey stone, and the way the detail combines with complex shapes and angles to feast the eye. It was also a tremendous feat of engineering, with the great train shed covered by a single span of iron and glass.

St Paul's, Covent Garden 🏛 †

*The Piazza, WC2. Map **10**F11. Tube Covent Garden.*

As the Duke of Bedford neared completion of his *Covent Garden* development, money became tight, and so he instructed Inigo Jones to build an economical church, suggesting as a model something like a barn. Jones defiantly declared that he would build "the handsomest barn in Europe", and today it stands as the sole surviving element of the piazza. In fact it cost a small fortune, but the barn analogy is not entirely inappropriate to the extreme simplicity of what was London's first entirely Classical parish church, completed in 1638. The main features are the overhanging eaves and the superb Tuscan portico, ironically never used as an entrance as the altar was moved in 1636 and a smaller door made at the rear in Bedford St. Today it is the 'actors' church', and every so often a grand theatreland funeral adds another monument to the collection.

St Paul's Cathedral ▥ † ★

Map 12F14. Entrance and movement restricted during services. Tube St Paul's.

There are a very few great churches in the world which strike all visitors, whatever their religious convictions, as a sublime witness to man's ability to reach towards the infinite. St Paul's was built as both a religious and secular statement of London's faith and self-confidence after the devastating Great Fire of 1666, and almost 300yr later it was to soar alone amid the total destruction of the surrounding buildings in the Blitz, preserved miraculously to breathe fresh hope into the beleaguered Londoners.

No building so clearly demonstrates Sir Christopher Wren's prodigious skill and energetic inventiveness: detail is used with characteristic Baroque exuberance but always subordinated to the highly controlled overall scheme which makes the cathedral so harmonious. The dominant dome still defies the encroaching modern buildings.

The current cathedral is the third to stand on this site, and not the largest. The first was founded in 604 and periodically enlarged until destruction by fire in 1087. A medieval cathedral was constructed in the 11th–12thC; in the 13thC it was enlarged, and in 1315 a huge spire was completed. It was one of the great churches of medieval Europe, with a spire that reached 489ft (149m) from the ground, taller and longer than the present St Paul's. (For a fine model, see *London, Museum of*.)

Decline set in as the Middle Ages waned, however. The spire burned down in 1561 and was not replaced. The building in general fell into bad repair and became used more as a market place than as a place of worship. The central aisle, 'Paul's Walk', was a famous social forum. In 1634, Inigo Jones carried out substantial repairs, but the medieval structure continued to deteriorate, and in 1666 Christopher Wren came up with his first scheme for drastic renovations. In the same year, the Great Fire destroyed most of London, raging in St Paul's for several days and reducing it to ruins.

Given the task of reconstructing the cathedral, Wren proposed sweeping away what remained of the medieval building and starting afresh. He began with daringly modern designs which were rejected by the ecclesiastical authorities. In the end, he was forced to return to the basic plan of a Gothic cathedral, even if not in appearance, and his design of 1675 was just that: with a nave, aisles, a crossing, transepts and a chancel, all forming a Latin cross. But the crossing was to be covered by a dome rather than a tower or spire, the first in England, following the example of the great Renaissance churches of

Italy. Wren also fought for, and won, the freedom to alter the 'ornamentation' of the cathedral, which in effect left him able to design the building's appearance as he went along.

Wren's **exterior** actually owes much to Inigo Jones' *Banqueting House*. There are two storeys, with pilasters decorating rusticated walls and a balustrade at the top – a first stroke of ingenuity, for the aisles behind the exterior side walls are only one storey high, as in a Gothic cathedral. The upper is thus a false wall (hence the blank niches instead of windows) connected to and supporting the walls of the nave by means of flying buttresses inside – an entirely Gothic device, but out of sight.

In Paul's Walk, at one time . . . shall you see walking the Knight, the Gull, the Gallant, the Upstart, the Gentleman, the Clown, the Captain, the Applesquire, the Lawyer, the Usurer, the Citizen, the Cheater, the Puritan, the Cut-throat, the High-men, the Low-men, the True-men and the Thief – of all trades and professions some, of all countries some.
Thomas Dekker, *Seven Deadly Vices of London*, 1604

The E end of the cathedral, containing the chancel, was built first. It has a rounded end, thus forming an apse as in a medieval church, but with a curved roof-line giving a Baroque flourish. This effect is echoed in the curved porches to the N and S transept facades, but these have more solidly Classical pediments at the roof line. The W end, the ceremonial entrance, was built later (1706–8), with massive towers at either side – the ornate tops to these are the most complex elements in the whole building, architecture handled as sculpture. The central portico is on two storeys with pairs of Corinthian columns, another emphatically Baroque motif. All this serves to balance the solemnity of the **dome**, suitably weighty and dignified as the dominant element of the composition. It is arguably the most beautiful dome in the world, 365ft (111m) high to the tip of the lantern and 100ft (30m) across inside.

The quality of the carving of such elements as the garlands just below the frieze, or the capitals to the columns and pilasters, is superb. The sculptures, too, are well executed. The reliefs in the transept pediments are by G.B. Cibber and Grinling Gibbons, the statues by Francis Bird, who also carved the relief in the W pediment showing the *Conversion of St Paul*.

The area around St Paul's has been effectively spoiled by modern developments. Views of the cathedral are cut off by uninspired or ugly modern buildings, and traffic whistles around alarmingly close to the walls. There remain, however, the fine **railings** that surround the churchyard, made in 1714 and an early example of the use of cast iron. In front of the portico stands a statue of *Queen Anne*, made in 1886 to replace the original of 1709–11 by Bird (but did the original look so like Queen Victoria?). In the churchyard gardens to the NE is **St Paul's Cross**, a bronze structure of 1910. Two of the old cathedral buildings survive, both designed by Wren: to the S is the little **Deanery** of 1670, and to the N the larger red-brick **Chapter House** of 1712–14. To the E, still inside the road, is the tower and elongated onion spire of the ruined church of St Augustine, designed by Wren in 1680–83, now attached to the new buildings of the celebrated St Paul's Choir School.

The **interior** gives an impression of the great bulk of the structure, but this is offset by the height of the nave and by the

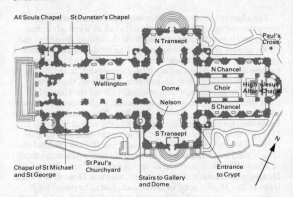

St Paul's Cathedral

All Souls Chapel   St Dunstan's Chapel

Paul's Cross

N Transept

N Chancel

Wellington

Dome

Choir

High Jesus Altar Chapel

Nelson

S Chancel

S Transept

N

Chapel of St Michael and St George

St Paul's Churchyard

Stairs to Gallery and Dome

Entrance to Crypt

vast open space at the very centre beneath the dome. The roofs are supported on a series of shallow cupolas, and the decorative elements are richly and finely carved, but limited in extent to the capitals of the pilasters, with garlands between, and geometrically patterned bands around the cupolas. The emphasis is on the sweeping drama of the Baroque. The eye is led along the nave or aisles, or across the transepts, and there seems to be a calculated attempt to create vistas with a sense of distance, focusing on the open space beneath the dome but leading ultimately towards the long chancel beyond the crossing. A great deal of light enters the cathedral from the clerestory windows of the nave, windows that are invisible from the outside because of the false upper storey of the external wall.

Walk to the left from the main w entrance. The small **All Soul's Chapel** contains **Lord Kitchener's monument** of 1925, one of the more effective of the cluster of memorials to national heroes introduced since about 1790, with an effigy of the soldier in deathly white marble. The **St Dunstan's Chapel** follows behind a superbly carved wooden screen of 1698. Outstanding monuments are to *Lord Leighton*, the leading Victorian painter, and to *General Gordon* of the Sudan. In one of the arches further along this N aisle is the great **monument to the Duke of Wellington**, erected in the mid-19thC and the most elaborate in St Paul's, with an equestrian statue of the duke on top of the canopy. The N transept is reserved for private prayer; it contains a number of monuments to the fallen heroes of the Napoleonic Wars, and the marble font, carved in 1727 by Francis Bird.

At this point the **crossing** can be admired, the focal point of the entire design. It is a huge space, with the circle of the **dome** supported on eight massive arches. The mosaics in the spandrels are Victorian, in the style of Michelangelo's Sistine Chapel frescoes, and there are Victorian statues in the niches above the Whispering Gallery. The breathtaking dome itself actually consists of three layers: an outer skin, a cone supporting the masonry of the lantern and a shallow domed ceiling. This is painted with illusionistic architectural frescoes in monochrome depicting scenes from the life of St Paul, by Sir James Thornhill, dating from 1716–19. Monuments in the crossing include those to *Dr. Johnson* (in an unlikely toga) and *Sir Joshua Reynolds*, first president of the *Royal Academy*. The lectern was made in 1720 but the pulpit is modern.

The **chancel**, stretching off towards the high altar, makes a sumptuous display, although it is not at all as Wren left it: the gaudy and fussy mosaics that decorate the ceiling date from the 1890s and are really not in keeping. The modern baldacchino, attempting to follow Wren's original scheme for a high altar canopy as a focal point, is only partly successful, in an unhappy marriage with the ceiling decorations. However, the **choir stalls and organ case**, which originally closed the chancel off from the crossing, are quite magnificent, with exquisite carving by Grinling Gibbons, made in the 1690s. The chancel aisles can be visited, giving a fine close-up view of the rear of the stalls and of Jean Tijou's extraordinarily fine **wrought-iron gates**, again of the 1690s but moved to their present site in 1890. Behind the altar is the Jesus Chapel, now a memorial to the American dead of World War II. Returning along the S chancel aisle **John Donne's monument** shows the poet, who was Dean of St Paul's from 1620–31, wrapped in his shroud, just as he posed for it during the (soon justified) bouts of melancholy before his death in 1631. It is the only monument to survive from the medieval cathedral.

Returning back towards the crossing, the S transept includes several military monuments, of which *Sir John Moore's* (1851) is the most moving, although *Lord Nelson's* includes a fine portrait. In the S aisle is a striking example of high Victorian religiosity, a late version of Holman Hunt's painting *Light of the World*, and a fine wooden screen of 1706 in front of the **Chapel of St Michael and St George**.

Crypt

Entrance from s transept 🚇 *Open Apr–Sept Mon–Fri 10.00–16.00, Sat 11.00–16.00; Oct–Mar Mon–Fri 10.00–15.00, Sat 11.00–15.00.*

The piers and columns support a crypt the size of the whole cathedral, a quiet and dignified place crammed with monuments to national figures. A few battered remains can be seen of monuments surviving from before the 1666 Great Fire, but the majority are from the 19th–20thC. By far the most impressive are the **tombs of Wellington**, a massive porphyry block on a granite slab, and **Nelson**, an elegant black sarcophagus originally made for Cardinal Wolsey in 1524–29 but denied him after his fall from royal favour. Other monuments include numerous generals and admirals, and in 'Painter's Corner', the tombs of *Turner* and *Reynolds* and monuments to *Van Dyck*, *Constable* and *William Blake*. Wren himself is buried nearby.

The **Treasury of the Diocese of London** also has an exhibition in the crypt, containing elaborate vestments, illuminated medieval manuscripts from the cathedral library, and some fine plate from London churches of the 16th–20thC.

Whispering Gallery and Dome

Stairs in s transept 🚇 *Hours as crypt.*

The stiff climb to the gallery inside the dome is repaid with stupendous views of the concourse below and the painted inner dome. The acoustics which give it its name enable the slightest sounds to be heard across the span; the traditional trick, much loved by children, is to whisper against the wall and wait for the sound to travel round to the next auditor.

The next section of the ascent is not for the faint-hearted, with steps winding up throughout the struts supporting the outer dome. The stunning views from the **Golden Gallery** at the base of the lantern make the 542 steps worthwhile.

St Stephen Walbrook 血 † ☆
Walbrook, EC4. Map 13F16. Tube Bank.

Although a parish church, its position behind the *Mansion House* means that St Stephen Walbrook is also the Lord Mayor's church. It is appropriately grand for this ceremonial function, with a simple exterior giving way to a magnificent structure inside, with Corinthian columns, and eight richly-moulded arches supporting a coffered dome. Wren built the church in 1672–79 and it is thought that he was trying out some ideas for *St Paul's Cathedral*. The contrast with his *St Mary Abchurch* is illuminating, for here the dome is not used to create a simple, large space but to contribute to the series of constantly changing views as the visitor moves through the columns. The tower is slightly later, 1717, and the crypt survives from the 15thC.

Science Museum ★
Exhibition Rd., SW7 ☎ *589–3456. Map 15J5* ☒ ▣ ♿
Open Mon–Sat 10.00–18.00, Sun 14.30–18.00. Tube South Kensington.

The Science Museum originated in 1857 within the great South Kensington museum complex conceived by Prince Albert. It was separated off from the *Victoria & Albert Museum*, housing the products of art rather than science, in 1909. Its present building, solemn and functional, was constructed in 1913, with the *Geological Museum* and *Natural History Museum* nearby.

On entering the ground floor, the first major item to be encountered is the Foucault Pendulum on the left, hanging from the very high roof and slowly proving by its deviation that the earth rotates. The development of motive power is then covered in the East Hall, a large room with galleries above on three levels and a glass roof. Industrial machinery, vast and now seemingly crude in its construction, shows the development of steam power in the 18thC. By contrast, a huge mill engine of 1903, with a great gleaming fly-wheel, shows the continuing use of steam into the 20thC. A gallery to the rear covers electric power rather more modestly. A new dramatically staged exhibition then introduces exploration, with full-scale models of the most modern space and underwater craft. The following section on transport is a great favourite, with famous steam locomotives such as Stephenson's *Rocket* of 1829 and the magnificent *Caerphilly Castle* of 1923 outstanding; the fascination with the visible working parts explains why something as messy and noisy as a steam train should have such a romantic appeal – there is something of the scientist in all of us. There are also horse-drawn carriages, motor cars and fire engines. Below the rear part of the museum there is an exciting **Children's Gallery**, with many practical displays – almost everything has a lever to pull or a button to press. One universally popular device demonstrates the generation of electricity by giving an electric shock. Domestic appliances are also found on this floor.

The displays on the upper floors (the galleries around the central East Hall and a few separate rooms) cover a great many aspects of science in turn. On the first floor, industrial processes such as iron and steel or glass manufacture and also agriculture are prominent. Most striking is the new display entitled 'The Challenge of the Chip', demonstrating the revolutionary new microprocessor technology.

On the second floor, subjects range from chemistry to nuclear physics to computers; there are some superb **models of ships**. Fascinating new exhibitions on the third floor cover photography and cinematography, as well as more theoretical areas such as heat and temperature. Stairs lead up to the excellent Wellcome Medical Museum, where the history of medicine and its most up-to-date manifestations are shown in spirited dioramas. Here too is the **National Aeronautical Gallery**: see the 'Flying Bedstead'; war fighters; Amy Johnson's 'Gipsy Moth', and the first ever jet plane.

Sir John Soane's Museum

13 Lincoln's Inn Fields, WC2 ☎ *405–2107. Map* **11E12** 📷
✗ *Sat 14.30 or by arrangement. Open Tues–Sat 10.00–17.00. Tube Holborn.*

Nothing could be further from modern ideas of museum display than Soane's Museum, for the great architect left his house as a museum on his death in 1837 on the condition that nothing be changed. His enormous collection of pictures, architectural fragments, books, sculptures and miscellaneous antiquities is crammed into every available space, giving some idea of his eccentricity as well as his tastes.

Born in 1753, Soane lived at no. 12 Lincoln's Inn Fields from 1792, in a plain Georgian house he designed himself. In 1812–14 he added the much more elaborate no. 13 with its grand facade, rebuilding no. 14 to complete a balanced design in 1824. The interior, joined between the three houses, is the most ingeniously complex layout, offering numerous vistas through the houses, both laterally and vertically, as several of the rooms and yards extend through two or more storeys. Mirrors are carefully placed to create additional illusory space. Most exciting are the paired **Dining Room** and **Library**, and the lovely domed **Breakfast Room**.

The fascination of the great number of objects on display from fossils to furniture is only increased by the capricious, even humorous, way in which they are jumbled together. Among them are several important works of art, as well as Soane's own architectural models. In the **Picture Room** are Hogarth's original paintings for two series, *The Rake's Progress* and *The Election*, 12 paintings in all, and elsewhere a Canaletto and a Turner. In a first floor Drawing Room is Watteau's *Les Noces*. Outstanding is the beautiful alabaster **sarcophagus**, covered with hieroglyphics, of Seti I, a pharaoh who died in 1290 BC, for which Soane paid the then princely sum of £2,000.

Soho ☆

Map **10**F–G. *Tube Piccadilly Circus, Tottenham Court Road, Leicester Square.*

Every city has its low-life area, of course, but in few are the red lights woven into a texture of such richness and variety as in London's Soho. These densely packed little streets in the heart of the West End, bounded by Oxford St., Regent St., Shaftesbury Ave. and Charing Cross Rd., are famous for their nightlife, their restaurants, the best delicatessens in London, their seedy but famous pubs, but, above all, for the gloriously cosmopolitan mix of their people and trades.

Much has been heard in recent years about the decline of Soho, for its thriving sex industry has threatened to engulf the area's other amenities. Even a pub where Dylan Thomas used to drink himself into oblivion has become a sex cinema.

However, the destruction has now largely been halted and there are clear signs that respectable businesses are returning, with fashionable restaurants and shops prospering. And Soho wouldn't be Soho without a scattering of sex parlours.

Within Soho there are two squares reminding us of its early development in the 17thC: **Golden Square** in the E was founded in 1673, and some 18thC houses survive around its undistinguished gardens with a 1720s statue of *Charles II*; but more impressive is **Soho Square**, laid out in 1681, with the few survivals of early buildings largely disguised by later additions, but offering a pleasant garden with a half-timbered summer house and a 17thC statue of *Charles II*. On its S side, in Greek St., is Soho's finest house, **The House of St Barnabas**(🖾 open Wed 14.30–16.15, Thurs 11.00–12.30), a luxurious 1746 town house with a plain exterior but a magnificently decorated Rococo interior, with rich plasterwork on walls and ceiling. Soho's other public open space is **St Anne's churchyard**, a little park in Wardour St. overlooked by a splendid tower of 1801–03 surviving from the church ruined in the war.

The southern part of Soho crosses Shaftesbury Ave., a busy street of many theatres, to London's **Chinatown**, centred on Gerrard St., small, authentic and packed with excellent restaurants. But Soho's heart, with marvellous French, Italian and Spanish delicatessens, together with fine butchers, fishmongers and wine merchants, is found further N on **Brewer St.**, **Old Compton St.** and **Berwick St.**; the latter is also an excellent open-air fresh food market, becoming more expensive and exotic at its continuation in Rupert St., s through sexy Walker Court. To the N of Old Compton St., Dean St., Frith St. and Greek St. have fine little restaurants, pubs and clubs, such as **Ronnie Scott's** for jazz (see *Nightlife*). In Wardour St., the respectable British movie industry has its centre. Throughout, blue plaques mark apparently run-down buildings with famous associations: Blake was born in Marshall St., Chopin gave recitals in Meard St., and in Frith St., Marx worked, Baird first demonstrated television, and Hazlitt died.

The northeastern part of Soho has less character: Carnaby St. was the Mecca of the Swinging Sixties, but most of its current visitors wonder why everyone else is a tourist.

Somerset House 🏛

Strand, WC2 ☎438–6622. Map 11G12. Fine rooms open only during temporary exhibitions. Tube Aldwych, Temple.
The boldly Classical style of this riverside frontage was created by Sir William Chambers in 1776–78, and strongly carved details stand out from the Portland stone facing. The entrance is from the *Strand*, through a triple arch into a courtyard. In its time it has housed learned societies like the Royal Academy and, until recently, the *Registry of Births, Deaths and Marriages*.

South Bank Arts Centre

Map 11G12. Tube Waterloo.
The plans for a national arts centre were formulated in the years after World War II, and crystallized when the general dereliction of this South Bank site was developed for the Festival of Britain in 1951, with the first stages of the Festival Hall and National Film Theatre ready for the event.

The **Festival Hall** is one of Britain's outstanding post-war buildings. Not finally completed until 1956, its impressive glass facade makes full use of its panoramic riverside location. Like later South Bank buildings, however, the exterior is more massive and monumental than appealing, and it is the interior which is most successful. This has a complex arrangement of spaces, efficiently and attractively laid out, with public areas offering views over the river, bars, restaurants and the great concert hall itself, seating almost 3,000, with near perfect acoustics. The **Queen Elizabeth Hall** and **Purcell Room**, seating 1,100 and 372 respectively, were completed next to the Festival Hall for smaller concerts in 1967. The **National Film Theatre**, under Waterloo Bridge, which now has two cinemas, shows an always interesting programme of historic and contemporary movies. The **Hayward Gallery**, next to the bridge, was opened in 1968, and puts on an important series of art exhibitions organized by the Arts Council. The latest addition, the *National Theatre*, continues the Brutalist theme.

See also *Nightlife*.

Southwark Cathedral ▥ † ☆
Map 13G16. Tube London Bridge.
This Gothic church is under siege from the encroaching railway viaducts, covered market and *London Bridge* that crowd to within a few yards of its walls, but it is still one of the most important medieval buildings in London. The tower is the best feature, dating from the 14th–15thC, with pinnacles of 1689.

It was founded as the Augustinian priory of St Mary Overie (meaning 'over the water') in 1106, becoming the parish church of St Saviour after the Reformation and a cathedral only in 1905. The priory burned down in about 1212 and was replaced with a Gothic structure, of which the present chancel and retro-choir were complete by 1220. Since then, restoration has been necessary periodically, the chancel of 1890–97, in a medieval style, being the latest major reworking.

Interesting features include the **ceiling bosses** from the 15thC, opposite the present main entrance, graphically carved with heraldic devices or grotesque figures. The rebuilt **chancel** actually shows very well the beauty and purity of early Gothic architecture, with its layers of perfectly proportioned arches. Behind the high altar, a superbly rich **reredos** dates from 1520.

The monuments in the church are of enormous interest, although several have been crudely painted in restoration. Look out for *John Gower*, a medieval poet and friend of Chaucer, who died in 1408, a wooden effigy of a knight of about 1275, and *Richard Humber* (died 1616) with his fashionably dressed wives. Next to the N transept is a chapel (rebuilt in 1907) devoted to John Harvard, founder of the great American college, who was baptized here in 1607. The **Nonesuch Chest**, in the retro-choir, is an outstanding example of 16thC furniture in the Classical Renaissance style. In the S aisle, there is a memorial of 1912 to William Shakespeare.

Speakers' Corner
Map 8G7. Tube Marble Arch.
Speakers' Corner in the NE tip of *Hyde Park* offers the dubious spectacle of numerous wild-eyed eccentrics haranguing small groups of spectators on everything from hell fire to Utopia. Established as late as 1872 as a place where such holding-forth could be tolerated without arrest, it has in recent years begun to attract more serious attention thanks to exiles from countries where free speech is denied. It is at its busiest on Sun.

Staple Inn 🏛

Holborn, EC1. Map 11E13. Tube Chancery Lane.

This is what Elizabethan London looked like: close to the
entrance of *Gray's Inn* is a remarkable survivor, a pair of timber
houses dating from 1586 forming the facade to Staple Inn, a
former Inn of Chancery. The two buildings together look like a
quaint jumble of haphazardly-placed beams and gables, with
charming overhanging storeys and oriel windows. Through the
gateway on the left, the courtyards of the Inn (now housing the
Society of Actuaries) can be entered. Dr. Johnson lived at no. 2
in 1759–60, where he supposedly wrote *Rasselas* in a week to
pay for his mother's funeral.

Stock Exchange

*8 Throgmorton St., EC2 ☎588–2355. Map 13F16 🎥 📷 with
flash ✗ Open Mon–Fri 9.45–15.15; film six times a day
(check times). Tube Bank.*

Jobbers and brokers, bulls and bears, on the nod or hammered;
the heart of *The City* beats to a mysterious rhythm, and this
institution, where negotiable securities are traded, is as eclectic
and xenophobic as its language. The Stock Exchange has been
functioning since 1773, when it replaced the Royal Exchange
and coffee houses as the centre of trade, and moved to a building
on the present site in 1802, next to the other bastion of The City,
the **Bank of England**. Rebuilding from 1967 created the
modern floor which today can be viewed from a public gallery.

Strand

Maps 10&11G11&12. Tube Charing Cross.

'Strand' means river bank, and that is what this street was until
the embankment was built in 1864–70; the old **watergate** still
stands in Victoria Embankment Gardens. Once the main route
from Westminster to The City, it was lined with great houses,
and is today a motley collection of theatres, shops and hotels.

Its E end begins at Temple Bar, on the edge of The City,
continuing the direction set by *Fleet Street*. On the N side are
the splendid Victorian Gothic *Royal Courts of Justice* with an
attractive tangle of buildings opposite.

The church of **St Clement Danes** occupies an island in the
middle of the road, built by Sir Christopher Wren in 1680–82,
with the stone tower completed by James Gibb in 1719. Entirely
wrecked by a bomb in 1941, the church has been restored with
exceptional skill and is now the church of the Royal Air Force.
Behind is a statue to *Samuel Johnson* erected in 1910, while to
the front is a more pompous monument to *Gladstone* of 1905.

The **Aldwych** follows on the N side of the street, an ambitious
planning scheme begun in 1900. Its crescent shape is made up
of massive, sombre buildings in heavy Edwardian style,
including Australia House and the BBC's Bush House. The
exquisite church of *St Mary-le-Strand* occupies another island
in the middle of the road at this point, with the 1971 concrete
facade of King's College almost opposite. *Somerset House*
comes next on the S side, just a little further along from the
Aldwych. Two large hotels are a little further W: the art deco-ish
Strand Palace (Simpson's ultra-traditional restaurant opposite)
and the famous Savoy (see *Hotels*). Several theatres are to be
found along the N side of the Strand from here, in a section
largely given over to bustling shoppers. The W end, opening on
to *Trafalgar Square*, is marked by *Charing Cross*, with the
remarkable **Coutts' Bank building** opposite.

Strawberry Hill 血

Strawberry Vale, Twickenham ☎ *892–0051. Map 20D3*
📷 🅿 *Open Jan–Easter, Easter–June, Oct–Dec Wed, Sat
afternoons; prior appointment necessary. Train to Strawberry
Hill from Waterloo.*

At a time when country houses were being built in cool Classical
style, Horace Walpole's Strawberry Hill, built in Twickenham,
sw of London, in 1749–76, was revolutionary. Although
influential in the 19thC, its curious 'Gothick' is entirely 18thC –
a Rococo plaything, a complex melange of turrets and
battlements. Walpole's attempt to revive the Gothic spirit was a
total failure. What he produced instead was a quaint pastiche, a
style now named after this house. The interior of the house is
most effective, carved, moulded and painted in complex detail.
The entrance and staircase are particularly splendid. Now St
Mary's Training College for teachers, it could not present a
greater contrast with the nearby *Ham House* and *Hampton
Court.*

Syon House 血

Brentford, Middlesex ☎ *560–0881. Map 20C3* 🖼 🎐 🗶 🅿
*Open Apr–Sept Sun–Thurs 12.00–16.15; gardens daily
10.00–18.00, sunset if earlier. Tube Gunnersbury.*

Syon House was originally a convent, founded by Henry V in
1415 and exceptionally rich until suppressed by Henry VIII in
1534. In 1547, it was taken over by the Lord Protector, the
Duke of Somerset, who transformed it into a large mansion on
the pattern of a hollow square. Somerset went to the scaffold in
1552 as did his successor to Syon, John Dudley, and also Lady
Jane Grey, who set out from the house to be Queen of England
for eight days in 1553. Since 1594, the Percy family, Dukes of
Northumberland, have held the house.

In 1762, Robert Adam was brought in to 'modernize' the
Tudor house, thus creating the extraordinary contrast between
the plain square exterior with battlements and corner towers,
and the incomparable interior. As at *Osterley Park* nearby, the
centrepiece to Adam's planning is the **Great Hall**, a cool and
elegant room with restrained Classical decoration in stucco,
including Doric columns, giving the house a dramatic entrance.
To complete the scholarly effect, there are genuine Roman
statues and some copies of famous antique models, including a
fine bronze version of the *Dying Gaul.* Adam's intention was to
create a sequence of pleasurable contrasts: the next room, **The
Ante Room**, is altogether more lavish, with rich gilding, dark
green marble columns and a brightly-patterned floor in
coloured artificial stone. The suite of state rooms continues the
contrast, with **Dining Room**, **Red Drawing Room** and **Long
Gallery** all in different, variously elaborate styles; some
furniture is gilded, some is in beautifully inlaid wood. In the
Red Drawing Room there is a fine carpet designed by Adam,
and in the Long Gallery landscape panels by Zuccarelli.
Paintings in the house include works by Van Dyck, Lely and
Gainsborough.

The gardens, remodelled in the late 18thC by the great
Capability Brown, take in many rare botanical specimens, as
well as many carefully planned vistas. The **Great Conservatory**
was added in 1830, with its large, almost oriental, glass dome,
and now contains an aviary and aquarium. In the park there is
also an experimental butterfly house, where British and tropical
specimens can be seen all year round under glass.

Tate Gallery ★

Millbank, SW1 ☎*821–1313, recorded info* ☎*821–7128.
Map* **18**K11 ◫ *K* ▣ *Open Mon–Sat* 10.00–17.50, *Sun*
14.00–18.00. *Tube Pimlico.*

Appropriately for a gallery famous for modern art, the Tate was
founded by the modern type of patron, a businessman, when in
1892 the sugar millionaire Sir Henry Tate gave his collection of
British paintings to the nation, together with funds to build a
special gallery. In fact, only later, in 1916, was the decision
taken to add modern foreign art, largely because at the time the
Tate was seen as an adjunct to the *National Gallery.* Several
extensions have increased the available space many times over,
recently in the large galleries opened in 1979, and with the new
Charles Clore extension opening in 1986. The two collections,
British and modern art, are now exhibited adequately and
distinctly, although the British collection is more complete.

The British collection

This is shown in **Rms. 1–23**, to the left of the entrance. The
first rooms (**Rms. 1 and 8**) cover the 16th–17thC, when foreign
artists working in England, such as Holbein and Van Dyck,
ruled the roost. A few works, such as the superb portraits by
William Dobson, show what a benign influence Europeans
could be.

In the 18thC, a truly national school appeared, particularly
with William Hogarth (**Rm. 2**), whose eye for contemporary life
was unrivalled. His *Study of the Heads of Six Servants* shows a
great and original understanding of the ordinary people making
up his household, whereas *Calais Gate* reveals his biting satire.
In the 18thC (**Rms. 4–5**), with Reynolds and Gainsborough,
two contradictory approaches to portraiture emerged, although
in the end both artists concentrated on pleasing their sitters.
Reynolds favoured a grand, Classicizing manner (as in *Three
Ladies Adorning a Term of Hymen*), while Gainsborough
concentrated on charm and prettiness with his extraordinarily
fluent technique. The Tate has good examples of the
development of landscape painting in the 18thC: Richard
Wilson's *Cader Idris* and Gainsborough's *Suffolk Landscape
with a Cornfield* demonstrates an emerging naturalism. Two
other important artists of the 18thC should not be missed:
George Stubbs (sporting and animal scenes, including the finest
horses ever painted), and Joseph Wright of Derby (highly
individual night scenes closely bound up with advances in
science and industrialization, such as his *Experiment with an Air
Pump*).

In the 19thC, British art for a time was free of the need to
imitate continental masters. Turner's bequest of his works to
the nation is partly on show in **Rms. 8–9**, and **12–13**, a dazzling
display of light and colour, revealing an unmatched
understanding of nature in all its moods and prefiguring the
Impressionists' innovations of several decades later. The late
works, such as the studies of *Norham Castle*, are outstanding.
Constable, too, in studies and finished works such as *Flatford
Mill*, showed an appreciation of the real appearance of the
countryside which was revolutionary in his time. By contrast,
Rm. 7 shows the eccentric mysticism of William Blake and his
followers, most effectively in a darkened room. The Pre-
Raphaelites are fashionable again and proudly displayed in
Rms. 16–17, rather than being consigned to the basement:
Millais' *Ophelia* and Rossetti's *Beata Beatrix* are the most
famous. Victorian painting is now admired and the Tate has an

admirable selection in **Rms. 14–15**, from John Martin's apocalyptic *The Great Day of His Wrath* to Frith's *Derby Day*, with its unbelievably complex story-telling detail. From the later 19thC, Whistler stands out (**Rm. 28**). This American painter working in England placed great emphasis on abstract pictorial qualities such as colour harmony.

The modern collection

The Tate's modern collection, occupying **Rms. 28–46** to the right of the main entrance, gives an effective, if patchy, coverage of the main currents in 20thC art. The gallery's purchasing policy is a subject of continuing controversy.

The collection starts with the Impressionists and Post-Impressionists (**Rm. 29**) with all the major figures represented with works of varying quality. Degas' bronze *Little Dancer*, Van Gogh's *The Chair and the Pipe*, and Gauguin's *Faa Iheihe* are notable. Two important masterpieces by pioneering artists of the Fauve group are in **Rm. 31**: Derain's *Port of London* and Matisse's late collage *The Snail*. **Rm. 30** is devoted to the Bloomsbury Group of British artists, more noted for their writings than their derivative paintings. This represents a general fault in the Tate's hanging policy, for British artists consistently have more space than they deserve in the modern collection. Cubism, short-lived but vitally important, is demonstrated with a few works of high quality of Picasso and Braque in **Rm. 32**, together with Futurism. The move to complete abstraction is shown by Delaunay, Kandinsky and Mondrian in **Rm. 35**. The gallery has some excellent Expressionist works in **Rm. 39**, including Munch's *Sick Child* and Grosz's *Suicide*. Important works by Picasso, the giant of modern art, are in **Rm. 38**, including the famous *Three Dancers* in his unique version of the Surrealist style. The Surrealists themselves, Miro, Ernst, Magritte and Dali, are in **Rm. 42**. American Abstract Expressionism, the most influential post-war art movement, is represented in **Rms. 40–41**, with Jackson Pollock's *Yellow Islands* prominent. The two most important contemporary British artists, Bacon and Hockney, are in **Rm. 44**, and Naum Gabo (the Tate has a leading collection) in **Rm. 45**. Arguably the high point of the modern collection comes with **Rm. 46**, entirely devoted to a group of powerful abstract canvasses by Mark Rothko in sombre black and purple; they serve as a potent reminder of the achievements of modern art.

The remaining rooms of the new extension are given over to fine **temporary exhibitions** (■ hours may be extended), generally of both contemporary artists and historical subjects.

Temple 🏛 ☆

Map **11**F13. *Tube Temple.*

It can be easy to miss the gateway to the Inner and Middle Temples amid the bustle of *Fleet Street*, yet behind them lies a large and relatively peaceful enclave of historic buildings and gardens down towards the Thames. The Temple is named after the Knights Templar, a religious order founded in the Middle Ages to further the Crusades, who came to this site – then outside The City walls – in about 1160. They were disbanded in 1308, but not before they had constructed a great complex of monastic buildings of which the chapel survives. Some time in the 14thC, the buildings were taken over by lawyers, and there they have remained, today organized into two of the four *Inns of Court*.

The red-brick **Middle Temple Gateway** was built in 1684 to
a design using Classical motifs, and leads through to Middle
Temple Lane, lined with chambers and courtyards. Much was
destroyed by war-time bombing, although some buildings date
back to the 17thC and beyond. Outstanding is the **Middle
Temple Hall** of 1562–70 (📷 open Mon–Sat 10.30–12.00,
15.00–16.00), expertly restored and retaining a superb
hammerbeam roof and **oak screen** from the Elizabethan
period, with Doric columns and arches, and finely-carved
figures. It is likely that Shakespeare himself appeared in the
performance of *Twelfth Night* given here in 1602.

To the E, narrow alleys lead through to the **Inner Temple**.
Here, the most important building is the **Templar church**, one
of London's most interesting medieval structures. It is one of
five circular churches in England, based on the Church of the
Holy Sepulchre in Jerusalem. The round nave was begun in
about 1160 and completed by 1185, one of the earliest Gothic
structures in England. The chancel is of about 1220–40, in a
more unreservedly airy Gothic style. On the floor of the nave are
nine 13thC effigies of knights in Purbeck marble.

The **Inner Temple Gateway**, leading back to Fleet St., is an
attractive half-timbered house of 1610–11, restored in 1906.
On an upper floor is Prince Henry's Room, with an elaborately
decorated plaster ceiling. The Prince of Wales Feathers and the
initials 'PH' suggest the connection with James I's son.

Tower Bridge
SE1 ☎407–0922. Map 13G&H17 📷 ✳ ◀€ *Open Apr–Oct
Mon–Sat 10.00–18.30; Nov–Mar Mon–Sat 10.00–16.45.
Tube Tower Hill.*

With its towers and drawbridges, this landmark has become a
symbol for London. Built in 1886–94, it is the most easterly
bridge over the Thames, and though designed so that large
ships can pass beneath its easily raised roadway, it is
deceptively graceful when viewed from a distance. Enter by
the N tower to visit the glass-enclosed walkway which leads
across to the S tower where there is a small exhibition. The
views are splendid, with Butler's Wharf downstream, *HMS
Belfast* to the W and *St Katharine's Dock* on the N bank.

Tower of London 🏛 ★
EC3 ☎709–0765. Map 13G17 📷 *summer* 📷 *winter* ✗ *Open
Mar–Oct Mon–Sat 9.30–17.45, Sun 14.00–17.45; Nov–Feb
Mon–Sat 9.30–16.00. Tube Tower Hill.*

The Tower's great keep rises from its complex accretion of
massively fortified walls, moats, towers and bastions, and today
its forbidding but thrilling appearance is often used as a symbol
for London. The best views are from Tower Hill to the N and W,
by All Hallows church, from *Tower Bridge*, or perhaps from
the river itself, on a boat trip from Tower Pier (see *Useful
addresses* in *Basic information*). The Tower is London's most
substantial medieval monument, steeped in a bloody past and
containing a superb collection of arms and armour together
with the priceless Crown Jewels. As a result, it is a prime tourist
attraction and is often crowded; a visit near to opening time is to
be recommended.

It was founded by William the Conqueror just inside the
Roman wall at the E end of London following his arrival in 1066,
to encourage the loyalty of the townspeople as much as to
defend them. William's castle was initially a wooden structure,

but from about 1077 the great stone White Tower began to rise, to be completed by 1097 in the reign of the Conqueror's son, William Rufus. At this time, the White Tower stood alone, joined to the river by an enclosed bailey, but Richard the Lionheart began to build a curtain wall in the late 12thC, a process continued in the reign of Henry III. Edward I (1272–1307) completed the transformation of the Norman stronghold into a fully-fledged medieval castle; the White Tower was now surrounded by a continuous curtain wall with 12 towers. The moat surrounding the whole was up to 120ft (38m) wide, with a barbican on the far side guarding the drawbridges. This is substantially as the Tower is today.

Until the reign of James I (1603–25) the Tower was a leading royal residence. Its strength meant that it was also used as a principal armoury and house for royal treasure. These functions have continued, and the Tower still holds the Crown Jewels and weaponry amassed over the ages. The Tower's security also commended it as a prison, and kings and queens have kept many of their most notable enemies within its walls: Anne Boleyn, Sir Thomas More, Elizabeth I (while a princess), Sir Walter Raleigh and, most recently, Rudolf Hess during World War II.

The continuous traditions of the Tower have cloaked it in rich ceremonial. It is guarded by the Yeomen Warders, or 'Beefeaters', a company founded by Henry VII in 1485, who still wear Tudor costume, with blue tunics carrying the sovereign's monogram on the chest and broad, flat caps. On ceremonial occasions, a more elaborate scarlet version of the same dress is worn. Together with guardsmen from the Regular Army, Yeomen Warders participate in the **Ceremony of the Keys** at 22.00 each day, formally locking up the Tower for the night (see *Calendar of events* in *Planning*). Another tradition hangs around the six ravens that live inside the Tower's walls – these are kept jealously, with a meat allowance, because of a legend that the Tower will fall when the ravens depart.

The outer fortifications

The main entrance to the Tower is, as in the Middle Ages, to the w, near the river. Evidence can be seen of the medieval causeway that led up to the vanished Lion Tower, so called because it housed the royal menagerie – lions and leopards included – until 1834. The whole entrance defence work, or barbican, was originally surrounded by water and reached by a drawbridge. Another drawbridge led to the **Middle Tower**, the present outer gateway, an 18thC reconstruction. From here, a causeway leads across the broad moat (once with another drawbridge) to the gate in **Byward Tower**, built by Edward I. The moat was drained in 1843 and is now grassed over. Byward Tower leads into the corridor between the curtain walls, with the angled **Bell Tower** on the left, probably built soon after 1200 by King John, one of the oldest surviving parts of the curtain defence. Farther along on the right is the notorious **Traitors' Gate**, through which royal barges and boats bearing prisoners (or provisions) could enter the castle.

The inner buildings

The inner precincts of the Tower can be entered through the gate in the **Bloody Tower** opposite, overlooked by the heavily fortified round structure of **Wakefield Tower** to the side. The Bloody Tower is by tradition the site of the murder of the young princes by their uncle, Richard III, in 1485, hoping to secure his succession to the throne, although modern historians are less certain about the event than was Shakespeare. Inside the tower, a winch used to raise the portcullis can be seen and two rooms are furnished as they might have been when Sir Walter Raleigh was imprisoned here. Other notable prisoners included Thomas Cranmer, Archbishop Laud, and the notorious Judge Jeffreys, who died here in a fit in 1689.

The great open space enclosed by the fortifications of the curtain walls can now be appreciated. On the right is a portion of 12thC wall, surviving from the Norman bailey, only exposed in 1940 when a bomb destroyed a 19thC building. When the top of the steps ahead is reached, the **Queen's House** (not open to the public), a pretty half-timbered structure begun in about 1540, is on the left. In its rooms, Guy Fawkes was tortured following the 1605 Gunpowder Plot. To the N is the entrance to **Beauchamp Tower**, used again and again as a prison. The interior is covered with carved graffiti, giving witness to the suffering of prisoners. Nearby is the **Chapel of St Peter ad Vincula**, built in the early 16thC on a 12thC foundation, in Perpendicular Gothic style. It retains some late medieval monuments. Beyond the chapel, **Bowyer Tower** contains a display of torture instruments.

The Crown Jewels ★

Nearby begin the long queues for the Crown Jewels, the Tower's greatest single attraction. The lines move quickly so you cannot expect more than a brief look.

Kept below the 19thC Waterloo Barracks, the jewels are reached through a suitably dramatic pair of polished steel doors. Inside, the Tower's best-guarded prisoners ever, the fire and brilliance of the stones are even more spectacular than their reputation or their worth. Almost all the royal regalia was melted down or sold off by Cromwell, so most of what is left dates from after the 1660 Restoration. The display begins with a selection of plate, massive and ornate pieces in silver-gilt; look out for the fabulous **wine cooler** of 1829, gilded state maces and bejewelled swords. The rich vestments of the knightly orders are on display, but put in the shade by the coronation robes of the sovereign, elaborately covered in gold embroidery. The Crown Jewels themselves are in the next room. Two items of coronation regalia survive from the Middle Ages: an exquisite **spoon**, probably made for King John's coronation in 1199; and a much restored early 15thC **ampulla** in the form of an eagle (from which the anointing oil is poured). The **Royal Sceptre** contains the largest diamond ever cut (530 carats), one of the 'Stars of Africa' from the Cullinan diamond found in 1905. Another piece was added to the **Imperial State Crown**, originally made in 1838, which also incorporates an immense and beautiful ruby, probably the one given to the Black Prince by Pedro the Cruel after the Battle of Najara in 1367 and worn by Henry V at the Battle of Agincourt. The oldest crown is 'King Edward's', made for Charles II's coronation in 1660. It weighs 5lb (2.3 kilos) and is worn by the sovereign at coronations. The **Queen Mother's Crown**, made for her coronation in 1937, contains the ancient Kohinoor diamond, which was bought by the British Crown in 1849 and was recut in 1852 to its present size of 109 carats.

The White Tower and armouries

The dominant White Tower is the oldest and largest of the Tower's buildings; its massive walls are up to 15ft (4.6m) thick, supported by external buttresses and carrying square or curved turrets at the corners. The large semi-circular protruberance at the SE contains the apse of the chapel; the round turret on the NE corner contains a spiral staircase. The medieval facade was even starker – since then the decorative cones have been added and Wren enlarged the windows.

Inside are displays from the Tower's superb collections of arms and armour. On the first floor, the **Sporting and Tournament Galleries** contain crossbows, muskets, lances, swords and the specialized armour made for jousting, already in the late Middle Ages a leisurely exercise in archaism.

The **Chapel of St John** on the second floor is the finest example of early Norman architecture in England, almost totally without ornament, massive and severe. More armour is displayed in the other two rooms; notice the awesome bulk of a suit made for a giant almost 7ft (2.13m) tall.

The third floor rooms contain outstanding examples of Tudor and later armour, with several suits that belonged to Henry VIII, growing progressively larger as their owner grew older and grosser. The ceremonial armour of the 17thC is decorated to absurd degrees – a suit belonging to Charles I of 1630 is chased and gilded over its entire surface. Stairs descend to ground level where a fine selection of hand-guns, uniforms and cannons from various periods can be seen. The oriental armour, including fine examples from India, China, Japan, even Africa, is housed in the **Waterloo Barracks**, worth visiting in particular for the elaborate elephant armour captured at the Battle of Plassey in 1757. Of many interesting cannons and other artillery pieces scattered throughout the Tower's enclosures, note a Turkish bronze cannon of 1530–31.

Trafalgar Square
Map **10**G11. *Tube Charing Cross.*

Trafalgar Square is known as a rallying point for political demonstrations and New Year's Eve revelries, or even as a sanctuary for pigeons. When Nash began its redevelopment in the 1820s, it already had the fine equestrian statue of *Charles I* on the site of *Charing Cross*, and the superb church of *St Martin-in-the-Fields*. Since then, the surrounding architecture has let down Nash's vision: the *National Gallery*, added on the high N side in 1832–38, is too small in scale to make the triumphant statement its site demands, and Admiralty Arch (1911), a monument to Queen Victoria which saves its best face for *The Mall*, is equally uninspired. Still, it does allow Nelson to steal the show, as Nash intended; he was placed atop the 170ft (52m) granite column in 1842. The base is decorated by spirited reliefs made from the guns of ships captured at Trafalgar, and the justifiably famous lions added by Landseer in 1858–67.

Victoria & Albert Museum ★
Cromwell Rd., SW1 ☎ *589–6371. Map* **15**J5 ☒ ▣ ☀ *Open Mon–Thurs, Sat 10.00–18.00, Sun 14.30–18.00. Closed Fri. Tube South Kensington.*

Probably the world's greatest museum of the decorative arts, it is a vast storehouse of extraordinarily varied treasures. While fine art is emphatically included, the reverence of the art gallery is absent. The 'V&A' is thus a lively, informal place, and one of London's most popular museums. The range of the exhibits is overwhelming, including everything from entire furnished rooms brought from the great houses of Britain and the Continent to spoons, shoes or locks.

The museum is, however, a labyrinth of galleries and passages in which it is easy to become lost, and around which it is almost impossible to plan a coherent or comprehensive tour. But, to an extent, this drawback contributes to the museum's appeal, for even regular visitors know that no matter how often they come, there are still new treasures to be discovered.

The initial impetus and finance for the Victoria & Albert came from the Great Exhibition of 1851, the profits of which were used to purchase the large site in South Kensington on which it stands. Under the enthusiastic direction of Prince Albert's friend, Sir Henry Cole, it first opened as the Museum of Ornamental Art in 1852, temporarily at *Marlborough House*, dedicated to fostering the 'application of fine art to objects of utility', but, in 1857, the museum moved to its iron and glass construction at South Kensington.

Almost from the first, Cole's ideals became diluted by the desire to fill the museum with great works of art. In 1865 Raphael's tapestry cartoons arrived from the Royal Collection. In 1888, the Constable Collection was bequeathed by a member of the great painter's family, adding another fine art element of the greatest importance but having little to do with the museum's intention. Before long, the museum felt free to acquire any item of aesthetic or historical interest.

Similar uncertainties have dogged the museum's building programmes, contributing to the sense of confusion. After 1863, the red-brick buildings were constructed around the gardens in a northern Italian Romanesque style with terra cotta and mosaic ornament. The leading artist, Lord Leighton, and the firm of William Morris contributed to the decoration of the interior, but shortage of funds prevented the scheme being completed. The library, especially attractive and now the **National Art Library**, was completed by 1882. But all this was haphazard and without any underlying plan. The final phase came in 1899–1900 with Sir Aston Webb as architect, after which the museum reopened as the Victoria & Albert. From this time date the great facades along Cromwell Rd.

It is not possible to suggest a complete route through the V&A – the result would be both difficult to follow and exhausting. Instead, two particularly well-displayed but contrasting departments are proposed as the starting and ending points – the Jones Collection and Constable Collection – and suggestions are made for sections to be visited in between. Visitors should stay alert on their travels for the countless minor surprises that the museum has to offer. Good large plans of the galleries are available at the main entrance. Note that the collection is supposedly arranged into 'primary collections', cutting across the arts of a given culture or period, and less important 'study collections', grouped by material.

Begin from the main entrance by turning left and following the signs for the **Jones Collection**, a dazzling display of French interior decoration, painting, furniture, ceramics and other decorative arts. Elaborate furniture, some of which belonged to Marie-Antoinette, is inlaid with brass or with finely-grained woods, or covered with enamelled panels. The rich, aristocratic mood is complemented by paintings such as Boucher's *Portrait of Madame de Pompadour*. German, Dutch and Italian decorative arts on display echo the French Rococo of the 18thC. The 17thC follows, just as elaborate but more solemn in mood. Several Dutch cabinets, inlaid with complex floral designs, are outstanding, as are German metalwork or Venetian glass.

121

At the end of these splendidly laid-out galleries steps lead up to the section devoted to the Renaissance, a series of rooms grouped around the court containing the gardens. In a less organized collection, some superb works stand out. There is a statue, for example, by Giovanni Bologna of *Samson and a Philistine*, a full-size marble composition of Mannerist complexity. From the High Renaissance, there is the famous elegantly gilded **Antico miniature bronze** of Meleanger (c.1500), and from the 15thC several important **reliefs by Donatello**, the greatest sculptor of the early Renaissance, including an exquisite and moving *Dead Christ tended by Angels*. Rooms on the side of the gallery opposite the garden have been restored to their original decoration; one was carried out by William Morris' workshops. Another has tiles by Minton and stained glass designed by James Gamble.

The northern Renaissance is also well covered. Particularly beautiful are two late Gothic carved limewood angels, made as candlesticks by Tilman Reimenschneider in the early 16thC. At the end of the gallery of Gothic art is a vast and gruesome Spanish altarpiece of the early 15thC, showing scenes from the life of St George, which, according to this account, consisted almost entirely of hideous torture. Be sure to study the **Syon Cope** closely – this early 14thC example of *opus anglicanum* needlework is one of the finest pieces of embroidery ever executed.

Also on the ground floor is the large and stunning **costume court ☆** with one of the world's great clothing collections of everyday garments and high fashion. It is a subject visitors relate to instantly, of course, but note that even some outfits of a decade or two ago can seem as strange as an 18thC ball gown or Jacobean court dress. Above this is the collection of **musical instruments**, especially strong in the 16thC keyboards such as virginals and the first harpsichords, many with exquisite carving and inlaid work.

A huge gallery nearby exhibits the seven **Raphael cartoons ★** on permanent loan from the Royal Collection. These vastly influential designs of the *Acts of the Apostles* were carried out in 1516–19 as designs for tapestries for the Sistine Chapel in the Vatican. Next to this room, the **woodwork collection** reflects the early educational purpose of the museum, but includes interesting items, such as a complete 17thC timber house front. A similar impression is given by the **cast courts**, housing old models.

Oriental arts are also represented on the ground floor, although even the large galleries allow room for only a small part of the V&A's great holdings. From India, there are several beautiful temple sculptures on show. More unusual is **Tipoo's Tiger**, a large wooden model of a tiger mauling a European, identified as British by his red coat; made in about 1790 for an anti-British sultan, it has organ pipes which simulate the groans of the victim. Outstanding is the exquisite **jade wine cup** made for Shah Jahan in 1657, with a lotus flower base and a graceful antelope head as the handle. The **Islamic gallery** is dominated by the vast **Ardabil Carpet** of 1540, from a Persian mosque, and some superb lacquered pottery. Outstanding in the **Chinese Collection** is an incredibly elaborate carved lacquer throne of the mid-18thC, ceramic and jade horses of more than 1,000yr earlier, and finely-embroidered court costume, all testifying to the unchanging sophistication of Chinese art. The **Japanese paintings** are heralded by a dramatic pair of tigers, looking a little like Chinese dragons, and there follow painted screens with misty landscapes or galloping samurai.

The important **British Art Collection** stretches through sizeable galleries on two upper floors to the left (or w) of the main entrance. First encountered is the furniture, especially beautiful, but generally simpler than the continental equivalents, often relying more on shape and the quality of the wood than on elaborate decoration. Several complete rooms transplanted into the museum include the massively Baroque gold and white **Music Room from Norfolk House** (mid-18thC) and Robert Adam's much more delicate **Glass Drawing Room from Northumberland House** (1773–74). Two beds dominate the furniture: the huge Elizabethan **Great Bed of Ware**, which became instantly legendary for its size and was mentioned by Shakespeare; and a chinoiserie fantasy by Chippendale of 1750–55. Especially beautiful are several **miniatures**, a form of painting which reached its peak in 16th–17thC England, including Nicholas Hilliard's famous *Young Man Amongst Roses*. The same artist is thought to have produced the miniature on the **Armada Jewel**, produced for Elizabeth I in 1589 to celebrate the destruction of the Spanish Armada, and the highlight of a fine jewellery collection. British decorative arts are brought right up to 1914, and there are several important examples of the work of William Morris and the Arts and Crafts Movement which had so much influence on modern British design.

Before leaving, make sure that you visit the **Henry Cole Wing**, opened in 1984 at the rear of the museum to the w. Here you will find the **Ionides Bequest**, largely but not entirely of 19thC paintings, and with several important works: a Degas ballet scene, Millet's *Wood Sawyers*, Burne-Jones' *Day Dream*, Gainsborough's portrait of his two young daughters, and works by Turner are outstanding. Here is also the **Constable Collection** which presents the best coverage anywhere of the work of the most English of painters, providing a refreshing, open-air view for even the most jaded visitor. The fleeting effects of the changing weather of the English countryside are here shown more convincingly than ever before or since. Clouds rush over Hampstead Heath, rainbows hover over Salisbury Cathedral and the trees of Suffolk rustle in gentle breezes, Besides finished paintings there are some superb small oil and watercolour 'sketches'.

Next to the Henry Cole Wing, in the main body of the museum, is the **Boilerhouse Project**, created by Terence Conran to promote discussion about the practice of design in relation to consumer products – an aim close to the V&A's original brief. It houses temporary exhibitions, often imaginative, on the application of design in the modern world.

Wallace Collection ★

Hertford House, Manchester Sq., W1 ☎ *935-0687. Map 9E8* ☐☎ *Open Mon–Sat 10.00–17.00, Sun 14.00–17.00. Tube Bond Street.*

Flying in the face of the renowned English insularity, this magnificent monument to Francophilia is, in fact, arguably the finest selection of French art to be found outside France, together with many other paintings and objets d'art of exceptional quality. It is a great private art collection of the 19thC 'frozen' in the grand house equipped by its wealthy owner to contain it.

Hertford House in Manchester Sq. was built for the Duke of Manchester in 1776–88 and acquired by the Second Marquess of Hertford in 1797. After some years as the French Embassy, it was used as a picture store by the Fourth Marquess who did most to build up the fabulous collection while living in Paris, adding to that of his father. He bequeathed both house and works of art to his natural son, Sir Richard Wallace, who returned to London and transformed Hertford House in the 1870s into a showcase for the collection. In 1897, his widow left it to the nation and it was opened as a public gallery in 1900. It thus reflects the tastes of three generations of Victorians.

The finest objects are on the first floor, which should be seen first. Large paintings by Boucher are on the walls of the top landing, full of the frivolous eroticism of the Rococo court style. Turning to the left, **Rm. XII** contains several scenes of Venice by Guardi and Canaletto. **Rms. XIII–XV** are devoted to Flemish and Dutch art, including fine studies by Rubens. Look out for Potter's animal scenes – even the cows have personality. Caspar Netscher's *Lace-Maker*, quietly realistic, is serenely haunting; the landscapes include marvellous works by Hobbema, and Rembrandt's eerie *Landscape with a Coach*. **Rm. XVI** is a large picture gallery built by Sir Richard Wallace, containing many outstanding works: Titian's *Perseus and Andromeda*, Rubens' deeply human portrait *Isabella Brant*, and Velazquez's cool *Lady with a Fan* are the most important. Works by Rembrandt, as always, stand out, including a buoyant *Self-portrait* and a deeply sympathetic *Portrait of Titus*, his son; also Reynolds' famous portrait of the beautiful courtesan *Nelly O'Brien* and Frans Hals' *Laughing Cavalier*.

Among the superb examples of the richly ornate Rococo furniture is a roll-top desk made by J.H. Riesener for the King of Poland in the 1760s, and a chest of drawers made for Versailles by Charles Cressent. **Rm. XVII** contains an impressive collection of gold boxes, mostly elaborate French 18thC work. Some of the best French Rococo pictures are in **Rms. XVIII–XIX**, leading in an unparalleled procession through Watteau, Lancret, Pater, Boucher and Fragonard and complemented by richly decorated furniture in the same style, much of which came from French royal palaces. Watteau's *Lady at her Toilet* and Fragonard's *Swing* sum up the leisured mood and Boucher's *Portrait of Madame de Pompadour* shows unexpected candour. **Rm. XX** contains the best public collection of works by R.P. Bonington, an English artist working in France in the early 19thC – the clear light of his seascapes is exquisite. **Rms. XXI–XXII** contain more French works, the furniture deserving most attention.

The ground floor is more an Aladdin's cave of miscellaneous treasures, many grouped into specialist collections of great merit – of armour, miniatures or pottery, for example. There is a splendid collection of terra cotta statuettes, mostly from the Italian Renaissance, and a unique cabinet of wax portraits. Furniture, including works attributed to the great A.C. Boulle, and Sèvres porcelain, continue the French bias of the collection. Italian majolica pottery, and Limoges enamels of the Renaissance are as well represented here as anywhere in the world. Paintings include works by Murillo, Canaletto, Guardi and Andrea del Sarto. From all this rich diversity, the **arms and armour** stand out. It is a remarkable collection of elaborately wrought and decorated items – look out for the northern Italian body armour and helmet of about 1620–35.

Westminster

Map 18H–J. Tube Westminster.

Even the visitor who has never heard of Westminster can
instantly appreciate the significance of this most stately of
London's districts for, like its long-time rival *The City*, it has
remained almost free from residential invasion and is devoted to
business, in this case government. Its activity is dominated by
the mother of parliaments at the Palace of Westminster (see
Westminster, Palace of) attended by the officialdom of
Whitehall. Next to the Houses of Parliament is the great church
of *Westminster Abbey*.

Parliament Square, an open space created at the time of the
building of the Palace of Westminster, is appropriately studded
with statues of great statesmen: *Disraeli*, *Palmerston*, *Abraham
Lincoln*, *Winston Churchill*. Surrounding the square, apart from
Westminster Abbey and the Palace of Westminster, there is the
Middlesex Guildhall (Neo-Gothic of 1906–13) and the Home
Office. In front of the abbey is the smaller church of **St
Margaret**, founded as the parish church of Westminster
possibly as early as the 11thC and now the parish church of the
Houses of Parliament, and always a fashionable place for
weddings (Pepys, John Milton and Churchill were all married
here). The present building dates from the early 16thC
although it was restored almost out of recognition in the 18thC.
Among its interesting monuments is the tomb of *Sir Walter
Raleigh*; the E window is Flemish 16thC.

To the E of Parliament Sq., just S of Birdcage Walk and *St
James's Park*, is **Queen Anne's Gate**, with some of the best
early 18thC houses in London, and a statue of *Queen Anne*
dated 1708. In Victoria St., two important landmarks are
Westminster Cathedral and **New Scotland Yard**, the
Metropolitan Police's modern headquarters. There is an
attractive enclave to the S of Westminster Abbey, with Georgian
houses in Cowley St. and Lord North St. The latter opens into
Smith Sq., which includes some 18thC survivors on its E side,
and in the centre of the square one of the most magnificent
Baroque churches in London, **St John's**, built in 1714–28, a
massive and monumental structure. It was burnt down during
World War II but has been restored and often hosts concerts.

Earth has not anything to show more fair . . . .
The City now doth, like a garment, wear
The beauty of the morning; silent, bare,
Ships, towers, domes, theatres, and temples lie
Open unto the fields, and to the sky;
All bright and glittering in the smokeless air . . . .
Never saw I, never felt, a calm so deep!
The river glideth at his own sweet will:
Dear God! The very houses seem asleep;
And all that mighty heart is lying still!
                    Wordsworth, *On Westminster Bridge*, 1802

Westminster Abbey ⏥ † ★

Broad Sanctuary, SW1 ☎ *222–5152. Map 18I11* ▨ *Royal
chapels* ⚑ ✗ *Mon–Fri 9.00–16.00, Sat 9.00–14.00,
15.45–17.00. Tube Westminster.*

Since William the Conqueror chose the new, incomplete
Westminster Abbey for his coronation as king of his new
subjects on Christmas Day, 1066, it has been the scene of the

coronation, marriage and burial of British monarchs, a place of tribute to Britain's heroes, and in every way Britain's mother church. While *St Paul's Cathedral* belongs to London, Westminster Abbey belongs to the nation. It is also, of course, one of Britain's finest Gothic buildings, a soaring and graceful offering to God, with a strikingly unified interior.

The date of Westminster Abbey's foundation is uncertain. Legend takes it back to the 7thC; in any case, there was certainly a religious foundation here by the 9thC. In 1050 Edward the Confessor began work on a large new abbey church, in the Norman style, and it became a Benedictine monastery attached to the new Palace of Westminster.

Work continued on the Norman buildings well into the 12thC, and remains can be seen in the ruined infirmary chapel of St Catherine to the S of the present abbey church. In 1245, Henry III began a vast new building programme in the latest French Gothic style of the cathedrals of Amiens and Reims. Work proceeded quickly and the chancel, transepts and part of the nave were complete by 1259, together with the chapter house. The great speed of the construction gave the building a remarkable unity of style and, when work was resumed more than a century later in 1375, it was decided that the existing parts should be imitated in the rest of the nave.

The mid-16thC was a time of religious upheaval, which first threatened and then confirmed the abbey's role. The royal connection preserved it from destruction at the dissolution of the monasteries and, in 1540, Henry VIII made it a cathedral, with its own bishop. Queen Mary, briefly restoring Catholicism, turned it back into a monastery in 1556. The permanent establishment of the protestant Church of England came under Elizabeth I, who gave it the status of a collegiate church independent of both the Bishop of London and the Archbishop of Canterbury in 1560. It thus became a Royal Peculiar, a great church serving Crown and State.

The building of Westminster Abbey did not end with the Middle Ages, although what has come since has tended to detract from its beauty. In 1698, Sir Christopher Wren began the designs for the W towers and facade. These were continued by Nicholas Hawksmoor and completed in 1745 – in pseudo-Gothic style but sitting uneasily all the same with the existing structure. In the 19thC, restoration work was carried out on a substantial scale – much of it destroying the medieval detail. Thankfully, more recent restoration work has concentrated on conservation rather than 'improvement'.

The exterior

Cleaning is now revealing the beauty of the abbey's soft Reigate stone. The W facade, with the main entrance, is perhaps the most dramatic approach, although Hawksmoor's towers are insubstantial – just too narrow and too high to suit the medieval facade – and their provenance can be detected in the Baroque stonework above the clock face and matching round windows in the opposite tower.

The abbey looks best from the N; the N transept forms a tremendous centrepiece, with its great triple porch and huge rose window, framed by a superb series of flying buttresses. Unfortunately, all the stonework is a product of 19thC restoration and only indicates in a general way the detail that was there before.

To the E lies the far more elaborate exterior of Henry VII's chapel, entirely covered with dense late Gothic tracery. The outer walls have turrets capped with pepperpots and connected to the chapel's nave by delicately-pierced flying buttresses, and the nave is topped by a pierced balustrade and narrow pinnacles, all creating a wonderfully decorative effect. To the s of the chapel can be seen the earlier, much plainer chapter house. The pointed roof is 19thC.

The area around Westminster Abbey once formed a part of it and was densely covered with buildings. The open space to the NW was the Sanctuary, where anyone could seek the Church's protection in medieval times; as a result it became packed with timber buildings inhabited by felons on the run. The s of the abbey was made up of the monastic buildings, and the cloister remains, but this is best visited from within the abbey, as is the Chapel of St Faith. Other monastic buildings to the s of these are now incorporated in Westminster School, a leading public school that has evolved from the monastery's teaching function. To the N is Dean's Yard, now an open space, which can be entered through a 19thC arch to the w of the abbey. Until the 18thC it was covered over by monastic buildings.

The interior

The abbey is entered from the w, immediately presenting the visitor with a stunning view along the nave. Sweeping exaltedly upwards, it is very like a French Gothic cathedral, much higher and narrower than other English churches, supported on piers of dark Purbeck marble. Above the main arches is the triforium containing a gallery (unlike the French style); then the clerestory containing the windows, beneath the gracefully vaulted ceiling, completing the majesty. The western end of the nave was built last to match the style of the 13thC work to the E; the huge, plain window above the w door is late 15thC.

Set in the floor ahead of the entrance is a memorial to *Winston Churchill* with the **Tomb of the Unknown Warrior** beyond; the brass lettering is made from cartridges brought back with the body from the World War I trenches. On the first pier of the nave to the right hangs a famous and rare medieval **portrait of Richard II**, probably painted in 1398. Both the aisles are filled with monuments, jumbles of marble statuary, both good and bad. In the s aisle, that to *Colonel Townshend*, killed at the Battle of Ticonderoga in the American War of Independence, is of particular merit. It was designed by Robert Adam and made soon after 1759. The N aisle is even more crowded with monuments. Most notable is that to *Charles James Fox* of 1823. Look out also for the small kneeling wall effigy of *Mrs Jane Hill* of 1631, with *Death in a Shroud* and the *Tree of Life* above. Buried in the nave are David Livingstone, the explorer, and the engineers Thomas Telford and Robert Stephenson, among many other national figures. The E end of the nave is closed by a brightly-coloured Neo-Gothic choir-screen of 1848. On the left in one of its arches is the monument to *Isaac Newton* of 1731, one of the finest sculptures in the abbey, designed by William Kent and carved by J.M. Rysbrack.

The rest of the abbey is reached through a gate in the N aisle. Memorials to scientists cluster near Newton's tomb: Lister, Darwin, Faraday, Rutherford; musicians including Elgar, Vaughan-Williams and Benjamin Britten are commemorated by plaques in the floor near Purcell's monument. In the N transept the monuments come thick and heavy, and include those to 19thC statesmen. The architecture is of Henry III's time (1216–72), except that the great rose window was heavily restored in the 19thC. In the E of the transept, among several

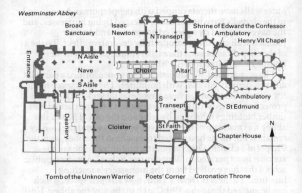

Westminster Abbey

older monuments, is one of the most impressively carved and imaginatively conceived of all – that to *Mrs J.G. Nightingale*, made by Roubiliac in 1761. It shows a grim figure of Death pointing a lance at the unfortunate lady, who died after being struck by lightning. The fine monument to *Sir Francis Vere* of 1609 is also remarkable.

At this point notice the **crossing**, with its temporary ceiling where a tower should rise. The wooden pulpit is early 17thC. To the w, the choir stalls are overdone Victorian Gothic, and to the E is the sanctuary, with an elaborately gilded reredos of 1867. To its right are rare and important early 14thC wall paintings, together with an early Renaissance Italian altarpiece. The medieval monuments to the right and left of the sanctuary are best seen from the ambulatory. Particularly fine is that to the *Earl of Lancaster* of 1296.

Before approaching the centrepiece of the whole abbey – the chapel and shrine to Edward the Confessor – visit the superb **Henry VII's chapel** at the E end of the abbey. Begun in 1503 and completed in 1512 by Henry VIII, it is in the much more richly elaborate Gothic style of the late Middle Ages, a mature, sophisticated farewell flourish. The whole surface is adorned with carvings – there are more than 100 statues, and the ceiling is a marvel of delicate tracery. The choir stalls are equally finely-carved in wood – be sure to inspect the misericords, carvings that are visible when the seats are folded up. Henry VII's tomb in the chapel was started in 1506 in the same rich Gothic style, with a bronze screen. For the monument within, however, the Italian Pietro Torrigiano produced the first Renaissance sculpture in England in 1512–18; the heads of the corner angels are especially beautiful.

Henry VII's chapel has its own subsidiary chapels and aisles. In the N aisle is the joint tomb of *Elizabeth I*, completed in 1606 with a suitably stern effigy, and her hated rival *Mary Queen of Scots*. Beyond are two monuments to daughters of James I. The s aisle contains several Tudor monuments rather grander than that to Queen Elizabeth herself. The easternmost chapel is dedicated to the R.A.F. with a commemorative window.

From Henry VII's chapel, **Edward the Confessor's shrine**, which is situated just behind the main altar of the abbey, is reached by a bridge, and entered past the wooden effigy and chantry chapel of Henry V, a Gothic structure of the early 15thC. Only the base remains from the magnificent tomb built by Henry III to contain the remains of the Confessor, but there is enough of the gold mosaic to indicate how splendid it must have been. It was made by an Italian artist in about 1270, as was the fine mosaic floor and Henry III's own similar tomb. Also in the chapel is the **coronation throne** of 1300–01, where almost every monarch since William I has been crowned. It contains, under the seat, the **Stone of Scone**, the mystical coronation stone of the Scottish kings, captured by Edward I in 1297. Legends identify it with Jacob's pillow when he dreamt at Bethel, and also as a holy stone in Ireland. It was certainly in use as a coronation stone for Macbeth and other Scottish kings from the 9thC. Its symbolic value persists: in 1950 it was stolen by Scottish nationalists but was recovered a year later. Beside the throne are the state sword and shield of Edward III, and all around are the tombs of the medieval monarchs, some of the finest sculpture surviving from this period in England.

After this holy of holies, the chapels of the S ambulatory are an anticlimax. In the ambulatory itself are the remains of a 13thC painted retable, with a well-preserved figure of *St Peter* on the extreme left. St Edmund's Chapel contains a fine effigy of *William of Valence*, Henry III's half-brother, of 1296. Look for the lovely miniature alabaster effigies of a knight and his lady.

The S transept has two beautiful carved angels from the mid-13thC in the spandrels of the main arch, but is more famous as **Poet's Corner**. Here are buried, or commemorated, many of the greatest writers in the English language. The best monument, *Geoffrey Chaucer*, was placed here in 1555, but probably includes older elements. More recent poets commemorated include Ben Jonson, Milton, Blake and Longfellow, and a very undistinguished statue of *Shakespeare*. Browning, Byron, Tennyson and Henry James have plaques in the floor. On the S wall are two fine late 13thC wall paintings, discovered in 1936.

In the S choir aisle a doorway leads through to the cloister, as dignified as a monastic cloister should be. The earliest part is to the E and N, dating from the 13thC and among the oldest parts of Henry III's work on the abbey; the cloister was finished in the 14thC, and much restored in the 19thC. It now contains a brass-rubbing centre, where copies can be made from replicas of medieval brass monuments. On the E side, a passageway leads through to the **chapter house** ▥ ☆ (open daily Oct–Feb 9.30–15.30, Mar–Sept 9.30–18.00), an exquisitely symmetrical octagon, with its vaulted roof supported on a slender Purbeck marble pier. It was built c.1250 and has been well restored to its medieval state, with beautiful red and gold tiles decorating the floor, and wall paintings. The chapter house was used throughout the Middle Ages for the occasional meetings of Parliament. To the N of the entrance is the small chapel of St Faith, with a high vaulted roof and, behind the altar, a well-preserved painting, probably late 13thC.

Beyond the chapter house is the **Norman Undercroft**, where the **Abbey Museum** (▨ open daily 10.30–16.30) houses a display of the abbey's history. Apart from examples of carving, there are a number of royal funeral effigies. Those of the Middle Ages are wood, later ones are wax, clothed in contemporary costume. Armour from Henry V's funeral is particularly interesting.

Westminster Cathedral 🏛 † ☆
Ashley Pl., SW1 ☎ *834–7452. Map* **17***J9. Tube Westminster, Victoria.*

When designs were being considered in the late 19thC for the Roman Catholic Cathedral of Westminster, intended to be London's most important Catholic church, a Neo-Gothic structure at first seemed the inevitable choice. In the end, however, an early Christian approach was courageously adopted, against all the prevalent dictates of the era. The result of this far-sighted decision is a building of great originality, a strange Byzantine basilica unique in London and cleverly avoiding a false comparison with nearby *Westminster Abbey*.

The cathedral was built under the direction of J.F. Bentley between 1895–1903, using as a model Santa Sophia in Istanbul, together with some Italian Renaissance ideas, the most striking of which is the huge campanile, similar to that of Siena Cathedral but in red brick with lighter stone striping. The top of the tower, 273ft (83m) high, can be visited in summer.

The interior is deeply impressive, with a massive open space created by the great nave, supporting a roof of four shallow domes, pure Byzantine in inspiration. The decoration is still incomplete, with rough brick exposed above the lower levels contributing to the solemn effect. The piers of the nave are giant columns of dark green marble, supposedly from the same quarry as those in Santa Sophia. Other marbles, dramatically patterned in grey and black, cover the walls, and over the altar is a great baldacchino of even more brightly-coloured marble, but again to a restrained design. It is intended that eventually the whole interior be covered with mosaics; unfortunately, those parts completed do not reflect the grandeur of the overall conception and tend towards fussiness. The outstanding works of art in the cathedral are the **Stations of the Cross**, reliefs carried out by Eric Gill in 1913–18.

Westminster, Palace of 🏛 ☆
Parliament Sq., SW1 ☎ *219–4272 (House of Commons), 219–3107 (House of Lords). Map* **18***I11* 🔲 ✿ 🏛
Visiting arrangements subject to repeated change, check first. During parliamentary sittings admittance to public galleries from St Stephen's entrance. Tube Westminster.
The effect is stunning: sheer size combines with immense variety and inventive detail to create an architectural triumph so instantly recognizable that it has come to symbolize the very system of government, representative democracy, housed within. In fact, this riverside complex of buildings is only the new home of the mother of parliaments, a high Victorian exercise in medievalism. The buildings are often known simply as the Houses of Parliament.

A royal palace was probably moved from Winchester to Westminster in about 1000, being established on the Island of Thorney in the marshes next to an existing monastery, and Edward the Confessor began an ambitious building programme in 1050–65, the monastery becoming *Westminster Abbey*. The Norman kings followed his lead and William Rufus, the Conqueror's son, built Westminster Hall in 1097–99, at the time almost certainly the largest hall in Europe. When in residence, medieval kings would call their councils of noblemen to meet at Westminster, a forerunner of the House of Lords. In 1265, a powerful baron called Simon de Montfort began the practice of calling additional councils of knights and burghers to represent the shires and towns. Meeting together from 1332, these subsequently became the House of Commons. A medieval king was not obliged to call a parliament, and only did so when he needed the co-operation of his lords and knights. In theory, they came to advise him, but, in practice, he needed their assistance in the raising of taxes. From this grew the fact, unpalatable to medieval monarchs, that the country could not be governed without the consent of lords and commons.

In the 16thC, when Henry VIII moved his residence to the nearby Whitehall Palace, the Palace of Westminster became the permanent and more exclusive base of Parliament, the Commons using from 1550 the abandoned royal chapel of St Stephen. Westminster Hall was not used for Parliament, however, but retained for the royal courts.

The 17thC saw the long struggle which would eventually lead to the constitutional pre-eminence of Parliament. In 1642 Charles I attempted to assert the royal power and crush the Commons, losing both crown and head in the process. Since his last desperate entry in 1648 to arrest parliamentary opponents, no monarch has entered the Commons. In 1660 Charles II was recalled to the throne and the struggle between King and Parliament was renewed. During the 18thC, the monarchy lost ground steadily and parliamentary government became a reality, with a prime minister appointed by the monarch according to the electoral wishes of the country.

In constitutional terms, Parliament consists of Monarch, Lords and Commons, all of whom have to assent to the laws by which the country is governed. But, by a process of recurring struggle, members of the Commons have come to have the dominant role – the Lords can now only delay legislation by one year and royal assent is never refused. The Lords is still the highest Court of Appeal in the land. A much criticized survival is that the Lords is still largely composed of hereditary peers, although an increasing number of peers are now created for life only. The system has developed slowly, through reforms and bitter struggles, with a unique combination of traditional ritual and democratic reality. Today, the palace is still a web of ancient regulations: there are opera hats in boxes in the Commons so that the hatless can comply with regulations.

Tightened security limits access to the interior of the palace. The medieval royal palace, with its 17th–18thC additions, was largely destroyed by fire in 1834. In 1840, rebuilding began, with only the old cloister, Westminster Hall and the crypt of St Stephen's Chapel being preserved. The architect was Sir Charles Barry, with the younger A.W.N. Pugin as his assistant. Barry was essentially a Classicist, forced to work in the Gothic idiom by the brief. Pugin, on the other hand, was a passionate medievalist – indeed, it was his meticulous drawings that won the commission. The House of Lords chamber was complete by 1847, the Commons by 1850. Both men died in 1852, and the work was not finally completed until 1860.

The most splendid views of the palace are from Westminster Bridge or across the river, taking in the great regular facade Barry constructed along the riverside, with large asymmetrical towers at either end: the huge square **Victoria Tower** to the s and the more slender and original **Clock Tower** to the N, the superb clock of which is Britain's most authoritative. Although this tower is often known as **Big Ben**, that name actually applies to the huge bell inside the clock itself, named after Benjamin Hall, Commissioner of Works at the time.

From the landward side, the visitor sees several different facades and views of the towers, spreading to N and S behind the central bulk of medieval Westminster Hall. Golden-brown Yorkshire limestone was chosen, but it was badly quarried and has needed constant repairs. Every part of the exterior is covered with tracery, statues and pinnacles, with a dominant pattern that echoes Henry VII's chapel over the road.

Of the few remaining medieval elements of the palace, **Westminster Hall★** is outstanding. The lower walls are the oldest part, dating from the late 11thC. In 1394–99, Richard II replaced the upper walls and roof with the remarkable structure seen today. It is one of the world's greatest timber constructions, and the apogee of English Gothic, a huge and beautiful oak **hammerbeam roof**, with wonderfully-carved tracery and angels on the ends of the beams. Statues of early kings, also dating from Richard II's reign, can be seen in niches. The only other survivor from the medieval palace is the **Jewel Tower**, across Abingdon St. and actually closer to the abbey. Strongly fortified and moated, it was built in 1365 as a royal treasure house, and was later used to store records.

There are two public entrances to the Victorian parts of the palace. For those wishing to 'lobby' their members of parliament (a practice whereby constituents can ask their representative to come to the lobby to discuss a particular issue), there is St Stephen's Porch beside the hall. This entrance leads above the medieval crypt, now the parliament chapel, and to the great lobby beneath an elaborate, spiral lantern which can be seen from outside. This entrance also gives access to the public galleries of the two debating chambers.

For the tour of the palace, which is sometimes allowed, entrance is made by the Norman Porch next to the Victoria Tower. The gate beneath the tower itself is used by the Queen only, for official ceremonies such as the **State Opening of Parliament** (see *Calendar of events* in *Planning*). The porch leads through to the **Robing Room**, a spectacular panelled chamber which amply demonstrates Pugin's effective use of Gothic and Tudor motifs; note especially the ornate fireplace. The **Royal Gallery** beyond is even more spectacular, with a colourful ceramic floor and a series of gift statues of monarchs.

Through the Prince's Chamber is the **House of Lords**, an absolutely stunning chamber surrounded by sumptuous red leather benches. The leather and wood, the rich colours, and the deep calm make it feel like a monumental clubland lounge, an analogy not altogether inappropriate for the more detached, learned deliberations of the upper house. The Lord Chancellor, who chairs the debates, sits on a red-covered woolsack, and behind him is the royal throne the Lords still maintain (the State Opening takes place in this chamber) beneath an extraordinarily fine gilded canopy, Pugin's masterpiece.

Beyond the Peers' Lobby, Central Lobby and Commons' Lobby is the **House of Commons** itself. It was burnt out during an air raid in 1941 and the entrance arch has been rebuilt, using some of the damaged stones, between statues of *Winston Churchill* and *Lloyd George*. The chamber itself was rebuilt in 1945–50 in a plainer style – neither Pugin-elaborated nor obviously modern. The governing party occupies the benches on one side, the opposition the other. Neither side is supposed to cross the red lines in the carpet, traditionally the distance apart of two drawn swords.

The rest of the Houses of Parliament, consisting of over 1,000 rooms and two miles of corridor, is not open to the public. It is a place of work: committees struggling over the details of legislation and MPs taking care of their constituency business. Restaurants and terraces for the MPs look out over the river, as does Pugin's magnificent **House of Lords Library**.

Whitechapel Art Gallery �

80 Whitechapel High St., E1 ☎ *377–0107. Map* **13***F18* 🔄
🔄 ⬛ *Open Tues–Sun 11.00–17.30. Tube Aldgate East.*

A scruffy parade of shops in the East End is an unlikely place to find one of England's most celebrated Art Nouveau buildings, but there it is, with a large arched doorway in a plain facade topped by a delightful foliage relief. It was built in 1897–99 by C. Harrison Townsend, a follower of the influential Arts and Crafts Movement, who also designed the Horniman Museum in *Dulwich*. The gallery currently enjoys a high reputation for staging important temporary exhibitions of modern art.

Whitehall

Map **10***G–H. Tube Charing Cross, Westminster.*

The word Whitehall is so firmly embedded in English that it is applied to people, institutions and buildings quite irrespective of whether they belong to the street of that name. Nevertheless, Whitehall has not changed as it is still lined by large government offices, and is still Britain's administrative centre. Running s from *Trafalgar Square* towards *Westminster*, it began to take on this character in the later 17thC, as government departments began building around the Royal Palace of Whitehall.

Before 1514, Whitehall Palace was York Place, a house belonging to the Archbishop of York. Henry VIII took it over from Cardinal Wolsey in 1530 and turned it into a huge rambling palace, and in 1619–25 Inigo Jones' magnificent *Banqueting House* was added, the only building that survives.

The northern end of Whitehall resembles any other commercial street in central London until the **Admiralty** is encountered on the w side, a brick building of 1722–26 with a large Ionic portico. In front is a handsome screen designed by Robert Adam in 1759–61 with winged seahorses surmounting the gates. Government buildings of about 1900 are followed by the Banqueting House, with the attractive Welsh Office, occupying a private residence of 1772, soon after. On the w side, opposite, is the *Horse Guards Parade* built in 1750–60 to William Kent's designs. Next to it is Dover House (the Scottish Office) with an elegant facade of 1787. Unfortunately, Whitehall at this point is dominated by the great bulk of the Ministry of Defence building, a Portland stone monster finished as late as 1959. Somewhere beneath it are Henry VIII's wine cellars, surviving from the old palace. The diminutive looking modern statues in front depict *Sir Walter Raleigh* and *Field-Marshal Montgomery*. Opposite is *Downing Street*.

From here, Whitehall becomes Parliament St., with massive 19thC government buildings in Italian Renaissance style. The Cenotaph of 1919, the national monument to Britain's war dead, is in the centre of Parliament St.

Beneath the offices, with a public entrance in King Charles St., are the fascinating **Cabinet War Rooms** (🔄 open Tues–Sun 10.00–17.50). This fortified bunker, deep in the bowels of the earth, housed Churchill's emergency centre of operations during the war. It can now be seen just as it was, with maps, telephones and even the great man's cigars on display.

133

Wimbledon

Map 20D4. Tube Southfields, Wimbledon, Wimbledon Park.
The modern tennis duels which have made this sw suburb
world famous had an earlier counterpart, on **Wimbledon
Common**, a large expanse of heath once notorious for settling
disputes of honour. The **All-England Tennis Courts**
themselves are in Church Rd., and the fortnight
championships in June – July transform the area, attracting
both tennis fans and those who come for the copious
strawberries and cream and champagne. Inside the splendid
ivy-clad main building is a **Lawn Tennis Museum** (🖾 open
Mon–Sat 11.00–17.00, Sun 14.00–17.00).

The Zoo 🏛 ☆

Regent's Park, NW1 ☎ *722–3333. Map 2B7* 🖾 ⚓ 🍴 ♿
*Open Apr–Oct Mon–Sat 9.00–18.00, Sun 9.00–19.00;
Nov–Mar 10.00–16.00. Tube Regent's Park, Mornington
Crescent, Camden Town.*
More properly named the gardens of the Zoological Society of
London, the zoo occupies an attractive portion of *Regent's
Park* bisected by the *Grand Union Canal*. Founded in 1826, it is
the oldest such institution in the world, and one of the most
important. Together with Whipsnade Park in Bedfordshire,
where the animals are kept in large open paddocks in the
countryside, London Zoo has no less than 5,000 species and, as
well as showing animals to the public, it enjoys worldwide
repute in the fields of conservation and animal medicine.

Innovation has changed the ways of showing animals, and
bold architectural experiments have displaced the old iron cage
approach. In many cases the animals are in larger compounds,
designed to reflect their natural habitats and separated from the
public by moats rather than bars. The most spectacular
example, the **Mappin Terraces**, were opened as early as 1914.
Here, an artificial mountain is divided up into layers, devoted to
pelicans in a pool at the bottom, with wild pigs, bears and
mountain sheep and goats on succeeding levels. Similarly, the
big cats can be seen at close range in their dens through glass or
watched as they roam their paddocks stocked with suitable
vegetation. These animals do not have that bored, lethargic
appearance that can make zoos so depressing. Precisely because
they are so active, the monkeys and apes in the **Michael Sobell
Pavilion** (opened in 1972) are perhaps the most enjoyable of the
zoo's creatures. More morbidly alluring is one of the world's
most extensive collections of reptiles and insects, poisonous
snakes and giant spiders.

Two special features are **The Moonlight World**, where
nocturnal animals can be seen behaving as if in the dead of
night, and the **children's zoo and farm**, with tame animals
which will give children rides or can be handled.

London Zoo also has some important examples of modern
architecture. The **Penguin Pool** of the 1930s used pre-stressed
concrete in a pioneering way, and still looks modern. The
Snowdon Aviary, opened in 1965, contains a variety of birds in
a large open space – superbly functional even if criticized for
looking rather like a collapsed radio mast.

The zoo has ambitious plans to modernize its display still
further – projected are a huge glass-fronted 'underwater world'
and a self-contained North American environment. With their
arrival over the coming few years, the remaining old-fashioned
cages will finally go.

Where to stay

London's hotels were described, in one well-bruited year, as the most expensive in the world, then 12 months later found themselves easing to a less-publicized 22nd position in the same *Financial Times* league table. It must be said, of course, that such calculations are greatly influenced by the value of the pound sterling against the visitors' currency, given to considerable fluctuation over recent years, though it is an inescapable fact that prices have recently taken another enormous leap.

The same differing viewpoints attend the hotels' reputations, while the most reflective judges argue that, at both ends of the price spectrum, standards are much the same as those elsewhere in Europe. Though London has not escaped the international trend towards the provision of fewer services, it might be contended that overall standards have improved in recent years.

Categories of hotel

At the most expensive end of the spectrum, what might be described as the grand old hotels of London bear witness to the Englishman's notion of style as an attribute not to be worn on the sleeve. They know that a gentleman does not have to prove anything, and neither do they. They assume that quality, though hideously expensive these days, is timeless, and so can seem old-fashioned to some. They were built for people with ancient country estates who needed a home-from-home in town. The traveller with the resources to understand this will enjoy them. Others may prefer something less English.

Most of the international chains have at least one establishment in London, offering the style of accommodation and service to which their regular patrons are accustomed, though at rather cosmopolitan prices. As most of them offer conference facilities, and are popular with the international businessman, advance booking is essential.

Two of the British chains, Grand Metropolitan and Trust House Forte, are increasingly international in their reach. The two are similar, though 'Grand Met' restricts itself more to the middle and upper range of hotel. Trust House Forte has nothing to do with the National Trust. Perhaps because the chain includes utilitarian as well as luxury hotels noisy opposition greeted its attempt to take over the Savoy group.

The cheaper type of British hotel is often known as a boarding house, or a 'bed-and-breakfast' (or simply 'B & B'). As this last name implies, the dining-room of such hotels, if they have one, is generally the least important of their services. However, at their best they are clean, comfortable and friendly, with all the charm of family-run hotels to be found throughout Europe, and can constitute a restful base.

Booking

If you want to choose the particular hotel you stay in, advance booking is essential, preferably at least a month in advance. Depending on the time of year, you might be lucky with short-notice reservations, but you might have to be flexible.

Advance booking of an inexpensive to medium-priced hotel can be arranged by writing to the **London Tourist Board**, 26 Grosvenor Gardens, SW1. Write at least six weeks in advance, suggesting a price bracket and any general preference for location, and the organization will then make a provisional booking in your name before writing to you to confirm it.

Hotels

A special good value promotion is run by the **British Tourist Authority**, embracing some 75–100 establishments in the capital from well-known hotels to no-frills bed-and-breakfast places. Details and booking forms from Thames Tower, Black's Rd., London W6, or from the many other British Tourist Authority offices throughout the world.

Given some flexibility, it is possible to make an instant booking at **London Visitor & Convention Bureau Information Centres** at Heathrow Airport or Victoria Station (see *Useful addresses* in *Basic information*).

Price

See *How to use this book* for the price guidelines corresponding to the symbols used in all hotel entries. London hotels usually charge by the person, rather than by the room, and sometimes include breakfast in the price, although it is increasingly only a 'continental breakfast' of toast or croissants and coffee, with a supplement for the fried 'English breakfast'. Check whether VAT (Value Added Tax) is included.

Service is usually included. If you are very pleased with the service, give a small tip to the chambermaid or receptionist.

Meals

The dining facilities range from some of the best restaurants in London to those which do not expect to attract most of their guests. What they nearly all offer, at extra cost, is the great British breakfast of bacon and eggs or kippers. Residential terms, with an evening meal included in the price, are rare.

Hotels classified by area

Bayswater/Paddington
Great Western Royal ▮▮▯
Royal Lancaster ▮▮▮▮
Belgravia/Knightsbridge
Basil Street ▮▮▯
Berkeley Hotel ▮▮▮▮ �
Capital ▮▮▮▮
Eleven Cadogan
  Gardens ▮▮▮▮
Hyatt Carlton
  Tower ▮▮▮▮ �
Sheraton Park Tower ▮▮▮▮ �
Bloomsbury
Imperial ▮▯ ❧
Jenkins ▯ ▯ ❧
Kingsley ▮▯ ❧
City
Great Eastern ▮▮▯
Covent Garden/Strand
Fielding ▯
Savoy ▮▮▮▮ �
Strand Palace ▮▯ ❧
Hampstead
Sandringham ▯
Swiss Cottage ▮▮▯
Kensington
Alexander ▮▮▯
Blakes ▮▮▮
Gore ▮▮▯ ❧
Kensington Close ▮▯ to ▮▮▯
Kensington Palace ▮▮▮
Onslow Court ▮▯ to ▮▮▯ ❧
Pembridge Court ▮▯ to ▮▮▯

Marylebone/West End
Berners ▮▮▮
Churchill ▮▮▮▮ �
Cumberland ▮▮▮
Durrants ▮▮▯ ❧
Merryfield House ▯ ▮
Montcalm ▮▮▮▮
Portman Court Hotel ▮▯ ▮
Portman Inter-Continental ▮▮▮▮
White House ▮▮▮ ❧
Mayfair
Britannia ▮▮▮▮
Brown's ▮▮▮▮
Claridge's ▮▮▮▮ �
Connaught ▮▮▮▮ �
Dorchester ▮▮▮▮ �
Grosvenor House ▮▮▮▮ �
Hilton ▮▮▮▮
Inn on the Park ▮▮▮▮ �
Inter-Continental ▮▮▮▮ �
May Fair ▮▮▮▮
Westbury ▮▮▮▮
Piccadilly
Athenaeum ▮▮▮▮
New Piccadilly ▮▮▮▮ �
Park Lane ▮▮▮▮
Ritz ▮▮▮▮ ▲
St James's
Dukes ▮▮▮▮
Stafford ▮▮▮▮
Victoria
Ebury Court ▮▯ to ▮▮▯
Goring ▮▮▮▮

Alexander

9 Sumner Pl., SW7
☎ *581–1591/5* ☏ *917133. Map*
15K5 ▮▮ ⚋ *34* ▭ *34* ▭ ▭ ▣
▣ ▨▨ *Tube South Kensington.*

Location: South Kensington. S.J.
Perelman once issued the entreaty
"Please don't give me nothing to
remember you by", but they
haven't forgotten his stays at The
Alexander; they named a room
after him. If he observed the
strangeness of a hotel in a street so
attractive that it is not allowed to
hang a sign, he didn't say so. The
Alexander is announced only by a
brass plate outside, and maintains
a similar note of restful discretion
inside. It is a Victorian house, in
which all bedrooms have been
impeccably modernized, with a
lovely, high-walled garden for the
use of guests. Those visitors who
have a bar at home will feel
comfortable in the self-service
lounge, operating on an honesty
system. Another insouciant touch
is the use of a taxi service to fetch
meals from restaurants, but the
Alexander's guests are more
inclined to seek out for themselves
the local *haute cuisine.*
▨ ✲ ▭ ▱ ⚓ ☗

Athenaeum

116 Piccadilly, W1 ☎ *499–3463*
☏ *261589. Map 9H8* ⚋ *112*
▭ *112* ▦▦ ▭ ▭ ▣ ▣ ▨▨
Tube Green Park.

*Location: West End, between
Mayfair and Green Park.* Although
it is especially well known for its
unrivalled selection of malt
whiskies, this smallish, pristine
1940s hotel is full of good ideas. A
quaintly-named Lady Athenaeum
Club makes sure lone female
travellers are welcomed and
pampered. Guests who want to jog
in the park are loaned tracksuits.
Attention to detail is the keynote.
If you have an afternoon nap, your
sheets will be changed again before
bedtime. Unlike so many present-
day hotels, the Athenaeum doesn't
stint on towels – there are mounds
of them, and luxury bathrooms too.
✲ ♿ ▭ ▱ ⚓ ☗

Basil Street Hotel

8 Basil St., SW3 ☎ *581–3311*
☏ *28379. Map 16/6.* ▮▮ ⚋ *96*
▭ *70* ▭ ⇌ ▭ ▣ ▣ ▨▨
Tube Knightsbridge.

*Location: Knightsbridge, behind
Harrods.* Much loved not only for
the high standard of service it
provides, but also for its depth of
personality. A woman's hotel in
the days when ladies came from the
country to do their shopping in
Knightsbridge, it still runs the
female counterpart to a
gentlemen's club. In the hotel,
however, guests of both sexes are
offered what the Basil describes
with some accuracy as "an island
of hospitality in our brusque,
modern world". Decorated with
British and oriental antiques, in an
Edwardian building part of which
was once the booking hall of a
station, the Basil has a cosiness that
belies its size; it remains small
enough to offer the personal touch,
but sufficiently large to provide the
services of a first-class hotel.
✲ ▭ ▱ ⚓

Berkeley Hotel 🏨

Wilton Pl., SW1 ☎ *235–6000*
☏ *919252. Map 16/7* ▮▮▮ ⚋ *159*
▭ *159* ▭ ▭ ▭ ▣ *Tube*
Knightsbridge.

*Location: Knightsbridge, opposite
Hyde Park.* Noel Coward's old
Berkeley is gone, yet much of its
character has re-emerged in the
new one, built by the same
management in 1972. "The last
really de luxe hotel to be built in
Europe", they claim. De luxe
rather than grand because, by
today's standards, it is small for a
hotel of this style. The hotel is
known for its service, organized
separately on every floor, has a
rooftop swimming pool, a sauna,
cinema, beauty salon and one of
London's better French
restaurants, as well as Le
Perroquet bar and the Buttery.
✲ ♿ ▭ ▱ ⇌ ⚓ ☗ ●

Berners

Berners St., W1 ☎ *636–1629*
☏ *25759. Map 10E10* ▮▮ ⚋ *235*
▭ *235* ⇌ ▭ ▣ ▣ ▣ ▨▨
Tube Tottenham Court Road.

Location: Off Oxford St. A
magnificent job of refurbishment
was carried out a few years ago in
this grand old hotel, the splendid
interior of which seems at odds
with its never having been famous
or fashionable. The location is
wrong for that, yet right for
shopping, and near to theatreland.
The rooms are spacious and
pleasantly decorated, and those
round the central well are very
quiet. A dozen rooms are specially
designed for the benefit of
handicapped people. The Berners
has a carvery-type restaurant.
✲ ♿ ▭ ▱ ✇ ⚓ ☗ ☗

137

Blakes

33–35 Roland Gdns., SW7
☎ *370–6701* ✆ *8813500.* Map
15K4 ▮▮▮ 🛏 50 ▭ 50 ⥮ AE ◉
◎ VISA *Tube South Kensington.*

*Location: South Kensington, off
Old Brompton Rd.* Mandatory for
media folk, who are suitably at
home in an hotel owned by a
designer. It shows, too, with that
beautiful birdcage, brass bedsteads
and a sunken bed in one suite. And
which other small London hotel
serves pastrami on rye? Worldwide
self-dialling telephones in every
room, one of the best hotel
restaurants in town, and what the
management describes as "all the
best services to be expected from a
first-class hotel", all in a Victorian
terrace.
🖾 ▭ 🖅 🥢

Britannia

*Grosvenor Sq. (entrance Adam's
Row), W1* ☎ *629–9400*
✆ *23941.* Map **9G8** ▮▮▮ 🛏 356 ▭
356 ⊟⊟ ⥮ AE CB ◉ VISA
Tube Bond Street.

*Location: Mayfair, near Oxford St.
and Hyde Park.* This very large
Georgian square, lined with
embassies, has largely been rebuilt
and restored, and there is little to
suggest that behind its facades lies
a large hotel. Even more
surprisingly, the Britannia was
built only in 1970, and its interior
is a well-achieved blend of original
and reproduction Georgiana.
Nonetheless, its built-in 'pub' can
claim to stand on the site where a
Cabinet meeting learned from a
horse-borne messenger that
Wellington had beaten Napoleon
at Waterloo. The hotel has
undergone extensive
refurbishment of late, with the
creation of fewer but more
spacious bedrooms. It now sports
an Anglo-American restaurant and
bar, and a Japanese restaurant,
Shogun.
‡ ▭ 🖅 🥢 🌱 🏺 ▾

Brown's

22–24 Dover St., W1
☎ *493–6020* ✆ *28686.* Map **9G9**
▮▮▮ 🛏 125 ▭ 125 ⥮ AE CB ◉
◎ VISA *Tube Green Park.*

*Location: Mayfair, near Bond St.
and Piccadilly.* The original Mr
Brown was butler to Lord Byron,
and the hotel he founded became
the most renowned among those
which set out to be London
homes-from-home for the gentry.
It still retains this character in the
charm, individuality and style of
its rooms, though many are, by
modern standards, rather small
and gloomy. Theodore Roosevelt
was married from Brown's, and
FDR and Eleanor honeymooned
there; the Dutch Government in
exile declared war on Japan and
Queen Wilhelmina and Princess
Juliana stayed here. Brown's still
takes pride in maintaining the
privacy of its guests, but life is
inevitably less serene in the late
20thC. It is now owned by the
Trust House Forte chain.
🖾 ‡ ▭ 🖅 🏺

Capital 🏨

Basil St., SW3 ☎ *589–5171*
✆ *919042.* Map **16I6** 🛏 56
▭ 56 ⊟⊟ ⥮ AE CB ◉ ◎ VISA
Tube Knightsbridge.

*Location: Knightsbridge, behind
Harrods.* So friendly and informal
that the designation 'luxury hotel'
seems unfairly intimidating. Yet
this sophisticated little modern
hotel is the sort of place that
provides each guest with a
toothbrush and bathrobe, leaves a
rose for every lady, and has a
concierge who attends to every
need. Newly redecorated public
rooms and reception area highlight
the feeling of intimate luxury.
Most of the rooms can be joined to
make suites, and its layout makes
for privacy. It is thus ideal for
families, though for reasons which
are harder to pin down, it is also
popular with Grand Prix drivers.
The Capital has a very good
French restaurant (see
Restaurants).
‡ ⅗ ▭ 🖅 ▾

Churchill 🏨

30 Portman Sq., W1
☎ *486–5800* ✆ *264831.* Map
8F7 ▮▮▮ 🛏 489 ▭ 489 ⊟⊟ ⥮
AE CB ◉ ◎ VISA *Tube Marble
Arch.*

Location: Off Oxford St. The
glittering, marbled foyer is a
suitably impressive introduction to
this modern luxury hotel, part of
the Loews group, which sits in a
busy but elegant square behind
Selfridge's store. The public
rooms and the thickly-carpeted
bedrooms are in a more relaxed,
but equally sumptuous, Regency
style. The Churchill has a good
French restaurant, and a 24hr
lounge for drinks and snacks.
Service is efficient, unobtrusive
and faultless.
‡ ⅗ ▭ 🖅 🥢 🏺

Claridge's 🏨
Brook St., W1 ☎ 629–8860
🕾 21872. Map 9F8 ▥▥ ☎ 205
and 55 suites 🛏 260 ⬜ ⇄ AE
🔘 🔘 VISA Tube Bond Street.
Location: Mayfair, near Oxford St.
Visiting royals and statesmen are
inclined to choose Claridge's
which, despite its fame, is
imperturbably discreet. No bar,
because such trappings don't fit a
country house, even if it is in the
middle of London. Drink in the
sitting room (not 'lounge' – it isn't
an airport), where a small orchestra
plays at lunchtime and in the
evening. Nor would it be very
dignified to publish a tariff, so they
don't. Lots of Art Deco, but the
tone is better set by log fires in the
suites. A guest who has been
shopping returns with a brace of
pheasants; without batting an
eyelid, the porter carries them for
her as if they were Gucci suitcases.
‡ ☐ 🖾 🦞 🛎

Connaught 🏨
16 Carlos Pl., W1 ☎ 499–7070.
Map 9G8 ▥▥ ☎ 90 🛏 90 ⬜ ⇄
🔘 Tube Bond Street.
Location: Mayfair, near Hyde Park
and Oxford St. The finest of
London's grand old hotels,
according to its devoted following,
and certainly the best
gastronomically (see Restaurants).
The Connaught is smaller than
other hotels in its peer group, and
accordingly offers a little less in the
way of facilities and services, but
that kind of expansiveness isn't its
style; the luxury is more personal.
Likewise, the cosy public rooms
make a virtue of their intimacy.
The clubby atmosphere fits this
part of Mayfair.
‡ ☐ 🖾 🦞 🍷

Cumberland
Marble Arch, W1 ☎ 262–1234,
reservations 723–2036 🕾 22215.
Map 8F7 ▥▥ ☎ 910 🛏 910 ⬜
AE CB 🔘 🔘 VISA Tube Marble
Arch.
Location: Oxford St., near Hyde
Park. This bustling hotel at the
busy end of Oxford St. became
something of a London institution
in its days as flagship of the old Joe
Lyons group. It has been sprucing
itself up since it was subsumed into
the Trust House Forte chain, and
has acquired country house suites
on one floor to match its English
restaurant (with English wines) and
roast-beef carvery. There's
even grouse on the Glorious

Twelfth (of Aug), but such
flourishes don't alter the fact that a
hotel so cavernous inevitably feeds
off tour parties, conventions,
exhibitions and receptions.
‡ ☐ 🖾 🛎

Dorchester 🏨
Park Lane, W1 ☎ 629–8888
🕾 887704. Map 9G8 ▥▥ ☎ 265
and 4 roof garden suites 🛏 269
▤▤ partial ⬜ ⇄ AE CB 🔘 🔘 VISA
Tube Hyde Park Corner.
Location: Overlooking Hyde Park.
With its stately terraces, the
Dorchester looks like an ocean
liner that has somehow been
moored on Park Lane. Bought in
1985 by the world's richest man,
the Sultan of Brunei, the hotel has
been revamped without
diminishing its grandeur. The
large, spacious public rooms
include a bar with a pianist, and
there is a roof garden. The
considerable facilities extend to a
hotel bakery. The bar in each room
is well stocked with champagne
and Jack Daniel's. In service, the
mood is one of detached efficiency.
(See Restaurants.)
‡ ⅃ ☐ 🖾 🦞 🛎 🍷 ♫ ⅌

Dukes Hotel
34–36 St James's Pl., SW1
☎ 491–4840 🕾 28283. Map 9H9
▥▥ ☎ 41 and 11 suites 🛏 52 ⬜
⇄ AE CB 🔘 🔘 VISA Tube Green
Park.
Location: St James's, near Green
Park and St James's Palace. In a
gas-lit courtyard, a small but
rather grand hotel occupying what
was once presumably someone's
Upstairs-Downstairs town house.
Dukes was pleased when an
enthusiastic guest described it as
"the smallest castle in England".
Only in London could a location
be so pretty and tranquil yet so
close to the throbbing heart of the
city. Despite its being almost
claustrophobically small, Dukes
offers full hotel facilities, including
24hr service.
⬜ ‡ ☐ 🖾 🛎

Durrants Hotel ♥
George St., W1 ☎ 935–8131
🕾 894919. Map 9F9 ▥▥ ☎ 100
🛏 70 ⇄ AE 🔘 🔘 VISA Tube Bond
Street.
Location: Near Oxford St. In a
street which is, as its name
suggests, Georgian, this attractive
small hotel is perennially popular,
not least because it offers excellent
value. A portrait of a Durrant

Hotels

patriarch, dating back to 1782, hangs among the delightful collection of oils and prints. There are leather chairs and pretty desks in the writing room, antiques on sale to guests, an open fire in the bar, Devenish beer in the bottle and sherry on draught, pheasant for dinner when it's in season, and brass bedsteads.

♨ ▢ those rooms with bath ⌨ ♨⚫

Ebury Court
26 Ebury St., SW1 ☎ *730–8147. Map* **17J8** ▢ *to* ▥ ☎ *39* ▭ *12* ⌧ ⌨ **VISA** *Tube Victoria.*

Location: Victoria/Pimlico.
Cottagey, quaint and under the proud eye of the owners, Mr and Mrs Topham, who have been there since the 1930s and live on the premises. To be a guest is thus to stay in the Topham's home. Their full English breakfast includes haddock and kippers, there is home-baked bread and roast duckling for dinner at the weekends. In order to have a drink though, it is necessary to pay a nominal fee to join the Topham's club; this is no place for libertines, despite one or two four-poster beds. In the foyer, a list is posted detailing the times at which the Guards pass on their way to Buckingham Palace; they are best seen from a balconied first-floor room.
♨ ▢ ⌨

Eleven Cadogan Gardens
11 Cadogan Gdns., SW3 ☎ *730–3426* ⓣ *8813318. Map* **16J7** ▥ ☎ *58* ▭ *58* ⌧ *Tube Sloane Square.*

Location: Belgravia, near Sloane Square. So discreet that it has no sign even on the door, which is kept locked. No wonder it is favoured by diplomats. Late Victorian exterior, with decor to match: a glorious marble fireplace in one room; a drawing room with open fire. Full English breakfast in bed, and they'll send out for a bottle of champagne (the establishment has no liquor licence); they'll even deliver you to the airport in a Rolls.
⌧ ⌨ ♨⚫ ⚓

Fielding ♣
4 Broad Court, Bow St., WC2 ☎ *836–8305. Map* **10F11** ▢ ☎ *26* ▭ *26* **AE** ⓓ ⓒ **VISA** *Tube Covent Garden.*

Location: Covent Garden. Henry Fielding, author of *Tom Jones*, was a magistrate at the nearby Bow St. court, hence the name of this inexpensive hotel in a pleasant pedestrianized corner of Covent Garden. Another writer, Graham Greene, is an occasional guest, as are a good sprinkling of other well-known faces who wish to keep a low profile, including performers at the Royal Opera House. An ambience full of character, and a parrot to greet guests at the hotel. The rooms are in general inexpensively decorated, and there are mostly showers rather than baths. The owner and his family are in attendance.
▢ ⌨ ♨⚫

Gore ♣
189 Queen's Gate, SW7 ☎ *584–6601* ⓣ *296244. Map* **15I4** ▥ ☎ *56* ▭ *56* ⌧ **AE** ⓓ ⓒ **VISA** *Tube South Kensington.*

Location: Kensington, near the Albert Hall and Hyde Park. With ivy outside, potted plants inside, and cane furniture in the more expensive rooms (with beautifully tiled modern bathrooms), this warm and welcoming hotel reflects the tastes of its enthusiastic owners, who are usually on hand. One honeymoonish room has a four-poster, real log fire and leaded windows, but the Gore also caters for many business visitors from Continental Europe. There is a small, intimate bar, and a coffee-shop which is open throughout the day.
♨ ▢ ⌨ ☗

Goring
15 Beeston Pl., Grosvenor Gdns., SW1 ☎ *834–8211* ⓣ *919166. Map* **17J9** ▥ ☎ *90* ▭ *90* ⌧ ⌧ **AE** ⓓ ⓒ **VISA** *Tube Victoria.*

Location: Victoria, near Buckingham Palace. A book on Buckingham Palace written by the hotel's founder is provided for each guest along with the Bible, and royal carriages may occasionally be seen calling at the Goring to collect diplomat guests. The thorough-minded Mr Goring was the first hotelier in the world to fit all of his rooms with central heating and baths, and he would undoubtedly be pleased to know that the hotel is still in the family three generations later. There are, after all, few full-service hotels of this size still in private hands. Some of the original furniture, including brass bedsteads, is still in use, and the policy has clearly been to renovate rather than replace. The public rooms are more elegant, and inviting, with an excellent writing room, a small bar and a good restaurant that is worth sampling.

‡ ☐ ⌧ ⁒ ☫ ☗ Ⴤ

Great Eastern

Liverpool St., EC2 ☎ *283–4363*
☏ *886812. Map* **13E17** ▥ ☙ *157*
▭ *129* ▦ ⚏ AE CB ◉ ◉ VISA
Closed Christmas. Tube Liverpool Street.
Location: The City. Away from the West End (though only a few stops on the tube), and in the heart of old London. Handy, too, for those wishing to travel on to the eastern counties of England or to Continental Europe. There is a genuinely traditional quality about railway hotels like this one. Spacious, high-ceilinged bedrooms, though with twin beds more available than doubles, and simple fittings. Some bedrooms have wash basins, but the majority also have bathrooms, usually with big, deep baths, though often without showers. High ceilings in the public rooms, too, with ornate mouldings. A magnificent stained-glass dome hangs over the carvery (one of three restaurants in the building). The cocktail bar and the hotel's pub serve real cask-conditioned ale to suit discerning beer drinkers.

‡ ☐ ⌧ ☗ Ⴤ

Great Western Royal

Praed St., W2 ☎ *723–8064*
☏ *263972. Map* **7F5** ▥ ☙ *165*
▭ *165* ▦ ⚏ AE CB ◉ ◉ VISA
Closed Christmas. Tube Paddington.
Location: Paddington. When the great engineer Brunel built this hotel, he intended it to be the starting point of journeys by way of his adjoining, and architecturally magnificent, station and Great Western Railway, via Bristol and his Great Western steamship, to New York. It has slumbered a little since then, but has in recent years smartened itself up. After a period of ill-advised Scandinavian affectations, it is returning to solid Englishness, as befits its magnificent marble bathrooms, though ice-making machines on every floor are a useful hands-across the Atlantic gesture.

‡ ☐ ⌧ ☗ Ⴤ

Grosvenor House ▦

Park Lane, W1 ☎ *499–6363*
☏ *24871. Map* **8G7** ▥ ☙ *472*
and *150 suites* ▭ *628* ▦ ⚏
AE CB ◉ ◉ VISA *Tube Marble Arch.*
Location: Mayfair, overlooking Hyde Park. The flagship of the Trust House Forte group is something of a modern-day grand hotel in its scale and in the extent of its service and facilities, which include a solarium, gymnasium and jacuzzi. Built in 1928 as apartments, a social centre during the Second World War when it accommodated American officers, the Grosvenor House is famous for its huge banqueting room. There's a pianist to accompany afternoon tea at which, despite the grandeur of the place, the atmosphere is relaxing and children are welcome. A well-run hotel.

‡ ☖ ☐ ⌧ ◁∈ ⇌ ☫ Ⴤ ♫ ꙮ

Hilton

22 Park Lane, W1 ☎ *493–8000*
☏ *24873. Map* **9H8** ▥ ☙ *509* ▭
509 ▦ ⚏ ⚏ AE CB ◉ ◉ VISA
Tube Hyde Park Corner.
Location: Mayfair, overlooking Hyde Park. Great excitement when the 28-storey new Hilton presented itself in Park Lane in the early 1960s, and some controversy about its modern style and proportions; today, it is part of the scenery, with its Trader Vic's restaurant and bar almost an institution. Improvements have recently been carried out and there is now a food and drink service in the Lobby Lounge, as well as the British Harvest restaurant serving English Specialities. The Roof Restaurant, with its marvellous views, remains, and the room service still offers Middle Eastern gastronomic specialities. The rooms have very large beds but are otherwise quite simple. The public areas are very busy, with theatre, secretarial and British Airways ticket desks.

‡ ☐ ⌧ ◁∈ ☫ Ⴤ ꙮ ●

Hyatt Carlton Tower ▦

2 Cadogan Pl., SW1 ☎ *235–5411*
☏ *21944. Map* **16J7** ▥ ☙ *236*
▭ *236* ▦ ⚏ AE CB ◉ ◉ VISA
Tube Knightsbridge, Sloane Square.
Location: Between Knightsbridge and Chelsea, off Sloane St.
Whether your requirement is for enormous breakfasts or a kosher dinner (and guests range from rock

stars to foreign politicians), American-cut beef or contemporary French cuisine, the Carlton Tower can meet your wishes, and you can always make your penances on the tennis court. Perhaps the most refreshing touch of luxury is the soap from Floris, the Jermyn St. perfumiers, but the hotel has always had an individuality, notwithstanding spells under the Sonesta, and now Hyatt, banners. The very building itself is distinctive, a handsome rectangular structure with a matching 15-floor tower that looks more 1930s than 1960s (which it is), and the location, in a quiet square, has a character of its own.

⌂ ♯ ☐ ◻ ↙ ⟨≼ ⁓ ☺ ♨ ♈

Imperial

Russell Sq., WC1 ☎ 837–3658, *reservations 278–7871*
☎ 263951. *Map* **10E11** ▯▯ ↺ 447
▭ 447 ⌂⌂ ⛁ ⟶ Ⓐ Ⓔ ⒸⒷ Ⓞ Ⓒ Ⓓ �𝚅𝙸𝚂𝙰
Tube Russell Square.
Location: Bloomsbury, near the British Museum. This modern, purpose-built hotel is the flagship of a small group owned by one family. It stands on the site of a previous Imperial hotel which was famous for its Turkish baths. The present Imperial is much more functional, but provides well-equipped accommodation in a convenient location.

♯ & ☐ ◻ ☺

Inn On The Park 🛏

Hamilton Pl., Park Lane, W1
☎ 499–0888 ☎ 22771. *Map* **9H8**
▮▮▮▮ ↺ 200 and 28 suites ▭ 228
▤▤ ⛁ ⟶ Ⓐ Ⓔ ⒸⒷ Ⓞ Ⓒ Ⓓ 𝚅𝙸𝚂𝙰 *Tube Hyde Park Corner.*
Location: Mayfair, overlooking Hyde Park. The only European hotel in the Four Seasons group, built in 1970, kept in superb condition, and favoured by stars, though it is better known as the home of Howard Hughes during one of his most demanding years. Despite its being such a recent building, the Inn On The Park has architecturally a 1950s look, and some of its suites are in a 1930s style, though each is individually appointed, and the hotel is lavishly furnished with antiques. In the Queen Anne-ish lounge, ten different teas are offered, with a pianist or harpist to provide additional soothing. Service in the hotel is outstanding, and there are two good restaurants.

♯ & ☐ ◻ ↙ ☺ ♈

Inter-Continental 🛏

1 Hamilton Pl., Hyde Park Corner,
W1 ☎ 409–3131 ☎ 25853. *Map*
9H8 ▯▯ ↺ 500 ▭ 500 ▤▤ ⟶
Ⓐ Ⓔ ⒸⒷ Ⓞ 𝚅𝙸𝚂𝙰 *Tube Hyde Park Corner.*
Location: Hyde Park Corner, overlooking Hyde Park. Very much the American style of luxury hotel, despite its now being owned by the large British group Grand Metropolitan: spacious rooms, often with separate sitting areas; individual heating and air-conditioning controls; dual-voltage; doorbell; telephone extension in the bathroom, free in-house movies, not to mention scales and a clothesline. A coffee house with sufficient privacy for breakfast meetings, and no wonder female executives seem to favour this hotel, with its Aquascutum and Cartier shops. Excellent cocktail barman, and excellent restaurant, Le Soufflé. Rolls-Royces available for hire.

♯ & ☐ ◻ ⟨≼ ☺ ♈ ☺ ♨ ♈

Jenkins 🛏 ❀

45 Cartwright Gdns., WC1
☎ 387–2067. *Map* **4C11** ☐ ↺
12. *Closed Christmas. Tube Russell Square.*
Location: Bloomsbury. The academic ambience is no doubt due to the owners' links with the University. The hotel has been in the same family for 25yr, and is still tended with justifiable pride. Fresh flowers, attractive fabrics, horse-hair mattresses, and fine china cups in the breakfast-room. Freshly ground coffee, and little china pots for the jam. There are several bed-and-breakfast hotels in this Georgian crescent, most of them rather better than average, with a tennis court available for guests.

⌂ ↙ ⁓

Kensington Close

Wrights Lane, W8 ☎ 937–8170
☎ 23914. *Map* **14I3** ▯▯ to ▮▮▮ ↺
530 ▭ 530 ▤▤ ⟶ Ⓐ Ⓔ ⒸⒷ Ⓞ
Ⓒ 𝚅𝙸𝚂𝙰 *Tube Kensington High Street.*
Location: Kensington High St. With goldfish ponds in its award-winning garden (with tables in the summer, and illumination in the evening), a swimming pool (evenings only), squash courts, sauna and even 'health' cocktails, this is the ideal hotel for a keep-fit freak. This Trust House Forte hotel in a converted apartment

block is otherwise a rather sprawling and conventionally modern building.

Kensington Palace
De Vere Gdns., W8 ☎ *937–8121* ☏ *262422. Map 15/4* ▥ ☎ 298 ▭ *298* ▤ ☞ AE ◉ CD VISA *Tube Kensington High Street.*
Location: Opposite Kensington Gardens. Beautifully and lavishly refurbished a few years back as one of the London showpieces of the Scottish group Thistle Hotels (it also operates the Cadogan, Lowndes, Selfridge and Tower hotels in London, among others). In true Scottish style, kippers and black pudding are proudly featured on the breakfast buffet menu, and they can be enjoyed in a gardenish coffee shop overlooking the park, French restaurant, and cocktail bar with pianist, attractive and comfortable rooms. The hotel is much used by airline staff and businessmen.

Kingsley ♣
Bloomsbury Way, WC1 ☎ *242–5881* ☏ *211517. Map 10E11* ▥ ☎ 146 ▭ *146* ☞ AE CD ◉ VISA *Tube Tottenham Court Road.*
Location: Bloomsbury, near British Museum. Warm and inviting hotel, ideal for families, offering accommodation at good-value prices in a very convenient location. The Kingsley is a full-scale hotel, with a bar and carvery restaurant, although small by the standards of its owners, the Trust House Forte group.

May Fair
Stratton St., W1 ☎ *629–7777* ☏ *262526. Map 9G9* ▥ ☎ 322 ▭ *322* ▤ ☞ AE CD ◉ VISA *Tube Green Park.*
Location: Mayfair, just off Piccadilly. The most entertaining hotel in London. With its own inbuilt theatre and cinema, the May Fair continues to pursue the performing arts, though in a lower key than it did during the big band era, with its long-gone Candlelight Room. The rooms are well-decorated with huge beds and attractive bathrooms – you can even have a spa bath if that is what turns you on. An Intercontinental hotel.

Merryfield House ▣
42 York St., W1 ☎ *935–8326. Map 8E6* ▭ ☎ 7 ▤ *7. Tube Baker Street.*
Location: Marylebone, near Oxford St. According to the proprietress, "This isn't a luxury hotel – no complimentary handkerchiefs – but I'll boil yours for you and hang them out. I have to go now; I'm having lunch with one of the guests, a widow who is here on her own." A friendly guest-house, immaculately kept.

Montcalm
Great Cumberland Pl., W1 ☎ *402–4288* ☏ *28710. Map 8F7* ▥ ☎ 104 and 12 suites ▭ *116* ▤ ☞ AE CB ◉ CD VISA *Tube Marble Arch.*
Location: Near Marble Arch and Oxford St. Frederick Forsyth's favourite London hotel, behind its Nash facade, evinces all the pampering luxury and style required by the man of action. The lavish leather sofas in which to relax, and the military chests with recessed brass handles, quietly set the style, with spiral staircases within the suites.

New Piccadilly ▨
Piccadilly, W1 ☎ *734–8000* ☏ *25795. Map 10G10* ▥ ☎ 260 and 30 suites ▭ *290* ▤ ☞ AE CB ◉ CD VISA *Tube Piccadilly Circus.*
Location: Near Piccadilly Circus. Reopened in late 1985 after a lavish year-long refurbishment programme, the Piccadilly has been transformed into a top-class luxury hotel. The *fin-de-siècle* extravagance of the interior, protected by preservation orders, has been restored to its former glory, while the pillared roof terrace has been glassed in to create a stunning conservatory-style brasserie. Businessmen in particular will be lured by the extensive conference facilities, and the basement health club complex, with pool, gym, squash courts and turkish baths.

Onslow Court
109–113 Queen's Gate, SW7 ☎ *589–6300* ☏ *262180. Map 15J4* ▥ to ▥ ☎ 170 ▭ *170* ☞ AE ◉ CD VISA *Tube South Kensington.*
Location: South Kensington. This

Hotels

former temperance hotel has undergone some major changes of late. In 1980, the hotel group, which then owned it, introduced alcohol, in the form of a bar. Since then, the hotel, in a typical, elegant Kensington terrace, has returned to private ownership and an extensive programme of refurbishment has been carried out. Rooms are categorized as standard or superior, and are large and well-fitted. Though the hotel has been totally updated, with all the services a tourist is likely to need, the traditional flavour has been retained.
⬛🔲💺🏊♥️🍸

Park Lane

Piccadilly, W1 ☎ 499–6321
☏ 21533. *Map* **9H8** ▥ 🎡 269
and 54 suites 🛏 323 🍽 *partial*
🔲💺 🅰🅴 🅾 🆔 🆅 *Tube Green Park.*
Location: Piccadilly, overlooking Green Park. This lovely old establishment is the largest privately-owned hotel in London. From its needlessly misleading name (Piccadilly is every bit as grand as Park Lane), the hotel is full of quirkiness and character. The French restaurant is decorated with carved panelling from J.P. Morgan's home, and the ballroom is a magnificent consummation of the Art Deco themes which pervade the hotel. Rooms are spacious, with walk-in closets and often with mahogany, 1920s-style beds. The beauty salon offers aromatherapy.
⬛🔲💺🏊♥️🍸♪

Pembridge Court

34 Pembridge Gdns., W2
☎ 229–9977 ☏ 298363. *Map*
6G2 🔳 *to* ▥ 🎡 32 *and 2 suites*
🛏 34 🍽 🅰🅴 🅲🅱 🅾 🆔 🆅 *Tube Notting Hill Gate.*
Location: Notting Hill, 1 mile (1.5km) w of centre. The Notting Hill locals who enjoy the French cooking and countrified ambience of Caps restaurant aren't always aware that this is part of a hotel. Caps in fact doubles as a breakfast room, apart from which there is only a small lounge and bar and the rooms, small but bright, impeccably kept, and comfortable. The hotel is owned by two doctors and their son, who runs it and has very much a family feeling. The clientele includes antique dealers who visit **Portobello Road** market (see *Shopping*).
🍽🔲💺♥️♥️

Portman Court Hotel 🏨

28–30 Seymour St., W1
☎ 402–5401. *Map* **8F7** 🔳 🎡 30
🛏 10 🅰🅴 🅾 🆔 🆅 *Tube Marble Arch.*
Location: Near Marble Arch and Oxford St. Small bed-and-breakfast hotel, ordinary and basic, but offering competitive prices for the very handy location. There are scores of hotels like this in London but the Portman Court is especially central.
♿

Portman Inter-Continental

22 Portman Sq., W1 ☎ 486–5844
☏ 261526. *Map* **8F7** ▥ 🎡 262
and 16 suites 🛏 278 🍽 🍽
🅲🅱 🅾 🆔 🆅 *Tube Marble Arch.*
Location: Oxford Street. The well-respected Rotisserie Normande has been replaced by Truffles, with luxurious food, including truffled specialities and an excellent wine list. An astonishing change of mood occurs on Sunday, when the restaurant presents a Creole brunch, with a restorative Ramos Fizz if you need one, and a jazz accompaniment. Apart from that, the Portman is very much the modern hotel, with the accent on the kind of service and facilities required by the well-heeled businessman. Its sister hotel is the **Inter-Continental**, in Park Lane.
⬛♿🔲💺♥️🍸♪

Ritz 🏨

Piccadilly, W1 ☎ 493–8181
☏ 267200. *Map* **9G9** ▥ 🎡 139
and 18 suites 🛏 157 🍽 🅰🅴
🅲🅱 🅾 🆔 🆅 *Tube Green Park.*
Location: Near St James's and Green Park. The first hotel to bear the name of César Ritz was in Paris, and he brought with him the architectural style of the Rue de Rivoli when he opened this London establishment at the beginning of the 1900s. He even imported French craftsmen to work on the Louis XVI interior. In the early days of the Ritz, the Prince of Wales used to dance there; later it became a favoured lunch place for Noel Coward, and post-war residents included millionaires like Getty and Gulbenkian. With the disappearance of such grandiosity, the Ritz has faced the difficult task of adapting itself to a less richly textured world. Sadly, one of its two famous bars has long gone, but other features are happily

immovable, like the staircase and rotunda; the restaurant (see *Restaurants*), with its magnificent view and *trompe l'oeil* ceiling, and the spectacular Palm Court, with its ornate marble fountain. The decor and furnishings in the Palm Court have been restored, and afternoon tea is served there. The Ritz has been through patchy times recently but it has now definitely re-established itself as one of the world's great hotels.

‡ □ ⌂ ✿ ♨ ⛤ ♈ ⋒

Royal Lancaster
Lancaster Terrace, W2
☎ 262–6737 ⓣ 24822. Map **7**G5
▥▥▥ ⌂ 436 ▭ 436 ▤▤ ⌂ (AE)
(○) ☎ VISA *Tube Lancaster Gate.*

Location: Bayswater, opposite Kensington Gardens. A comfortable and well-maintained modern hotel in the Rank group, in an excellent location, from which some rooms have lovely views of the park. The rooms are well-appointed, and the hotel has an informal café serving pasta dishes and grills, as well as Anglo-French restaurant.

‡ ⚵ ⌂ ✿ ⛤ ♈

Sandringham
3 Holford Rd., Hampstead, NW3
☎ 435–1569. Map **21**C4 □
⌂ 14 ▭ 2. *Tube Hampstead.*

Location: Hampstead, N of centre, near the heath. Every guest believes this bed-and-breakfast hotel is his or her own secret, but it turns out to be quite well known – unsurprisingly, in the light of its being owned by Mrs Dreyer whose friendliness and helpfulness has enhanced the visit of many a stranger to London. Dried flowers on the tables, well-filled china cupboards, a breakfast-room overlooking the garden. Small, immaculate rooms, with baths and showers. A Victorian house in a villagey Hampstead street, with panoramic views of London. Perhaps because Hampstead has so many bookshops, the Sandringham is popular with academics.

⌂ ✿ ♨ ⛤

Savoy ▥
Strand, WC2 ☎ 836–4343
ⓣ *reservations 24234. Map*
11G12 ▥▥▥ ⌂ 153 *and 49 suites*
▭ 202 ▤▤ *partial* ▭ ⥂ (AE) VISA
Tube Charing Cross.

Location: Strand, near Covent Garden and South Bank. The Earl of Savoy built a palace on this site

in 1245, and the present hotel was opened in 1869 by Richard D'Oyly Carte, who first staged the operettas of Gilbert and Sullivan in the adjoining Savoy Theatre, which is still functioning. With its tucked-away entrance at the front, and gardens facing the Thames at the back, the Savoy is full of extravagant treats. An open fire greets guests, afternoon tea is served in a garden setting with a new gazebo, and recent renovation has uncovered yet more 1920s features. The emphasis is on thorough hotel-keeping and comfort, with Irish linen sheets on the beds, and mattresses made by the Savoy's own workshop. Most bathrooms have marble floors and satisfyingly deep tubs. There are two restaurants to choose from, the famous Grill, now re-establishing itself after a bad period, and the Savoy restaurant.

‡ □ ⌂ ✿ ♨ ⛤ ⟨ ⛤ ⛤ ♈ ⋒ ♨

Sheraton Park Tower ▥
101 Knightsbridge, SW1
☎ 235–8050 ⓣ 917222. Map
16I7 ▥▥▥ ⌂ 265 *and 30 suites* ▭
295 ▤▤ ⌂ ⥂ (AE) (CB) (○) (○) VISA
Tube Knightsbridge.

Location: Knightsbridge/Belgravia, near Hyde Park. European flagship of the group, and very much the metropolitan, luxury type of Sheraton, as opposed to some of the smaller ones in American provincial cities. The hotel towers above Knightsbridge in an outwardly ugly cylindrical shape. All the rooms have a view, and are spacious and luxurious. Guests range from Bob Hope to Bjorn Borg, and the hotel provides accommodation for groups of visitors from blue-chip corporations, but as a matter of policy it does not accept conventions. Superb bathrooms, beauty salon, barber's shop and valeting service to keep guests well-groomed. The recently revamped dining room now boasts excellent and imaginative cuisine.

‡ ⚵ □ ⌂ ♨ ⟨ ⛤ ♈

Stafford
St James's Pl., SW1 ☎ 493–0111
ⓣ 28602. Map **9**H9 ▥▥▥ ⌂ 60 ▭
60 ⥂ (AE) (○) *Tube Green Park.*

Location: St James's, near Green Park. Elegant and discreet hotel in gentlemanly St James's, where almost every house is of historical interest. The Stafford's 300yr-old wine cellars once belonged to St

Hotels

James's Palace (and the hotel today has the distinction of employing not one but two Master Sommeliers). Much of the interior is in the style of Adam, though the brickwork facade is much later. The building once housed the Public Schools Club, and during World War II accommodated American officers and French resistance workers. It is a beautifully kept hotel, with four comfortable salons which are hired out for business meetings.

Strand Palace ♣
369 Strand, WC2 ☎ *836-8080* ⊗ *24208. Map* **11** *G12* ▥ ☎ *774* ▭ *774* ⚎ AE CB ⊕ ⊙ VISA *Tube Covent Garden.*

Location: Strand, near Covent Garden. When it was built in the early part of this century, a 900-bedroom hotel was by definition a palace. Now, the Strand has slimmed a little, been extensively modernized, and turned its attention to a different business: that of providing good value accommodation. It does so from a vantage point right opposite the *Savoy*, in a location handy for many theatres and for city sightseeing. The Strand Palace has most of the facilities to be expected in a large hotel, though there is no room service. There are kettles in each room and a 24hr coffee shop, Neapolitan chefs in the *pizzeria*, and an american-style cocktail bar. It is a Trust House Forte hotel.

Swiss Cottage
4 Adamson Rd., NW3 ☎ *722-2281* ⊗ *27950* ▥ ☎ *72* ▭ *66* ⚎ AE ⊕ ⊙ VISA *Tube Swiss Cottage.*

Location: Swiss Cottage, N of centre, near Hampstead. An exquisite little hotel, with its original oils, Staffordshire pottery, Tabriz rugs, Victorian furniture and grand piano. The Tea House suite, a tiny cottage in the garden, is a unique delight. With 24hr room service, a sauna and a resident Austrian pastrycook this is a most unusual small hotel, in a pleasant quarter of N London.

Waldorf Hotel
Aldwych, WC2 ☎ *836-2400* ⊗ *24574. Map* **11** *F12* ▥ ☎ *310* ▭ *310* ⚎ AE ⊕ ⊙ VISA *Tube Aldwych.*

Location: N side of the Aldwych. Exemplifying the Edwardian era with its crystal chandeliers, marble floors and vast pot plants, the Waldorf is a comfortable hotel, offering both old-world charm and excellent service and facilities. These include mini-bars in the bedrooms, a video channel for in-house movies, a hairdresser and valet service. There is a *thé dansant* on Fri and Sat.

Westbury
Conduit St., W1 ☎ *629-7755* ⊗ *24378. Map* **9** *G9* ▥ ☎ *225* and *15 suites* ▭ *240* ⚎ ▦ *partial* AE CB ⊕ ⊙ VISA *Tube Bond Street.*

Location: Mayfair, near Bond St. and Oxford St. The first Westbury Hotel, on Madison Avenue, New York, was named by a polo buff after the ground on Long Island. Like its New York counterpart, the London Westbury still has a bar called the Polo, and its martinis are of American dryness. When it opened in 1955, the London Westbury was the first hotel in Britain to be operated by an American chain, but since 1977 it has been owned by Trust House Forte. Its library-style lounge, with an open fire in winter, and its comfortable rooms nonetheless sustain the feeling of a 1950s American hotel.

White House ♣
Albany St., NW1 ☎ *387-1200* ⊗ *24111. Map* **3** *D9* ▥ ☎ *587* ▭ *587* ⚎ AE CB ⊕ ⊙ VISA *Tube Great Portland Street.*

Location: Near Regent's Park. A handy location for sightseeing, shopping, and taking relaxing walks in the park, though this is not a hotel area. The White House is a well-appointed hotel, offering 24hr room service and all the other amenities of a luxury hotel at more modest rates. The fact that the preferences and whims of guests are kept on computer gives some indication of the rate of repeat bookings, though it also suggests a high rate of occupancy by business visitors. Despite its name, the White House is a British hotel (the building is actually shaped like the Union Jack), and is owned by the Rank group. The block is large enough to shrug off the traffic which swarms around it.

Eating in London

Recent years have seen something of a revival of English cooking, blighted two centuries ago by the disruption of the world's first industrial revolution. The invasion by foreign cuisines, with the French in the van, was thorough, but now the ethnic diversity of London's restaurant world is being tempered by the resurgence of the native table. Many eating places display the rose symbol of the Taste of England scheme, promoted by the English Tourist Board, indicating that they serve local specialities and use fresh local produce. Some are even asked by the tourist board to eschew the spurious French menu terminology, often over-employed in the past.

There are, of course, some excellent French restaurants of unimpeachable authenticity in London, and equally notable standard-bearers of many another national cuisine. Even local cooking illustrates London's propensity for absorbing outside influences. Those who can muster the appetite to begin the day with the great British breakfast might find that the kippers come from Scotland, the bacon from Ireland (or, more lately, Denmark), and the tea from India. This is a meal which draws upon the tradition of home cooking, like that other British speciality, high tea (see *Cafes and tearooms*); to sample them the visitor should go to one of the grand old hotels rather than a restaurant.

So much is the blind Folly of this Age, that they would rather be imposed on by a French Booby, than Give Encouragement to a good English Cook!

Mrs Glasse, *The Art of Cookery*, 1747

The English are traditionally eager carnivores, and feast day dishes are still usually some sort of roast meat. The South Downs of Kent and Sussex produce the finest English lamb and mutton. It's odd that Sussex also claims to have invented the steak-and-kidney pudding, when the most famous beef is produced far away in Hereford or Scotland. Presumably it was the time taken to transport the beef that led, in the days before refrigeration, to its being preserved by pickling, hence the Londoners' beloved boiled beef. There seems to be less doubt about the origins of sweet puddings and pies, filled with the apples, cherries and soft fruits of Kent and Essex.

Among geographical influences on London's own specialities, the Thames is paramount. Cockles, mussels and whelks are sold for immediate consumption by vendors in many open markets (see *Shopping*). Shellfish from the estuary and beyond are very much the capital's own love, and the ritzier diners of Mayfair throng to oyster bars like **Bentley's**, Swallow St., W1; City folk have **Sweeting's**, Queen Victoria St., EC4. Fish specialities like whitebait and eel were originally pulled from the river itself. Street sellers still offer jellied eels, while the stewed version is the stock in trade of the pie-and-mash shop, one of London's own 'ethnic' eating places, usually to be found near a street market.

Whisper it not, but that other tradition, fried fish and chips, was brought to Britain by immigrants from Italy and Belgium respectively, and they seem to have met in the North of England. Still, Londoners do make good fish and chips; apart from fashionable places like **Geale's** or **Sea Shell**, the capital is well endowed with fish and chip shops of varied quality.

147

Restaurants

Choosing a restaurant

London has at least 2,000 fully accoutred restaurants. Like most things in the city, their keynote is diversity. Geographically, too, there are no hard-and-fast rules, although the areas best served by good restaurants are Covent Garden, Soho, Chelsea and South Kensington.

As a great city not only of its old empire but also of Western Europe, London is richly cosmopolitan. The ubiquitous Italians of London are a remarkable number of fashionable restaurants in the middle to upper price brackets, many of which are notably similar in style: quarry-tiled floors, white-painted walls, foliage, discreet spotlights, a fairly basic menu and cheerful waiters. This trattoria style was popularized in the sixties; more recent fashions include the new style in *haute cuisine* which seems to have been established by the Roux brothers, and the up-market French restaurant with the ambience of a brasserie.

From farther afield are the various cuisines of which Chinese and Indian are the most obvious. As in many cities, 'ethnic' eating can be remarkably good, and excellent value. Chinese and Indian restaurants in particular have also become known for producing good 'take-aways', and late at night a Londoner might simply declare that he is going "for an Indian" or "for a Chinese". These two and other ethnicities are manifest in dozens of inexpensive restaurants, and a few grander ones: Gerrard St. (W1) for Chinese; the Post Office Tower area (W1), Westbourne Grove (W2) or Hammersmith (W6) for Indian; and Charlotte St. (W1) for Greek.

London also boasts humbler eating places, many doing their trade mostly by day. The pub is certainly more likely to serve meals at lunchtime, and is usually cheap; the fare will range from French bread and cheese to, typically, steak-and-kidney pie or shepherd's pie. Wine bars also offer inexpensive eating, some of them content to serve quiche and pâté, others stretching to full meals. At a pace more agreeable than fast food, and in a restaurant ambience, chains like Pizza Express, Bistro Bistingo and Bistro Vino offer good value. The carvery types of dining-room in some hotels are also good value, providing a selection of roast meats, often for a set price.

When to eat

Restaurants in the West End and The City are busy at lunchtime, with a largely business clientele, but those dining for pleasure tend to come out at night, usually 20.00 or 21.00. Restaurants close after lunchtime, re-open at about 18.00–19.00, and wind down after about 22.00–23.00. The more famous and well-established restaurants are nearly always booked up before they open; it is usually possible to find somewhere good to eat on the spur of the moment, but the careful diner will always reserve a table first.

Price

Set-price menus are relatively uncommon in London, although appearing more often of late. On all menus look out for items which might bump up the quoted or apparent price: check whether VAT (Value Added Tax) and service are included, and whether salads and vegetables are going to be expensive. Pre- and after-dinner drinks can also prove costly – don't be afraid to ask. If service is not included, and you are happy with your treatment, give a tip of 10–15%.

Wine and food

Wine is one area where French dominance continues. Italian and German white wines are also almost universally available, and Spanish and Californian wines are to be found on several lists. There is a small, and growing, English wine industry, producing mainly white wine, rarely on offer in London.

Away from the mainstream of Anglo-French-Italian cooking, wine might not always be the best bet; beer goes well with Indian and much oriental food, and jasmin tea can be ordered with a chinese meal.

Aperitifs and after-dinner drinks

The English have long been leading consumers of fortified wines, and have played a leading part in the sherry and port trade. If there is a traditional aperitif in England, it is dry sherry, which whets the appetite perfectly; however, London restaurants will generally be able to cater for most tastes.

After dinner, the English gentleman traditionally 'takes' port. it is one of the longest-lived wines, and develops great complexity – do not dismiss it as a 'sweet' drink. Alternatives usually available are brandy, liqueurs, or perhaps malt whisky.

Vintage chart

A guide to the major areas and the general qualities of recent vintages. See key below.

	1975	1976	1977	1978	1979	1980	1981	1982	1983	1984
Red Bordeaux										
Médoc/Graves	●	◑*	○*	●	●	●*	◑*	●	●	○
Pomerol/St-Emilion	●	●*	○*	●	●	●*	◑*	●	●	○
White Bordeaux										
Sauternes & sweet	●	●*	○*	◑*	◑*	◑*	◑*	●	◑	○
Graves & dry	●*	◑*	○*	●*	◑*	◑*	◑*	●*	●	◑
Red Burgundy and neighbours										
Côte d'Or	○*	●	○*	●	◑*	◑*	○	●	●	◑
Beaujolais		●*	○*	●	●*	◑*	○*	●*	●◑*	◑*
White Burgundy and neighbours										
Côte d'Or	◑*	●*	◑*	●*	◑*	◑*	◑*	◑	●	◑
Chablis	●*	●*	◑*	●*	◑*	◑*	◑*	◑	●	◑
Alsace	●*	●*	○*	●*	●	◑*	◑*	◑*	●	◑
Rhône	○*	●*	◑*	●*	●*	◑*	◑*	○*	●	◑

Best vintages of other wines

Italy. Chianti: 1971, 1975, 1977, 1978, 1979, 1980, 1982; Piemonte: 1971, 1975, 1978, 1979, 1980.

Germany. Mosel: 1975, 1976, 1979, 1983; Rhine: 1975, 1976, 1977, 1979, 1983.

Spain. Rioja: 1970, 1974, 1976, 1978, 1982.

California. Red: 1973, 1974, 1975, 1977, 1978, 1980, 1981; White: 1977, 1979, 1980, 1981.

Vintage port: 1960, 1963, 1966, 1967, 1970, 1975, 1977.

Key: ● above average to outstanding ◑ average
○ acceptable * for drinking now

Restaurants

Restaurants classified by area

Battersea
L'Arlequin ▮▮▮ Fr
Chez Nico ▮▮▮ Fr
Bayswater
Le Chef ▮ to ▮▮ Fr
Kalamares ▮ Gr
Belgravia/Knightsbridge
Capital Hotel ▮▮▮ ⌂ Fr
Hyatt Carlton Tower ▮▮▮ ⌂ Fr
Ménage à Trois ▮▮ to ▮▮▮ Fr/Eng
Mr Chow ▮▮ to ▮▮▮ Ch
St Quentin ▮▮▮ Fr
Salloos ▮▮▮ Pak
San Lorenzo ▮▮▮ to ▮▮▮ It
Shezan ▮▮▮ Pak
Camden Town/Euston
Diwana Bhel Poori ▮ ❀ ● Ind
Nontas ▮▮ Gr
Chelsea/South Kensington
Bagatelle ▮▮ Fr
Bangkok ▮▮ Th
Brinkley's ▮▮ Eng/Fr
Busabong ▮ to ▮▮ Th
La Croisette ▮▮▮ Fr fish
Dan's ▮▮ to ▮▮ Eng/Fr/It
Daphne's ▮▮ Fr
Drakes ▮▮▮ to ▮▮▮ Eng
Eleven Park Walk ▮▮▮ It
English House ▮▮▮ Eng
La Famiglia ▮▮ It
Gavvers ▮▮▮ ⌂ Fr
Hilaire ▮▮▮ Fr
Hungry Horse ▮▮ Eng
Ma Cuisine ▮▮▮ Fr
Meridiana ▮▮ to ▮▮ It
La Nassa ▮▮▮ It   439 Kings Rd
Nikita's ▮▮ to ▮▮▮ Rus
Paper Tiger ▮▮ to ▮▮ Ch
Read's ▮▮ to ▮▮ Eng
San Frediano ▮▮ It   Fulham
Le Suquet ▮▮▮ Fr fish
Tai-Pan ▮▮ to ▮▮ Ch
La Tante Claire ▮▮ to ▮▮▮ Fr
Walton's ▮▮ to ▮▮▮ Eng/Fr   117 Walton
City
City Tiberio ▮▮▮ It
Le Poulbot ▮▮▮ to ▮▮▮ Fr
Sweetings ▮▮ Eng
Covent Garden/Strand
Ajimura ▮▮ ❀ Jap
Calabash ▮▮ Afr
Food for Thought ▮ ❀ ● Eng
Inigo Jones ▮▮ to ▮▮ ⌂ Fr
Interlude de Tabaillau ▮▮▮ Fr
Joe Allen ▮▮ to ▮▮ Am
Luigi's ▮▮ It
Mon Plaisir ▮▮ Fr
Porter's ▮▮ Eng
Simpson's-in-the-Strand ▮▮ to ▮▮▮ Eng
East End
Bloom's ▮▮ Je

Hammersmith
Anarkali ▮▮ Ind
Hampstead
Keats ▮▮▮ Fr
Islington/King's Cross
Ganpath ▮ Ind
M'sieur Frog ▮▮ Fr
Kensington/Notting Hill
Ark ▮ ❀ Fr
Bombay Brasserie ▮▮▮ ❀ Ind
Geale's ▮ ● Eng
Leith's ▮▮▮ Eng
Obelix ▮▮ Fr
192 ▮ ❀ Fr/Eng
Marylebone/West End
L'Etoile ▮▮ to ▮▮▮ Fr
Gaylord ▮▮ Ind
Little Akropolis ▮▮ Gr
Odins ▮▮ Eng
Rue St Jacques ▮▮▮ Fr
Sea Shell ▮ ❀ ● Eng
Surprise ▮ Am
Mayfair
Cecconi's ▮▮▮ It
Chicago Pizza Pie Factory ▮ Am
Connaught Hotel ▮▮▮ ⌂ Fr
Dorchester ▮▮▮ ⌂ Eng/Fr
Le Gavroche ▮▮▮ ⌂ Fr
Hard Rock Cafe ▮ Am
Tandoori of Mayfair ▮▮ Ind
St James's/Piccadilly
Bentley's ▮▮ Eng
Cafe Royal ▮▮▮ ⌂ Fr
Le Caprice ▮▮ Eng/Fr
Langan's Brasserie ▮▮▮ Fr
Ritz ⌂ Eng/Fr
Suntory ▮▮▮ Jap
Wilton's ▮▮▮ ⌂ Eng
Soho
Bianchi's ▮▮▮ It
La Capannina ▮▮ to ▮▮ It
Chuen Cheng Ku ▮▮ ❀ Ch
Cranks ▮ ❀ ● Eng
L'Escargot ▮▮ to ▮▮▮ Fr
Gallery Rendezvous ▮▮ Ch
Gay Hussar ▮▮ to ▮▮▮ Hung
Au Jardin des Gourmets ▮▮ to ▮▮ Fr
Kettners ▮ to ▮▮ It/Am
Manzi's ▮▮ ❀ It fish
Melati ▮ to ▮▮ Indo/Malay
Poons ▮ to ▮▮ Ch
Rasa Sayang ▮▮ Indo/Malay
Red Fort ▮▮ Ind
Soho Brasserie ▮ to ▮▮ Fr
Victoria/Pimlico
Memories of China ▮▮▮ Ch
Tate Gallery Restaurant ▮▮ to ▮▮ Eng
Westminster
Lockets ▮▮ Eng

Key to types of cuisine

Afr African	Fr French	Indo Indonesian	Pak Pakistani
Am American	Gr Greek	It Italian	Rus Russian
Ch Chinese	Hung Hungarian	Jap Japanese	Th Thai
Eng English	Ind Indian	Je Jewish	Turk Turkish

Ajimura ♣

51–53 Shelton St., WC2
(Covent Garden) ☎ *240–0178.*
Map **10**F11 ▢▢ ⌷ ■■ AE ⊙ ▣
VISA *Closed Sat, Sun lunch. Tube*
Covent Garden.

London's Japanese community of
around 20,000 has 30 or 40
restaurants to its name, many of
them well-respected if generally
expensive. Ajimura is
gastronomically one of the best, in
a handy place, with a varied
clientele and a set meal which is,
for this type of food, very
reasonably priced. The menu
changes from time to time, but
includes standard favourites like
sukiyaki tempura and *sashimi* as
well as less conventional dishes.

Anarkali

303–305 King St., W6
(Hammersmith)
☎ *748–1760/6911* ▢▢ ⌷ ■■ AE
⊙ ▣ VISA *Tube Ravenscourt Park.*

Anarkali was one of the first Indian
restaurants in London to win
widespread gastronomic attention,
and it inspired the others. Its
cooking is Punjabi, with a
tendency to creaminess,
exemplified by the excellent
chicken *korma*. Start with
outstanding *samosas*, and have
niramish vegetable. A
distinguished former chef gives his
name to **Aziz**, 116 King St., W6
☎ *748–1826*, handy for the Lyric
Theatre.

Ark ♣

122 Palace Gardens Terrace, W8
(Kensington) ☎ *229–4024. Map*
6G3 ▢▢ ⌷ ⊙ ▣ VISA *Closed*
Sun lunch, Easter and four days at
Christmas. Tube Kensington High
Street.

This funky wooden hut looks most
unpromising, but is regarded with
great affection by a loyal clientele
as the nearest thing in London to a
French bistro, with prices which
are by local standards reasonable.
Posters, photographs and
paintings on the walls. Very hearty
servings of basic bistro food from a
short menu: good soups, sea bream
with fennel, medallions of beef
with tarragon, and very acceptable
wines in a list of equally sensible
brevity. There are two Arks; this
wooden one is fractionally less
expensive, but nonetheless
gastronomically held in slightly
higher regard than its sister at 35
Kensington High St., W8 ☎
937–4294.

L'Arlequin

123 Queenstown Rd., SW8
(Battersea) ☎ *622–0555. Off*
Map **17**M8 ▢▢ ⌷ ■■ *lunch* ▣ ⊙
VISA *Closed Sat, Sun, three weeks*
Aug. Tube Clapham Common.

Dark and dingy Queenstown Rd. is
the unlikeliest setting imaginable
for a top-class restaurant, yet not
content with just one, **Chez Nico**,
it has spawned another,
L'Arlequin (and **Lampwicks**, at
No. 24 and **Alonso's** at No. 32 are
not to be sniffed at either). This
soberly pretty, rather formal little
restaurant is beautifully run by
Geneviève Delteil, while her
husband Christian creates such
light and inventive delicacies as
asparagus mousse, *feuilleté* of
scallops and leeks in a shellfish
sauce or beef with bone marrow
and grapes and wonderful sorbets.
The wine list is very expensive,
though the house wine is reliable.

Bagatelle

5 Langton St., SW10 (Chelsea)
☎ *351–4185. Map* **15**M4 ▢▢ ⌷
■■ *lunch* ▣ AE ⊙ ▣ VISA *Closed*
Sun. Tube Sloane Square.

Named after the Bagatelle in the
Bois de Boulogne, Paris. This one
may be in smart Chelsea, but it is
at the more recently gentrified far
end of the King's Road. The
potted plants fit the domestic style
of the neighbourhood, and the
kitchen matches élan with
simplicity: definitely French
cuisine, but with a taste for roasted
meats. Excellent cheeseboard.

Bangkok

9 Bute St., SW7 (South
Kensington) ☎ *584–8529. Map*
15J5 ▢▢ ⌷ *Closed Sun. Tube*
South Kensington.

The Bangkok pioneered Thai food
in London, and it still excels in the
extraordinary complexity of this
cuisine. When the menu says a dish
is spicy, it can usually be taken at
its word. This unobtrusive little
restaurant can become very
crowded, but devotees don't mind.
You might start with excellent
satay, followed by sweet and sour
pork or stir-fried beef with ginger
and mushroom sauce.

Bentley's

11 Swallow St., W1 (Piccadilly
Circus) ☎ *734–4756. Map*
10G10 ▢▢ ⌷ AE CB ⊙ ▣ VISA
Closed Sun. Tube Piccadilly
Circus.

Oyster bars and fish restaurants of

Restaurants

long-established reputation abound in London. Some have tended to live on their reputation, but Bentley's has remained solidly reliable. Although the restaurant's ownership changed in 1981, oysters are still provided by the family's beds near Colchester.

Bianchi's
21a Frith St., W1 (Soho)
☎ 437–5194. Map *10F10* ▮▮ ▭
▮▮ ⚫ ⚫ *VISA Closed Sun. Tube Tottenham Court Road.*
Bright young movie actors, authors and agents for years favoured lunch upstairs at Bianchi's, where a motherly *maitresse d'* personified the Italian family dining-at-home feeling which was the greatest charm of the restaurant. She was 'poached' by a rival establishment, but Bianchi's still represents more earthily than its many rivals the deeply-rooted Italian character that has proven to be the most durable ethnic strain in Soho. The restaurant's popularity with media people is especially apposite in that the inner upstairs room was the scene of John Logie Baird's first demonstration of television. Downstairs has never been favoured, though the room there is very pleasant. The pasta dishes are reliable, and *Fritto misto* makes a good starter.

Bloom's
90 Whitechapel High St., E1 (East End) ☎ 247–6001/6835. Map *13F18* ▮▮ ▭ ▭ *Closed Fri eve, Sat, Jewish hols, Christmas Day. Tube Whitechapel.*
While Manhattan's Jewish families were migrating from Lower East to Upper West Side, London's were making an almost identical journey. Even Bloom's restaurant opened a branch in Golders Green, NW11, but its soul remains in Whitechapel, where the nostalgia is thicker than the *borscht* and noisier than the *matzos*, and the waiters as crotchety as any on Lower East Side. Eat here on Sun after visiting **Petticoat Lane** and **Brick Lane** markets (see *Shopping*).

Bombay Brasserie
Courtfield Close, Courtfield Rd., SW7 (Kensington) ☎ 370–4040. Map *15J4* ▮▮▮ ▭ *lunch* ▬ ▤ ▼ ♫ *AE* ⚫ ⚫ *VISA Tube Gloucester Road.*
For sheer scale and lavishness,

with a huge conservatory leading off the palatial 1920s main dining room, this European vanguard of India's thoroughbred Taj Hotels group must rank as one of London's most imposing restaurants. But the food impresses too: regional home cooking (Goa, Bombay, Punjab), changing daily, with such delights as halibut *ambotik*, crab *malabar*, mutton *achari* and superb *gulab jamun*. The staff is cosmopolitan and excellent. Open every day of the year, with last orders at midnight. The set price buffet lunch is outstanding value.

Brinkley's
47 Hollywood Rd., SW10 (Chelsea/South Kensington) ☎ 351–1683. Map *15L4* ▮▮▮ ▭ ▬ ▬ ⌂ ▤ *AE* ⚫ ⚫ *VISA Closed lunch, Sun. Tube West Brompton.*
Hardly a secret, but not very well known for a restaurant of such qualities. John Brinkley is very much one of the new generation of young restaurateurs, bringing both professional skill and flair to an establishment which is original in both menu and ambience. Starters include *ménage à trois* (hot pastries of Camembert, Roquefort, Boursin); main courses range from *sole meunière* to suprême of chicken with spinach, watercress and herbs; puddings (as the menu likes to call them) from crêpes to home-made sorbets. Mahogany furniture, with Moroccan touches, a womb-like downstairs, and eating in the garden in summer.

Busabong
331 Fulham Rd., SW10 (South Kensington) ☎ 352–4742. Map *15L4* ▮▮ *to* ▮▮ ▭ ▭ *Fri and Sat eve AE* ⚫ ⚫ *VISA Closed Christmas. Tube South Kensington.*
Thai boxing, sword-fighting and dancing on Fri and Sat evenings present the colourful side of this multi-faceted restaurant. The entertainments are in the Khantok Room, where diners sit on cushions at low tables; more conventional seating is provided in the Tubtim Room, and there is what is described as 'fast food' in the Marokot Room. Its more expensive pleasures have in the past attracted gossip-column audiences, though a more reliable supply of Singha Beer, and better coffee, would be welcome refinements.

Café Royal ⌂
68 Regent St. W1 (Piccadilly Circus) ☎ Grill Room *439–6320* Map *10G10*. ▥ ⌷ ▰ ⬛ ⬛ AE CB 𝄐 ⓓ ⓒ VISA *Tube Piccadilly Circus.*
Oscar Wilde's name is the one most bandied about, but the Café Royal is remembered as the haunt of many wits, writers and artists in the late 1800s and early 1900s. The 1890s interior of the Grill Room is as dazzling as ever, but the Café Royal is long past the bloom of youth. Nor does its formal mood encourage bohemian impetuosity. The cuisine is classical French, with some excellent fish dishes, and prices are predictably haughty. The Café Royal's Le Relais restaurant has now been transformed into the Nicols restaurant, where a carvery-style buffet has been created mainly to attract groups of businessmen before they retire to the Café Royal's private function rooms.

Calabash ●
38 King St., WC2 (Covent Garden) ☎ *836–1976*. Map *10G11* ⬛ ⌷ AE 𝄐 ⓒ *Closed Sat lunch, Sun, Christmas Day. Tube Covent Garden.*
The Africa Centre offers Black and Muslim studies, exhibitions and the Calabash restaurant, which has the feel of an Oxbridge refectory, despite African rugs on the walls and exotic taped music. The service tends to be languid, and the menu is very limited indeed, but still spans both former British and Francophone Africa. Specialities include African stews, and fish dishes, and there are North African wines and Tusker beer.

La Capannina
24 Romilly St., W1 (Soho) ☎ *437–2473*. Map *10F10* ⬛ *to* ⬛ ⌷ AE 𝄐 VISA *Closed Sat lunch, Sun. Tube Leicester Square, Piccadilly Circus.*
A good example of the type of unpretentious, inexpensive, friendly Italian restaurant in which Soho specializes. Well-prepared basic Italian dishes like *gnocchi*, *raviolini*, *crespolini*, sea-bass with fennel, beef braised in Barolo, rabbit in white wine.

Capital Hotel ⌂
22 Basil St., SW3 (Knightsbridge) ☎ *589–5171*. Map *16I7* ▥ ⌷ ▰ ▤ ⬛ AE CB 𝄐 ⓓ ⓒ VISA *Tube Knightsbridge.*
One of the finest hotel restaurants

in London, though by no means the best-known. French cuisine, decidedly *haute*, as are the prices. The kitchen has flair as well as more basic virtues such as reliability, and the food, such as *mousseline de coquilles St-Jacques à la crème d'oursins* and *carré d'agneau aux herbes de Provence*, is beautifully presented. The dining room, redecorated of late by Nina Campbell, has been given the full treatment, all pink and festooned and candlelit.

Le Caprice
Arlington House, Arlington St., SW1 (Piccadilly) ☎ *629–2239*. Map *9G9* ⬛ ⌷ AE 𝄐 ⓓ VISA *Closed Sat lunch. Tube Piccadilly Circus.*
Long famous as a restaurant, Le Caprice was given a new image a few years ago, and now, all chrome and glass and black-and-white Bailey photographs, it's as fashionable a rendezvous for West End glitterati as Langan's across the road. The food is surprisingly good and just right for the ambience: steak tartare, onion tart, rack of lamb, imaginative salads, Grand Marnier soufflé. And it's perhaps the best place in London for Sunday brunch.

Cecconi's
5 Burlington Gdns., W1 (Mayfair) ☎ *434–1509*. Map *9G9* ▥ ⌷ ▤ AE 𝄐 ⓒ *Closed Sat lunch, Sun. Tube Piccadilly Circus.*
So Venetian, in the grand hotel mood, that surely the lone diner in the corner is Thomas Mann (or Dirk Bogarde)? Signor Cecconi was at the Cipriani, and he even brought with him the Bellinis, not to mention ten champagnes and three sparkling waters, as well as a faithful clientele of extremely well-heeled Italians. The food, which is also Venetian, of course, is always dependable without being exceptional, which cannot be said for the prices.

Le Chef
41 Connaught St., W2 (Bayswater) ☎ *262–5945*. Map *8F6* ⬛ *to* ⬛ ⌷ ▭ ⬅ ⓒ *Closed Sat lunch, Sun, Mon, Aug. Tube Marble Arch.*
Outdoor pavement tables are hard to find in London, though the idea has gained a little ground in recent years. When the weather is favourable, the handful of gingham-covered tables outside Le

153

Restaurants

Chef bring a soupçon of Paris to the streets of London. The menu also brings flavours from other regions of France, and a distinct quality of home cooking, both deriving from the diligence of the resident proprietors. Quality can be uneven, though the pungent fish soup with wine is always excellent.

Chez Nico Battersea
129 Queenstown Rd., SW8 (Battersea) ☎ *720–6960. Off Map 17M8* ▥ ▭ ▤ AE ◎ VISA *Closed Sat, Sun, three weeks Aug, week of Easter and Christmas. Tube Clapham Common.*

The gratitude felt toward Nico Ladenis by the diners of South London has made him into a legend. His blessing to them has been to pioneer gastronomy on the 'wrong' side of the river, first in Dulwich and now in Battersea. He did so in a way which made diners feel they had been invited into his home, while at the same time offering them highly imaginative French cooking. After the success of his first enterprise, Mr Ladenis has moved to larger premises outside London, and while remaining patron of Chez Nico Battersea, has handed the reins to his gifted assistant, Philip Britten.

Chicago Pizza Pie Factory
17 Hanover Sq., W1 (Mayfair) ☎ *629–2669. Map 9F9* ▭ ▭ *Tube Oxford Circus.*

Chicago adman Bob Payton left his London job to do his own thing and he does it with zest. His huge pizzas are of the deep-dish style, soft and seductive if a little bland. Doggie bags are cheerfully produced for leftovers. Music is taped from a Chicago radio station and there are video tapes of baseball and other all-American games.

Chuen Cheng Ku ♥
17 Wardour St., W1 (Soho) ☎ *734–3281. Map 10G10* ▭ ▭ ▬ AE ◎ ◎ VISA *Tube Leicester Square.*

Dim sum snacks, served in wobbly basketwork pagodas, are a popular lunch among the workers of Soho, not to mention the local Chinese community. The long-time favourite scene of such pleasures is the Chuen Cheng Ku, locally known as the CCK, which also has a respectable gastronomic reputation for other types of

Cantonese dish. It is not necessary to book; the CCK has the advantage of apparently endless floors, each with countless rooms, so that the restaurant can expand magically to accommodate Soho's appetite.

City Tiberio
8 Lime St., EC3 (City) ☎ *623–3616. Map 13F16* ▥ ▬ ▬ ▤ AE ◎ ◎ VISA *Closed evening, Sat, Sun. Tube Bank.*

The City is not very well served with good restaurants, but this is one, the snag is that it opens only at lunchtime. The City Tiberio is typical of the more expensive type of London trattoria, with a relaxing atmosphere and good wine list.

Connaught Hotel ⌂
Carlos Pl., W1 (Mayfair) ☎ *492–0668. Map 9G8* ▭ *restaurant* ▬ *Grill Room* ▬ ◎ *Grill Room closed Sat, Sun. Tube Bond Street.*

The *nouvelle cuisine* flirtations of chef Michel Bourdin brought quite a frisson to this widely respected home of more conventional dining, without disturbing the marriage of French flourish and English tradition which characterizes the menus of most grand hotels in London. Bourdin's is a feat not to be underestimated in an establishment as clubby (one critic called it sombre) as this. His offerings include the superb *rendezvous du pêcheur*, *quenelles* of sole with two sauces, wild duck with peaches and soft-boiled quails eggs in little pastry boats surrounded by *hollandaise* sauce. Service is always superbly orchestrated.

Cranks ♣ ☕
8 Marshall St., W1 (Soho) ☎ *437–9431. Map 10F9* ▭ ▭ *Closed Sun. Tube Oxford Circus.*

Vegetarian restaurant which has over the years become the best-known in London, helped no doubt by its ironic name, but also by its thoroughgoing approach to the joys of wholefood. Less of a true restaurant than a self-service lunch place, but its popularity brooks no argument as well as ensuring that it gets very crowded. Plain wooden tables, and a shop for wholefood, accessories and books. Branches in Covent Garden market and at 9–11 Tottenham St., W1.

Restaurants

La Croisette
168 Ifield Rd., SW10 (Chelsea/South Kensington) ☎ *373-3694. Map 14L3* 🍴 🎴 🃏 ᴬᴱ *Closed Mon and Tues lunch. Tube West Brompton.*

French fish restaurants of outstanding quality are a relatively new but most welcome addition to the London gastronomic scene, thanks to Alberto Bracci and Pierre Martin, who started with La Croisette. The basis of the menu is fresh, seasonal fish, flown in if necessary, but never from a deep-freeze. Great attention is paid in preparation to the character of the type of fish, so that sauces are always complementary and light, and never drowning. Shellfish is a particular speciality, and *plateau de fruits de mer* the crowning glory – too substantial for some diners.

Dan's
119 Sydney St., SW3 (Chelsea) ☎ *352-2718. Map 15K5* 🍴 *to* 🍴 🎴 🃏 ᴬᴱ 🄰 *Closed Sun evening. Tube South Kensington.*

Fashionability and high gastronomic standards do not always coincide but when Dan Whitehead opened up in Chelsea, at the beginning of the 1980s, he was successful on both counts. From the outside, it looks like a bow-fronted shop; inside, it has two small rooms and a pretty garden, in which tables are set during the summer. The kitchen is of what might yet come to be known as the Chelsea school: ravioli filled with crab, sole stuffed with broccoli and steamed over Noilly Prat, sweetbreads with amaretto, and a menu which changes regularly.

Daphne's
112 Draycott Ave., SW3 (Chelsea/South Kensington) ☎ *589-4257/584-6883. Map 16K6* 🍴 🎴 🃏 ᴬᴱ 🄰 🄵 *Closed lunch, Sun. Tube South Kensington.*

Highly-regarded French restaurant with a penchant for game dishes, classical cuisine, and careful but usually inspired innovation. Smart without being pretentious.

Diwana Bhel Poori ♥ 🍽
121 Drummond St., NW1 (Euston) ☎ *387-5556. Map 4C10.* 🃏 🎴 ᴬᴱ 🄰 🄵 *Tube Warren Street.*

Deliciously spicy vegetarian Gujerati (western Indian) cooking at Indian rather than English prices. The set lunch *thali* is satisfying and filling; or try crispy *samosas* and *dose* – long pancakes with a savoury filling. Drink *lassi* or fruit juice or bring your own wine. Surroundings are very basic and seating is hard and cramped, but that doesn't deter from the spotless hygiene and good food. There's more space and less bustle at the 50 Westbourne Grove, W2 branch ☎ 221-0721. Or try the branch in Rue St-Lazare, Paris.

Dorchester △
Park Lane, W1 (Mayfair) ☎ *629-8888. Map 9G8* 🍴 🃏 🎴 *Terrace* 🍽 🎴 ᴬᴱ 🄰 🄲 🄰 🄵 *Terrace closed lunch and Sun evening. Tube Hyde Park Corner.*

The celebrity of Swiss *Maître Chef des Cuisines*, Anton Mosimann, has brought fresh and much-deserved attention to this grand hotel. Not only has *haute cuisine* flourished under M. Mosimann, but he also supervised the most welcome innovation of a restaurant serving exclusively British dishes, the **Grill Room**. The *haute cuisine* is to be found in the evenings only in the **Terrace** restaurant, with softly romantic decor by Alberto Pinto, with a dance floor and pianist. Mosimann's policy of what might be termed inspired simplicity is especially evident in the British dishes, such as halibut in dry cider and roast duckling with cucumber.

Drakes
2a Pond Pl., SW3 (Chelsea/South Kensington) ☎ *584-4555/6669. Map 15K5* 🍴 *to* 🍴 🃏 🎴 ᴬᴱ 🄰 🄵 *Tube South Kensington.*

Game, English-style, but within a bright and innovative menu, at a very fashionable restaurant. Sauces and stuffings are likely to be made with fruit, marmalade or chestnuts, and there are some splendidly sweet English puddings; on Sundays spit roast beef is on offer. The same blend of tradition and invention is manifested in the interior design, though modernity wins, and the atmosphere is airy rather than intimate.

Eleven Park Walk
11 Park Walk, SW10 (Chelsea/South Kensington) ☎ *352-3449. Map 15L4* 🍴 🃏 🎴 ᴬᴱ *Closed Sun. Tube South Kensington.*

Northern Italian: the menu, a

155

Restaurants

goodly sprinkling of the diners, and the chic. Relaxed and friendly ambience. Apart from excellent pasta dishes like *taglioni*, and *crespelle*, there are such simple delights as *crudités* with *bagna cauda*, *bollito misto*, and several game dishes.

English House
3 Milner St., SW3 (Chelsea)
☎ *584–3002. Map* **16***J6* **IIII** ◨
■ *lunch* ➤ **AE** ⊕ **CD** **VISA** *Tube Sloane Square.*
Here is Georgian cooking under the eye of historian, food writer and TV chef Michael Smith. The rooms are small and intimate and manners more refined than in Georgian times. Typical dishes include delicious chilled Stilton soup, and venison with juniper berries.

L'Escargot
48 Greek St., W1 (Soho)
☎ *437–2679. Map* **10***F10* **IIII** *to* **IIII** ➤ **AE** ⊕ **CD** **VISA** *Closed Sun. Tube Tottenham Court Road.*
Soho rejoiced when young wine importer Nick Lander gave a new lease of life to the venerable Escargot. He and his wine-writer wife Jancis Robinson have created a global selection of wines, but the food is, as chef Martin Lam puts it, "modern English, obviously influenced by French". The downstairs brasserie-type menu is a lighter version of what's on offer to the media-folk in the upstairs dining rooms. Graphically-arresting snail-trails on the carpets, and marbled *eau-de-nil* walls to the lofty skylights. Its life-force is *maîtresse d'* Elena, enticed from **Bianchi's**.

L'Etoile
30 Charlotte St., W1 (West End)
☎ *636–7189/1496. Map* **10***E10* **IIII** *to* **IIII** ➤ ■ **AE** ⊕ *Closed Sat, Sun, three weeks in Aug. Tube Goodge Street.*
Old-fashioned *bourgeois* French restaurant which could be in Paris, a pervasive feeling which is intensified by the excellence of the wine list and in no way diminished by the establishment's cosmopolitan touches, or its long years of residence in a neighbourhood better known for its Greek tavernas. Nor has the sumptuous intimacy of L'Etoile been dimmed by the proximity of noisy and inexpensive neighbours.

La Famiglia
7 Langton St., SW10 (Chelsea)
☎ *351–0761. Map* **15***M4* **IIII** ◨
AE ⊕ **CD** **VISA** *Tube South Kensington.*
Southern Italian outpost of restaurateurs Alvaro and Corrado, in the World's End neighbourhood of Chelsea, a needlessly pessimistic name, as several restaurateurs have found it a congenial district in which to establish themselves; Alvaro's fishier **La Nassa** is just around the corner. La Famiglia is longer-established, with good pasta and that slightly boisterous friendliness that usually characterizes his establishments. The odd celebrity can often be spotted among the diners.

Food for Thought
31 Neal St., WC2 (Covent Garden) ☎ *836–0239. Map* **10***F11* ◨ ◨ **CD** *Closed Sun. Tube Covent Garden.*
Youthful vegetarian restaurant so popular that Covent Garden lunchers queue in the street for the privilege of eating in the cramped cellar. Good salads, soups and pastas as well as hot vegetarian dishes. Open until 20.00.

Gallery Rendezvous
53 Beak St., W1 (Soho)
☎ *734–0445. Map* **9***G9* ◨ ◨ ■
AE ⊕ **VISA** *Tube Piccadilly Circus.*
Diners don't necessarily always want an ethnically-authentic ambience when they eat the food of a particular culture, and the creators of the Rendezvous chain perhaps had that in mind when they created their calm, spacious restaurants in which to serve Peking-style food of genuine quality. The set menus are the best value.

Ganpath
372 Grays Inn Rd., WC1 (King's Cross) ☎ *278–1938. Map* **5***C12* ◨ ◨ **CD** *Closed Sun. Tube King's Cross St Pancras.*
South Indian food is very different from that of the northern part of the sub-continent, which is more commonly found in Britain. Southern cooking is usually (though not always) hotter, and this particular restaurant also gives it a vegetable emphasis, though fish and meat dishes are available on a menu which is authentic, interesting, and varied. Gracious service, too, but don't go too late – the restaurant starts to close

around 22.30. Try spiced green bananas, *avial* (vegetables in coconut and yogurt) and *masala dosa*.

Le Gavroche △
43 Upper Brook St., W1 (Mayfair)
☎ 730–2820. Map **9F8** ▮▮▮▮ ▭ ▭
▤▤ CB ⊕ CD VISA *Closed Sat, Sun.*
Tube Bond Street.

For the money you could fly to Paris, but even there you wouldn't get the wonderful creations of Albert and Michel Roux. The brothers are from Charolles, in Burgundy, and theirs is widely regarded as one of the two or three best French restaurants in London. The menu is sufficiently varied to meet most requirements, and it does list a few popular classics among the heavenly sauces and soufflés, mousses and *mousselines*. Although Le Gavroche doesn't specialize in fish, its *mousseline* of lobster and *turbotin au porto* are notable delights. Burgundian the brothers may be, but their lengthy wine list pays equal homage to Bordeaux. Service is attentive, courteous and helpful, and the ambience unstuffy.

Gavvers ♣
61–63 Lower Sloane St., SW1 (Chelsea) ☎ 730–5983. Map **16K7** ▮▮▮ ▭ ⊕ *Closed lunch, Sun, one week Christmas. Tube Sloane Square.*

There are few restaurants where fixed price means what it says, but this young relation of **Le Gavroche** is one of them. From the crisp vegetable canapés to the final cup of coffee not a single extra creeps on to the bill. Included in the price is a half bottle per person from a small but excellent selection of house wines. The Parisian chef, who has his vegetables brought by lorry from France, changes his imaginative *nouvelle cuisine* menu every Monday. Gavvers also boasts excellent service and an intimate ambience, but would be more comfortable if the tables were better spaced.

Gay Hussar
2 Greek St., W1 (Soho).
☎ 437–0973. Map **10F10** ▮▮ to ▮▮▮ ▭ ▭ *lunch* ▤▤ *Closed Sun. Tube Tottenham Court Road.*

The name pre-dates any sexual connotation, and persuasions are more obviously political in this famous plotting place. It is an irony that a Hungarian emigré establishment should be so well patronized by leading Socialist politicians, but they obviously enjoy such central European sustainers as cherry soup, pressed boar's head, goose, mallard, dumplings and lemon cheese pancakes. A considerable choice at modest prices on the lunch menu. Victor Sassie orchestrates proceedings with panache.

Gaylord
79 Mortimer St., W1 (West End)
☎ 580–3615. Map **9E9** ▮▮▮ ▭ ▭
▤▤ AE ⊕ CD VISA *Tube Oxford Circus.*

The first Gaylord was in Delhi, but the London branch, which opened in 1966, has probably done most to spread the name of this family of restaurants, with their own delicate style of Indian *haute cuisine*. The Gaylords boast that they open for lunch and dinner '365 days a year'. The *pilaus*, lamb *pasanda* and *korma* dishes are an impressive introduction to Indian cooking for the timid or sceptical.

Geale's ☀
2 Farmer St., W8 (Notting Hill)
☎ 727–7969. Map **6G2** ▭ ▭ CD
Closed Sun, Mon, three weeks July. Tube Notting Hill Gate.

Fish and chips should be eaten out of a newspaper held hotly in the hand, in the course of a winter's evening stroll; every true Briton knows that in much the way that all Americans prefer their franks to be served at a ball-game. The notion of a fish-and-chip restaurant is to the purist heresy enough, and a fashionable one defies the logic of the world's greatest take-out food. Geale's became fashionable when it was patronized by people like then-soccer star George Best, in search of simple pleasures. Success hasn't spoiled the place, which remains very basic, with excellent fish, notwithstanding such nonsense as a wine list (better tea would be more appropriate) and rather half-hearted desserts. No bookings.

Hard Rock Cafe
150 Old Park Lane, W1 (Mayfair)
☎ 629–0382. Map **9H8** ▭ ▭ ☎
Tube Hyde Park Corner.

The best hamburgers in London, by common consent and, in fact, better than most in the United States. Steaks, sandwiches, chilli in winter, American beer, and good ice-cream. Not a place for conversation, though; it might better be called the Loud Rock Cafe. No reservation, and often a queue.

Hilaire
68 Old Brompton Road, SW7 (South Kensington) ☎ 584–8993. Map **15**J5 ▮▮ ▬ ▤▤ [AE] [✆] [CD] [VISA] *Closed Sat lunch, Sun. Tube South Kensington.*
From the canapé that arrives at your table as you sit down, to the individual hand towels and Floris soap in the loos and the chocolate truffles served with the coffee, no detail is forgotten in this new and deservedly acclaimed restaurant. The understated décor and crisp white tablecloths provide a perfect background for excellent food prepared by young chef Simon Hopkinson. The set menu changes fortnightly and offers a varied but beautifully balanced selection of dishes, amongst which you may find *boudin blanc en croûte aux morilles* to start, followed by excellent *steak au poivre* and passion fruit *bavarois*. Hilaire is owned by the ambitious Kennedy Brookes chains – "but left to its own devices". The best tables are upstairs, away from the windows.

Hungry Horse
196 Fulham Rd., SW10 (Chelsea/South Kensington) ☎ 352–7757 Map **15**L4 ▮▮ [✉] [AE] [✆] [CD] [VISA] *Closed Sat lunch. Tube South Kensington.*
English food like mother used to make, with some interesting regional touches. The Hungry Horse led the way, in the 1960s, before English food became fashionable again, and its authentic menu is as appetizing as ever including delicious kedgeree, jugged hare and treacle tart. The atmosphere is less English, more bistro-ish, in a vaguely Italianate setting.

Hyatt Carlton Tower ⌂
Cadogan Pl., SW1 (Belgravia) ☎ 235–5411. Map **16**I7 ▮▮ [✉] ▬ ▤▤ [AE] [✆] [CD] [VISA] *Tube Sloane Square.*
Two excellent but quite different restaurants under one roof in this pleasant, relaxing hotel. The one offers roast beef, American cut, in impressive quantity and quality; the other contemporary French cuisine, school of Bocuse, of the highest standards. The beef is to

be found in the recently redecorated Rib Room which also has an oyster bar: the *haute cuisine* in the Chelsea Room, whence its *maître d'* and chef make frequent forays to all parts of France to keep sharp their gastronomic wits.

Inigo Jones ⌂
14 Garrick St., WC2 (Covent Garden) ☎ 836–6456. Map **10**G11 ▮▮ to ▮▮ [▭] ▬ ▤▤ ▬ [AE] [✆] [CD] [VISA] *Closed Sat lunch, Sun. Tube Covent Garden.*
Some *nouvelle cuisine* in a menu which changes monthly, is mainly French and, for the most, contemporary; excellent wines too. Very expensive, though there is a set-price menu at lunchtime and for a pre-theatre dinner. An interestingly-designed restaurant which has some attractive souvenirs from the building's days as a stained glass factory.

Interlude de Tabaillau
7–8 Bow St., WC2 (Covent Garden) ☎ 379–6473. Map **10**F11 ▮▮ ▬ ▬ ▤▤ [AE] [CD] [VISA] *Closed Sat lunch, Sun, one week Aug. Tube Covent Garden.*
A fairly new French restaurant with considerable aspirations, set up by a former **Le Gavroche** chef, neatly placed for *après*-opera diners. Early diners may be warned that their table will be needed for half-past ten and service has been known to be disorganized, to put it mildly. The mouth-watering set menu offers a choice of five starters (inventive but rich), ten main courses (rather too creamy sauces), a good sweet trolley and an excellent cheese board. Half a bottle of wine per person from a choice of seven is included in the price, and there is also a full wine list. At lunchtime the choice is less, but cheaper. The interesting interior design creates a sociable warmth.

Au Jardin des Gourmets
5 Greek St., W1 (Soho) ☎ 437–1816. Map **10**F10 ▮▮ to ▮▮ [▭] ▬ ▬ [AE] [✆] [CD] [VISA] *Closed Sat lunch, Sun. Tube Tottenham Court Road.*
Although it is especially noted for its fine wines – one of the best lists in London, acquired with great care and served with love – this elegant, discreet classical French restaurant has for years been a Soho favourite. Specialities are crustaceans and game.

Restaurants

Joe Allen
13 Exeter St., WC2 (Covent Garden) ☎ *836–0651. Map 11F11* □ *to* □ ▢ □ ▤ ☒ *Tube Covent Garden.*

Branch of the New York restaurant, and very similar in style and decor, though somehow less intimate and more bustling. Very popular with journalists and actors, more for its social ambience than its food. Sizeable menu on a chalkboard, with salads, burgers (called 'chopped steak'), etc., and American desserts. Cocktails at the bar. Open until 1.00.

Kalamares
76–78 Inverness Mews, W2 (Mega) and 66 Inverness Mews W2 (Micro) (Bayswater) ☎ *727–9122. Map 6G3* □ □ ▥ ▤ ▦ *Closed lunch, Sun. Tube Bayswater.*

An unprepossessing mews leads to these two ever-popular Greek tavernas. Micro, nearest, is smaller, rather cramped, unlicensed and cheaper; Mega, farther down, is more spacious. The food at both is equally good, the atmosphere relaxed and very jolly. An incomprehensible menu is patiently decoded by helpful waitresses (although it would be simpler to print translations). Starters tend to be more exciting than main courses: try deep-dried squid, *melitzanes skordalia* (fried aubergine with garlic dip) and the spicy sausages. Wine is Greek too.

Keats
3 Downshire Hill, NW3 (Hampstead) ☎ *435–3544 Map 21C4* ▦ □ ▢ ▤ ▥ ▦ ▧ *Closed lunch, Sun. Tube Hampstead.*

In bookish Hampstead, even the restaurants look like libraries, but such an erudite and worldly district is most exacting in the matter of gastronomy. The classical French menu, which might include such delights as *châteaubriand aux trois sauces* and wild duck, features new dishes every month, prepared to very high standards, and the wine list is outstanding.

Kettners
29 Romilly St., W1 (Soho) ☎ *437–6437/734–6112. Map 10F10* □ *to* □ ▢ □ ▤ ☒ ▧ ▥ ▦ ▧ *Tube Leicester Square, Tottenham Court Road.*

A famous London restaurant in days gone by, Kettners is now home to yet another Pizza Express (there are 18 branches in London, at two of which, **Pizza on the Park**, 11 Knightsbridge, SW1 ☎ 235–5550 and **Pizza Express**, 10 Dean St., W1 ☎ 437–9595, live jazz can be heard nightly). This is all to the good, since it means that those with only a few pounds to spend can enjoy their tasty pizzas and hamburgers in splendidly plush surroundings (avoid the modern, tiled dining room if you can). There is also a champagne bar and cocktail lounge with pianist, where you may be serenaded by Alfredo, the singing *maître d'*.

Langan's Brasserie
Stratton St., W1 (Piccadilly) ☎ *493–6437. Map 9G9* ▦ ▥ ▤ ▢ □ ▦ *Closed Sat lunch, Sun. Tube Green Park.*

Michael Caine, the archetypal knowing Cockney, was one of the founding members of this headquarters of London's café society, where the famous are not only sketched on the menu but also seated at the tables. Londoners have always enjoyed the watering-holes, such as **Odins**, established by extrovert Irish restaurateur Peter Langan.Even though Peter Langan is now only rarely in evidence, having decamped to warmer climes, his buzzing and crowded brasserie has lost none of its pizazz and, under the aegis of chef Richard Shepherd, the food remains surprisingly superior. Enjoy an interesting menu (recommended are spinach soufflé, *frisée au lardon* and profiteroles with chocolate sauce), the art of David Hockney and Patrick Procktor, and sometimes jazz in the downstairs bar.

Leith's
92 Kensington Park Rd., W11 (Notting Hill) ☎ *229–4481. Map 6G2* ▦ □ ▢ ▤ ▥ ▤ ▥ ▦ *Closed lunch, Aug hol weekend. Tube Notting Hill Gate.*

A school of food and wine, a farm growing produce for the restaurant, and an impressive *oeuvre* as a cookery writer, all underpin the work of Prue Leith and her partners in this Victorian building, with an interior by expatriate American architect Nathan Silver. The result is almost sepulchral in both ambience and the respect accorded to food by the kitchen and diners alike. Leith's is a temple of the very best English food of an especially inventive (though nonetheless usually simple) style, served from a very short menu. The restaurant is well known for its trolley of cold starters, on which a typical item might be smoked trout pâté parcels wrapped in smoked salmon. Stilton soup is a favourite, perhaps followed by charcoal-grilled lamb steak with thyme. Superb vegetables, an excellent, if expensive, wine list, and delicious desserts like ginger syllabub.

Little Akropolis
10 Charlotte St., W1 (West End)
☎ *636—8198. Map 10E10* ▥▯ ▭
ⒶⒺ ⊙ ⒸⒹ ⓋⓈⒶ *Closed Sat lunch, Sun, three weeks Aug. Tube Goodge Street.*

Comfortable, old-established restaurant offering carefully-prepared Greek dishes at medium prices. Very good *avgolemono*, excellent *kleftiko*, and rose-petal pancakes.

Lockets
Marsham Ct., SW1 (Westminster)
☎ *834—9552. Map 18H11* ▥▥ ▭
◼️ ▰ ⒶⒺ ⊙ ⒸⒹ *Closed Sat, Sun. Tube Westminster.*

Members of Parliament like Lockets not only because it is convenient for the Palace of Westminster but also because it provides traditional English food of mostly excellent quality. Just the place to take a counterpart from Brussels or a visiting Congressman who might choose mousse of Arbroath smokies, spiced beef cooked in ale, or duck with black cherries.

Luigi's
15 Tavistock St., WC2 (Covent Garden) ☎ *240—1795. Map 10G10* ▥▯ ▭ ▱ ⒸⒹ ⓋⓈⒶ *Closed Sun. Tube Covent Garden.*

Theatregoers who exit stage east, in the Strand/Covent Garden/Drury Lane area, flock to Luigi's, a bustling old favourite on several floors. Typical Italian menu, with good *pastas* and *zabaglione*.

Ma Cuisine
113 Walton St., SW3 (Chelsea/South Kensington) ☎ *584—7585. Map 16J6* ▥▥ ▭ ⒶⒺ ⊙ *Closed Sat, Sun, one month July—Aug. Tube South Kensington.*

Patron Guy Mouilleron is no longer the chef at this excellent and popular restaurant, but Jean Claude Audertin has maintained the standards of his boss, if not always the inspiration. Daily special dishes are announced at the table, according to what was fresh in the market that morning, although their prices have to be guessed at and a knowledge of French is a bonus. Ma Cuisine is small and intimate, not to say crowded, and sometimes it is necessary to book a week ahead.

Manzi's ✿
1 Leicester St., WC2 (Soho)
☎ *734—0224. Map 10G10* ▥▯ ▭
ⒶⒺ ⊙ ⒸⒹ ⓋⓈⒶ *Closed Sun lunch. Tube Leicester Square.*

This Italian fish restaurant has been a much-loved London institution for more years than anyone can remember, including Mr Manzi. Its atmosphere is less overtly Italian than between-the-wars 'Continental'. Downstairs, Manzi's is all bustle and lunchtime or pre-theatre dining. Upstairs, the Cabin Room is calmer, for post-theatre dinners, or romantic assignations. Good starters, excellent scallops, sole, crab, lobster, simply prepared. Custardy strawberry flan is an essential sweet. Unpretentious and good value.

Melati ☕
21 Great Windmill St., W1 (Soho)
☎ *437—2745. Map 10G10* ▭ *to* ▥▯ ▭ ▰ *Tube Piccadilly Circus.*

Excellent Indonesian food, with some Malaysian/Singaporean dishes, in a little Soho spot not far from the original Melati in Peter St. ☎ 437—2011. *Satay*, of course, with the distinctive flavour of lemon grass powder, but also a wide variety of soups, noodle dishes, seafood and vegetarian specialities. Very helpful staff.

Memories of China
67—69 Ebury St., SW1 (Victoria)
☎ *730—7734. Map 17J8* ▥▯ ▭
◼️ ▤▤ ⒶⒺ ⊙ ⒸⒹ ⓋⓈⒶ *Closed Sun. Tube Victoria.*

The gastronomic memories are those of Ken Lo, the best-known writer on Chinese cooking in London. He also has a cookery school, and a shop round the corner from the restaurant selling Chinese spices and kitchen utensils. The restaurant features regional dishes, especially from the North, as well as some more innovative creations. The overall style of cooking inclines to the light and crispy or crunchy, and the airy, cool interior seems to match it. On the menu you will find Shantung hand-shredded chicken in garlic sauce, Shanghai long-cooked braised knuckle of pork, barbecue of lamb in lettuce puffs and iron-plate sizzled chicken.

Ménage à Trois

15 Beauchamp Place, SW3 (Knightsbridge) ☎ *589–4252/ 584–9350. Map 16/6* ⬛⬛ *to* ⬛⬛⬛ ⬛ ▬ ⬛ᴬᴱ ⬛ ⬛ ⬛ᵛᴵˢᴬ *Closed Sun. Tube Knightsbridge.*

Just the spot for lunch after a hard morning's shopping at Harrods. The 'all starters and puddings' menu is perhaps better suited to daytime rather than evening eating and to delicate female rather than voracious male appetites. Certainly it's popular amongst Sloane Ranging women for an intimate *tête à tête* where, between scintillating pieces of gossip, they can sample light, intricate and utterly delectable dishes, prettily presented *à la mode*. Two dishes apiece, perhaps the trio of creamed eggs followed by baby fillets of lamb, beef and veal in a curry cream sauce, or terrine of lobster, salmon and broccoli followed by stuffed boned quail in pastry, will just keep the wolf from the door; any more and the price becomes exorbitant for such tasty but insubstantial fare.

Meridiana

169 Fulham Rd., SW3 (South Kensington) ☎ *589–8815/25. Map 16K5* ⬛⬛ *to* ⬛⬛⬛ ⬛ 🍷 🎵 ⬛ᴬᴱ ⬛ ⬛ *Closed Sun. Tube South Kensington.*

Downstairs, from mid-evening, lovers of Art Tatum or Earl Hines can enjoy the moody inventions of the pianist Alan Clare in the small, friendly bar. Upstairs, on summer days, there's a terrace on which to dine. The food is not as good as that in nearby **San Frediano**, but Meridiana's charm is an informality which dates back to the Swinging Sixties. A good place to take children for Sun lunch, when the ice cream is free.

Mon Plaisir

21 Monmouth St., WC2 (Covent Garden) ☎ *836–7243. Map 10F11* ⬛⬛ ⬛ ▬ *lunch. Closed Sat, Sun, Aug. Tube Covent Garden.*

The cheese board at Mon Plaisir is

so good that one day a diner will order it for all four courses. The notion has been discussed, but no one has yet dared risk the wrath of the staff who can at times be very Parisian. The cuisine is more tuned to country cooking such as *coq au vin* and *escargots Bourguignons*, and the atmosphere is bistro-ish. Mon Plaisir is on the edge of the Covent Garden area in something of a no-man's land, but by no means inconvenient, and it has for years been everyone's favourite secret. Small, intimate, and pleasantly busy.

Mr Chow

151 Knightsbridge, SW1 (Knightsbridge) ☎ *589–8656/ 7347. Map 16/6* ⬛⬛ *to* ⬛⬛⬛ ⬛ ⬛ᴬᴱ ⬛ᶜᴮ ⬛ ⬛ ⬛ᵛᴵˢᴬ *Tube Knightsbridge.*

In the late 1960s, when fashion decreed that to be trendy a restaurant must have exuberant Italian waiters and an Apicella-style interior, Chow had a good idea. Why not do that, with Italian waiters, but serve the food of his native China, particularly Peking? It turned out that, while people certainly wanted to follow fashion, they didn't necessarily want to eat *mozarella* every night; the rest is history.

M'sieur Frog

31a Essex Road, N1 (Islington) ☎ *226–3495. Map 21C5* ⬛⬛ *to* ⬛⬛⬛ ⬛ *Closed lunch, Sun, three weeks in Aug, one week at Christmas. Tube Angel.*

The neighbourhoods of NE London are not the best-served gastronomically, but fashionable Islington does its bit. M'sieur Frog is a well-respected bistro serving robust, often northern, French cooking, in a warm, friendly atmosphere. Typical dishes might include *gigot Bretonne* and *ris de veau à la Normande*.

La Nassa

438 King's Rd., SW10 (Chelsea) ☎ *351–4118. Map 15L4* ⬛⬛ ⬛ ⬛ᴬᴱ ⬛ ⬛ ⬛ᵛᴵˢᴬ *Tube West Brompton.*

Alvaro's restaurants are ephemeral but compulsive. Wherever he goes with his excitable and welcoming crew of waiters, his devotees follow. At La Nassa, even the frog's legs are designed as 'shapely' but the jokes on the menu mercifully stop there. So does the meat, since La Nassa, despite its greenhousy decor, is essentially a

Restaurants

fish restaurant, although of late a few meat dishes have appeared on the menu. Suitably Italianate dishes include squid in vermouth sauce and sea bass with rosemary. Even the *linguine* is served with fish sauces.

Nikita's
65 Ifield Rd., SW10 (Chelsea/ South Kensington) ☎ *352–6326. Map 14L3* ▮▮ *to* ▮▮▮ ⬚ AE ⬚ ⬚ *Closed lunch, Sun. Tube West Brompton.*

Pepper vodka? Tarragon vodka? At least ten versions of the Slav spirit, and often more, are served at this predictably lively Russian restaurant. The atmosphere is that of a bistro with subdued lighting; the prices are definitely those of a restaurant; but no one leaves without having been infused with at least one sort of spirit. Nor does anyone leave hungry, after dill-flavoured chicken *consommé* with dumplings, veal with caviar, and pancakes with chilled cream. If you want a bit of peace and quiet, ask for one of the booths when you book.

Nontas
16 Camden High St., NW1 (Camden Town) ☎ *387–4579* ▮▮ ⬚ AE ⬚ ⬚ *Closed Sun. Tube Camden Town.*

The Greek Cypriot ethnic neighbourhoods of London are Camden and Kentish Towns and points NW, and throughout this area are inexpensive local restaurants of greatly varying quality. In Camden Town, Nontas is an excellent local Greek restaurant, full of life, with very flavoursome cooking and good lamb and fish dishes, varied *mezze* and delicious Hymettus honey and yogurt to finish what should be a most pleasant meal.

Obelix
294 Westbourne Grove, W11 (Notting Hill) ☎ *727–4695. Map 6F1* ⬚ ⬚ ⬚ *Tube Ladbroke Grove.*

French fast-food, handily sited in the middle of **Portobello Rd**. market (see *Shopping*). French savory pancakes, known as galettes, with a very wide range of appetizing fillings, washed down with Normandy cider, and followed by sweet *crêpes*, make a sustaining and unusual snack meal at a modest price and in a useful location.

Odins
27 Devonshire St., W1 (Marylebone) ☎ *935–7296. Map 9E10* ▮▮ *to* ▮▮▮ ⬚ *Closed Sat lunch, Sun. Tube Regent's Park.*

Peter **Langan's** other place, less excitable than the restaurant that bears his name, and more private. Restful and engrossing in its collection of paintings, gastronomically reaches very high standards at times. Don't miss the wonderful chocolate pudding to finish.

192 ✿
192 Kensington Park Rd., W11 (Notting Hill) ☎ *299–0482. Map 6G1* ▮▮ ⬚ ⬚ AE ⬚ *VISA Closed Sun evening. Tube Ladbroke Grove.*

Though it's probably meant to be stunning, the all-glass front of this restaurant-cum-wine bar is somehow rather uninviting, as is the self-consciously stylish post-modern/'50s interior, with its mainly blank eau-de-nil walls and tightly packed seating. What does impress is the wine and the food, which for their price are very good value: the bill, which includes no hidden extra charges, is usually a very pleasant surprise. The menu changes daily according to the chef's forays in the market, but there are often excellent warm salads, perhaps of quail or duck livers. Ask for a table upstairs for preference.

Paper Tiger
10–12 Exhibition Rd., SW7 (South Kensington) ☎ *584–3737. Map 15J5* ▮▮ *to* ▮▮▮ ⬚ ⬚ AE ⬚ ⬚ *VISA Tube South Kensington.*

Szechuan food has not really caught on in London, despite the overall great popularity of Chinese cooking. So, for its Szechuan dishes alone, such as bang-bang chicken and crispy duck, Paper Tiger was a welcome addition to the scene. It also has some Peking dishes, and is much more comfortable, airy and relaxing than a cellar restaurant, even one so meandering, has any right to be.

Poons ✿
4 Leicester St., WC2 (Soho) ☎ *437–1528. Map 10G10* ⬚ *to* ⬚ ⬚ *Closed Sun. Tube Leicester Square.*

One of Chinatown's best establishments: good, tasty dishes; smart, clean café-style surroundings; efficient service. Poons' speciality is wind-dried food – salty but moreish sausages, pork and duck – as well as excellent Singapore-style noodles, steamed scallops, eel with pork and garlic, or sweet and sour *wun-tun*. Poons have also reopened their branch in Covent Garden at 41 King St., WC2 ☎ 240–1743. Next to the Leicester St. branch, at No. 3, is another highly recommended Chinese restaurant, **Joy King Lau** ☎ 437–1132.

Porter's
17 Henrietta St., WC2 (Covent Garden) ☎ *836–6466. Map* **10G11** 📮 🍴 *lunch* 💳 💳 *Closed Sun. Tube Covent Garden.*
The raised pie is one of the principal themes of traditional English cooking, and it has the natural advantage that it can be pre-prepared and is easy to handle. Thus it makes an ideal dish for quick lunches in a busy restaurant, as Porter's has discovered. The same is true of soups and potted meats, which go to make up an emphatically traditional but quickly-served menu at a restaurant which arrived with the revival of Covent Garden.

Le Poulbot
45 Cheapside, EC2 (City) ☎ *236–4379/248–4026. Map* **12F15** 💳 *to* 💳 💳 💳 💳 💳 *Closed evenings, Sat, Sun. Tube St Paul's.*
Haute cuisine's only outpost in The City, and inevitably a popular place in which to plot or consummate a big business deal. Very discreet, and excellent, as might be expected from one of the Roux brothers' establishments (see **Le Gavroche**). Lunch only, with a short menu which changes daily. Superb cheese board.

Rasa Sayang
10 Frith St., W1 (Soho) ☎ *734–8720. Map* **10F10** 💳 📮 *eve* 💳 💳 💳 *Closed Sat lunch, Sun. Tube Tottenham Court Road.*
The Singaporean specialities of the Rasa Sayang have won a considerable following in Soho, and devotees have followed the restaurant as it changed addresses and metamorphosed from a cosy little place to something fancier. This journey entailed the manifestation of surroundings which owe at least some of their

inspiration to an airport lounge, but the food remains as good as ever. In addition to the basic Singaporean dishes, with their coconut emphasis, there are also peanutty Indonesian specialities and spicier Penang confections, making for some interesting combinations if two or more people are dining. The colourful, icy sweet drinks and desserts are an acquired taste.

Reads
152 Old Brompton Rd., SW5 (South Kensington) ☎ *373–2445. Map* **15K4** 💳 *to* 💳 📮 🍴 *lunch* 💳 💳 💳 💳 💳 *Closed Sun evening, two weeks Christmas. Tube South Kensington.*
This is a charming restaurant, pretty and filled with flowers. The atmosphere is convivial and unstuffy, generated by the informal but dedicated approach of the proprietors. "We hate restaurants which are nothing but shrines to good food," says co-owner Keith Read, who has built up an interesting and well-explained wine list (he particularly recommends his Pomerols) and orchestrated the efficient, friendly table service. His young wife Caroline is the talented chef. Though she says she is still learning her trade, the food, described as "English . . . with imagination" is accomplished and beautifully presented with some good ideas, such as *millefeuille* of fresh frogs' legs or deliciously stuffed rare fillet steak. Try to find room for a pudding, or at least a home-made *petit four*. Roast beef lunch on Sundays.

Red Fort
77 Dean St., W1 (Soho) ☎ *437–2115/2525 Map* **10F10** 💳 📮 🍴 🍷 💳 💳 💳 💳 *Tube Leicester Square.*
Indian restaurants have gone upmarket. At least in London, flock wallpaper and piped music are definitely out, to be replaced instead by Osborne and Little wallpaper and cocktail bars, or alternatively an evocation of the last days of the Raj. This and the **Bombay Brasserie** are vanguards of the new-wave 'Indian' and both have proved successful. in neutral, soothing surroundings, on two floors, the Red Fort dispenses above-average if not outstanding North Indian

cooking, which tends to be uneven. Good starters, prawn dishes, quails marinated in yogurt, Goan-style fish and vegetable dishes. To drink – stick to lager if you can; the wine list is unadventurous and pricey.

Ritz ⌂
Piccadilly, W1 (Piccadilly)
☎ *493–8181. Map 9G9* ▥▥ *to* ▥▥
▢ ▰ AE CB ⊕ CD VISA *Tube Green Park.*

London's prettiest dining room can now boast food that almost, if not quite, lives up to the ravishing pink and marbled Empire surroundings. The kitchens have been streamlined and the menu taken in hand, and some real gems can be found on it such as the fish sausages, wild mushroom soup and chocolate mousse. Service lacks the almost balletic efficiency and the courtesy of some other top London hotels.

Rue St Jacques
5 Charlotte St., W1 (West End)
☎ *637–0222. Map 10E10* ▥▥ ▢
AE ⊕ CD VISA *Closed Sat. Sun. Tube Goodge Street.*

With its sophisticated, glossy decor, its almost faultless culinary offerings and its lavish prices, this restaurant has already established itself as one of London's best, although it opened only in 1984. Chef Gunther Schlender (who was at the now defunct Carrier's for many years) rekindles the jaded palettes of businessmen with elastic expense accounts and society ladies alike with such delights as guinea fowl in a caramel glaze with mangoes, sole with ginger-and-cream sauce, sweetbreads with wild mushrooms *en brioche* . . . Altogether a classic restaurant very much in the modern style.

St Quentin
243 Brompton Rd., SW3 (Knightsbridge) ☎ *589–8005. Map 16I6* ▥▥ ▢ ☉ ▤ ▤ AE ⊕ CD VISA *Closed Mon, Sun eve. Tube Knightsbridge, South Kensington.*

Brasseries in London, like **Langan's** and St Quentin, have the bar and ostensibly casual air of their French counterparts in the late 1800s – all mahogany and mirrors. But they are, in truth, highly fashionable restaurants. This one has been known to serve Mick Jagger and Princess Margaret on the same evening.

Some of the brasserie tradition is retained nonetheless by the weekend custom of serving breakfast croissants and patisserie in the afternoon. Main courses are excellent, starters perhaps less so, and the wine list short but good. Service excellent.

Salloos
62–64 Kinnerton St., SW1 (Belgravia) ☎ *235–4444. Map 16I7* ▥▥ ▢ ▰ AE ⊕ CD VISA *Closed Sun. Tube Knightsbridge.*

A rare Pakistani restaurant. The ethnicity is a matter of some pride to patron 'Salloo' Salahuddin, who also has a restaurant in Lahore. What it really indicates is the food of the NW corner of the sub-continent, with an emphasis on kebabs and other roasted meats. Although there are ethnic touches, the restaurant is basically modern in design, and smart but subdued. Specialities include lamb in wheatgerm, chicken in cheese and tandoori quails.

San Frediano
62 Fulham Rd., SW3 (South Kensington) ☎ *584–8375. Map 15K5* ▥▥ ▢ ▰ ▤ ▤ AE ⊕ CD VISA *Closed Sun. Tube South Kensington.*

The friendly and caring service in this extrovert and somewhat Tuscan restaurant doesn't seem to have faded since it first became popular more than a dozen years ago. The food is good, too; arguably the best among this style of Italian trattoria, at prices which represent excellent value. Mouth-watering cold table, and excellent Italian wines.

San Lorenzo
22 Beauchamp Pl., SW3 (Knightsbridge) ☎ *584–1074. Map 16I6* ▥▥ *to* ▥▥ ▢ ⌂ *see below. Closed Sun. Tube Knightsbridge.*

Once the most fashionable of Italian restaurants of London, but today such a distinction is harder to bestow. Much loved for its conservatorial interior and roof which opens in summer. Favoured dishes include *crudités* with *bagna cauda* and veal San Lorenzo.

Sea Shell ♣ ●
51–53 Lisson Grove, NW1 (Marylebone) ☎ *723–8703. Map 8E6* ▢ ▢ ✳ *Closed Sun, Mon. Tube Marylebone.*

Once it was a humble fish-and-

chip shop, then people started
coming in Rolls-Royces, and now
it is a restaurant. The Sea Shell
offers a notably wide variety of
excellent quality fried fish in
generous helpings – not only the
traditional cod and haddock but
also skate, plaice, sole, and others –
followed by better apple pie than
might be expected. Proud, friendly
service. Queuing; no booking.

Shezan
*16–22 Cheval Pl., SW7
(Knightsbridge)*
☎ 589–7918/0314. Map **16**/6 ▮▮▮
▭ ▦ _AE_ ⊕ ⊚ _VISA_ Closed Sun.
Tube Knightsbridge.
Widely regarded as the best of the
'gourmet' restaurants from the
Indian sub-continent, though the
delicacy of its spicing and
individual approach to one or two
dishes can disappoint the diner
who prefers something more
ethnic. The intention is to provide
Pakistani *haute cuisine*, and the
clientele is this coolly smart,
almost austere, restaurant seems to
include many successful
businessmen from the sub-
continent. Pleasing choices from
the menu include *murg tikka
Lahori*, *kofta Kashmiri* and *pulao
Lizazi*.

Simpson's-in-the-Strand
100 Strand, WC2 (Strand)
☎ 836–9112. Map **11**G12 ▮▮ to
▮▮▮ ▭ _AE_ ⊕ ⊚ _VISA_ Closed Sun.
Tube Covent Garden.
The most famous home of roast
beef, saddle of lamb, Aylesbury
duck, and other traditional English
favourites. The roast meats are
brought on a trolley and carved at
the table. Good English apple pie,
or finish the meal with a savoury
like angels on horseback, oysters in
bacon on toast. Very male
atmosphere.

Soho Brasserie
*23–25 Old Compton St., W1
(Soho)* ☎ 439–3758. Map
10F10 ▭ to ▮▮ ▭ ▦ ☷ _AE_
⊚ _VISA_ Tube Leicester Square.
The moment the blue and cream
doors of this brewery-owned
establishment were opened a few
years ago, it became the newest
place in the area to see and be seen,
whether taking a croissant or a
cocktail in the front bar (with small
tables and chairs, not stools) or a
more substantial meal in the
restaurant behind. If you are
looking for a light but tasty lunch

this is a good choice: the bar menu
includes excellent fish soup (be
warned: you'll be treated like a
leper after you've eaten the
pungent accompanying *rouille*),
good cheese and charcuterie. The
restaurant menu has its moments
too: the turbot and brill dishes are
particularly recommended for the
discerning diner.

Suntory
*72 St James's St., SW1 (St
James's)* ☎ 409–0201. Map **9**H9
▮▮▮▮ ▭ ▦ _AE_ ⊕ ⊚ _VISA_ Closed
Sun. Tube Green Park.
In surroundings of simple
elegance, with cool Japanese
screens, Suntory dispenses Shabu-
Shabu dishes in one room, and
Teppan cooking in another. The
restaurant is owned by the
Japanese vineyard, distilling and
brewing company Suntory, and is
something of a showpiece of the
country's cuisine, in preparation,
presentation and service. On the
menu, all dishes are described in
detail in English, and service is
helpful.

Le Suquet
*104 Draycott Ave., SW3
(Chelsea/South Kensington)*
☎ 581–1785. Map **16**J6 ▮▮▮ ▭
🏠 _AE_ Closed Mon lunch, Tues
lunch. Tube South Kensington.
While its companion **La
Croisette** has a set menu, Le
Suquet is à la carte; beyond that,
the differences between these fine
French seafood restaurants are
minor. The atmosphere is very
French, as is the service, but it is
the quality of the fish, and the
cuisine, that have made these
restaurants so successful. Treat
yourself to the huge *plateau de
fruits de mer*, or perhaps to *filet de
loup bordelaise* or *raie au beurre
noir*. It is essential to book for both
lunch and dinner.

Surprise
*12 Great Marlborough St., W1
(West End)* ☎ 434–2666. Map
9F9 ▮▮ ▭ _AE_ ⊕ ⊚ _VISA_ Closed
Sun evening. Tube Oxford Circus.
An American restaurant, and
proud of being 'all-American'
gastronomically. The food
includes chowder, *jambalaya*,
applejack pork, and hot fudge
brownies. There are American
paintings on the wall, the interior
design is modern, and the bustly
atmosphere is partly restaurant,
partly coffee-shop.

Restaurants

Sweetings
39 Queen Victoria St., EC4 (City)
☎ 248–3062. Map **12**F15 ▯▢▱
*Closed evening, Sat, Sun. Tube
Mansion House.*

Unchanged for 150yr, Sweetings
remains an old friend to countless
pin-striped City workers who
jostle for a seat at the bar or in the
small back dining room with its
communal tables (there are no
bookings). They are there for fish,
prepared in a no-nonsense British
way, without fuss or frills: oysters,
shellfish salads, delicious crab and
salmon sandwiches and so on. For
pudding there are such favourites
as jam roly-poly, bread-and-butter
pudding and spotted dick.

Tai-Pan
*8 Egerton Garden Mews, SW3
(Chelsea/South Kensington)*
☎ 589–8287/584–2499. Map
16J6 ▮▮▯ ▢▱ ▤ ▦ ▣ ▩
▥▧ *Tube South Kensington.*

Hunan cooking was introduced to
London by the Tai-Pan at the
beginning of the 1980s, and the
restaurant takes great pride in its
authentic dishes in this style. A
genuinely exotic menu includes
frogs' legs Hunan, tigers' whiskers
and squirrel fish. There are also
Szechuan and Peking dishes, in a
short menu which always features
daily specials. A busy restaurant,
with an expensive clientele, in an
airy basement.

Tandoori of Mayfair
37a Curzon St., W1 (Mayfair)
☎ 629–0600/493–7166 Map
9H8 ▮▮▯ ▢▱ ▤ ▦ ▣ ▩ ▥▧ *Closed
Sun. Tube Green Park.*

Tandoori cooking, employing a
clay oven, became popular in
London at the end of the 1960s,
and has remained so ever since.
The Tandoori of Mayfair has been
serving this type of Indian food
since the early days, and still
specializes in the style. The
charcoal-fired oven imparts its
own character to *tikka* starters,
tandoori main courses, and the
essential accompaniment of *nan*
bread.

La Tante Claire ♣ ⌂
*68 Royal Hospital Rd., SW3
(Chelsea)* ☎ 352–6045. Map
16L6 ▮▮▯ *lunch* ▮▮▯ ▢▱ *lunch*
▤ ▣ *Closed Sat, Sun, two
weeks Easter, two weeks
Christmas, three weeks Aug. Tube
Sloane Square.*

It was the Roux brothers' **Le**

Gavroche that gave birth to
Pierre Koffman's Tante Clair, and
any argument as to which is the
finest restaurant in London are
inclined to polarize between these
two. Both are noted, as *haute
cuisine* surely should be, for their
exquisite and complex sauces. The
distinguishing features of Tante
Claire are its fish dishes, and its
more innovative approach, while
convinced supporters probably
find it more intimate. It can be
booked up weeks in advance,
especially in the evenings. The set
lunch remains excellent value, and
gives lesser mortals the chance to
savour London's *haute cuisine.*

Tate Gallery Restaurant
Millbank, SW1 (Pimlico)
☎ 834–6754. Map **18**K11 ▮▮▯ *to*
▮▮▯ ▢▱ ▣ *Closed evening, Sun.
Tube Pimlico.*

Not a museum snack bar but a full-
scale restaurant with a
considerable reputation, an
excellent wine list, and
commensurate prices. Nor can a
seat be relied on after a morning in
the Tate Gallery; it is advisable to
book. Appropriately, the central
theme is old English cooking, often
from original recipes, with
specialities such as buttered crab
and Joan Cromwell salad, although
the overall approach of the kitchen
is by no means insular.

Walton's
*117 Walton St., SW3 (Chelsea/
South Kensington)* ☎ 584–5297.
Map **16**J6 ▮▮▯ ▢▱ ▤▥ ▦ ▣▣
▤ ▣▢ ▣ ▣ ▥▧ *Closed Sun
evenings. Tube South
Kensington.*

Renowned for its plush and
privacy. Its menu is basically
French, but with British touches:
Stilton soup; *noisettes* of Welsh
lamb with lobster meat and
*béarnaise sauce; moneybags of
curried mussels.*

Wilton's ⌂
55 Jermyn St., SW1 (St James's)
☎ 629–9955. Map **10**H10 ▮▮▯ ▢▱
▤ ▣ ▣ ▥▧ *Closed Sat, Sun,
three weeks July–Aug. Tube
Green Park.*

Clubby and rather male, this old-
established restaurant has recently
moved location, but the general
atmosphere and standard of food
remain unchanged. The English
menu is traditional, relying on
prime fresh ingredients simply
prepared.

Cafes and tearooms

Britain's colonial adventures made her controller of the world's tea trade; united with a rich tradition of cakes, biscuits and breads, this resulted in an institution nobody has copied – afternoon tea. The traditional meal is a substantial affair, with cakes, toasted teacakes or crumpets, perhaps even fish or cold meat. Popular today is the 'cream tea': scones, jam and whipped cream. It is more than mere refreshment – it is a graceful, sometimes even formal, social occasion.

Most of the better hotels offer a traditional afternoon tea between about 15.30–17.30. Taking tea there is a uniquely metropolitan experience. A choice of India or China tea, or Earl Grey, camomile or even tilleul (linden or lime-blossom) if you care to ask is offered at the **Ritz Hotel**, W1 (it is essential to reserve); on Sun afternoons at the Ritz there is a *thé dansant* – also at the **Waldorf**, WC2, on Fri and Sun. Those who enjoy the full gastronomic delights favour **Brown's Hotel**, W1, and the **Hyde Park Hotel**, W1, but those more concerned with the drink itself incline to the Ritz and to the **Savoy** group (which includes **Claridges** and the **Connaught**, both W1, and the **Berkeley**, SW1), which has its own blend. At La Chinoiserie in the **Hyatt Carlton Tower** , SW1, and on Sat and Sun in the Savoy, there is a harpist; piano accompaniment is on hand at most grand hotels.

One of the most stylish locations in which to take afternoon tea is **Fortnum & Mason**, Piccadilly, in the Fountain restaurant, which serves excellent sandwiches, salads and cakes. Among the department stores which offer afternoon tea, **Harrods** also provides a pianist, and has a fairly expensive set price for which you can eat as much as you like. Opposite Harrods, on Brompton Rd., SW3, is a branch of **Richoux**, at which rather high prices are matched by a expensive ambience.

The opening of a tea shop may not seem a headline-maker, but the 1981 revival of the **Lyons Corner House**, Strand, WC2, a long established institution, made waves in the London media, and attracted afternoon queues for weeks afterwards. Upstairs, Lyons is happy to serve at any time of day an order comprising nothing more than a cup of tea ('cuppa'), perhaps with a Chelsea bun, although egg and bacon or a snack are available. Downstairs, lunches are served, and orders for just tea are taken only between 15.00–17.30. Whether in the abrasive 1980s the company can sustain the idea of a relaxed atmosphere, with very low prices, and adequate, if slightly fast-foodish, quality on busy sites, only time will tell.

The upstairs-downstairs arrangement is followed in a slightly different manner at the **Ceylon Tea Centre**, 22 Regent St., W1. Upstairs for waitress service, down for cafeteria, but at either level it is possible to order a solo 'cuppa', and there is an excellent choice of different teas. Lunches are also available. The **India Tea Centre**, 343 Oxford St., W1, even serves curries. Since the classic English teas are blends of Ceylon and India, these establishments offer as authentic a selection as can be sampled on the spot. Unfortunately, The City, where the tea trade has its roots, now has only countless anonymous snack bars.

London has long been sufficiently cosmopolitan to have a number of good patisseries. For gossipy ambience, try **Valerie**, 44 Old Compton St., Soho, W1; for privacy and good pastries, visit nearby **Maison Bertaux**, 28 Greek St., W1; for excellent pastries, **Maison Bouquillon**, 45 Moscow Rd., W2.

Pubs

In most countries, it is difficult for even the experienced traveller to visit a strange town and immediately spot a place where it will be possible to relax and, with luck, meet a few friendly natives. Apart from the welcome, each painted sign outside a pub heralds a singularity of identity which is its quintessential charm.

The public house contrives to be unmistakable whatever its origins, and pubs can vary considerably. Being one of England's older cities, London has pubs which grew out of every period of the country's history, and their names reveal their backgrounds. A pub which stands on the site of a colonial Roman taverna may be called The Vines or The Grapes; a hostel for workers on some medieval construction project might be The Builders, The Castle or The Bridge; a monastery hospice for pilgrims, The Angel or The Salutation. Though the term 'public house' was not used in official language until the mid-1880s, that's what they all are, whether they were built as coaching inns, Georgian coffee houses or gin palaces for the new city-dwellers of the Victorian period.

The first purpose of the pub is to provide for conversation in an informal setting, and most London pubs do concentrate on just that, though, as in Shakespeare's time, there are hostelries which present live entertainment. There are plenty of pubs, too, which serve meals, but a greater number employ the impenetrable pork pie as a defence against would-be diners, thus freeing themselves to concentrate on the serving of drink, which is the second purpose of the pub.

What to drink in the London pub? The fact that England's national spirit is London Dry Gin is easily overlooked, perhaps because the average publican's skills in the matter of mixed drinks don't stretch much further than the addition of tonic.

The true stock-in-trade of the pub is beer. Because London is so close to the hop gardens of Kent, it has long had a tradition of especially 'hoppy' beers. Two London breweries, Whitbread and Watneys, are national giants, while the truly local breweries are small firms, Fuller's (London Pride) and Young's. The latter in particular have championed the unique British tradition of having their beer conditioned at the pub, in the cask, whence it is drawn by a hand pump or 'beer engine' at a natural cellar temperature. An ale should never be cold, but served like a red wine, which surprises many tourists.

Another puzzler for foreigners is the lack of waiter service, though you may find it in some 'lounge' bars. The public bar is where you will find the darts board, and the purist who likes to stand up while he enjoys his pint, and to drink it from a straight, handle-less glass.

Drinking laws

Britain's inconvenient drinking laws are better known. They were devised during the First World War to curb drunkenness and have survived all efforts to reform them. Inner London pubs open from 11.00 until 15.00 and from 17.30 until 23.00. Outer London pubs do everything half an hour earlier. In the financial and commercial heart of The City, pubs may open at 17.00 for the evening, and then close early, remaining shuttered at weekends as well. Ten minutes before closing, the barman sings out "last orders". Closing time is announced as "time gentlemen please", and customers are given a final ten minutes to drink up.

Central London

Anglesea
Selwood Terrace, SW7.
(Kensington) Map **15**K5
On Chelsea borders. Drink outside
in summer. Inside, a pewter beer
engine dispenses such country
specialities as Brakspeare's and
Ruddle's. Fairly basic pub snacks.
Nearby on the corner of Old
Church St. and Fulham Rd.,
publican-turned-novelist Sean
Tracey entertains literati and
artists in the delightfully scruffy
Queen's Elm.

Black Friar
174 Queen Victoria St., EC4.
(Blackfriars) Map **12**F14
The astonishing interior, in
marble, alabaster, bronze and
copper, with friezes depicting
bacchanalia among the friars who
gave the neighbourhood its name,
dates from 1905–24 and is an
outstanding manifestation of the
later period of the Arts and Crafts
Movement. This busy pub, with
seats outside, is handy for the
Mermaid Theatre (see *Nightlife*)
and for *Fleet Street* and *The City*.
Don't miss the tiny nook at the
back of the main bar. A good range
of real ale is served. Closed Sat
evenings and all day Sun.

Bunch of Grapes
207 Brompton Rd., SW3.
(Knightsbridge) Map **16**I6
This pub, w of Harrods, on the way
to the *Victoria and Albert
Museum*, has a beautiful Victorian
interior, with grapes carved in
wood, leaded-glass partitions and
'snob screens' to prevent bar staff
from eavesdropping on your
conversation. Pleasantly dark,
with intimate little bar at the back.
Country beers from Everard's and
Wells. Substantial hot snacks
available.

Cheshire Cheese
Wine Office Court, EC4.
(Fleet St.) Map **11**F13
The pub is on the N side of Fleet
St., and scribes from the street of
saints and sinners still favour Dr
Johnson's old pub for its low-
ceilinged friendliness and
Marston's beer, despite its
inevitably being a tourist haunt.
No food in the pub, but the
adjoining restaurant offers its
famous steak, kidney and game
pudding in winter, and a similar
pie in summer. Reservations are
advisable.

French House
49 Dean St., W1.
(Soho) Map **10**F10
The definitively picaresque Soho
hangout, in which even the bar
staff fit the image. Visitors either
adore 'The French' or wholly fail to
be engaged by its perverse charm,
but true Soho-lovers have been
loyal for decades. Bare except for
fading photographs of French
boxers and stage stars, and the
pewter water-cooler (for your
pastis). Indifferent beer and
unexciting wine; try the
champagne. 'The French', like
such neighbouring pubs as **The
Swiss Tavern** in Old Compton
St., the **Coach and Horses** in
Romilly St., and **The Sun and 13
Cantons**, Gt. Pulteney St., is a
reminder of Soho's ethnic past.

George
77 Borough High St., SE1.
(Lambeth) Map **12**H15
This type of inn, with galleries
from which patrons could watch
shows presented by strolling
players in the courtyard, inspired
the layout of the first theatres,
including Shakespeare's Globe.
The George is the last galleried inn
in London, and only a part of it still
stands. It is most attractive and
comfortable, with four small bars,
one serving bar food, as well as two
restaurants. Wethered's Bitter is
dispensed from a 150yr-old beer
engine.

Grenadier
18 Wilton Row, SW1.
(Belgravia) Map **17**H8
At Hyde Park Corner, down a tiny
unpromising mews called Old
Barrack Yard. Said to have been
the Duke of Wellington's local.
You can drink outside this pretty
pub, and eat full meals inside at
reasonable restaurant prices.
Ruddle's County beer.

Guinea
30 Bruton Place, W1.
(Mayfair) Map **9**G9
In the heart of London, a tiny,
basic pub that would pass for a
village local if it weren't full of
advertising account executives and
book editors. Hard to find, down a
mews, but worth the effort. The
adjoining restaurant serves
excellent beef and good claret, but
is very expensive indeed. The
Guinea is a Mayfair outpost for
Young's brewery in much the way

169

that a nearby mews pub, the **Star Tavern**, Belgrave Mews West, SW1, just off Belgrave Sq., is a showpiece in Belgravia for Fuller's brewery.

Lamb and Flag
Rose St., WC2.
(Covent Garden) Map **10**F11
The poet Dryden dubbed this pub 'The Bucket of Blood' after being mugged in the adjoining alley. It's as dark and poky as ever, but you will meet none more intimidating than the graphic design crowd, spreading themselves almost into Garrick St.

Magpie and Stump
18 Old Bailey, EC4.
(City) Map **12**F14
The lawyers regularly to be seen drinking here can no longer watch the fruits of their labours; the pub was once a vantage point from which to view public executions, and the neighbourhood's Newgate Prison has long gone. But the *Old Bailey* (the Central Criminal Court) is still very much in business. The pub, rebuilt in 1931 but still rich in atmosphere, serves Charrington's IPA.

The Olde Watling
29 Watling St., EC4.
(City) Map **12**F15
In the shadow of *St Paul's Cathedral*, a Wren-built pub restored in the course of this century. Oak-beamed and very busy, serving City types with draught Bass, and traditional English pies.

Red Lion
2 Duke of York St., SW1.
(Piccadilly) Map **10**G10
Behind Simpson's store and gentlemanly Jermyn St. Said to be the best example of a small Victorian gin palace. Burton's beer, hot snacks.

Salisbury
Cecil Court, St Martin's Lane, W1. (Trafalgar Sq.) Map **10**G11
Art Nouveau bronze nymphs and equally decorative predominantly male clientele inhabit this spectacular theatreland pub. Draught Guinness. Cold buffet.

Sun
63 Lamb's Conduit St., WC1.
(Bloomsbury) Map **10**D12
Specialist beer pub offering never less than a dozen out-of-town brews, usually ranging from

Bateman's Good Honest Ales (Lincolnshire) to Timothy Taylor's Ram-Tam (Yorkshire). Landlord Roger Berman will proudly show you his cellars (book in advance) when he is not too busy slaking the thirsts of medics from Great Ormond St. Hospital, or feeding them tasty hot snacks. Further along this charming little street is the **Lamb**, said to have been Dickens' local (see *Dickens' House*), which has an attractive Victorian interior. Young's is the beer that is served here.

Barnes

Sun
Church Rd., SW13
The village pond lies opposite, alive with ducks and fringed with weeping willows and oak trees. There are seats by the pond, but you could just as well sit outside the pub with a pint of Taylor Walker's beer. Inside, it is low-ceilinged and cosy. Remarkably rural for a place which is a double-decker bus ride (no. 9) from Piccadilly. Barnes has lots of interesting pubs. Just down the High Street are the **Bull's Head** for jazz, and the **White Hart** for its riverside verandah. Both sell Young's beer.

Epping Forest

Traveller's Friend
496 High Rd., Woodford Green
Epping Forest is a rural part of the London area rarely visited by tourists, yet full of interest. This pub, within reach of Woodford Station on the tube (Central line), is a good starting point for a visit to the area. It also offers Victorian snob screens and a rare opportunity to sample Ridley's beer.

Greenwich

Cutty Sark
Ballast Quay, SE10
Named after the famous tea clipper, which is permanently berthed nearby, this pub is Georgian in style, and dates from the early 1800s. It serves draught Bass. Another nautical public house, which is situated nearby, at 60 Greenwich Church St., is the **Gipsy Moth**, serving Taylor Walker beer. Greenwich also has a fine Victorian pub in the **Rose and Crown**, 1 Croom's Hill, serving Courage's beer on traditional handpumps.

Hammersmith

Dove
19 Upper Mall, W6
Riverside pub, with terrace, just
upstream from the splendid
Hammersmith Bridge. Part of the
pub was built by George III's son,
Prince Augustus Frederick. Rich
in historical and literary
associations. Fuller's beer. Closer
to the bridge is the **Blue Anchor**,
13 Lower Mall, W6, with a fine
pewter bar and enormous beer
engine serving Courage's beer.

Hampstead

Bull and Bush
North End Way, NW3
Popularized in song by a star of the
19thC music hall, Florrie Forde.
The 'Bull' recalls the days when it
was the site of a farm, and the
'Bush' was a clump of trees planted
when it was the home of Hogarth,
the cartoonist and moralist.
Among the notables who have
drunk here, in the intervening
years, Dickens perhaps forges the
link between the earthiness of the
music hall and the artiness of
Hampstead. The pub is not far
from Hampstead Heath, has its
own garden, and serves Taylor
Walker beer. There are two other
historically interesting pubs
nearby: **Jack Straw's Castle**, also
in North End Way, and the
Spaniards Inn, Spaniards Rd.

Flask
Flask Walk, NW3
Among the well-known
Hampstead pubs, this is the best-
liked locally. It is a genuine
neighbourhood pub, with
interesting tiling inside and out, a
lively regular clientele, and
Young's beer. It is in a pretty
alleyway, near a couple of
bookshops, just round the corner
from Hampstead tube station.
There is another **Flask** across the
Heath at 77 Highgate West Hill,
N6, full of historical interest, and
serving Taylor Walker beer. Both
take their name from the flasks
once used to carry water from wells
in Hampstead.

Richmond

Orange Tree
45 Kew Rd., Richmond
Theatre pub opposite Richmond
station (for details of shows
☎ 940 – 3633). Victorian, large
and rambling, yet somehow

intimate. Young's beer and good
range of bar meals. Richmond has
several good pubs; also especially
recommended is the **Old Ship**, 3
King St. (which faces the main
George St.), for its Young's beer
and its cheering, open fires in
winter.

Southwark

Goose and Firkin
47 Borough Rd., SE1
The beer is brewed in the cellar;
bitters with names like Goose,
Borough, Dogbolter and
Earthstopper bring in an
enthusiastic, young clientele.
Drinkers can see the brewery
through a window at the same
proprietor's **Fox and Firkin**, at
316 Lewisham High St., SW13,
further s. On the other side of
town, a third pub in this growing
mini-chain is the **Frog and
Firkin**, 41 Tavistock Crescent,
W11, not far from Portobello Rd.
A firkin is a nine-gallon cask.

Mayflower
117 Rotherhithe St., SE16
Close to the jetty whence the
Mayflower set sail, this well-
restored pub, with a verandah over
the river, serves Charrington's
IPA. Next door is the Wren church
of St Mary's. In the same dockland
area is one of Pepys' favourite
pubs, the **Angel**, at 101
Bermondsey Wall East, SE16,
serving Courage's beer.

Wapping

Prospect of Whitby
57 Wapping Wall, E1
Recently completely refurbished
and still desperately touristy pub
in old dockland, though the history
and location are genuinely
interesting. The nearby **Tower of
Ramsgate**, 62 Wapping High St.,
E1, is a more honest-to-badness
pub, where hanging once took
place. This East End riverside area
always had a marrow-chilling
mood which has been heightened
by economic depression.

Woolwich

Village Blacksmith
Hillreach, SE18
Since the Nag's Head in
Hampstead closed down, this is the
only house in the capital run by the
consumerist Campaign for Real
Ale, offering the drinker a wide
selection of hand-pumped beers.

Nightlife

After dark, the most evident activity in the West End of
London (The City dies after the evening rush hour) is theatre-
going. It is far less formal and self-conscious than in some
European cities, but even Broadway can hardly match the
elegant bustle of Shaftesbury Avenue as the black cabs deposit
and reclaim theatre-goers. Although the best seats for a big
show can be expensive, the London theatre does offer its
patrons a wide range of prices, so only the most determinedly
philistine visitor fails to catch at least one production. (Those
with a busy schedule might also note that many theatres present
a matinee on Sat and one mid-week day.)

For the Londoner, and for the visitor who thinks of it, a drink
in a pub is a likely part of an evening at the theatre, either as a
rendezvous beforehand or for a nightcap afterwards; that may
depend upon whether you eat before or after the show. Since
most of the West End theatres are near either Soho or Covent
Garden, these two neighbourhoods are the most convenient,
and consequently the most lively, after dark. Don't be put off
by the seediness of Soho; it has lots of reasonably-priced
Chinese (Gerrard, Lisle and Wardour Streets) and Italian (Frith
St.) restaurants, and is a safe place to walk, provided you avoid
the darkest alleys. For a simple stroll, Covent Garden might
seem more relaxing. Elegant Mayfair has a villagey enclave
called Shepherd Market, with pleasant pubs, restaurants and
ladies of the night (or, often, of the broad daylight), whose
presence is not excessively assertive. Elsewhere, Mayfair is, in
general, an area of expensive restaurants, private clubs and
casinos. The main nocturnal area out of the centre of town is
outrageous Chelsea; along King's Rd. and Fulham Rd. parade
the latest trends, strolling (or skating, or whatever) in and out of
pubs, wine bars and lively restaurants.

The closing hours of pubs and restaurants, and the paucity of
late-night transport, have won London a reputation which it
only partly deserves for being insufficiently nocturnal. Like an
ageing, dignified actress, London cherishes its beauty sleep,
but isn't above the occasional exploit in the small hours. The
essential precaution is to lay plans carefully. Be aware that
nightclubs may require membership to be arranged in advance;
and after midnight, summon a cab from the restaurant or
nightclub, rather than expecting to pick one up on the street.

Ballet and opera

Royal Opera House ▥
Bow St., WC2 ☎ *240–1911 (info), 240–1066 (bookings).
Map **11**G11. Matinees Thurs and Sat.*
Covent Garden was always a nocturnal enclave, and its more
recent crop of wine bars and restaurants have helped retain at
least a hint of that. 'Covent Garden' is art critics' shorthand for
the Royal Opera House, one of the most historically interesting
theatres in London, with its Classical facade on Bow St. and its
box office in Floral St. It is now one of the world's most
important venues for opera and ballet, and the greatest artists
appear regularly. Originally named the Theatre Royal, its
establishment derived from the first permissions granted by
King Charles II for the opening of playhouses after the
Restoration. The theatre of Kean and Kemble was twice
burned down before the present building was completed in

1858. The Royal Opera and Royal Ballet both perform at Covent Garden in seasons of alternating productions. Postal bookings open about six weeks before the beginning of a season, and tickets are quickly snapped up, but 65 seats up in 'the gods' (very high in this theatre) are held until the day of the performance. Each person is permitted only one ticket, and there can be long queues, sometimes overnight.

Sadler's Wells Theatre
Rosebery Ave., EC1 ☎278–8916 (info and booking). Map 5C13. Matinees Thurs and Sat.

It is a strange name for a theatre, and Islington is perhaps an unlikely location. The site was originally a garden in which there was a health-giving well, and its owner, whose name was Sadler, opened a 'musick house' there in 1683. The theatre is the base for the Sadler's Wells Royal Ballet company, and has guest seasons including Gilbert and Sullivan productions. It was the original home of the company which became the Royal Ballet, and of the English National Opera.

London Coliseum
St Martin's Lane, WC2 ☎836–7666 (info), 836–3161 (booking). Map 10G11.

The theatre which houses one of London's largest auditoriums is barely visible from the street, but its illuminated globe stands out in the night skyline. For a long time a music hall, it now houses the English National Opera, whose prestigious large-scale productions are usually sung in English.

Bars
The traditional cocktail bar is most easily found in hotels. The **Savoy**'s inspired the famous *Savoy Cocktail Book*, and is believed to have been the first cocktail bar in Europe. The drinks are good, but ambience a little lacking. The **Park Lane Hotel**, the **Inn on the Park** and the **Hyde Park Hotel**, all W1, have good cocktail bars, as do many other hotels.

The younger generation of cocktail bar, featuring confections like the Margarita, Tequila Sunrise or Pina Colada, often doubles as a short-order restaurant, and may be obliged by law to ensure that at least a pastrami sandwich is consumed by each drinker. The definitive example is **Peppermint Park**, at 13 Upper St Martin's Lane, WC2 ☎836–5234. The very well-known **Zanzibar**, 30 Great Queen St., WC2 ☎405–8199, is a private club, and visitors must be introduced by a member.

A change of mood is offered by the wine bar. The traditional type, which grew out of wine merchants' shops, is typified by **El Vino**, 47 Fleet St, EC4, haunt of journalists and lawyers. It is a male chauvinist establishment at which, although waitress service is extended to both sexes, ladies may not obtain their drinks at the bar.

There was a second growth of wine bars during the 1970s, and these are much more numerous. The most extrovert example, jostling with magazine folk and models, is **Brahms and Liszt** (Cockney rhyming slang for the risqué 'pissed', meaning drunk) at 19 Russell St., Covent Garden, WC2. For excellent wines and good food, visit the **Cork and Bottle**, 44–46 Cranbourne St., WC2; and, for Knightsbridge or Sloane St. shoppers, the **Ebury Wine Bar**, 139 Ebury St., SW1 is pleasant and well-run. It is not necessary to eat in wine bars, but most provide a range of cold and some hot food.

Casinos

London does have casinos, but their numbers have in recent years declined drastically in face of regulatory activity by the Gaming Board. Several famous names have vanished, or had their licences suspended, and the future of others is uncertain. It is the more urbane type of casino, usually found in the Mayfair or Knightsbridge districts, which has fallen foul of the Board, but one or two brasher places still brightly proclaim their presence in Soho. Those casinos which have remained in business are not permitted to advertise, which includes mentions in guide books, but they are usually known to hotel concierges. In order to visit a casino, you must either join, which takes 48hr, or be the guest of a member.

Cinema

London has an enormous selection of cinemas, but a lesser choice of films. Two chains, **Odeon** and **ABC**, dominate, and concentrate on box office hits. Art house films are more likely to be shown by independents, so check the *London Standard* or *Time Out* for the following: the **Curzon**, Curzon St., W1 ☎499–3737; the **Gate** cinemas, Brunswick Sq., WC1 ☎837–8402, 87 Notting Hill Gate, W11 ☎221–0220, and Camden High Street, NW1 ☎267–1201; the **Camden Plaza**, 211 Camden High St., NW1 ☎485–2443; the **Chelsea Cinema**, King's Rd., SW3 ☎351–3742; and the **Academy**, at 165 Oxford St., W1 ☎437–2981; (for foreign films) **Screen on the Hill**, 203 Haverstock Hill, NW3 ☎435–3366; **Screen on the Green**, 83 Upper St., N1 ☎226–3520; **Screen on Baker St.**, 96 Baker St., NW1 ☎935–2772; and the **Minema**, 45 Knightsbridge, SW1 ☎235–4225.

In Notting Hill, there's the offbeat **Electric Screen**, 191 Portobello Rd., W11 ☎229–3694. The **Institute of Contemporary Arts**, more commonly known as the ICA ☎930–3647, in The Mall, SW1, has a cinema; and the true celluloid freak heads for the **National Film Theatre** ☎928–3232, in the *South Bank Arts Centre*. It has two cinemas presenting a wide range of films, with retrospectives on the work of individual directors and performers.

Concerts
Classical music

The two most important concert venues are the Royal Albert Hall and the Festival Hall (in the *South Bank Arts Centre*) – each belongs to a different era of optimism and grand gestures.

Royal Festival Hall, Queen Elizabeth Hall, Purcell Room ▥

South Bank, SE1 ☎*928–3191 (info and booking). Map 11G12.*

The **Festival Hall**, built for the Festival of Britain in 1951, is part of the Greater London Council *South Bank Arts Centre* with the **Queen Elizabeth Hall** and the **Purcell Room**. Said by Toscanini to have the finest acoustics in the world, the Festival Hall itself, with 3,000 seats, presents concerts by the leading British and international symphony orchestras. The Queen Elizabeth Hall, which has 1,100 seats, stages chamber music, string quartets and other small ensembles. The 372-seat Purcell Room presents solo performances and other small events. You can see and hear perfectly from all seats, so the cheaper ones are often a good buy. All three halls offer not only classical music but also pop and jazz. Early evening conversations with celebrities of the music world are held in the Waterloo Room of the Queen Elizabeth Hall.

Royal Albert Hall 血
Kensington Gore, SW7 ☎ *589–3203 (info), 589–8212 (booking). Map 15I4.*
The Albert Hall, named after the Prince Consort, is a spectacular manifestation of Victorian architecture, facing Kensington Gardens and the Albert Memorial. It is self-financing, operating independently under Royal Charter. Its best-known annual event is its 'Proms' ('promenade concerts'), founded in 1912 to bring the classics to a wider audience by recapturing the spirit of informal performances in London pleasure gardens. The centre of the circular hall is cleared of seats for the Proms season, which runs from mid-July to early Sept, and a cheap ticket allows you to stand and wander at your leisure while you enjoy the music. Tickets are available at the door on the evening of the performance, except in the case of the Last Night of the Proms, a social event characterized by youthful nostalgia, which is booked up long in advance.

Although a wide range of classical music is performed at the Albert Hall, its keynote is eclecticism. The Hall plays host to pop singers, wrestlers, and the annual Miss World contest.

The new **Barbican Centre** (see *Theatres p178*) is now the regular home of the London Symphony Orchestra, which gives concerts regularly throughout the year.

There are several smaller halls. **Wigmore Hall**, Wigmore St., W1 ☎935–2141, is a famous small concert hall almost within earshot of Oxford St., featuring primarily soloists, many of whom make their London debut there, and early music and Baroque recitals. **Holland Park Court Theatre**, Holland Park, W8 ☎602–2226, presents light opera and orchestral music in summer in the only remaining wing of the 17thC **Holland House**. There is no advance booking. **Kenwood Lakeside** ☎633–1707, is a venue for large-scale orchestral performances on Hampstead Heath on summer weekends. By the lake near Kenwood House is an orchestra shell which has accommodated the Royal Philharmonic and London Symphony, among others. It is possible to reserve a deck chair, or to sit on the grass. There are also performances of chamber music in the **Orangery** of **Kenwood House**.

There are also a number of more offbeat venues, such as the cushion concerts held at the **Royal Academy** ☎379–6722, during its Summer Exhibition of paintings; open only to those aged between 14 and 25, beyond which dignity does not permit people to sit on the floor. There are lunchtime recitals at some of London's most attractive and interesting churches, including **St Martin-in-the-Fields**, and the famous boys' choir of **St Paul's** can be heard during Sun services at the Cathedral.

Folk music
The English Folk Dance and Song Society, at **Cecil Sharp House**, 2 Regent's Park Rd., NW1 ☎485–2206, has performances on Sat at 19.30; and there is traditional English Morris Dancing at **Westminster Abbey**, in front of the main gate of Broad Sanctuary, at 20.00 on summer evenings. British, Irish and American folk music is performed in a variety of clubs and pubs, with dates listed in *Time Out* and *City Limits*.

Jazz

Big-name jazz is always available in London, despite the fact that there are only a few venues. Almost every well-known name in international jazz has played at **Ronnie Scott's Club**, 47 Frith St., W1 ☎439–0747. It looks and feels like a club, and stays open until 3.00, but anybody can enjoy the jazz; meals and drinks are served. The Jazzcentre Society ☎580–8532 presents Mon performances at the **100 Club**, 100 Oxford St., W1 ☎636–0933.

On every evening of the week except Mon, leading British musicians, and occasional guests from other countries, perform at the **Pizza Express**, 10 Dean St., Soho, W1 ☎439–8722. Its companion **Pizza on the Park**, 11 Knightsbridge, SW1 ☎235–5550, has jazz every evening except Sun. Both restaurants belong to the same jazz-crazed owner, who is also active in the Soho community conservation movement. Jazz cognoscenti have an affection for a pub called the **Bull's Head** ☎876–5241, despite its being in an unlikely villagey setting on the river at Barnes, SW13. It offers fine jazz nightly, and especially on Sun lunchtimes, 12.00–14.00, and serves Young's splendid beer.

Rock

London has an ever-lively and ever-changing rock scene. Clubs, concerts and pub dates are listed in *Time Out* and in rock newspapers like *Melody Maker*. All the major rock venues are 30–45min from the West End. They are the **Odeon**, Hammersmith, Queen Caroline St., W6 ☎748–4081; the **Rainbow**, 232 Seven Sisters Rd., N4 ☎263–3148; the **Earls Court Exhibition Centre**, SW7 ☎385–1200; and the **Wembley Arena**, Middlesex ☎902–1234. **Upstairs at Ronnie's**, 47 Frith St., Soho, W1 ☎439–0747, is above the famous jazz club. Also in Soho is the long-established **Marquee** club, 90 Wardour St., W1 ☎437–6603. In Covent Garden, the **Rock Garden**, a club and hamburger bar, is at 6–7 The Piazza, WC2 ☎240–3961. The **Camden Palace** is a converted cinema at 1a Camden Rd., NW1 ☎387–0428. Rock in pubs is a changing scene, but the **Half Moon**, 93 Lower Richmond Rd., SW15 ☎788–2387, and the **King's Head**, Fulham, 4 Fulham High St., SW6 ☎736–1413 are particular favourites with fans.

Nightclubs

If nightingales still sing in Berkeley Square, their songs are directed at the habitués of **Annabel's**, at no. 44 ☎629–3558. "The world's best nightclub", says London's most garrulous gossip columnist, Nigel Dempster. Hermetically discreet, expensive, and an introduction from a member is almost essential. This and other similar clubs are not impossible to get into, but you must arrange something in advance.

Inside will be music and dancing, according to the current fashion, bars, and, in the more exclusive clubs, good meals will be served. Similar proscriptions apply to other haunts of royals and pop stars, like **Raffles**, 287 King's Rd., Chelsea, SW3 ☎352–1091; **Tokyo Joe's**, Clarges St., Mayfair, W1 ☎409–1832; **Stocks**, 107 King's Rd., SW3 ☎351–3461; and **Tramp**, 40 Jermyn St., SW1 ☎734–3174. It is in the nature of such diversions to be affected by fashion –discos have been known to open and close with alarming swiftness, or to announce a violent shift from one trend to another. Such shifts

are best monitored through the several gossip columns of the
London Standard, and the glossy magazine *Harper's & Queen*.

The (Roof) Gardens, 99 Kensington High St., W8
☎937–8923, on top of the old Derry and Toms department
store, has long been a stylish vantage point. Disco queen Regine
failed with a nightspot here, then youthful music magnate
Richard Branson took over, and put in charge Carinthia West,
one-time girlfriend of Mick Jagger. There is special free
introductory membership for holders of American Express,
Diners Club and Visa cards.

Among nightspots open to anybody is **Dingwalls**, Camden
Lock, NW1 ☎267–4967, an unpretentious and youthful spot
for live music (reggae, rock, R&B, jazz), open until 2.00. No
reservations, so get there before 22.00. The **Empire Ballroom**
in Leicester Sq., WC2 ☎437–1446, is an old-style dance hall;
big-band alternates with American disco music and roller disco
on Sun afternoons; open until 2.00, and 3.00 at weekends.
Another famous old dance hall out of town, now catering for all
tastes, is the **Hammersmith Palais**, 242 Shepherds Bush Rd.,
W6 ☎748–2812. More exclusive is **Legends**, 29 Old
Burlington St., Mayfair, W1 ☎437–9933, inspired by New
York's Studio 54, with disco, French cuisine, and prices that
are not prohibitive. Non-members are admitted at the
discretion of the doorman, as at **Stringfellows**, 16 St Martin's
Lane, WC2 ☎240–5534. Glass dance-floor, suede walls and
lots of chrome set the tone for what is intended to be an
elegantly casual clientele. Proprietor Peter Stringfellow has
also transformed the old Talk of the Town into the popular
Hippodrome, Charing Cross Rd., WC2 ☎437–4311,
particularly lively on Fri and Sat; dress up. '**Heaven**',
Underneath the Arches, Villiers St, WC2 ☎839–3863, is the
best gay nightclub with mixed nights on Tues and Thurs.
Villa dei Cesari, 135 Grosvenor Rd., SW3 ☎828–7453,
offers dinner and dancing, in an opulent Roman-style
restaurant, overlooking the river near the Chelsea
Embankment; an expensive treat. Also recommended for
dinner and dancing: **La Bussola**, 42 St Martin's Lane, WC2
☎240–1148.

Theatres

Despite financial pressures, London remains one of the major
world centres of theatre, and the British still produce many of
the greatest actors. The theatre scene can be split into three
broad categories: companies subsidized by the state, in
impressive buildings, producing serious drama to the highest
standards; commercial theatres, mainly built at the turn of the
century in a style of cosy splendour, mounting lighter plays and
musicals; and fringe or club theatres, which might do anything
anywhere, but should not be missed by serious theatre-goers.
The major subsidized theatres usually have several plays in
repertory at one time; most other theatres have a single play
running as long as it is successful.

A booth on the w side of Leicester Sq., WC2, has half-price
seats to same-day shows with spare tickets in West End
theatres. There is a small service charge, a maximum of four
seats per person, and there can be a long queue, but it is a good
deal. Many theatre bars welcome advance bookings for interval
drinks, a system which saves the crush, frustration and thirst.
Most theatres close on Sun. Cheaper seats in some of the older
theatres may allow only a partial view.

The National Theatre ⅲ
Upper Ground, South Bank, SE1 ☎ *633–0880 (info),*
928–2252 (booking). Map **11***G13.*
The National Theatre company, originally under the direction
of Laurence Olivier, began its life at the Old Vic in the Waterloo
Rd. Sir Peter Hall took over in 1973 ready for the opening of
the new, purpose-built theatre, a modern architectural
landmark, in the *South Bank Arts Centre*. 'The National'
actually comprises three theatres within one building. The
largest, the **Olivier**, has an amphitheatre setting; the
Lyttelton has a proscenium stage; and the **Cottesloe** is a
studio theatre. The three present a wide range of classical and
modern, British and international works. Before performances
there is live music in the foyers, picture galleries are open, and
there are early evening lectures, poetry readings and short
plays, from 18.00. Although many performances are heavily
booked, the National always retains some seats for sale on the
day, and has reduced-price standby tickets. There are also
backstage tours.

Barbican Theatre (Royal Shakespeare Company)
Barbican Centre, EC2. Map **11***E15* ☎ *628–8795.*
The finest productions of the world's greatest dramatist, many
would say. In any case, the RSC enjoys worldwide repute. This
is its new London base, which complements its Stratford home
(see *Excursions*), where many of the theatre's productions
originate. Besides Shakespeare, the company also performs a
wide variety of standard and new plays. With *Nicholas Nickleby*
and *The Greeks*, the company pioneered productions in which
one major work spanned two or three performances. It also runs
a studio theatre, **The Pit**, in the Barbican, which books through
the same box office.

The Royal Court Theatre
Sloane Sq., SW1 ☎ *730–1745. Map* **16***J7.*
Despite its name, this theatre has a distinguished record of
anti-establishment drama. George Bernard Shaw's plays were
presented here in the 1920s and 1930s; and John Osborne, the
original 'angry young man', and Arnold Wesker made their
names here in the 1950s and 1960s. John Arden, Edward Bond
and David Storey are more recent examples. There is also a
smaller **Theatre Upstairs** ☎ 730–2554.

The oldest theatre in London is the **Theatre Royal**, Drury
Lane, WC2 ☎ 836–8108, which specializes in musicals and hit
shows. The most elegant is the **Theatre Royal**, **Haymarket**,
SW1 ☎ 930–9832, presenting a high standard of 'legitimate'
theatre. Both date back to the Restoration. The most famous is
probably **The Palladium**, Argyll St., W1 ☎ 437–7373, which
has a policy of family entertainment, and plays host to most of
the top international stars. **Regent's Park Open Air Theatre**,
NW1 ☎ 486–2431, presents Shakespearean works throughout
the summer.

'Off West End', **The Mermaid**, Puddle Dock, EC4
☎ 236–5568, is a much-loved subsidized theatre run by Sir
Bernard Miles in what was a blitzed warehouse on the Thames.
It is a notably friendly and unpretentious place, with a string of
great successes to its name.

A few of the more permanent fringe theatres are listed
below; publications such as *Time Out* will give details of the

smaller, more transient ones. An exquisite 1895 auditorium
has been lovingly retained inside a modern concrete shell at the
Lyric, Hammersmith, King St., W6 ☎741–2311, offering
serious classical and modern drama. Neighbours are
Riverside Studios ☎748–3354 and **The Bush** ☎743–3388,
a pub theatre. Another pub theatre is the **King's Head**, 115
Upper St., N1 ☎226–1916. Other well-regarded venues away
from the centre include the **Hampstead Theatre Club**,
Swiss Cottage, NW3 ☎722–9301, and the **Greenwich
Theatre**, Crooms Hill, SE10 ☎858–7755.

Other theatres include:
Adelphi (commercial)   Strand, WC2 ☎836–7611
Albery (commercial)   St Martin's Lane, WC2 ☎836–3878
Ambassadors (commercial)   West St., WC2 ☎836–6111
Apollo (commercial)   Shaftesbury Ave., W1 ☎437–2663
Apollo Victoria (commercial)   Wilton Rd., SW1 ☎828–8665
Arts Theatre Club (commercial)   6/7 Gt Newport St., WC2
☎836–3334
Astoria (commercial)   157 Charing Cross Rd., WC2
☎734–4287
Cambridge (commercial)   Earlham St., WC2 ☎836–6056
Cockpit (fringe)   Gateforth St., NW8 ☎402–5081
Comedy (commercial)   Panton St., SW1 ☎930–2578
Criterion (commercial)   Piccadilly Circus, W1 ☎930–3216
Duchess (commercial)   Catherine St., WC2 ☎836–8243
Duke of York's (commercial)   St Martin's Lane, WC2
☎836–5122
Fortune (commercial)   Russell St., WC2 ☎836–2238
Garrick (commercial)   Charing Cross Rd., WC2 ☎836–4601
Globe (commercial)   Shaftesbury Ave., W1 ☎437–1592
Her Majesty's (commercial)   Haymarket, SW1 ☎930–6606
ICA (club)   The Mall, SW1 ☎930–3647
Jeanetta Cochrane (subsidized)   Southampton Row, WC1
☎242–7040
Lyric (commercial)   Shaftesbury Ave., W1 ☎437–3686
Mayfair (commercial)   Stratton St., W1 ☎629–3036
New London Theatre   Drury Lane, WC2 ☎405–0072
Old Vic (commercial)   Waterloo Rd., SE1 ☎928–7616
Palace (commercial)   Shaftesbury Ave., W1 ☎437–6834
Phoenix (commercial)   Charing Cross Rd., WC2 ☎836–8611
Piccadilly (commercial)   Denman St., W1 ☎437–4506
Players Theatre Club (club)   Villiers St., WC2 ☎839–1134
Prince Edward (commercial)   Old Compton St., W1
☎437–6877
Prince of Wales (commercial)   Coventry St., W1 ☎930–8681/2
Queen's (commercial)   Shaftesbury Ave., W1 ☎734–1166
St George's (commercial/fringe)   49 Tufnell Park Rd., N7
☎607–1128
St Martin's (commercial)   West St., WC2 ☎836–1443/4
Savoy (commercial)   Savoy Court, WC2 ☎836–8888
Shaftesbury (commercial)   Princes Circus, WC2 ☎379–5399
Strand (commercial)   Aldwych, WC2 ☎836–2660
Theatre Royal, Stratford East (commercial)   Gerry Raffles Sq.,
E15 ☎534–0310
Vaudeville (commercial)   Strand, WC2 ☎836–9988
Victoria Palace (commercial)   Victoria St., SW1 ☎834–1317
Whitehall (commercial)   14 Whitehall, SW1 ☎930–7765
Wyndhams (commercial)   Charing Cross Rd., WC2
☎836–3028

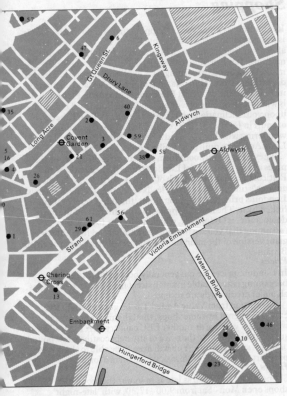

Shopping

It is nothing as mundane as shopping that you do in London. It is promenading in the fashionable King's Rd. on a Saturday afternoon after having been busked at in Portobello Rd. in the morning. It is listening to the spiel in Petticoat Lane street market on a Sunday morning. It is exploring the world's biggest department store, **Harrods**, in Knightsbridge, and comparing its food with the exotica at **Fortnum & Mason** in Piccadilly. It is window-dreaming of jade and jewels in Bond St. Depending upon your inclinations, it is the sensation of silk in **Liberty**, or of snuff in Jermyn St. It is relaxing in Covent Garden and wondering whether you need a French horn (**Paxman**, 116 Long Acre) or a quill pen (**Philip Poole**, 182 Drury Lane).

These neighbourhoods form a jigsaw stretching five or six miles across the centre of London from Chelsea in the w to Petticoat Lane in the E. Each of them is worth half a day of anyone's time, and every one leads to another. None of them is London's principal shopping street, though several of them are linked by it. The main shopping thoroughfare, and the most democratic, is Oxford St., which itself runs from w to E (assuming that you see the most traditional end first). It is a giant version of the main shopping street of every town or city in Britain.

Prices

In London, prices are not generally negotiable, although bargaining is acceptable in some street markets. In most shops, all major credit cards are accepted.

Exemption from Value Added Tax on goods bought for export is offered by some shops, though this is not always workable if you live in another EEC country. VAT can add a substantial amount to the price of any item costing a few pounds or more, so do enquire. You will need to be able to show your passport, and the shop will ask you to fill in a form.

Hours

Shops do not stay open as late as in some other countries. Most shops open Mon–Sat from 9.00–17.30, with 'late-night' shopping once a week. The Chelsea and Knightsbridge area stays open until 19.00 on Wed, and Oxford Street until 20.00 on Thurs. Some consolation is that few shops close for lunch. Some shops in Bond St. and a few others in the West End close on Sat. Central London shops do not as yet open on Sun although new laws may change that in future.

Although central London has few 'local' or corner shops, inner-city neighbourhoods have plenty, and they often open until mid-evening, or even midnight, and on Sun.

Antiques

At the top end of the price range, and for the best that money can buy, visit the famous specialists in Bond St., W1, and the adjoining streets and arcades. Examples range from the **Antique Porcelain Company**, at 149 New Bond St., to **The Leger Galleries**, for old masters, at 13 Old Bond St., or **Sac Frères**, for amber, at 45 Old Bond St. The serious buyer will also want to head out to Kensington Church St., W8, which has several high-quality shops. At the s end of this hilly street, **Scalpay**, at no. 32b, deals in icons; further up is **The Lacquer Chest**, at no. 75; at the Notting Hill end, **Philip and Bernard Dombey** sell antique clocks at no. 174. Nearby is Westbourne Grove, W2, for cheaper antiques, and for interesting shops like

Dodo, at no. 185, which deals in interesting old advertising materials. The New King's Rd. beyond World's End has also become peppered with quality antique shops, and, farther on, the Wandsworth Bridge Rd. with shops dealing in pine.

In recent years, several permanent, indoor antique markets have been established. In the Bond St. area, **Gray's Mews Antique Market** is at 1–7 Davies St., W1; there are about 300 stalls, in a pleasant, well-appointed former factory building, with a lot of Art Nouveau and Deco, and an excellent stall for tin toys. Across Oxford St., Gee's Court or Duke St. leads to the old-established market in **Barrett St.**, W1, with silver, jewellery, antiques and bric-à-brac.

Among the indoor markets, the insiders prefer **Alfies**, rather isolated from shopping areas in Marylebone, at 1 Church St., NW8, selling old lace, antique photographic equipment, genuine antique street signs, with the added interest of the bustle, gossip and dealing. The other neighbourhood for indoor markets is Chelsea/Kensington. The **Chelsea Antique Market**, at 245 King's Rd., SW3, is a maze of stalls, run by seasoned dealers in all types of antiques. **Antiquarius**, 135 King's Road at the corner of Flood St., has always been very conscious of trends.

(See also *Street markets p188*.)

Auction houses

Auctions are a part of London's metropolitan life. If you fancy taking a look, don't be intimidated by newspaper stories of six-figure bids; most items go for much less, and, if you keep your hands firmly on your lap, you can enjoy the auction without parting with any money. It is not necessary to reserve a seat. Sales are listed on the back page of *The Times* each day, and there are always viewing days beforehand. The most renowned salerooms are the following.

Bonhams   Montpelier St., SW7 ☎584–9161. Especially good for furniture and paintings. You may pick up a bargain.
Christies   8 King St., SW1 ☎839–9060. One of the two great names. Fine art, and speciality auctions, including wine sales. Christie's other saleroom at 85 Brompton Rd., South Kensington, SW7, is worth visiting for less expensive items of general interest.
Phillips   7 Blenheim St., W1 ☎629–6602. Prices usually in the medium range. Objets d'art, and various collectibles.
Sotheby's   34/5 New Bond St., W1 ☎493–8080. The other great name, and the biggest. Fine art, porcelain, jewellery, costume, books, Victoriana and decorative arts.

Books

The street for the bibliophile is Charing Cross Rd., ./C2, with numerous shops, including **Foyles** (one of the world's biggest) at no. 119, and the excellent **Waterstones** next door. In fascinating alleys like Cecil Court, hours pass quickly in the secondhand book shops. Regular shops of particular interest are **Zwemmer** at no. 76–80, for art, architecture and cinema; and **Collet's** at no. 64–66, for political and philosophical works of the Left. Away from Charing Cross Rd., **Hatchards**, in Piccadilly, is a pleasant, well-stocked general bookshop. For the academically-inclined, **Dillon's University Bookshop**, 1 Malet St., Bloomsbury, is highly recommended. **The Children's Book Centre**, in **Young World**, 229 Kensington High St., W8, has a huge stock for children up to age 13.

China

The English invented bone china, and the famous names display themselves proudly in Regent St., W1, especially Wedgwood and Spode at **Gered**, no. 158. There is an even more opulent display at **Thomas Goode**, 19 South Audley St., W1, with its Minton elephants within range of the hunting rifles across the road at the gunsmith's **James Purdey & Sons**. China, glassware, and all sorts of elegant household goods can be found at the **General Trading Company**, 144 Sloane St., SW1, near Sloane Sq., and at department stores like **Liberty**, **John Lewis**, **Selfridges** and **Harrods**, (see *p186*). For its selection, **Chinacraft**, in Regent St., W1, New Bond St., W1, and branches, is noteworthy; and for bargains, try the **Reject China Shop**, 33–35 Beauchamp Pl., SW3.

Clothes
Clothes for children

Britain's maritime tradition is upheld even for children by **Rowes**, at 17 Old Bond St., W1, which began by making clothes for the children of naval families. This traditional line shares the shop with such children's classics as button-bar shoes and velvet-collared tweed coats. Visit **Liberty** (see *Department stores p186*), **Zero Four**, in South Molton St., W1, and **Little Horrors**, 16/22 Cheval Pl., SW3.

Clothes for men

Savile Row is the place for suits, Jermyn St. for accoutrements, definitive addresses for the English gentleman.

In Savile Row, W1, the appositely named **H. Huntsman and Sons**, at no. 11, is famous for riding clothes, and has been a tailor to royalty for more than a hundred years; very expensive, and no credit cards. Other renowned names in Savile Row include **Gieves & Hawkes**, at no. 1, **Anderson & Sheppard** at no. 30, and **Tommy Nutter**, fraternized by Elton John and Mick Jagger, at no. 18. For classic and casual suits, try **Blades of Savile Row**, at 8 Burlington Gardens, W1. Also nearby is **Austin Reed**, 103 Regent St., W1, and **Aquascutum**, 100 Regent St., W1. At 35 Dover St., W1, **Crolla** sells wonderfully *outré* clothes for men (and women) in beautiful rococo brocade prints. And **Paul Smith** in Covent Garden, at 43 Floral St., is another trendy menswear shop that has made a name for itself.

In Jermyn St., SW1, a man can no longer sweat out a hangover in the Turkish baths, but he can still have a shave and haircut, buy himself a clean shirt, and prepare to face the world. It is still a male street, in the debonair sense of the word. Buy moustache wax or a badger-hair shaving brush at **Ivan's**, no. 20, or an antique meerschaum at **Astleys**, no. 109. Top-quality shirts are available from **Harvie and Hudson**, at nos. 77 and 96, or the extrovert **Turnbull and Asser**, at no. 71. For a bowler hat (a 'derby' to Americans), for townwear, where better to go than the originators of the style, **James Lock**, nearby at 6 St James's St., SW1. For a tweed cap, visit **Bates**, at 21a Jermyn St., where the shop's late cat (it died in 1921) watches you from a glass case. Of the department stores **Simpson's**, 203 Piccadilly, W1, is most noted for menswear.

Clothes for women

Young British designers are very much in the international limelight these days, and London's importance as a fashion centre has never been greater.

The Bond St. area has the premises of internationally-known British designers like the romantic **Bill Gibb** at 17 Old Bond

St., W1; **Zandra Rhodes**, weaving fantasies from chiffon at 14a Grafton St., W1; and the 'Royal Wedding' **Emanuels**, at 26a Brook St., W1. No one would consider visiting any of these establishments unless provocatively clad in lingerie by **Janet Reger** of 2 Beauchamp Pl., SW3, or at least feeling able to afford to be.

For more accessible creations, nearby South Molton St., W1, is browsily full of interesting clothes and best known for high fashion and sporty items at the several **Browns** shops. Similar lines and accessories abound in St Christophers Pl., W1, just across Oxford St.

Head w via Knightsbridge, Sloane St. and Brompton Rd., dropping in to department stores like **Harvey Nichols**, Knightsbridge, SW1, and **Harrods' Way In** boutique (see *Department Stores p186*) for a wide range of British designer clothes, en route to **Laura Ashley** for blossoming 'country' smocks and blouses (9 Harriet St., SW1, and branches), finally reaching Beauchamp Pl., SW3. This pretty little street is crammed with fashion, from smart **Caroline Charles** at no. 11, by way of ethereal **Monsoon** at no. 53 to **The Beauchamp Pl. Shop** at nos. 37 and 55, selling British and foreign designer clothes respectively.

King's Rd., Chelsea, SW3, is best known these days for the bizarre, and often ephemeral, but it never fails to offer a wide variety of visual stimuli. Punk was popularized at no. 153, at a shop originally called 'Acme Attractions' then renamed **Boy**. Some of the most flamboyant attractions are grouped round a shop which is named after its location, **World's End** (but remembered by early punks as 'Seditionaries'), at no. 430; look out for the high-speed clock which whirls around backwards.

The best furs can be bought at a price at **Calman Links**, 149 Brompton Rd., SW3 – you can visit the workshops upstairs. Alternatively, hire one for an evening from **Moss Bros.**, Bedford St., WC2. For hats, the centre of the **Frederick Fox** millinery business is a tiny salon at 26 Brook St., W1.

(See also *Department stores p186*. All have women's fashion departments.)

Knitwear

The hugely successful Italian chain, **Benetton**, have branches all over London, including 23 Brompton Rd., SW3. British specialities, such as chunky knits and tweeds, can be bought from **Ireland House Shop**, 150 New Bond St., W1. **The Scotch House**, 2 Brompton Rd., SW3, 84 Regent St., W1, and branches, is the shop for Fair Isle, Shetland, Pringle, Ballantyne and tartans. More imaginative sweaters are to be found at **Scottish Merchant**, 16 New Row, Covent Garden; artisan, handmade designers' sweaters in beautiful patterns and colours. Visit **Peal & Co.** for cashmere and luxury, in majestic Burlington Arcade, W1, one shop for women and men. More economical are the branches of **Westaway and Westaway**, 65 Great Russell St., and 29 Bloomsbury Way, both WC1, famous for bargains, and **Marks and Spencer** (see *Department stores p186*).

Outerwear

For both men and women, tweed jackets, high-quality trench coats and double-breasted raincoats are the specialities at **Aquascutum**, 100 Regent St., W1. Plaid-lined raincoats and fine cashmere coats are the hallmarks of **Burberrys**, 18–22 Haymarket, SW1. Complete the outfit with a stick or umbrella from **James Smith & Sons**, 53 New Oxford St., WC1.

185

Crafts

The **British Crafts Centre**, 43 Earlham St., Covent Garden, WC2, sells original ceramics and jewellery. Also in Covent Garden, on Sat, is Britain's largest display of crafts, at the Jubilee Market. If you feel you need to know a little more before you go shopping for this particular type of merchandise, visit the **Crafts Council**, 8 Waterloo Pl., SW1, off Pall Mall – not a shop but an exhibition centre. Another specialist craft shop is the **Craftsman Potters' Shop**, Marshall St., W1, on the site of William Blake's house in Soho, noteworthy for stoneware. Nearby, at 17 Newburgh St., W1, is the **Craftwork Gallery**, with a wider range of products, including knitwear and weaves. **The Design Centre**, 28 Haymarket, SW1, is an essential port of call for those interested in contemporary British products.

Department stores

Household names abound, especially along Oxford St., where **Selfridges** introduced the American concept of the department store in 1909. Closer to Oxford Circus, a much more British response can be seen in the sober but reliable **John Lewis**. Four stores are tourist attractions in themselves.
Fortnum & Mason   181 Piccadilly, W1, is an aristocratic and exotic grocery store with tail-coated assistants, founded by a footman to Queen Anne, and famous for preserves, biscuits, and the like. Have afternoon tea in the Fountain restaurant. The upstairs floors are devoted to fashion and other items.
Harrods   Knightsbridge, SW1 (actually in Brompton Rd.), is the biggest and best-known department store. Imperial flourishes like the zoo have been trimmed, but the food hall still feels and looks like Britain's greatest provision merchant's. Harrods will get you anything, even if it has to be ordered. In fashion and home-making, a very wide range of tastes is met.
Liberty   Regent St., W1, gave its name to a design style embracing fabrics, silver, glassware and furniture during the Art Nouveau period. 'Liberty prints' and 'Liberty silks' are still renowned. This heritage is evident, as are the store's origins as an importer of oriental goods, although today's range of merchandise is much wider. Worth a visit just for its 1924 mock-Elizabethan building.
Marks and Spencer   458 and 173 Oxford St., W1, and branches. It is for knitwear and other items of mainly British, well-made clothing that visitors go to M & S, and local office workers shop there for superb convenience food. Whatever you buy, it will be good value. It is not a department store in the traditional sense of the word, but what a metamorphosis from the utilitarian 'Marks & Sparks' of the past!

Fine art

The commercial galleries are predominantly in two short and elegant streets, Cork and Albemarle, in Mayfair, W1, and in nearby parts of Bond St. Of special note is **Thomas Agnew & Son**, 43 Old Bond St., selling paintings from all periods. For contemporary art, go to **Browse and Darby**, 19 Cork St., **Christies**, 8 Dover St., and **Marlborough Fine Art**, 39 Old Bond St., which often deals in the really big names. The occasional gallery has opened in Covent Garden, WC2.

Food and drink

Don't visit London without 'laying down' an English Christmas pudding from one of the great department stores (see above).

Their food halls offer an experience which is uniquely metropolitan, even if the biscuits come from Bath or Carlisle, the shortbread and whisky from Scotland. There is an especially Scottish flavour about the food hall at **Barker's**, Kensington High St., W8, and all these stores have well presented gift packs of teas and other specialities. Their hampers, which can be sent abroad, are costly but fabulous.

Gourmet foods also dazzle the eye at **Hobbs**, 3 Garrick St., Covent Garden, WC2. All these shops and food halls incorporate excellent wine merchants; a specialist vintner of note is the old-established **Berry Bros. & Rudd**, 3 St James's St., SW1, whose shop contains a superb pair of antique scales. For the finest selection of Scotch whiskies (single malts, not the commercial blends), go to the **Soho Wine Market**, 3 Greek St., W1.

Other specialist food shops include the following.

For chocolates **Bendicks**, who hold the royal warrant, at 55 Wigmore St., W1, 3 Grosvenor St., W1 and branches; **Charbonnel et Walker**, 31 Old Bond St., W1; and **Prestat**, 24 South Molton St., W1.

For the best English cheese and ham **Paxton & Whitfield**, 93 Jermyn St., SW1.

For health foods, including a superb range of breads **Cranks**, 8 Marshall St., W1, or the extraordinary selection of shops in **Neal's Yd.**, Earlham St., Covent Garden, WC2.

Household

Conran, 77 Fulham Rd., SW3, and **Habitat**, 206 King's Rd., SW10, and branches, are the names that have dominated British household design in the past couple of decades. Habitat is also at 156 Tottenham Court Rd., W1, and with **Heal's**, at no. 196, now owned by the Conran empire. For more traditional furniture, try **Maples**, at no. 141.

Jewellery

London's diamond centre is Hatton Garden, EC1. The emphasis is on the trade, but some shops, like **R. Holt**, at no. 98, welcome the public. The royal jewellers are **Garrard**, at 112 Regent St., W1. Anything from a jewel box to a gold-plated toothbrush can be had at **Asprey**, 165 New Bond St., W1; in the same street is **Cartier**, at no. 175. For very fashionable jewellery, visit **Butler and Wilson**, at 189 Fulham Rd., SW3.

Music

The biggest record shop is **HMV**, 363 Oxford St., W1, with a vast stock covering all categories. Specialist shops include: **Virgin Records**, 14–16 Oxford St., W1, for British rock and for new wave; **Rough Trade Records**, some way out of the centre, geographically as well as musically, at 202 Kensington Park Rd., W11; **Collets**, 180 Shaftesbury Ave., W1, for British folk music and jazz; and jazz buffs will also want to see the famous **Dobell's Jazz Record Shop**, which has moved to 21 Tower St., W1, off Shaftesbury Ave. (☎240–1354). Classical music is available from **The Gramophone Exchange**, 80 Wardour St., Soho (☎437–5313); and from **Henry Stave**, 11 Gt. Marlborough St., W1.

Perfumers

All the international brands are best bought in department stores. For English flower perfumes, visit the old-established

Floris, 89 Jermyn St., SW1, or the fashionably traditional
Penhaligon's, 41 Wellington St., WC2.

Pharmacies

Harley Street's suppliers, **John Bell and Croyden**, nearby at 50
Wigmore St., W1, can meet any pharmaceutical need, and the
shop carries cosmetics. Homeopathic specialists **A. Nelson**,
at 73 Duke St., W1, by appointment to the Queen, has
wonderfully Victorian premises. For more conventional needs,
Boots and **Underwoods** have branches all over London.

Photographic

To buy a camera, try **City Camera Exchange**, 124 High
Holborn, WC1, or **Dixons**, 88 Oxford St., and branches. For
films, use the **Boots** or **Underwood** chains, which also develop
films fast. **Fotofast**, 150 Kings Cross Rd., WC1, and branches,
sells film, and has a six-hour processing service. **Foto Inn**
proposes a one-hour service at 35 South Molton St., W1.

   For emergency repairs: in Soho, **Advance Technical**, 24
Poland St., W1, and **Sendean**, 6 d'Arblay St., W1; near
Trafalgar Sq., **Technical Cameras**, 31 Whitcomb St., WC2.

Shoes

Fashion shoe shops abound in Bond and South Molton Streets,
W1. Men who want the best and can wait for it can order
bespoke boots fit for royalty from **John Lobb** at 9 St James' St.,
SW1; they keep on the premises a wooden last of every
customer. Sturdy, traditional footwear can be bought nearby at
Maxwell's, 11 Savile Row, W1, and slightly less expensively at
Tricker's, 67 Jermyn St., SW1. The Queen buys shoes from
Rayne, 15–16 Old Bond St., W1 (and branches).

Tobacco

Even non-smokers are charmed by the curio-filled premises of
Fribourg & Treyer, selling tobacco, snuff, and accessories like
spoons, at 214 Piccadilly, W1. **Dunhill** is not far away, at 30
Duke St., St James's, SW1.

Toys

The biggest toy shop in the world is **Hamleys**, 186 Regent St.,
W1. Parents who believe play should be educative favour **Galt
Toys**, within Liberty (see *Department Stores p186*). Victorian
reproductions are available at **Pollock's Toy Museum**, 1
Scala St., W1, and Covent Garden Market, WC2.

Street markets

The famous ones are still fun, but see some of the others, too.
London has 50 or 60 street markets and it is here that the town
best demonstrates its wit, wisdom, and elusive code. If you
demonstrate your own, you might knock prices down. You will
not find credit accepted, only English cheques, so take cash.
Portobello Road   Sat antique market, especially well known
for its silver. Easy to find – and to explore, since it is basically
one street – but it stretches for more than a mile. Lunch on
crêpes at **Obelix** (see *Restaurants*), or get a take-away health-
food snack at one of the shops near the road bridge. Start by
taking the underground to Notting Hill Gate, and walk via
Pembridge Rd., W11, following the crowd. Antiques and junk
come first, then freaky shops, and finally food, at the N end of
the street.

Petticoat Lane Middlesex St., E1. Junk market in the East End on Sun, and only one part of a maze of street trade where the patois embraces Cockney rhyming slang, Yiddish and Bengali. Serious bargain-hunters start at the improbable hour of 4.00 with the Cheshire St. (E2) and Brick Lane (E1) areas, where the action subsides well before 9.00. The more touristic Petticoat Lane itself (real name, Middlesex Street) is in full swing by then, and impossibly crowded by 11.00. Take lunch at Bloom's (see *Restaurants*); you'll have to queue, but after that early start, the chicken soup will be manna. The nearest underground stations are Liverpool Street and Aldgate East.

Camden Passage Camden Passage, N1. Wed morning and all day Sat for the good quality antiques; Tues for coins; Thurs and Fri for books. A permanent shop here, **Chiu**, at 10 Charlton Pl., N1, helped pioneer interest in Art Deco, something of a theme in the market, especially in the Athenai Arcade. Everyone goes to the Camden Head pub or Natalie's coffee shop. Otherwise lunch at M'sieur Frog or Sultan's Delight (see *Restaurants*). Go by underground to Angel, and walk up Islington High St.

Bermondsey (New Caledonian) Long Lane and Tower Bridge Rd., SE1, on Fri. The insiders' antique market, where the cognoscenti hunt by flashlight at 5.00 in the morning, grab their purchases by 8.30 at the latest, then retire for breakfast at the Rose Dining Rooms. As if that weren't a sufficiently daunting venture, the market is also hard to find – through such challenges, Bermondsey has remained a market for the seriously interested. Go by underground to London Bridge, and walk down Bermondsey St.

Camden Lock Camden High St./Chalk Farm Rd., NW1. Sun market with an entertaining mix of junk and attractions, including books, musical instruments, clothing and snacks. It stretches for a mile from Chalk Farm underground. The main market is by Regent's Canal.

Clothing sizes

When shops give clothing sizes in inches or centimetres, use the following conversion scale to determine the correct size

12 in	16	20	24	28	32	36	40	44	48
30 cm	40	50	60	70	80	90	100	110	120

When standardized codes are used, although these may be found to vary considerably, the following provides a useful guide.

Women's clothing sizes

UK/US sizes	8/6	10/8	12/10	14/12	16/14	18/16
Bust in/cm	31/80	32/81	34/86	36/91	38/97	40/102
Hips in/cm	33/85	34/86	36/91	38/97	40/102	42/107

Men's clothing sizes

European code (suits)	44	46	48	50	52	54	56
Chest in/cm	34/86	36/91	38/97	40/102	42/107	44/112	46/117
Collar in/cm	13½/34	14/36	14½/37	15/38	15½/39	16/41	16½/42
Waist in/cm	28/71	30/76	32/81	34/86	36/91	38/97	40/102
Inside leg in/cm	28/71	29/74	30/76	31/79	32/81	33/84	34/86

Men's and women's shoe sizes

UK/US sizes	3/4½	4/5½	5/6½	6/7½	7/8½	8/9½	9/10½	10/11½	11/12½
European	36	37	38	39	40	41	42	43	44

Biographies

A list of the famous whose names are linked with London would be endless. The following personal selection pays particular attention to those mentioned in this book.

Adam, Robert (1728–92)
The great Scottish Neo-Classical architect and designer brought new refinement to the town and country houses of London.

Albert, Prince (1819–61)
Queen Victoria's consort endeared himself to Londoners, despite his German origin. He left his stamp on the capital in the massive *Kensington* museum and learned society complex.

Bacon, Sir Francis (1561–1626)
The great philosopher and statesman of the Elizabethan and Jacobean period was a member of *Gray's Inn*.

Boadicea (died AD 61)
Now considered a national heroine, the warlike queen led her Icenie tribe against the Romans, razing London to the ground before her defeat. Her statue graces Westminster Bridge.

Browning, Robert (1812–89)
Apart from 15yr spent in Italy with his wife Elizabeth Barrett of Wimpole St. fame, the Victorian poet spent most of his life in London, largely by the *Grand Union Canal* at Little Venice.

Carlyle, Thomas (1795–1881)
Author of *The French Revolution* and in many ways the essential Victorian intellectual, Carlyle lived for 47yr in *Chelsea* in preference to his native Scotland. *Carlyle's House* is as he left it.

Charles I (1600–49)
The most ambitious of Britain's royal patrons ended his reign on the scaffold after defeat in the Civil War with Parliament. He was led to his execution from his own *Banqueting House*.

Charles II (1630–85)
Perhaps the most flamboyant of kings, Charles II enjoys enduring fame thanks to his indiscreet relationships with the likes of Nell Gwynne. More significantly, he was a great patron of the London theatre, developed the royal parks and presided over the rebuilding of *The City*.

Chaucer, Geoffrey (c.1340–1400)
The greatest of the medieval English poets was for many years a senior customs official of the port of London. The pilgrims of *The Canterbury Tales* set off from a Southwark inn.

Churchill, Sir Winston (1874–1965)
The steadfastness of the wartime national leader helped Londoners endure the horrors of the German bombing of their city – the Blitz. This he successfully organized from his secret cabinet war rooms beneath government buildings in Whitehall.

Constable, John (1776–1837)
The great painter of the English countryside lived for many years in *Hampstead*. Several of his finest works, on view at the *Victoria & Albert Museum*, show views of the Heath. He is buried in Hampstead parish churchyard.

Coram, Thomas (c. 1668–1751)
This bluff sea captain became one of the 18thC's leading philanthropists on his retirement, setting up the Foundling Hospital. The *Coram Foundation* displays works by the artists whom Coram enlisted into his fund-raising efforts.

Cubitt, Thomas (1788–1855)
To this energetic man can be credited some of the finest housing in London. Establishing the first modern building firm and

inventing the concept of 'speculative builder', he constructed much of *Bloomsbury* and *Belgravia*.

Dickens, Charles (1812–70)
In novels such as *Oliver Twist* and *The Old Curiosity Shop*, Dickens drew attention to the appalling social deprivations of Victorian London.

Edward the Confessor (c.1002–66)
This pious king began the Normanization of England that culminated in the Conquest. He also reinforced the importance of London by establishing his palace at *Westminster*.

Flamsteed, John (1646–1719)
The first Astronomer Royal, working largely at **Greenwich Observatory**, recorded no fewer than 3,000 stars.

Garrick, David (1717–79)
The English stage's greatest actor/manager, Garrick established the naturalistic style which modern acting takes for granted. Most of his performances were in *Covent Garden*.

Gibbons, Grinling (1648–1721)
Wren's master-carver decorated many of the great architect's outstanding buildings with incomparably naturalistic flowers, leaves, fruits, musical instruments – all sculpted in wood or stone with Baroque exuberance. The greatest profusion is to be seen at *St Paul's Cathedral* or *Hampton Court*.

Gibbs, James (1682–1754)
Continuing where Wren had left off, this Scottish architect introduced some of the more theatrical elements of the Italian Baroque to London church building. Excellent examples can be seen at *St Mary-le-Strand* and *St Martin-in-the-Fields*.

Gresham, Sir Thomas (1519–79)
Founder of the *Royal Exchange*, Gresham was one of the great merchants and financiers of the Elizabethan age, when London began to establish its dominance in international commerce.

Henry VIII (1491–1547)
The heavy hand of this powerful monarch was repeatedly felt in London – not least in the dissolution of the monasteries. Among more positive achievements, he moved the chief royal palace to *Whitehall* (giving Westminster to Parliament) and built up *St James's Palace* and *Hampton Court*.

Hogarth, William (1697–1764)
With the sharpest of all eyes for social foible or moral weakness, Hogarth in his paintings and engravings has given us an unforgettable picture of the seamier sides of life in 18thC London. *Hogarth's House* at *Chiswick* is now a museum.

Johnson, Dr. Samuel (1709–84)
The giant of 18thC letters patronized the pubs of *Fleet Street*, the coffee houses of *Covent Garden* and wrote his famous dictionary at *Dr. Johnson's House* nearby.

Jones, Inigo (1573–1652)
With this architect, the ideas of the Italian Renaissance came to England with extraordinary sureness and originality. Examples of his bold vision can be seen in the Queen's House at *Greenwich*, the *Banqueting House*, and *Covent Garden*.

Keats, John (1795–1821)
The perfect romantic poet, and a consumptive to boot, wrote much of his best work at *Hampstead* (see *Keats' House*).

Marx, Karl (1818–83)
Writing in German in the *British Museum*, the political economist whose theories have split the world down the middle lived for most of his life as an exile in *Soho* and N London. Pilgrims flock to where he is buried in Highgate Cemetery.

Biographies

Nash, John *(1752–1835)*

Marble Arch, Regent's Park and Carlton House Terrace in *The Mall* are the visible legacies of this Regency architect. Just as significant is the fine town planning scheme of which Regent St. forms the main axis.

Pepys, Samuel *(1633–1703)*

Recording the Great Plague and Fire of London, Pepys' diary is an outstanding social document, presenting an irresistible account of daily life in the 17thC city.

Prince Regent *(1762–1830)*

In many ways a ludicrous figure, the Regent (later George IV) led the nation in fashion and sport, and backed the ambitious town planning schemes of **John Nash**.

Seifert, Richard *(born 1910)*

This uncompromising architect's works are a dominant and controversial feature of the modern London skyline. **Centrepoint** at St Giles Circus is the best known: to the conservationists, it symbolizes uncontrolled speculative development.

Shakespeare, William *(1564–1616)*

The London stage saw the first productions of almost all the bard's plays – usually in the theatres of *Southwark*, where he worked, although sometimes in the halls of the *Inns of Court*.

Sloane, Sir Hans *(1660–1753)*

The *British Museum*, *Natural History Museum* and *Museum of Mankind* all ultimately owe their existence to this successful physician's vast collections, bequeathed to the nation.

Tyler, Wat *(died 1381)*

After his capture of the *Tower of London*, the leader of the great Peasant's Revolt of 1381 was personally killed by the Lord Mayor of London while attempting to parley with Richard II at Smithfield.

Wellington, Duke of *(1769–1852)*

The leading British general of the Napoleonic Wars, Wellington ultimately defeated Napoleon at the Battle of Waterloo. He went on to become an authoritarian prime minister, during which time he lived at *Apsley House*, now the Wellington Museum.

Whittington, Dick *(1358–1423)*

A rich merchant and the greatest medieval Lord Mayor of London, Whittington has passed into legend. In the quintessential rags-to-riches story, he paused in flight from the city on Highgate Hill (accompanied by his famous cat), when the bells of *St Mary-le-Bow* called him back to greatness.

William the Conqueror *(c.1027–87)*

Having defeated the English and declared himself their first Norman king, William consolidated by building the massive *Tower of London*.

Wolsey, Cardinal *(c.1473–1530)*

Promoted by Henry VIII but falling from favour when he failed to secure the king's divorce, this powerful churchman's palaces at *Whitehall* and *Hampton Court* were confiscated and became the favourite royal residences.

Wren, Sir Christopher *(1632–1723)*

The dazzling career of the greatest British architect includes a staggering number of major buildings, most of which are in London – a feat made possible by the ravages of the Great Fire of 1666. Numerous city churches, *St Paul's Cathedral*, major parts of *Hampton Court* and *St James's Palace* testify to his genius.

Sports and activities

For information on all sports: **Sportsline** ☎222–8000.

Athletics
Major athletic events are held at the **Crystal Palace National Sports Centre**, SE19 ☎778–0131. Information from **The Amateur Athletic Association**, Francis St., SW1 ☎828–9326.

Bicycling
This can be an effective way of exploring the city and one of the quickest ways of getting around. Bikes can be rented from **Bike UK Ltd**, Lower Robert St., off York Buildings, WC2 ☎839–2111 or **Dial-A-Bike**, 18 Gillingham St., SW1 ☎828–4040. For more serious cycling, contact the **British Cycling Federation**, 16 Upper Woburn Pl., WC1 ☎387–9320, or **London Cycling Campaign**, Tress House, 3 Stamford St., SE1 ☎928–7220.

Cricket
The most baffling of sports to the newcomer, but an integral part of the English summer; from Apr–Sept club matches are played all over London, in parks and on greens, mainly on Sat and Sun afternoons. First-class professional matches, also on weekdays, at **Lords** (the Middlesex club), NW8, ☎289–1615, and **The Oval** (the Surrey club), SE11 ☎735–4911. Both stage a test match every year: Lords in June, The Oval in Sept.

Fishing
Fishing in the Thames is forbidden unless you have a licence from the Thames Water Authority, obtainable through the **London Anglers Association**, Forest Rd. Hall, Hervey Park Rd., E17 ☎520–7477, which also handles licences for the **Lea Valley Reservoirs**, on the NE edge of London, the other main fishing spot in the city. It is also possible to fish in some of London's parks; licences from **The Royal Parks Department** , The Storeyard, Hyde Park, W2 ☎262–5484.

Football
Football (soccer) matches are generally played on Sat afternoons from Aug through to Apr, with some matches on midweek evenings. The FA Cup Final, the biggest single match, is played in May at **Wembley Stadium**, Middlesex ☎902–1234, also the scene of England's international matches, usually played on Wed evenings. The principal clubs are:
Arsenal   Highbury Stadium, Avenall Rd., N5 ☎359–0131
Chelsea   Stamford Bridge, Fulham Rd., SW6 ☎385–5545
Crystal Palace   Selhurst Park, Whitehorse Lane, SE25 ☎653–4462
Fulham   Craven Cottage, Stevenage Rd., SW6 ☎736–6561
Queen's Park Rangers   Loftus Rd., W12 ☎743–0262
Tottenham Hotspur (Spurs)   White Hart Lane, High Rd., N17 ☎808–1020
West Ham United   Green St., Upton Park, E13 ☎472–2740
Wimbledon   49 Durnsford Rd., SW19 ☎946–6311

Gardens
Apart from the parks and gardens that are open to the public, the **National Gardens Scheme**, 57 Lower Belgrave

St., SW1 ☎730–0359, runs a scheme whereby private gardens both in London and the country are open to the public for perhaps one day a year. The **Royal Horticultural Society** holds periodic shows in summer at its home in Vincent Sq., SW1, and stages the massive **Chelsea Flower Show** in May (see *Calendar of events* in *Planning*).

Golf

Most courses are private and will only allow you to play if you have an introduction from a member or from your own club. Public courses, however, will allow you to play on payment of a green fee, and will also hire out clubs. The most central are at:
Richmond Park   Roehampton Gate, SW15 ☎876–3205
Royal Epping Forest Golf Club   Forest Approach, Chingford, E4
Wimbledon Common   Camp Rd., SW19 ☎946–0294 (Mon–Fri)
    The only major professional venue near London is **Wentworth**, in Surrey.

Greyhound racing

Traditionally a pastime favoured by the London working man without his woman, 'the dogs' are now moving upmarket and at most tracks the races can be watched from a restaurant. Ring for times. London's venues are:
Catford   Ademore Rd., SE26 ☎692–2261
Hackney   Waterden Rd., E15 ☎985–3511
Harringay   Green Lanes, N4 ☎800–3474
Walthamstow   Chingford Rd., E4 ☎531–4255
Wembley Stadium   Middlesex ☎902–8833
Wimbledon   Plough Lane, SW19 ☎946–5361

Health Clubs

Among health clubs that do not require you to be a member is **Westside**, 201–207 Kensington High St., W8 ☎937–5386, which offers gymnasiums, saunas and beauty treatments. **The Sanctuary**, 11 Floral St., WC2 ☎240–9635, is for women only.
    Popular with office workers in Covent Garden at lunchtime are the dance/keep fit sessions at **The Dance Fitness Centre**, 11 Floral St., WC2 ☎836–6544, and **Pineapple**, 7 Langley St., WC2 ☎836–4004.

Horse racing

There are many large racecourses within easy reach of London: to the w, **Ascot** and **Newbury**; to the sw, **Sandown**, **Epsom** and **Kempton**. Any day except Sun. There are long overlaps between the summer (flat) and the winter (jumping) seasons. All races will be well covered in the daily newspapers, and it is possible to bet from betting shops that are not on the course.

Ice-skating

The major public rinks, which will hire skates are:
Queens Ice Skating Club   Queensway, W2 ☎229–0172
Richmond Ice Rink   Clevedon Rd., Twickenham ☎892–3646
Streatham Ice Rink   386 Streatham High Rd., SW16 ☎769–7861

Riding

Stables are conveniently located near major parks:
L.G. Blum   32a Grosvenor Crescent Mews, SW1 ☎235–6846, for Hyde Park.

Roehampton Gate   Priory Lane, SW15 ☎876–7089, for Richmond Park.

Several major show jumping events are held at Wembley, Middlesex ☎902–1234 (see *Calendar of events* in *Planning*).

Roller-skating

The best places to skate are on the Embankment between County Hall and The National Theatre, and also in Battersea Park. Indoor roller-skating areas that rent out skates include **Jubilee Hall**, Central Market Sq., WC2 ☎836–4835 and **Finsbury Leisure Centre**, Norman St., EC1 ☎253–4490. Check opening hours before you go.

Rowing

Rowing boats and sailing dinghies may be hired on the Serpentine, in Battersea Park and Regents Park, as well as on some stretches of the Thames. For rowing events see *Calendar of events* in *Planning*. For details contact the **Amateur Rowing Association**, 6 Lower Mall, W6 ☎748–3632.

Rugby

There are two versions of this tough game. Rugby Union, a 15-a-side sport, restricts its players to amateur status in the same way that athletics does. Matches are played on Sat afternoons from Sept–Apr, with international and major games taking place at the sport's headquarters at Whitton Rd., Twickenham ☎892–9303. The principal clubs are:

Blackheath   Charlton Rd., SE13 ☎858–1578
Harlequins   Twickenham (see above)
London Irish   The Ave., Sunbury-on-Thames ☎(76) 83034
London Scottish   Kew Rd., Richmond ☎940–0397
London Welsh   Kew Rd., Richmond ☎940–2420
Rosslyn Park   Upper Richmond Rd., SW15 ☎ 876–1879
Saracens   Green Rd., N14 ☎449–3770
Wasps   Repton Ave., Wembley ☎902–4220

Rugby League, the professional 13-a-side game, was traditionally restricted to the the N of England. However, one pioneering London club now plays on Sun afternoons: **Fulham**, Craven Cottage, Stevenage Rd., SW6 ☎736–6561.

Squash

Addresses from **Squash Rackets Association**, Francis St., SW1 ☎828–3064.

Swimming

Major indoor pools with all facilities include:
Chelsea Baths   Chelsea Manor St., SW3 ☎352–6985
Fulham Pools   Normand Park, Lillie Rd., SW6 ☎381–4494
Marshall St. Baths   W1 ☎439–4678
Oasis Pool   32 Endell St., WC2 ☎836–9555
White City Pool   Bloemfontein Rd., W12 ☎743–3401

For outdoor swimming during the summer, major pools are:
Hampstead Ponds   NW3 ☎435–2366
Parliament Hill Lido   NW5 ☎485–3873
The Serpentine   Hyde Park, W2 ☎262–5484

Tennis

Information from **The Lawn Tennis Association**, Palliser Rd., W14 ☎385–2366. For major annual tennis tournaments see *Calendar of events* in *Planning*.

195

London for children

Information

To find out what's on in London for children ☎246–8007 for a detailed recorded message or buy the inexpensive *Children's London* published by the London Tourist Board. For more specific questions ring **Kidsline** ☎222–8070 between 16.00–18.00 (9.00–16.00 during school holidays).

Many of London's museums have special features of particular interest to children and often produce questionnaires to make a child's visit more directly interesting.

Ways of seeing London

An ideal introduction to London, from a child's point of view, is to go on a Round London Sightseeing Tour in a double-decker bus. River trips to *Hampton Court* and *Greenwich* are also popular. (See *Useful addresses* in *Basic information* for departure points of buses and boats.)

Eating in London

Most restaurants accept children willingly and some less expensive restaurants will supply children's portions. Hamburger and other fast-food restaurants are plentiful.

Fares

On London Regional Transport, children under 5 travel free and children between 5–16 travel for a reduced fare, although children aged 14 and 15 need a photocard (available from any post office).

Christmas

Seeing the Christmas lights and decorations in London, particularly in Regent St. and Trafalgar Sq., makes a good early evening's entertainment. Children can also see Father Christmas at most large department stores during the season.

Parks

Hyde Park and Kensington Gardens (separated only by a road) are the most central and well-known of London's parks. As well as wide open spaces enabling large-scale games to be played, there are many more unusual attractions. Boats and cyclocraft can be hired on the Serpentine, part of which is cordoned off and used as a swimming area in the summer. Kensington Gardens also has unique Sun entertainments – men sail their model boats on the Round Pond, and there are kites to admire. Nearby is the playground donated by J. M. Barrie with its statue of *Peter Pan*. Another statue to look out for is the beautifully carved *Elfin Oak*, near Bayswater Rd., supposedly restored by the fairies (with a little help from Spike Milligan). Puppet shows are staged here on Aug afternoons.

Regent's Park also has rowing boats for hire, but the main attraction is the *Zoo*.

Hampstead Heath, though not particularly central, also offers wide open spaces as well as a deer park, a pond for model boats, an outdoor swimming pool and a playground.

Coram's Fields in Holborn is a park donated to children in London by Sir Thomas Coram – adults are only allowed in if accompanied by a child!

In addition to these parks are the many supervised adventure playgrounds, which have imaginative materials and equipment created by the children themselves. Information from **London Adventure Playground Association**, 28 Underwood Rd., E1 ☎377–0314. Younger children can go to the GLC-run **One O'Clock Clubs** where they can play with the equipment provided. Under-5s must be accompanied by an adult. Information from **Parks Department** ☎633–1707.

Theatres and cinemas

Some London theatres have special performances for children. *The Little Angel Marionette Theatre* 14 Dagmar Passage, Cross St., N1 ☎226–1787, shows regular puppet plays, on weekend afternoons and on weekdays during school holidays; performances for small children take place on Sat mornings. *Polka Children's Theatre* 240 The Broadway, SW19 ☎543–4888 stages regular plays for children, and has exhibitions of puppets and toys.
The Unicorn Arts Theatre 6 Great Newport St., WC2 ☎836–3334, also stages plays suitable for children aged between 4–12 on weekend afternoons.

During the school holidays in particular, major cinemas show a wide selection of children's films. Both the **National Film Theatre** and the **Institute for Contemporary Arts** cinemas (see *Nightlife*) have children's film clubs on weekend afternoons.

Funfairs and circuses

Touring circuses and fairs often come to London for bank holiday weekends (see *Public holidays* in *Basic information*) and usually take place in the larger parks. Information can be obtained from the **London Tourist Board** ☎730–3488. Fireworks and other celebrations on Nov 5 often include funfairs. See *Calendar of events* in *Planning*.

Brass-rubbing

This can be a fascinating way of passing a wet afternoon. The **London Brass Rubbing Centre**, St James's Church, Piccadilly, W1 ☎437–6023, has a large collection, and **Westminster Abbey**, SW1, and **All-Hallows-by-the-Tower**, Byward St., EC3 ☎481–2928 (open mid-May–Oct), also have facilities. In all cases, admission is free but you must pay for your materials.

Babysitters

Babysitters Unlimited 271–273 King St., W6 ☎741–5566
Childminders 67a Marylebone High St., W1 ☎935–2049
Junior Jaunts, 4a William St., SW1 ☎235–4700, offers to take your children around London for you; its tours, (10.00–16.00) are for groups of up to six children from 5–15.

Farms

There are a surprising number of farms in the Inner London area. The most interesting are:
Freightliners Paradise Park, Sheringham Rd., N7 ☎609–0467
Kentish Town City Farm 1 Crossfield Close, NW5 ☎482–2861
Mudchute Community Farm Pier St., E14 ☎515–5901
Spitalfields Project Buxton St., E1 ☎247–8762
Stepping Stones Farm Stepney Way, E1 ☎790–8204
Vauxhall City Farm 24 St Oswald's Pl., SE11 ☎582–4204

Toy shops See *Shopping*.

SPECIAL INFORMATION

Excursions

In Britain, all roads lead to London, and they can also be taken in the opposite direction, as can the commuter railway routes to such historically interesting cities as Canterbury, Salisbury and Winchester. London's hinterland covers the half-dozen 'home counties' of the SE and beyond to cities like Cambridge, Oxford and even Bath. These cities, and to an even greater extent Stratford, repay a weekend visit, with a little exploration on the way. All of them are popular with visitors, and at the height of summer are over-subscribed to the point of suffocation.

Stately homes around London

London's own countryside, where the nobility once had their stately homes, begins in the suburbs, then fans out into Epping Forest, the Thames Valley, the Downs, and the Chilterns. Much of this countryside can be reached by tube, and there are several 'country' homes open to the public within the capital, especially in West London (see houses at *Chiswick, Ham, Orleans* and *Syon* and *Osterley Park*). Beyond, there are about 50 houses and castles within 100 miles.

Audley End House   40 miles (64km) from London, 15 miles (24km) s of Cambridge ☎(0799) 22399. Drive through the pretty Roding Valley on the M11, or take the train from Liverpool Street to Saffron Walden, then a 10min local bus ride. Open April–Oct Tues–Sat, closed Mon and Good Fridays. One of the best examples of a Jacobean mansion, with extensive later work by Vanbrugh and Robert Adam. Much fine 18thC furniture, and a collection of stuffed birds. Large grounds, with a miniature railway.

Beaulieu (pronounced Bewlee)   80 miles (128km) from London, 14 miles (22km) s of Southampton ☎(0590) 612345. By car, A3, A31 or M3, A33. Train from Waterloo to Southampton, then bus. World famous for its **Motor Museum**, with 200 veteran cars, early Rolls, land-speed record breakers, and a monorail. The house, home of motoring enthusiast Lord Montagu, was built as the gatehouse of the 13thC Beaulieu Abbey, the ruins of which can be visited. Museum and ruins can be visited all year, as can the stately home. Nearby is the **Maritime Museum** at Buckler's Hard, a village with shipbuilding associations dating from Nelson's times, and the **New Forest**.

Broadlands   80 miles (128km) from London, 6 miles (10km) NW of Southampton ☎(0794) 516878. By car, as above. Train to Southampton, changing for Romsey. Open Apr–Sept Tues–Sat. The Prince and Princess of Wales spent part of their honeymoon at Broadlands, thus bringing public attention to the home of the late Lord Mountbatten, and in an earlier time of Lord Palmerston. Broadlands is now the home of Lord and Lady Romsey. There is a **Mountbatten exhibition** in the house, which is a Palladian mansion with landscaping by Capability Brown.

Chartwell   25 miles (40km) from London, 5 miles (8km) sw of Sevenoaks ☎(073278) 368. By car, A21, A233, B2026. Bus from Victoria Coach Station. Train to Sevenoaks from Charing Cross, then bus to Westerham, then a 25min walk. Open Apr–Nov Tues–Sat. Winston Churchill's country home for 40yr. Victorian, chosen for its tranquillity and views. Churchill's study and library can be visited. An unfinished canvas still stands in his studio in the beautiful gardens. Five

miles (8km) away are **Hever Castle**, trysting place of Anne
Boleyn and Henry VIII and 20thC home of William Waldorf
Astor (with Holbeins and a Titian), and **Penshurst Place**,
birthplace of Sir Philip Sidney (with a toy museum, costume
display, Italian gardens and nature trail), is also nearby.

Hatfield House   21 miles (33km) N from London
☎(30) 62823/65159. By car, A1000. Train from King's Cross
or Moorgate to Hatfield. Open daily Apr–Oct. Royal
mementoes dating back to Elizabeth I, paintings, tapestries and
armour, and special exhibitions on crafts and collectables.
Within the grounds is a part of the palace in which Elizabeth I
lived as a girl. Her Secretary of State, Robert Cecil, built
Hatfield House, and his descendant, the Marquess of
Salisbury, still lives there. Six miles (10km) N is **Knebworth
House**, begun in 1492 and completed in the 1800s, known for
its books and manuscripts, paintings and furniture, steam
railway and occasional rock and jazz concerts.

Leeds Castle   36 miles (57km) from London, 5 miles (8km) SE
of Maidstone. By car, A20 and M20. By train and bus, inclusive
ticket available from Victoria Station ☎(0622) 65400. Open
Apr–Oct Tues–Thurs, Sun; daily in Aug. Fairytale medieval
castle on two islands in a lake. Built about 1120, restored in the
1800s. Henry VIII converted it into a royal palace; Elizabeth I
was a prisoner here. A garden with many species of flowers is
named after another resident, Lord Culpeper, who was
Governor of Virginia in the 1600s and founder of the herbalist
shop.

Luton Hoo   30 miles (48km) from London, 2 miles (3km)
from Luton ☎(0582) 22955. By car, A1 (M1). Train from St
Pancras Station, then local bus. Fabergé jewels and mementoes
of Tsarist Court. Renaissance jewels, bronzes, porcelain, in a
house built by Robert Adam. Gardens by Capability Brown.
Open Apr–Sept Sun, Mon, Wed, Thurs, Sat.

Polesdon Lacey   20 miles (32km) from London, 2 miles
(3km) from Dorking ☎(31) 52048. By car, A24. Train from
Waterloo to Box Hill or Bookham, then a taxi, then bus plus walk.
The playwright Sheridan lived, gardened and farmed here, but
his house was demolished in the early 1800s and replaced by a
Regency villa. After having several private owners, the
property was bequeathed to the National Trust. The lovely
house, with a much-admired rose garden, contains a substantial
collection of porcelain, and paintings by Sir Joshua Reynolds
and Sir Henry Raeburn. The gardens are open all year, daily,
but the house in the afternoon only, Mar–Oct excluding Mon
and Fri.

Waddesdon Manor   38 miles (60km) from London, 5 miles
(8km) w of Aylesbury ☎(0296–651) 211. By car, A41. Train
from Marylebone to Aylesbury, then a taxi or bus, plus a
strenuous walk. Open Apr–Oct Wed–Sun afternoons.
Château-like house built by Baron Ferdinand de Rothschild.
Family mementoes, French royal furniture, carpets, paintings.
Extensive grounds with deer.

Wilton House   80 miles (128km) from London, 2½ miles
(4km) w of Salisbury ☎(072–274) 3115. By car, A30. Train-
and-bus excursions by British Rail Awayday from Waterloo
Station. Open Apr–Oct Tues–Sat. Whimsical Inigo Jones
house, with Chippendale and Kent furniture and Van Dyck
paintings. Wilton House's more offbeat attractions include
some 7,000 brightly-painted model soldiers and a lock of Queen
Elizabeth I's hair.

Bath

116 miles (186km) from London. Population. 85,000.
Getting there: By train, 70min from Paddington, trains
hourly; by car, 2hr, M4 to Junction 18, then A46. Tel. code
(0225) i Abbey Churchyard ☎ 62831.

One-day excursion: An effortless day out by comfortable high-speed train, with good views of gentle countryside, especially between the Vale of White Horse and the Lambourn Downs, and where the edges of the Cotswolds form a valley with the Marlborough Downs. Fast by car, too, though the temptation is to make it a weekend, with detours into the hills and stops at ancient sites like **Stonehenge** or **Avebury**, or canalside walks by the Kennet and Avon Canal.

The warm springs which gave Bath its name are said to have been discovered by King Lear's father, but their celebrity can more accurately be dated from the devotions of the Romans. The renewed enthusiasm for taking the waters in Georgian times spawned a second layer of history, and an architectural elegance which remains remarkable. Bath is easy to explore on foot and, being set amid hills like Rome itself, it best rewards those with willing legs. The centre of the city becomes very crowded in summer.

A first glimpse of that hillside majesty, embellished with Georgian crescents, is well taken from the train as it slows out of Brunel's tunnel at Box and rumbles towards Bath Spa Station. Out of the station, the immediate impression is uninteresting, but a walk straight ahead down Manvers St. leads to the Georgian Bath in **North** and **South Parades**. A left turn along North Parade leads to **Sally Lunn's Tea House**, after which a traditional English bun is named. The premises are said to be the oldest house in Bath, and the establishment is reputed to have been a haunt of Beau Nash, the dandy and arbiter of social graces who helped make Bath fashionable in Georgian times. Cut through York St. to the **Abbey Churchyard**, the heart of the city. The abbey itself was begun in the 15thC, but some of its most striking features are Victorian. Across the churchyard are the **Roman Baths** and **Pump Room**, completed in 1799 (open 9.00–18.00, Sun 11.00–17.00). A guided tour of the baths affords the opportunity to see the fruits of constant excavations there, ranging from coins to a sacrificial altar. On special occasions, it is possible to swim in the baths, and there are plans to restore the nearby treatment centre. The water can be sampled from a fountain in the elegant and restful Pump Room. Since the water tastes, in the words of Dickens' Sam Weller, like a "warm flat iron", it is perhaps as well that the Pump Room serves morning coffee and afternoon tea, sometimes to the accompaniment of string music.

The most spectacular Georgian homes were built on the hillsides to provide their owners with panoramic views. Walk along Bath St. (colonnaded to protect itinerant bathers), turning right at the end, then left into Sawclose, past the city's lively theatre and a restaurant area, up Gay St. to The Circus, then along Brock St. to the **Royal Crescent**, built 1765–75, where the house at no. 1 is open as a museum in summer (open Tues–Sat 11.00–17.00, Sun 14.00–17.00). Return via The Circus to the **Assembly Rooms**, home of an outstanding **Museum of Costume** (open 10.00–18.00, Sun 14.00–17.00).

Return downhill by Lansdown Rd. which becomes in turn Broad St. and High St., with the Guildhall and the covered market, noted for another of the city's culinary delights, the Bath Chap – this turns out to be a pig's jowl!

Such indulgences may subsequently call for a diet of Dr Oliver's remorselessly plain biscuits, for which the city is also known (the more luxurious chocolate-coated version seems at odds with his ascetic intentions), or simply a Bath bun. Determined walkers can do a little more shopping under cover of Pulteney Bridge, an Italianate delight designed by Robert Adam. This leads into another fine Georgian street named Argyle St., and thence to nowhere in particular except perhaps, at the end of Forrester Rd., a place where boats can be hired on the River Avon. At weekends, pleasure trips can also be taken on the Kennet and Avon Canal, from Sidney Wharf, near Bathwick Hill, or from the Top Lock, at the far end of North Parade Rd.

A unique attraction a couple of miles out of the city, at Claverton Down, is the **American Museum in Britain** (open Tues–Sun 14.00–17.00). This has Indian folk art, interiors of early American homes, including Shaker and Pennsylvania Dutch settings, relics of the West, and gardens which replicate George Washington's at Mount Vernon. The museum bakes its own selection of cakes and gingerbread, making for a delicious afternoon tea.

In town, Bath is especially well endowed with museums, catering for a wide variety of interests. Others include: **Burrow's Toy Museum**, York St.; the **Carriage Museum**, Bennet St.; the **Geology Museum**, 18 Queen Sq.; the **Herschel Museum** (astronomy and music), 19 New King St.; the **National Centre of Photography** in the Octagon, Milsom St. (the building itself merits a visit, and the street has elegant shops); the **Postal History Museum**, 8 Broad St.

Maritime enthusiasts might wish to see **SS Great Britain**, in the nearby city of Bristol. In the opposite direction, a drive into the Mendip Hills leads to the small city of **Wells**, with one of Britain's most beautiful cathedrals.

Hotels

The **Priory** ▐▐▐▐ (see below) and the **Royal Crescent Hotel** ☎319090 ▥ ▐▐▐▐ are especially comfortable and full of personal touches. The friendly **Pratt's**, South Parade ☎60441 ▐▌ and the more sophisticated **Francis**, Queen Sq. ☎24257 ▐▌ are both centrally placed. There are many bed-and-breakfast places along Pulteney Rd., and Wells Rd. Recommended is **Eagle House**, Church St., Bathford ☎859946 ▢ a Georgian mansion 3 miles (2km) outside Bath.

The Tourist Information Centre also has an accommodation register.

Restaurants

One of the most famous restaurants in England, the **Hole in the Wall**, is in Bath, at 16 George St. ☎25242 ▐▐▐▐ where fresh ingredients are inventively incorporated into a French-style menu. Rich but subtle sauces feature in the opulent restaurant at the **Priory Hotel**, Weston Rd. ☎331922 ▐▐▐▐ Less expensive is **Popjoys**, named after Beau Nash's mistress and in his house, serving English food at Sawclose ☎60494 ▐▌ Other well regarded places are **Woods**, 9–13 Alfred St. ☎314812 ▐▌ **Clarets** wine bar, 6–7 Kingsmead Sq. and **Flowers**, 27 Monmouth St. ▢ ▩ Or try **Evelyn Owens**, Bartlett St. or **Sweeney Todds**, 15 Milsom St. for a pizza.

Excursions

Brighton

53 miles (85km) from London. Population: 162,000.
Getting there: By train, 58min from Victoria, trains twice
hourly; by car, 2hr, A23 then M23. Tel. code (0273)
i Marlborough House, 54 Old Steine ☎ 23755; also at
King's Rd., on the seafront, in summer.

One-day excursion: The speed and frequency of the trains and
the labyrinthine quality of the roads out of South London deter
most day-trippers from taking a car, but weekenders might
wish to do so to explore the Downs and the Sussex countryside
around Brighton.

This seaside resort is beloved by eclectic Londoners for its wry
mix of Regency elegance and Graham Greenian seediness. A
day out in Brighton is an English experience. The craze for
sea-bathing in the late 1700s, and the Prince Regent's
subsequent attentions, gave Brighton a social status which it has
never entirely surrendered and to which its residents still cling.

The Regency terraces, squares and crescents provide the
elegance, crowned by the extravagant fantasies of the Royal
Pavilion, the exploration of which is an essential feature of a
first-time visit to Brighton. Such an Aladdin's cave of orientalia
is an appropriate centrepiece to a town noted for its antique
shops, the most celebrated of which, along with some
interesting fish restaurants, are in a neighbourhood called The
Lanes. Not far away, an antique electric railway, the first in
Britain, runs from one of the town's two Victorian piers along
the pebbly beach to the swimming pool and marina. The
journey can be continued by open-topped bus, or on foot, to the
village of Rottingdean.

From the railway station, Queen's Rd. and Trafalgar St. are
the boundaries of an antiques-and-boutiques area called **North
Laine**, which is less pretty but also less expensive than The
Lanes. Within this area, there is a Sat morning flea market.

A half-mile walk down Queen's Rd. leads to Church St. on
the left and the **local museum** (open Mon–Sat 10.00–17.45,
Sun 14.00–17.45) housing a major Art Deco collection as well
as English watercolours and old masters. Just beyond is the
Royal Pavilion (open daily 10.00–17.00). The royal flourish
was bestowed upon Brighton by the Prince Regent, later to be
George IV, who is said to have gone there to get away from his
father. While there in 1785 he secretly and illegally married a
Catholic, Mrs Fitzherbert, a twice-widowed commoner. The
Pavilion was his summer palace, though he left it soon after its
completion. The bizarre mock-Indian architecture, most of it
by Nash, derives from the fashionability of oriental themes
during a period of great trade with the East. There was room for
discordance within this preoccupation; the interior was
decorated in 'the Chinese taste'. The Pavilion affords visitors a
good hour's browse through eccentric splendour, with huge
dragons, exotic birds and chandeliers, in a whole series of room
settings.

From the Pavilion, one wanders into **The Lanes**, the
fashionable and fascinating shops of which often close on Sun,
but stay open late on Wed and Thurs. From there it is a few
minutes' walk down to the seafront. To the right, about half a
mile along the beach, is the West Pier, built in 1866, and a
century later the memorable setting for the film *Oh, What a
Lovely War*. The pier now stands forlorn, unsafe, closed to
visitors, and with an uncertain future. In that direction are

202

some fine Georgian buildings, notably in **Regency Square**, as Brighton blends into its sister town of Hove.

In a more central position on the seafront is the **Palace Pier**, built in 1891, a rich symbol of British seaside frolics. Nearby in King's Rd. Arches, Lower Promenade is a **Penny Arcade Museum** containing Edwardian machines, including working expositions of 'What The Butler Saw'.

Just to the left of the pier is the **Aquarium** (open daily 9.00–18.00), dating from 1872, with a Dolphinarium. From this point, **Volk's Electric Railway** begins its journey. The railway, named after its founder, was opened in 1883 but at its terminus now is the largest yachting marina in Europe. Visitors can walk along the breakwaters, and there are pleasure trips and deep-sea angling. Beyond the marina, the resort which once popularized bathing machines now has an area of beach set aside for those who prefer nudity. This bracing facility is a whistle away from England's most famous girls' school, **Roedean**, on the way to **Rottingdean**. There is a toy museum and Rudyard Kipling room at **The Grange**, Rottingdean, where the great writer lived towards the end of his life (open Mon–Sat 10.00–17.00, Sun 14.00–17.00; closed Wed).

Hotels

Brighton has an enormous selection of hotels, and the Tourist Information Centre has a booking service. Two famous Victorian seafront hotels are the **Metropole** ☎775432 ▮▮▮ – rather unfairly notorious for furtive weekend couples – and the **Grand**, bombed with tragic consequences by the IRA at the 1984 Conservative Party Conference and currently closed for extensive renovation. Both are in King's Rd., as is the **Old Ship Hotel** ☎29001 ▮▯ which has a fine ballroom.

Restaurants

In The Lanes, **English's Oyster Bar**, 29 East St. ☎27980 ▮▮▯ is something of an institution. Despite its name, it is a full-scale restaurant, but its set lunch is reasonably priced – it is advisable to book in advance. In King St., at no. 64 is **Wheeler's Sheridan Tavern** ☎28372 ▮▮▮ a branch of the famous London chain of fish restaurants, known for its sole. In Market St., at no. 22, is the **Ceres Health Foods Restaurant** ▯ which is a self-service establishment. At the edge of The Lanes, a tea shop called **The Mock Turtle**, at 4 Pool Valley, sells homemade cakes and lunchtime snacks. Elsewhere in Brighton, **Le Grandgousier**, 15 Western St. ☎772005 ▮▯ is a bistro offering good value, and **Le Français**, 1 Paston Pl., Kemp Town ☎680716 ▮▮▮▮ makes an excellent fish soup to head its fine French menu.

Outside Brighton

Walkers enjoy the South Downs, a range of chalk hills that runs just inland from Brighton and stretches for 80 miles (128km). A bus from the seafront to the crest of **Devil's Dyke** offers superb views and a half-hour walk to the **church at Poynings**. The Tourist Information Centre has detailed information on walks.

In the Sussex countryside, several towns and villages are worth a visit, including **Lewes** (with a castle, interesting pubs and good walks), **Sheffield Park** (for its Capability Brown gardens, and a full-scale steam railway), and **Arundel** (another castle, a sometimes grotesque museum of curiosities, housing a late-Aug arts festival).

Cambridge

54 miles (86km) from London. Population: 102,500.
Getting there. By train, about 75min from Liverpool Street
(direct) or King's Cross (with change, but faster route), two
or three trains hourly; by car, M11, 90min. Tel. code (0223)
i Wheeler St. ☎322640.

One-day excursion: Being linked to London by motorway,
Cambridge is easily reached by car. The town is encircled with
parking spaces, and cars should not be taken into the centre.

The first scholars came from Oxford to Cambridge in 1209, and
the first college, **Peterhouse**, was founded in 1284. Modern
times have seen the age of Leavis, the lion of literary critics, the
splitting of the atom by Rutherford and the work of Crick and
Watson in establishing the double helix structure of DNA. For
all its architectural similarities to Oxford, this 'younger' of
Britain's two great university cities is distinguished by the
larger scale of its colleges, its lower skyline (unlike Oxford, it is
not an industrial town), its paler stone, and its geographical
setting on the edge of flat and water-laced Fen country.
Cambridge makes good use of its river, the Cam or Granta,
along which half a dozen of its colleges are set. Most of the
colleges can be visited, and there are three tours daily, starting
from the Tourist Information Centre at 11.00, 14.00 and 15.00.
It is advisable to book an hour beforehand.

Close to the bus station is **Emmanuel College**, where John
Harvard was a pupil in the 1600s. Emmanuel's chapel is one of
several fine Wren buildings in Cambridge. Across St Andrew's
St., in Downing St., are the **Museums of Geology and
Archaeology**. Downing St. bends into Pembroke St., and
Pembroke College, which also has a Wren chapel. Parallel with
Pembroke St. is Botolph Lane, beyond which lies **Corpus
Christi**, with its fine 14thC collegiate building in Old Court.

Turn left from Pembroke St. into Trumpington St. for the
Fitzwilliam Museum (open Tues–Sat 10.00–17.00, Sun
14.15–17.00), which has an outstanding collection, including
paintings by Gainsborough, Turner, Rembrandt, Renoir and
Degas, drawings by Hogarth, Dürer, Michelangelo and
Leonardo, and Blake's illuminated books, as well as Roman,
Greek, Egyptian and Eastern antiquities and English pottery
and porcelain. Return along Trumpington St., turning left for
two more colleges, **St Catherine's** and **Queens'** (1448), the
latter with its Tudor courtyard, Cloister Court and
Mathematical Bridge.

Nearby, at Mill Lane (and further along, at Quayside),
rowing boats and punts can be hired on the river. Along this
stretch of the water are five more colleges, **King's**, **Clare**,
Trinity, **St John's** and **Magdalene**. The grassy bank facing the
first two of these colleges is known as The Backs.

King's College chapel is an outstanding example of
Perpendicular architecture, built between 1446–1515, with
glass by Flemish craftsmen. Among its treasures is *The
Adoration of the Magi*, by Rubens. Nearby on King's Parade is
the **Senate House**, a Georgian building in which the
University's 'Parliament' sits.

Clare College was founded in 1326, but the present building,
like a perfectly-proportioned tiny palace, was built in the 1600s.
It has lovely gardens opposite the elegant Clare Bridge. Trinity,
with its Great Court, fountain and many-windowed Wren
library, is the largest and richest of the colleges. Its alumni have

included Bacon, Byron, Macaulay, Tennyson and Thackeray. In the library are manuscripts by Tennyson, Thackeray and Milton. Two famous bookshops, **Heffers** and **Bowes & Bowes**, are in Trinity St., and nearby is **Belinda's**, for excellent teas and cakes.

St John's (1511), with its wedding-cake silhouette and Tudor gateway, is architecturally an acquired taste, but its 'Bridge of Sighs' is a splendid gesture. Properly known as New Bridge, it was built in 1831. St John's chapel was also built in the 1800s, by Sir George Gilbert Scott. At the end of this stretch of river, Magdalene College (1524), favoured by the aristocracy, has Samuel Pepys' library, in the original bookcases.

Across the road from Magdalene St., in Castle St., the **Folk Museum** (open Tues–Sat 10.30–17.00, Sun 14.30–16.30), in a converted inn, has an engrossing collection of domestic and agricultural objects from Cambridgeshire. In the opposite direction, in Bridge Street, is one of only five round churches in England, the **Church of the Holy Sepulchre**, modelled on its namesake in Jerusalem.

From Bridge St., turn left for **Jesus College**, which was once a convent. The windows in the chapel were designed by Burne Jones and made in the William Morris workshop. Behind the college are Jesus Green and Midsummer Common separated by Maid's Causeway and Short St. from another stretch of open grassland rather offhandedly known as Christ's Pieces.

Next to the railway station is another stretch of open grassland called Parker's Piece, with a restaurant called **Hobbs' Pavilion** which is popular with students. The restaurant is a converted cricket pavilion, and is named after the great batsman Jack Hobbs. Nearby, in Lensfield Rd., is the **Scott Polar Research Institute**, named after the explorer, with relics of expeditions. In the same part of the town, off Trumpington Rd., are the University's **Botanic Gardens**. These uncrowded and beautifully-scented gardens were laid out in 1846, primarily for the purposes of research.

Hotels

Student riots brought some unwelcome publicity to the **Garden House Hotel** Mill Lane ☎63421 ▥□ at the beginning of the 1970s, but guests with a nostalgic or vicarious interest can stay safely enough in what was already one of the city's best-known hotels, with a better-than-average restaurant, pretty gardens and river views. Also on the river is the smaller, comfortable **Arundel House**, in a Victorian terrace at 53 Chesterton Rd. ☎67701 ▯□ **The Blue Boar**, in Trinity St. ☎63121 ▯□ opposite the college, is rich in antiquity and a meeting place.

Restaurants

A disappointing city gastronomically, in which the most highly regarded restaurants are Chinese. **The Peking**, 21 Burleigh St. ☎354755 ▯□ has a hearty kitchen especially good on fish dishes; **Charlie Chan**, 14 Regent St. ☎61763 ▯□ serves Pekinese and Szechuan specialities. **Hobbs' Pavilion** ☎67480 □ serves crêpes, salads and its own ice-cream. Amazingly exotic decor and good food with Middle Eastern overtones can be found at **Xanadu**, Jesus Lane ☎31167 ▯□ While the selection of good restaurants is slim, several local pubs have good food. The **Fort St George** on Midsummer Common is one example, and the crankily English **Tickell Arms** at Whittlesford, 15 mins' drive away, is another.

Oxford

56 miles (90km) from London. Population: 109,000.
Getting there: By train, 60min from Paddington, trains
hourly; by car, 90min, A40 then M40. Tel. code (0865) **i** *St*
Aldate's ☎ *726871.*

One-day excursion: Oxford is a finely-crafted jewel of a city,
which has to be protected against incursion. There are several
pedestrian streets, a ring of car parks, and a 'Park and Ride' bus
service. Do not take a car into the centre.

It has been a university town since the 1200s, and has provided
its country with enough prime ministers to make a cricket team;
with writers ranging from Wilde to Tolkien, and with
adventurers from Raleigh to Rhodes. Oxford's colleges and
quadrangles dominate the centre of the city, rich in their
architectural diversity, though with a preponderance of Gothic
among their turrets, towers and dreaming spires. Some of the
colleges are walled, though most of them can be visited in the
afternoons (and all day during holidays, usually for a month
around Christmas and Easter, and St Giles, and July–Sept). As a seat of
learning, Oxford also has institutions such as the Bodleian
Library and Ashmolean Museum and famous bookshops.
There is punting on the river with unstrenuous walks by the
waterside. Beyond, the countryside reaches out to both the
Chiltern and the Cotswold Hills.

An impressive start to a day in Oxford might be at the
Ashmolean Museum (open Mon–Sat 10.00–16.00, Sun
14.00–16.00), one of Britain's finest museums, with riches
ranging from Michelangelo and Raphael drawings, by way of
silverware and musical instruments, to John Tradescant's
natural history collection. The Victorian Ashmolean building is
at the corner of Beaumont St. and St Giles, from which
Magdalen St. runs into Broad St., the address of the famous
Blackwell's bookshop (this and Foyle's in London are the two
most extensive bookshops in Britain); browsers are welcome.
Also housed in Broad St. is a small and friendly pub called the
White Horse.

On this stretch of walk are the rival colleges of **Trinity**, with
charming 17thC buildings and a rose garden, and **Balliol**,
founded in the 13thC and especially influential in the
development of the university, with a beautiful garden
quadrangle. Opposite Balliol on Broad St. is **Exeter College**,
the place of conception of the pre-Raphaelite Brotherhood.

To the right off Broad St. is the **Sheldonian Theatre**, the
first building designed by Wren in 1662. The theatre, modelled
on those of ancient Rome and named after its benefactor
Archbishop Sheldon, is used for university functions and
concerts. Behind it is the **Bodleian Library** (open Mon–Fri
9.00–17.00, Sat 9.00–12.30), named after Sir Thomas Bodley,
a diplomat who donated his own collection in 1598. This is said
to be the oldest library in the world, and contains three million
books. The part known as the Divinity School, with a beautiful
late Gothic low-vaulted ceiling, has folios and first editions of
works by Shakespeare, Milton, Swift and Pope, among others.
Also within the Bodleian is the **Radcliffe Camera**, a striking
domed rotunda designed by James Gibbs in 1739. To the left
across Catte St. is **All Souls College**, with its celebrated twin
towers by Hawksmoor. Behind All Souls is **New College**,
founded in 1379, with a magnificent chapel and parts of the
medieval city wall in its gardens; cream teas are served in the

hall in summer. If such delights are not available, try one of the tea shops in Holywell St. nearby.

Holywell St. leads into Longwall, from which the Magdalen deer park can be seen. Where Longwall reaches High St. a turn to the right along Merton St. leads to **Merton College**, with the oldest quadrangle in Oxford, dating from the 1300s. A turn to the left, through Christ Church Meadows, leads to **Magdalen College**, the most beautiful of the colleges with its Perpendicular bell-tower from which the choir sings at 6.00 on May Day morning. At Magdalen Bridge it is possible to hire a punt. From Rose Lane, a footpath runs round Christ Church Meadow, following the River Thames. Alongside Rose Lane are the **Botanic Gardens**, which date back to 1621.

Blenheim Palace: 8 miles (13km) from Oxford. The Churchills' ancestral home and nearby burial place would have a magnetic appeal even without the grand Baroque design of Vanbrugh and the landscaping of Capability Brown, but the combination of the historic with the aesthetic is irresistible.

The enormous Blenheim Palace and Park (open Mar–Oct 11.30–17.00) are at the small town of **Woodstock**, which has resonances quite different from those of its American descendant, and there are buses every half hour from Cornmarket. Apart from its assembly of Churchill artefacts, the palace has a large collection of tapestries, paintings, sculpture and furniture. Perhaps the most magnificent room is the Long Library, which contains more than 10,000 volumes as well as 17thC oriental porcelain, and has carvings by Grinling Gibbons.

The palace was built by a grateful Queen Anne for John Churchill, First Duke of Marlborough, to mark his victory over the French at the Battle of Blenheim in 1704. Winston Churchill, grandson of the Seventh Duke, was born there on Nov 30, 1874. He is buried in the churchyard at Bladon, on the edge of the park.

Hotels
For a city which attracts many visitors, Oxford does not flaunt its hotels, but the Tourist Information Centre ☎726873/4 does have a special telephone accommodation register. Among the better known hotels are the **Randolph**, Beaumont St. ☎247481 💵 with its Edwardian plush, and the **Ladbroke Linton Lodge**, Linton Rd. ☎53461 💵 with pleasant gardens. There are lots of bed-and-breakfast places around Abingdon Rd., St John's St. and Walton St. 7 miles (10km) E of Oxford is **Le Manoir aux Quat' Saisons** at Great Milton ☎(08446) 8881 💵💵 Raymond Blanc's much-praised hotel and restaurant.

Restaurants
There are several first-class restaurants in Oxford, all of them offering French cuisine: **Le Petit Blanc**, 272 Banbury Rd. ☎53540 💵💵 ♣ occupying Raymond Blanc's former premises; **Elizabeth**, 84 St Aldate's ☎242230 💵💵 and **La Sorbonne**, 130a High St. ☎241320 💵💵 ═ For Northern Italian food and the wines of the country, **La Cantina di Capri**, 34 Queen St. ☎47760 💵💵 is also recommended. For less expensive eating, cold buffet and Sun lunch, **Cherwell Boathouse** ☎52746 💵 on the river off Bardwell Rd. makes for a pleasant experience, as does **Brown's**, Woodstock Rd. ☎511995 💵 and **Gee's**, Banbury Rd. ☎511472 💵💵 an airy and light conservatory.

Stratford-upon-Avon

96 miles (154km) from London. Population: 22,000.
Getting there: By train, 2hr 30min from Paddington,
changing at Leamington Spa, trains hourly; by train and bus,
1hr 50min from Euston, changing at Coventry, trains hourly;
by car, 2hr 30min–3hr, A40, M40 to Oxford, then A34. Tel.
code (0789) i 1 High St. ☎293127, recorded info
☎67522.

One-day excursion or longer: An awkward journey, but still a
seemingly inescapable trip for visitors from overseas. Stratford
is not really within London's ambience, belonging less to the
South than to the Midlands, and is most comfortably visited as
part of a trip taking in **Warwick** or **Kenilworth** castles, **Coventry Cathedral**, or the northern part of the Cotswold Hills.

In the 16thC, as now, playwrights found their audiences and
their milieu in London, and Shakespeare was a metropolitan
writer. However, he was born in Stratford, retired and died
there, and was buried there. Soon after his death in 1616,
people started going to Stratford to see his birthplace, and today
they can also watch his plays performed by the Royal
Shakespeare Company during its long season. There is much
worth seeing in the town, despite exploitation which would
surely draw a satirical sting from the subject of its purported
devotions. There is little left of the Forest of Arden, setting for
several of the plays, except for the odd clump, but its trees
remain in the timbering of some fine Elizabethan and Tudor
buildings. When its streets are not sighing under the weight of
visitors, Stratford is a quiet and peaceful town, especially in
the evenings.

From the railway station, Alcester Rd., Greenhill St. and
Windsor St. lead to the half-timbered **Shakespeare's House** in
Henley St. (open Mon–Sat 9.00–18.00, Nov–Mar
9.00–16.30, Sun 13.30–16.30) where the playwright was born,
probably on April 23, 1564. The interior has been carefully
restored – notice the engraved signatures of pilgrims such as
Carlyle, Tennyson and Sir Walter Scott in the room where the
birth is said to have taken place.

A short walk along Henley St., High St. (past the family
home of John Harvard, founder of the University), and Chapel
St. is **New Place**, to which Shakespeare retired, and where he
died at the age of 52. The house no longer stands, but the
garden, laid out in the characteristic Elizabethan 'knot'
patterns, can still be enjoyed. Further along, when the same
thoroughfare has become Church St., is the **Shakespeare
Birthplace Trust**, which offers a combined ticket for the
several properties historically linked to the bard. Another of
these properties, just round the corner in Old Town, is **Hall's
Croft** (open Mon–Sat Apr–Oct 9.00–18.00, Nov–Mar
9.00–12.45, 14.00–16.00; Sun Apr–Oct 14.00–16.00; closed
Nov–Mar). This building is named after John Hall, who
married Shakespeare's daughter; its principal interest,
however, is the fact that Hall was a doctor, and the equipment
within provides a fascinating insight into the medical
techniques of the 17thC.

Old Town meets Trinity St. at the churchyard where
Shakespeare was buried. The gravestone is inscribed with an
imprecation, attributed to Shakespeare, to leave him in peace.
On the chancel wall is a monument, and at the font is a
reproduction of the register recording his baptism and burial.

Back along Southern Lane and Waterside, by the Avon, is the **Royal Shakespeare Theatre**. There were performances in Stratford even in the days of strolling players, but the first serious attempts to honour Shakespeare began in the late 1700s. The original Shakespeare theatre was built in 1879, and burned down in 1926. The present red-brick building was opened in 1932, and the Royal Shakespeare Company, one of the world's finest theatre companies, presents at least six Shakespearian productions in a season stretching from Apr–Dec or Jan.

The RSC also has a studio theatre in the town, known as **The Other Place**. Recorded booking information for both theatres can be obtained round the clock ☎(0789) 69191, for the box office ☎295623. The theatre has an interesting and informative picture gallery containing paintings of great actors in Shakespearian costume, in a surviving section of the original building. It also has extensive gardens. In the part near the church are rare trees and a court for Nine Men's Morris, an ancient game mentioned in *A Midsummer Night's Dream*; the part near the Shakespeare monument, called **Bancroft Gardens**, makes a pleasant picnic spot. A nearby shop called **Pargetter's** in Waterside makes its own delicious bread and lardy cake.

Two further scenes from the *Seven Ages of Shakespeare* are to be seen just outside the town. **Anne Hathaway's thatched cottage**, which was her home before her marriage to Shakespeare, is 2 miles (3km) away at **Shottery** (hours as Shakespeare's Birthplace). The contents include Shakespeare's 'second best bed', a four-poster which he willed to his wife. The cottage can be reached by a very pleasant walk along a signposted footpath from Evesham Pl.; there is also a bus service from American Fountain. A longer and sometimes muddy walk along a canal towpath N from Bridgefoot, or a short train journey, leads the 4 miles (6km) to **Wilmcote**, home of Shakespeare's mother, Mary Arden (hours as Hall's Croft). This was a typical Warwickshire farmstead, and was in use as such until 50yr ago. It still has an informality which makes it a revealing museum of English rural life.

Hotels

The thespian hotel, also enjoyed for its food and drink, is **The Arden**, at Waterside ☎294949 ⫴ which has a country house atmosphere. There are several other hotels in Stratford with this kind of ambience, though the rooms have usually been modernized. For the full modern treatment there is the **Moat House** at Bridgefoot ☎67511 ⫴ Bed-and-breakfast places tend to gather on the roads into Stratford from Oxford, Evesham and Alcester. The Tourist Information Centre has an accommodation register.

Restaurants

The **Royal Shakespeare Theatre** ☎69191 has its own restaurant and offers a package-deal ticket for a play and dinner ❧ ⫴ Or book in the morning for a pre-theatre dinner at the charmingly simple **Hill's**, 3 Greenhill St. ☎293563 ⫴ with delicious French-inspired cooking. After the theatre, Sheep St. has several late restaurants, Italian and Greek, among which the Greek **Christophi's** is a lively highlight ☎293546 ⫴ In the same street, there are good pub lunches at the **Rose and Crown**, while actors favour the **'Dirty Duck'** (**Black Swan**), at Waterside, near the theatre.

Windsor

21 miles (34km) from Central London. Population: 30,000.
Getting there: By train, 23min from Paddington, changing at
Slough for Windsor and Eton Central, trains hourly, or 50min
direct from Waterloo to Windsor Riverside, trains twice
hourly; by car, 1hr, M4 then A308. Tel. Code (95) from
London i Central Station (Apr–Dec) ☎*52010.*
One-day excursion: Windsor and Eton are compact and busy,
and surrounded by walking country. A car is not essential.

With its royal castle and Great Park, on a pretty stretch of the
River Thames, and with Eton, famous for its boys' school, just
across the footbridge, a visit to Windsor is, understandably, an
almost mandatory day trip for the visitor to London, or worth
even a hasty half-day. Hotels are not listed as Windsor is too
close to London to warrant an overnight stay.

Even in William the Conqueror's time it was within a day's
march of London, which is why he chose it for the site of one of
the nine castles with which he decided to encircle the city. Since
the Royal Family still spend time at **Windsor Castle** it is both a
national monument and a private home, and it is the largest and
oldest inhabited castle in the world. The precincts are open to
visitors, and there is admission to the State Apartments when
the Queen is not in official residence. There are walks in
Windsor Great Park, which stretches for 6 miles (10km) in the
direction of **Ascot racecourse**. A similar distance up the
willow-fringed river is Boulter's Lock, still much as it was when
Jerome K. Jerome described it in *Three Men in a Boat* in 1889,
and the town of **Maidenhead**.

A further couple of miles up river is **Cliveden House**, built
by Barry in 1851, once owned by the Astors, and on occasion
the breeding ground of political scandal. A small part of the
house is open to visitors on Sat and Sun afternoons in summer.
The magnificent gardens with beautiful views can be visited
from Mar–Nov Wed–Sun. Cliveden is close to the village of
Cookham, where the painter Stanley Spencer lived. One of his
paintings hangs in the church, and others are in King's Hall.

Across the river from Windsor, Eton High St. is dotted with
craft and antique shops.

Unless you intend to take a long walk in the Great Park or
along the river, the places of interest in Windsor and Eton are all
within a radius of about a mile. It is possible to take a perhaps
brisk look at each in the course of one day, and there are reasons
to see Windsor in the morning and Eton in the afternoon. From
Riverside Station, a walk along Datchet Rd. and Thames St.
leads to the castle. Central Station is closer; there is a large car
park opposite, housed in the ugly King Edward Court shopping
centre, and a walk up Peascod St. and Castle Hill leads to the
castle.

In the morning, the **Changing of the Castle Guard** can be
seen at 10.25. The new guard leaves from the Victoria Barracks
at 10.15 and marches along High St. to the castle. The old guard
returns by the same route at 11.00. On the High St. the
Guildhall (open daily 13.30–16.30), completed by Wren after
the death of the original architect, has an exhibition including
royal portraits.

Up Church Lane, in Church St., Nell Gwynne's house is now
a coffee shop called **Measures**, specializing in open
sandwiches. At the top of Church St., King Henry VIII Gate is
the main entrance to the castle. Straight ahead within the castle

is the finest example of Perpendicular architecture in England,
St George's Chapel (open daily 10.45–15.45, closed Jan),
where several monarchs are buried in the choir. The
architectural style, with external buttresses providing much of
the support, permits a spacious interior, with the light from
stained-glass windows filling the magnificent nave. There are
elaborate carvings in the nave and stalls. On the opposite side of
the castle precincts are the **State Apartments** (open daily
10.30–17.00, Oct–Mar 10.30–15.00, closed usually for a
month at Christmas and Easter, and for Ascot race week in
June), decorated with paintings from the royal collection,
including works by Van Dyck and Rubens, and with carvings
by Grinling Gibbons. There are also drawings by Leonardo da
Vinci and Holbein in the hall near the main entrance to the State
Apartments. Within the same complex are a **coach museum**
and an extraordinary delight, **Queen Mary's Dolls' House**,
also near the entrance. This has running water, working lifts
and a library with commissioned writings by Kipling and
miniature paintings. The house, designed by Sir Edwin
Lutyens, is on a scale of 12:1. From the castle, Long Walk runs
for 3 miles (5km) through Home Park to a statue of *George III*.
Beyond stretches Windsor Great Park, with Smith's Lawn,
where Prince Charles plays polo. Nearby, the **Savill Garden**
(open Mar–Nov 10.00–18.00, or sunset if earlier) contains a
large collection of rhododendrons, roses, herbaceous borders
and alpine plants, set in 35 wooded acres.

An exploration of the Great Park and Savill Garden may well
demand an afternoon, but the alternative is to return to the
town, and from Thames St. cross the footbridge (a pretty
Victorian structure in cast iron) to **Eton**, which may prove a less
crowded place in which to have lunch. The town of the boating
song and playing fields on which Britain's battles were allegedly
won instantly proclaims itself; from the bridge, the Eton
College boathouses can be seen on the left. In the High St. near
a splendid Victorian pillar box, and with punishment stocks
outside, is a timbered building dating from 1420, where cock-
fighting used to take place. Known as **The Cockpit**, it is now,
incongruously, an Italian restaurant. Among the antique shops
in the High St. is **F. Owen**, at no. 113, notable for militaria;
covering one wall of the shop are photographs of customers who
were Eton boys. **Eton College** (open daily 14.00–17.00,
Christmas, Easter and summer holidays 10.30–17.00), cradle
of great British poets and prime ministers, was founded in 1440
by Henry VI, and some of the oldest parts of the school can be
seen in a quadrangle called The Cloisters. The 15thC chapel in
the Perpendicular style contains wall paintings from the time of
its foundation.

Restaurants
Gastronomes will cut short their sightseeing to spend time and
money at the **Waterside Inn**, Bray, near Maidenhead
☎(0628) 20691 ▥▥ which is the country establishment of the
Roux brothers, owners of Le Gavroche in London (see
Restaurants). Windsor itself cannot match such gourmet
delights as the exquisite lightness of touch in the Waterside's
cuisine, though **La Taverna** at 2 River St., off Thames St.,
☎63020 ▥◨ is worth visiting for pasta and veal dishes. For the
determined sightseer, the schedule might favour a really
excellent snack at the **Eton Wine Bar**, or a hot pub lunch at the
Christopher, both in the High St., Eton.

Index

Individual hotels, restaurants and shops have not been indexed, because they appear in alphabetical order within their appropriate sections. The sections themselves, however, have been indexed. Similarly, streets are listed in the gazetteer and not the index, with a few notable exceptions, such as Fleet Street and Pall Mall, being indexed as well.

Page numbers in bold type indicate the main entry.

Index

Index

Index

Gazetteer of street names

Numbers after the street names refer to pages on which the street is mentioned in the book. Map references refer to the maps that follow this gazetteer.

It has not been possible to label every street drawn on the maps, although of course all major streets and most smaller ones have been named. However, some streets that it has not been possible to label have also been given map references in this gazetteer, because this serves as an approximate location which will nearly always be sufficient for you to find your way.

A

Abchurch Lane, EC4, 103, Map 13F16

Abingdon St., SW1, 131, Map 18I11

Adam's Row, W1, 138, Map 9G8

Albany St., NW1, 146, Map 3D9

Albemarle St., W1, 157, 186, Map 9G9

Albert Bri., SW3, 56, Map 16L–M6

Aldermanbury, EC2, 16, 70, Map 12E5

Aldwych, WC2, 41, 113, 179, Map 11F12

Argyll St., W1, 178, Map 9F9

Arlington St., SW1, 153, Map 9G9

Arthur St., EC4, 60, Map 13G16

Ashley Pl., SW1, 132, Map 17J9

B

Baker St., NW1 & W1, 17, 86, 174, Maps 2&8

Bankside, SE1, 47, Map 12G15

Barrett St., W1, 183, Map 9F8

Basil St., SW3, 137, 138, 153, Map 16I7

Bayswater Rd., W2, 196, Maps 6–8

Beak St., W1, 157, Map 9G9

Bear Gdns., SE1, 47, Map 12G15

Beauchamp Pl., SW3, 161, 164, 184, 185, Map 16I–J6

Bedford Pl., WC1, 48, Map 4E11

Bedford Sq., WC1, 41, 48, Map 4E10

Bedford St., WC2, 105, 185, Map 10G11

Beeston Pl., SW1, 140, Map 17J8

Belgrave Mews West, SW1, 170, Map 16I7

Belgrave Sq., SW1, 15, 38, 47, 170, Maps 16&17

Berkeley Sq., W1, 86, 176, Map 9G8

Berkeley St., W1, 16, Map 9G9

Bermondsey St., SE1, 189, Map 13H–I17

Berners St., W1, 137, Map 10F10

Berwick St., W1, 111, Map 10F10

Bevis Marks, EC3, 59, Map 13F17

Birdcage Walk, SW1, 40, 125, Map 18I10

Bishopsgate, EC2, 56, 59, 61, Map 13E17

Blackfriars Bri., SE1, 18, Map 12G14

Blackfriars Lane, EC4, 61, Map 12F14

Blenheim St., W1, 183, Map 9F8

Bloomsbury Sq., WC1, 19, 48, Map 4E11

Bloomsbury St., WC1, 41, Map 4E11

Bloomsbury Way, WC1, 41, 100, 143, 185, Map 10E11

Bond St., W1, 38, 87, 182, 183, 186, 188, Map 9F–G9 see also New Bond St. and Old Bond St.

Borough High St., SE1, 169, Map 12H15

Borough Rd., SE1, 171, Map 12H14

Bow Lane, EC2, 104, Map 12F15

Bow St., WC2, 29, 64, 140, 159, 172, Map 10F11

Bread St., EC4, 28, 57, Map 12F15

Brewer St., W1, 111, Map 10G10

Brick St., W1, 144, Map 9H8

Bridge St., SW1, 39, 40, Map 18I11

Broad Court, WC2, 140, Map 10F11

Broad Sanctuary, SW1, 125, 175, Map 18I11

Broad Walk, NW1, 96, Map 3C8

Broadway, SW1, 15, 16, Map 18I10

Broken Wharf, EC4, 59, Map 12G15

Brompton Rd., SW1 & SW3, 53, 77, 164, 167, 169, 183, 185, 186, Map 16I–J6

Brook St., W1, 38, 139, 185, Map 9F8

Brunswick Sq., WC1, 48, 63, Map 4D11

Bruton Pl., W1, 169, Map 9G9

Buckingham Gate, SW1, 40, 54, Map 17I9

Buckingham Palace Rd., SW1, 12, 40, 54, Map 17J8–9

Burlington Arc., W1, 185, Map 9G9

Burlington Gdns., W1, 84, 153, 184, Map 9G9

Bute St., SW7, 151, Map 15J5

Byward St., EC3, 58, 197, Map 3G17

C

Cadogan Pl., SW1, 141, 158, Map 16H7

Cadogan Sq., SW1, 55, Map 16J7

Camden High St., NW1, 16, 162, 174, 189, Map 3B9

Camden Passage, N1, 36, 189, Map 5B14

Camomile St., EC3, 59, Map 13E17

Canning Pl., W8, 77, Map 15I4

Cannon St., EC4, 60, Map 12F15

Carey St., WC2, 81, Map 11F12

Carlos Pl., W1, 139, 154, Map 9G8

Carlton House Ter., SW1, 26, 40, 84, 94, 192, Map 10H10

Gazetteer

LONDON

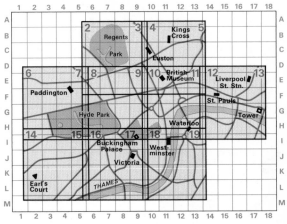

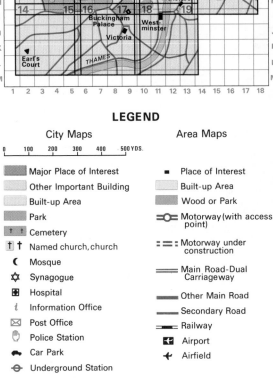

LEGEND

City Maps

0   100   200   300   400   500 YDS.

Major Place of Interest

Other Important Building

Built-up Area

Park

† †   Cemetery

† †   Named church, church

☾   Mosque

✡   Synagogue

✚   Hospital

i   Information Office

⊠   Post Office

�   Police Station

➤   Car Park

⊖   Underground Station

→   One Way Street

Footpath, arcade

10   Adjoining Page No.

Area Maps

■   Place of Interest

Built-up Area

Wood or Park

=O=   Motorway (with access point)

= = =   Motorway under construction

Main Road-Dual Carriageway

Other Main Road

Secondary Road

Railway

✈   Airport

✦   Airfield

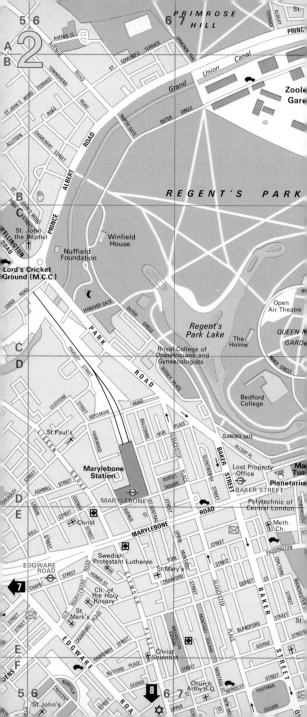

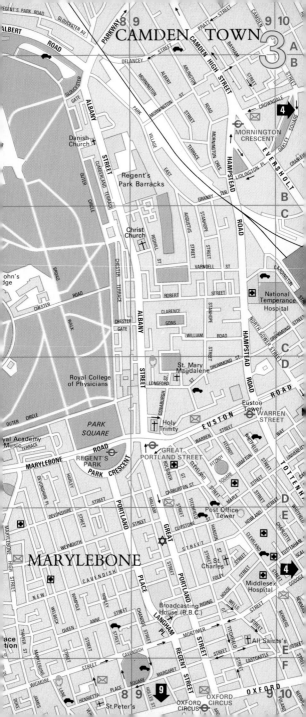

REGENT'S PARK ROAD
GLOUCESTER AV.
PARKWAY
PRATT
CAMDEN
ALBERT
ROAD
GLOUCESTER
DELANCEY
STREET
CAMDEN HIGH STREET
BAYHAM
CROWNDALE
4
MORNINGTON CRESCENT
OAKLEY SQUARE
EVERSHOLT
CRANLEIGH

ALBANY
STREET
CUMBERLAND TERRACE
Danish Church
GATE
ALBERT
MORNINGTON
ST.
PARK
VILLAGE
MORNINGTON
ROAD
STREET
STREET
ARLINGTON
MORNINGTON CRES.
TERRACE
EAST
HAMPSTEAD
LIDLINGTON PL.

OUTER
CIRCLE
Regent's Park Barracks
GRANBY TER.
ROAD
B
C

BROAD
CHESTER
ROAD
ohn's dge
CHESTER TERRACE
AUGUSTUS
STANHOPE
ROBERT
REGILL
ST.
Christ Church
VARNDELL
ST.
STREET
STREET
CLARENDON
STREET
National Temperance Hospital
WALK
CHESTER GATE
ALBANY
CLARENCE GDNS.
STANHOPE
WILLIAM
ROAD
STREET
HAMPSTEAD
NORTH GOWER STREET
DRUMMOND STREET
C
D

OUTER CIRCLE
Royal College of Physicians
STREET
PETERBOROUGH
LONGFORD
St. Mary Magdalene
Holy Trinity
DRUMMOND ST.
ROAD
Euston Tower
FUSTON
WARREN STREET
WARREN
ROAD

yal Academy Music
TERRACE
PARK SQUARE
REGENT'S PARK
ROAD
PARK CRESCENT
MARYLEBONE
GREAT PORTLAND STREET
BOLSOVER
GT.
CLEVELAND
FITZROY
SQUARE
WHITFIELD
GRAFTON
WAY
TOTTENH.
WAY

DEVONSHIRE PL.
HARLEY
STREET
PORTLAND
CARBURTON ST.
HALLAM
GREAT
MAPLE
Post Office Tower
HOWLAND
CLEVELAND
CHARLOTTE
TOTTENHAM
SCALA
D
E

MARYLEBONE HIGH STREET
DEVONSHIRE
STREET
WEYMOUTH
WIMPOLE
STREET
HARLEY
PORTLAND
CUBSTONE
GT.
STREET
TICHFIELD
HANSON
St. Charles
FOLEY
WELLS
Middlesex Hospital
BERNERS
GOODGE
4
E
F

MARYLEBONE
CAVENDISH
NEW
QUEEN
ANNE
WELBECK
STREET
PLACE
CHANDOS STREET
LANGHAM PL.
PORTLAND
Broadcasting House (B.B.C.)
RIDING
MORTIMER
STREET
TICHFIELD
All Saints's
EASTCASTLE
STREET

ace tion
THAYER ST.
MARYLEBONE
WIGMORE
JAMES
LANE
DUKE
VERE
HENRIETTA
St. Peter's
CAVENDISH
PLACE
HOLLES ST.
SQUARE
8
9
MARGARET
9
REGENT
STREET
OXFORD CIRCUS
OXFORD CIRCUS
OXFORD
POLAND
9
10

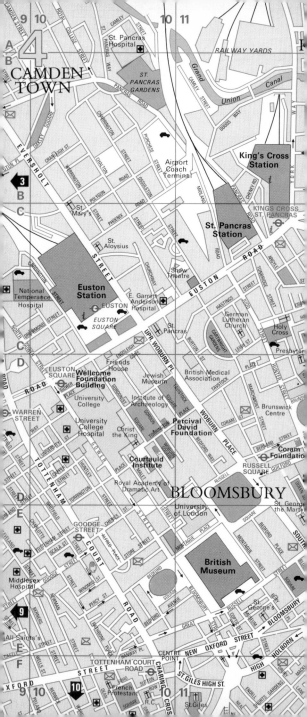

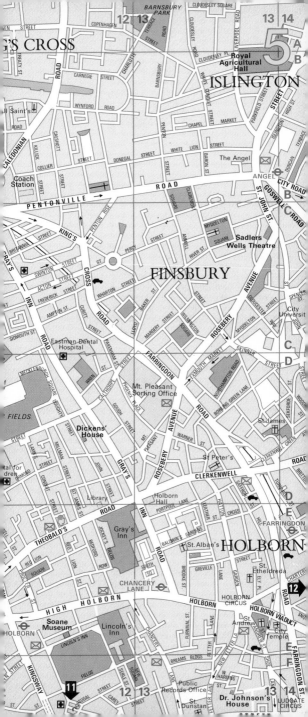

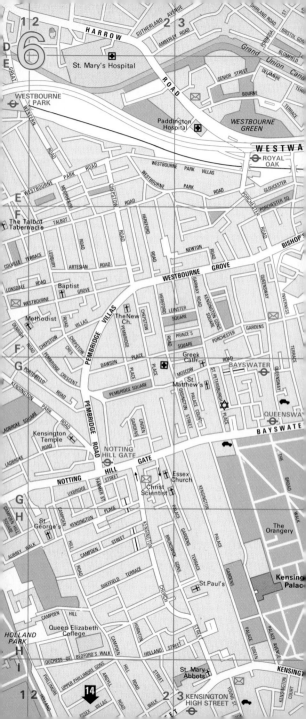

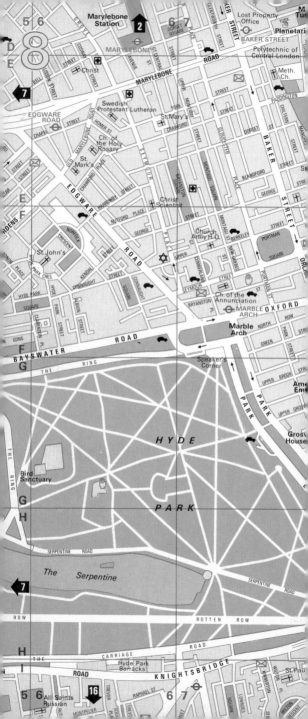

D 5 6 7

Marylebone
Station

Lost Property
Office

York
STREET
Planetari

BAKER STREET
Polytechnic of
Central London

E

MARYLEBONE

Christ
ROAD

PADDINGTON

Meth.
Ch.

7

Swedish
Protestant Lutheran

St Mary's
CRAWFORD

York
STREET

DORSET
STREET

CHILTERN
STREET

MANCHE
STER

EDGWARE
ROAD
CHAPEL

Ch. of
the Holy
Rosary

St.
Mark's

BLANDFORD

GEORGE

STREET

E

CRAWFORD

NUTFORD PLACE

GEORGE

Christ
Scientist

Church
Army H.Q.

PORTMAN
SQUARE

St.John's

KENDAL

CONNAUGHT

Seymour

Ch. of the
Annunciation
MARBLE
ARCH

ST.

OXFORD
ROW

HYDE PARK
SQUARE

ALBION
STREET

BRYANSTON

Marble
Arch

NORTH

GREEN

F

BAYSWATER
ROAD

Speaker's
Corner

UPPER BROOK

Ame
Emb

G

THE
RING

PARK

Gros
House

THE
RING

H Y D E

Bird
Sanctuary

P A R K

G
H

SERPENTINE   ROAD

The   *Serpentine*

7

ROW

ROTTEN   ROW

CARRIAGE
ROAD

H
I

THE
ROAD

Hyde Park
Barracks

KNIGHTSBRIDGE

St.P

5 6 All Saints
Russian

16

RAPHAEL ST.

TREVOR

6 7

MONTPELIER

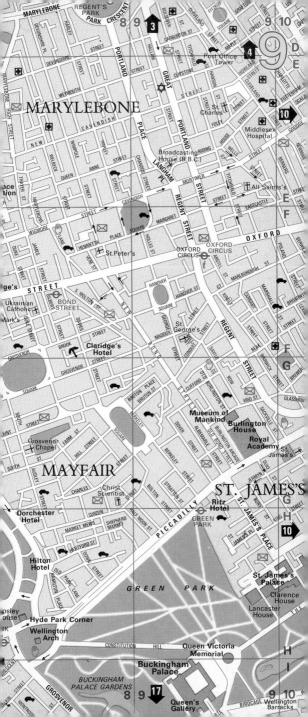

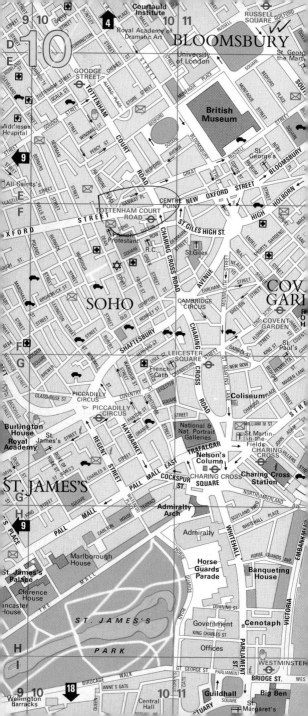

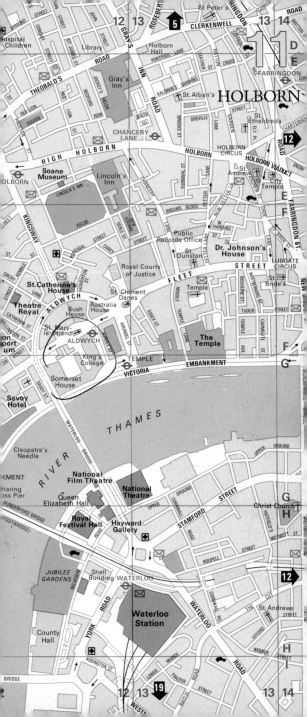

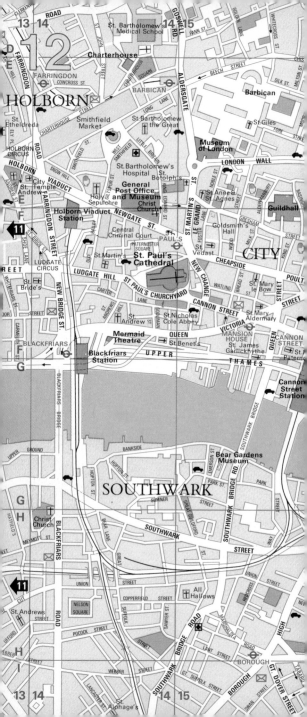

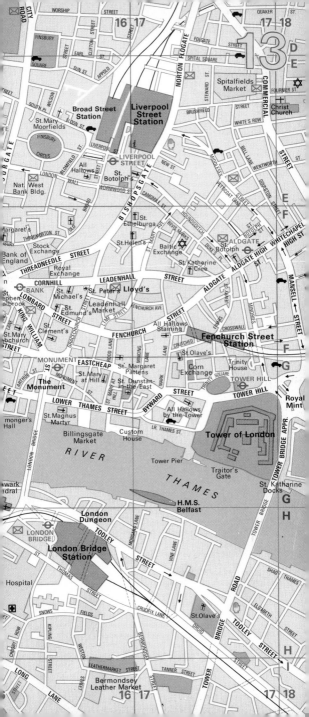

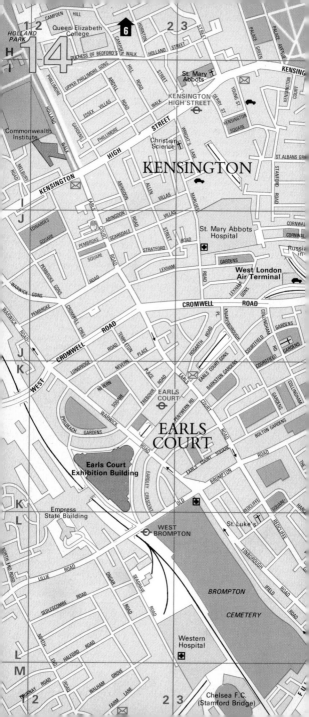

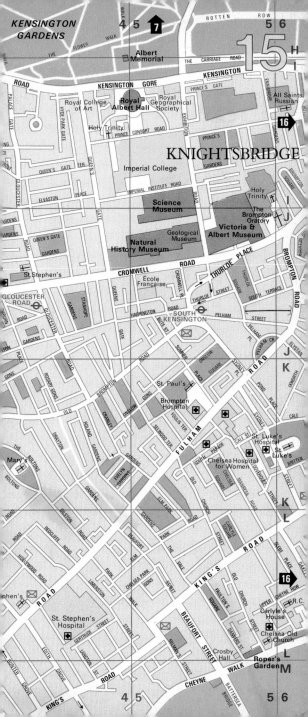

KENSINGTON GARDENS

ROTTEN ROW

4 5 7

5 6

Albert Memorial

15 H

THE CARRIAGE ROAD

KENSINGTON GORE

KENSINGTON

PALACE GATE

HYDE PARK GATE

ROAD

Royal College of Art

Royal Albert Hall

Royal Geographical Society

PRINCE'S GATE

All Saints Russian

16

Holy Trinity

PRINCE CONSORT ROAD

QUEEN'S GATE TER

KNIGHTSBRIDGE

PRINCE'S GARDENS

Imperial College

EXHIBITION ROAD

ELVASTON PLACE

IMPERIAL INSTITUTE ROAD

Science Museum

Holy Trinity

The Brompton Oratory

I J

GARDENS

QUEEN'S GATE GARDENS

Natural History Museum

Geological Museum

Victoria & Albert Museum

BROMPTON ROAD

St Stephen's

CROMWELL ROAD

École Française

THURLOE PLACE

SOUTH TERRACE

GLOUCESTER ROAD

QUEENS GATE

HARRINGTON ROAD

CROMWELL ROAD

THURLOE STREET

THURLOE SQUARE

SOUTH ROAD

PELHAM STREET

STANHOPE GARDENS

ROSARY GDNS

BUTE ST

SOUTH KENSINGTON

PELHAM PL

PELHAM CR

J K

GLOUCESTER ROAD

ROAD

SUMNER PLACE

ONSLOW SQUARE

PELHAM STREET

ROAD

ELLSTAN

K

OLD BROMPTON

ORANGE

ROLAND GARDENS

DRAYTON GARDENS

SELWOOD TER

FOULIS TER

St Paul's

Brompton Hospital

ONSLOW GDNS

SYDNEY

POND PLACE

CALE ST

St Luke's Hospital

CALE

Mary's

THE BOLTONS

EVELYN GARDENS

FULHAM

SOUTH PARADE

CHELSEA SQUARE

Chelsea Hospital for Women

MANRESA ROAD

DOVEHOUSE

St Luke's

BRITTEN STREET

K L

L

BILTON ROAD

ELM PARK GARDENS

PARK

CHURCH STREET

CARLYLE SQUARE

ROAD

GLEBE PLACE

REDCLIFFE ROAD

BEAUFORT STREET

THE VALE

ELM PARK ROAD

CHELSEA PARK GDNS

KING'S ROAD

PAULTON'S SQUARE

OLD CHURCH STREET

16

HOLLYWOOD ROAD

LIMERSTON STREET

UPPER CHEYNE ROW

Carlyle's House

CHEYNE ROW

hen's

ROAD

St. Stephen's Hospital

GERTRUDE STREET

LANGTON STREET

MILMAN'S STREET

BEAUFORT STREET

DANVERS STREET

Crosby Hall

Chelsea Old Church

Roper's Garden

L M

EDITH GROVE

BUNTER GROVE

KING'S ROAD

4 5

CHEYNE WALK

BATTERSEA

5 6

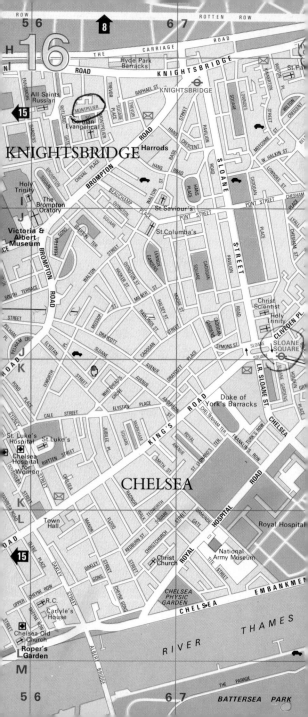

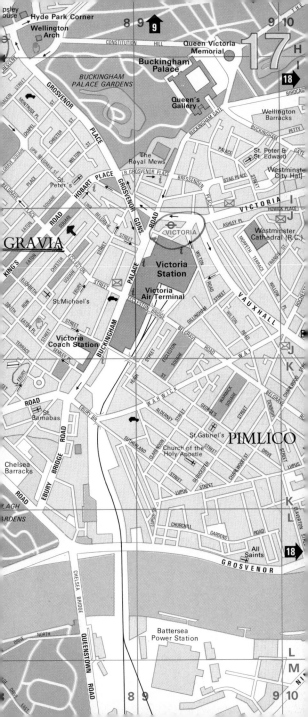

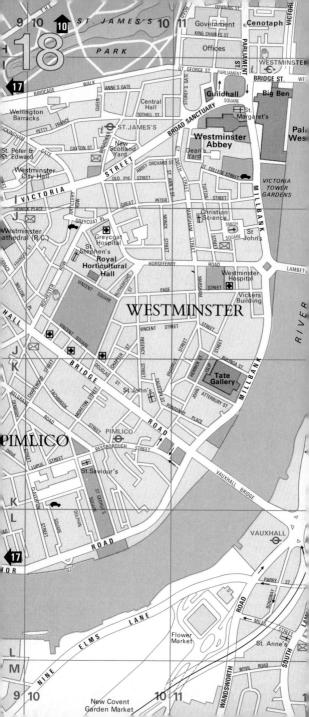

DOWNING ST.

Government
Offices
KING CHARLES ST.
Cenotaph

WESTMINSTER

BRIDGE ST. WE

ST. JAMES'S

PARK

PARLIAMENT ST.

GT. GEORGE ST.
PARLIAMENT

STOREY'S GATE

BIRDCAGE

WALK

ANNE'S GATE

QUEEN

Central
Hall
TOTHILL ST.

Guildhall

SQUARE

Big Ben

St.
Margaret's

Pal
Wes

Wellington
Barracks

PETTY FRANCE

CAXTON ST.

ST. JAMES'S

New
Scotland
Yard

BROADWAY

BROAD SANCTUARY

Westminster
Abbey

St. Peter &
St. Edward

Westminster
City Hall

BUCKINGHAM

GATE

STREET

ABBEY ORCHARD ST.

OLD PYE STREET

Dean's
Yard

GT. COLLEGE STREET

VICTORIA
TOWER
GARDENS

VICTORIA

HOWICK PLACE

ARTILLERY
ROW

GREAT

PETER

STREET

ST. ANN'S ST.

SMITH STREET

TUFTON STREET

MARSHAM

MILLBANK

LAMBET

J

Westminster
Cathedral (R.C.)

FRANCIS ST.

WILLOW

Greycoat
Hospital

GREYCOAT PL.

St.
Stephen's

Royal
Horticultural
Hall

ROCHESTER

ROW

VINCENT SQUARE

RUTHERFORD

ST.

HORSEFERRY

PAGE

ROAD

Christian
Science

SMITH
SQUARE

St.
John's

Westminster
Hospital

Vickers
Building

WESTMINSTER

RIVER

HALL

VINCENT SQUARE

VINCENT STREET

REGENCY

STREET

CHAPTER

DOUGLAS

ST.

STREET

ERASMUS ST.

HERRICK ST.

STREET

PAGE

MARSHAM

STREET

BULINGA ST.

Tate
Gallery

MILLBANK

J
K

BRIDGE

CHARLWOOD

ST.

TACHBROOK STREET

MORETON STREET

St. John's

CAUSTON ST.

JOHN

ATTERBURY ST.

PONSONBY

PLACE

BELGRAVE

ROAD

IRVINE

CLAVERTON

ROAD

LUPUS STREET

PIMLICO

St. Saviour's

BESSBOROUGH STREET

ST. GEORGE'S SQUARE

PIMLICO

DOLPHIN

STREET

VAUXHALL BRIDGE

K
L

ROAD

VAUXHALL

17

OR

NINE

ELMS

LANE

Flower
Market

ROAD

PARRY ST.

BONDWAY

MILES STREET

SOUTH LAN

St. Anne's

WYVIL ROAD

WANDSWORTH

L
M

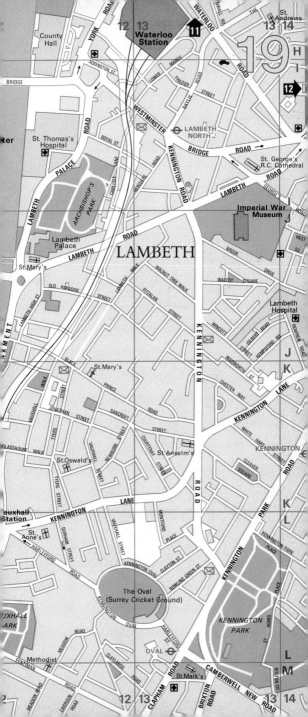

12 13
Waterloo Station

County Hall

YORK ROAD

ADDINGTON ST.

BRIDGE

LOWER MARSH

FRAZIER STREET

BAYLIS ROAD

WESTMINSTER BRIDGE ROAD

St. Thomas's Hospital

ROYAL ST.

LAMBETH PALACE ROAD

LAMBETH NORTH

KENNINGTON ROAD

St. George's R.C. Cathedral

CARLISLE LANE

HERCULES

ARCHBISHOP'S PARK

LAMBETH

GEORGE'S RD.

Imperial War Museum

J

LAMBETH PALACE

Lambeth Palace

WEST

ROAD

St. Mary's

LAMBETH ROAD

LAMBETH

OLD PARADISE STREET

LAMBETH HIGH ST.

LAMBETH WALK

FITZALAN STREET

WALNUT TREE WALK

WALCOT SQUARE

BROOK DRIVE

Lambeth Hospital

WINCOTT STREET

GILBERT ROAD

KEMPSFORD RD.

J
K

BLACK PRINCE ROAD

St.Mary's

WALK

STREET

PRINCE ROAD

SANCROFT STREET

COURTENAY STREET

BEACONSFIELD ST.

CHESTER WAY

KENNINGTON

KENNINGTON LANE

WHITE HART ST.

KENNINGTON ROAD

VAUXHALL WALK

JONATHAN STREET

TYERS STREET

NEWBURN STREET

VAUXHALL STREET

St. Anselm's

CLEAVER SQUARE

K
L

Glasshouse WALK

St.Oswald's

TYERS STREET

STREET

ROAD

Vauxhall Station

KENNINGTON LANE

St. Anne's

DURHAM STREET

VAUXHALL STREET

MONTFORD PLACE

KENNINGTON PARK

KENNINGTON PARK PLACE

HARLEYFORD ROAD

KENNINGTON OVAL

CLAYTON ST.

BOWLING GREEN ST.

KENNINGTON PARK

UXHALL ARK

**The Oval
(Surrey Cricket Ground)**

KENNINGTON OVAL

HARLEYFORD STREET

ST. AGNES PLACE

L
M

Methodist

FENTIMAN

MEADOW ROAD

CLAYLANDS ROAD

OVAL

St.Mark's

CAMBERWELL NEW ROAD

BOLTON RD.

MEADOW ROAD

CARROUN ROAD

CLAPHAM ROAD

BRIXTON ROAD

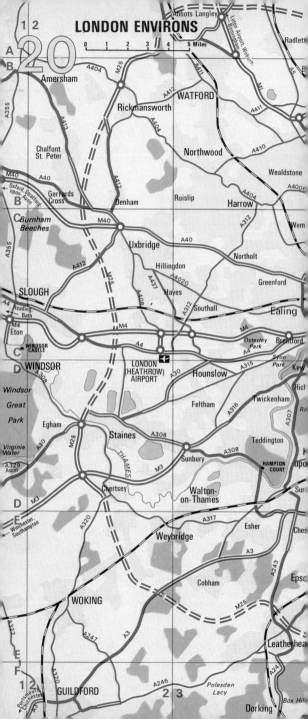

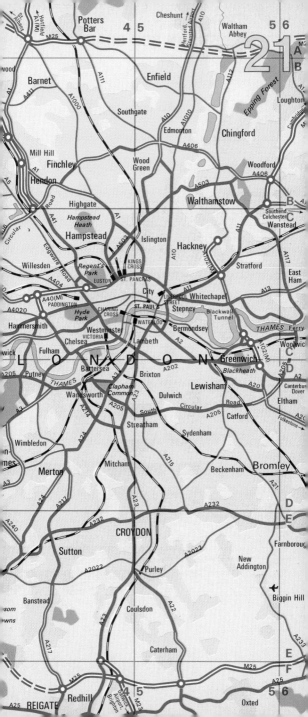

22 LONDON BUS CHART

	Aldwych	Angel	Baker St.	Bank	Chelsea / King's Rd.	Earls Ct.	Elephant and Castle	Euston	Hammersmith	Hampstead	Highgate	High St. Kensington	Holborn	Hyde Pk. Corner	Kew	King's Cross	Knightsbridge / Harrods
Aldwych																	
Angel	4, 171																
Baker St.	1, 13	30															
Bank	6, 9	43	13														
Chelsea / King's Rd.	11	22, 38	22, 30	11, 22													
Earls Ct.	30, 9	74, 38	30, 74	30, 9	31												
Elephant and Castle	1, 68	171	1, 176	133		A											
Euston	68, 77A	30, 73	18, 30	68	1,	30	68										
Hammersmith	11	73	27	9	11			73									
Hampstead	24, 176	24, 30	24, 30	24, 8	24, 22	24, 30	24, 176	24, 73	24, 73								
Highgate	134, 176	43	134, 30	43	134, 30	134	134	134	134	210							
High St. Kensington	9	73	27	9	31	31		73	9,	73	73, 134						
Holborn	68, 77A	38	8, 159	22	22, 30	68, 188	68, 77A	73	24	73, 134	9						
Hyde Pk. Corner	9	19, 73	30, 74	25	22	30, 74	14,	73	73, 24	73, 134	9,	73	19, 22				
Kew			27						27			27, 24, 134		27	C		
King's Cross	77A, 239	30, 73	30	73	30	45, 63	30, 73	73, 24	30, 134	73	77A	14, 73	73, 27				
Knightsbridge / Harrods	9	73	9		19, 30	30, 74	9,	14, 30	73	73, 73	73, 134	9	14, 73	22		14, 30	
Liverpool St.	6	43†	13	6, 9	22	22, 30	35		8, 68	9	18, 134	9	68	18, 45		9	22
Ludgate Circus	6, 9	4	18	6, 9	11		45, 63		8, 68	9	18, 134	9	68	18, 45		9	
Marble Arch	6, 15	73	30, 74	6, 8	22	74	12	30, 73	73, 24	73, 134	73,	7,	2, 25		8, 73	30, 73	6, 74
Monument	23, 501	43	23, 159	43	E	35, 95		F	43	501	23,	E	23, 77A	23		23	3
Notting Hill Gate		12, 27	27		31	31	12, 53	12, 73	24, 134	28, 31	9	52	27	73		12, 73	52
Olympia	9	73	27	9				73	27, 24, 134	73	9,	73	27		73	73, 137	
Oxford Circus	6, 15	73	13, 159	6, 22	73, 22	73, 30	53	73	73, 24	73, 134	73,	25, 73	73		73	73, 137	6
Oxford St. / Selfridges	6, 15	73	13, 159	6, 22	73,	74	12	73	73, 24	73, 134	73,	25, 73	73		73	73, 137	6
Paddington	15, 27	27, 73	27	15	23, 12		23, 12	27, 73	27, 24	27, 134	27	7	36, 368	27		368, 90	27, 73
Piccadilly Circus	6, 9	19	13, 159	6, 15	22		12, 53	14	9	14, 134	73	19, 22	14			14, 22	
Richmond			27			B	27		27, 24, 134	27		C	27			27, 73	
St. Paul's	6, 9	4	18	6, 9	11		141		8, 68	9	18, 134	9		68		9	18, 9
Sloane Sq.	11	19	19, 74	11	11, 22	19, 30		19, 73	11	137, 24	137, 134	19, 73	19, 22	137		19, 30	19, 137
South Kensington	14, 30	30	30	14, 49	49	30	14, 176		14, 30	14, 134	49	14, 9	30, 14			30, 14	14, 30
Tate Gallery / Millbank	77A, 88	73	28		2, 22	30	10	77A	73	1,		77A, 36	J		77A, 14		14
Tottenham Ct. Rd.	1, 176	73	176, 25	25, 22	1, 30	176		73	24, 134	7,	14, 73	24, 27		14, 73		14, 19	
Trafalgar Sq.	6, 9	172	1, 13	9	11		12, 53	14	9	24, 134	9	77A	14		77A, 9		
Victoria	11	38	2, 28	11	11, 7	30	176	11	24	25, 134	52	38	2, 36		24, 73	27	52, 1
Warren St.	176	30, 73	1, 176	25, 22	30	176		73, 24	24, 134	73, 7	73	27	73		14, 30		
Waterloo	5, 68	4	76, 501	11	K	177, 30	68, 155	24	176, 29	176, 134	5, 68	68	K		168A, 239	88, 1	
Westminster	77, 77A	172	159	11	11	500, 30	109, 155	11	24	29, 134		77A, 172	500	E	77A		

To find the route numbers of buses linking any two locations on this chart, follow the rows of squares horizontally and vertically to the square where the two rows meet. If a square is coloured you must change buses as indicated in the key.

Change at Aldwych
Change at High St. Kensington
Change at Hyde Pk. Corner
Change at Oxford Circus
Change at Tottenham Ct. Rd.
Change at Trafalgar Square
Change at Warren St.

* Buses run Mon-Fri only.
† From Liverpool St. walk along Eldon St.
to Moorgate for direct bus service (43).

The following journeys are difficult by bus, involving two changes and the alternative tube connections are suggested:
A   Bakerloo line to Embankment then change to District line
B   District line to Embankment then change to Bakerloo line
C   District line to Earls Ct. then change to Piccadilly line
D   Circle line to Sth. Kensington then change to District line
E   District line direct
F   Escalator link to Bank then change to Northern line
G   District line to Sth. Kensington then change to Circle line
H   Circle or District lines direct
I   Victoria line from Pimlico to Warren St. then change to Northern line
J   Victoria line from Pimlico to Victoria then change to District line
K   Bakerloo or Northern line to Embankment then change to District line

	Marble Arch	Monument	Notting Hill Gate	Olympia	Oxford Circus	Oxford St./Selfridges	Paddington	Piccadilly Circus	Richmond	St. Paul's	Sloane Sq.	South Kensington	Tate Gallery/Millbank	Tottenham Ct. Rd.	Trafalgar Sq.	Victoria	Warren St.	Waterloo
Monument	23, 6																	
Notting Hill Gate	12, 88	12, 23																
Olympia	73	27, 28																
Oxford Circus	6, 7	23	12, 88	73														
Oxford St./Selfridges	6, 7	23	27	27	7, 15	7, 15												
Paddington	7, 15	23	12, 88	9	6, 12	6, 12	15											
Piccadilly Circus	6, 15	E	27	27		27												
Richmond	6, 15	23	9	6, 15	15, 23	15												
St. Paul's	137	137/52	137/9	137	137	19, 22	E	11										
Sloane Sq.	30	H	49	14/73	30	14/36	14	14/19										
South Kensington	88	10	88	88	88	36	88	J	14/19									
Tate Gallery/Millbank	7,12/88	176/23	73	7, 8	7	14, 22	176/27	22	14	88								
Tottenham Ct. Rd.	12, 88	23	9	6, 15	15	6, 9	11	14	88	24, 29								
Trafalgar Sq.	2, 25	52	9	25	2, 25	36	38, 55	11	11	2, 14	25, 36	24, 29						
Victoria	30, 73	27	27, 73	73, 137	27	14	27	18	137	14, 30	24, 29	24, 29	24					
Warren St.	68, 6	501*/513*		1	1		4		176	176	24, 29	24, 29	176					
Westminster	12, 88	23	12, 88	12, 88	12, 88	E	11	11	500, 177A/14	88	24, 29	24, 29	24, 29	70, 76				

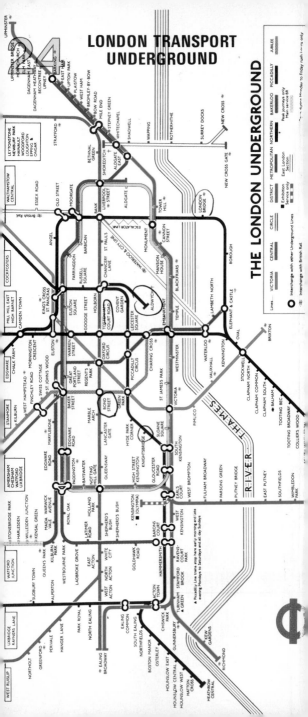

LONDON TRANSPORT UNDERGROUND

THE LONDON UNDERGROUND